CALIFORNIA SPLIT

RACING THROUGH THE SIXTIES

A MEMOIR

By Allan D. Brown

ABCOM PUBLISHING

Copyright © 2010 by **Allan D. Brown**

All rights reserved by the author. No part of this publication may be reproduced, stored in a retrieval system or transmitted in any form or by any means electronic, mechanical, photocopying, recording or otherwise, without the prior written permission of the author.

ISBN: 978-0-578-05542-8

**DEDICATED TO THE FREE SPIRTS
OF THE SIXTIES**

ALSO BY ALLAN BROWN

NEWS-DAZE (2006)
A novel of TV news

BERKELEY-DAZE (2007)
Memoir of a Frat Boy

SUN-STRUCK (2008)
Growing up in postwar California

CHASING AFTER PARADISE (2009)
A family journey through the South Pacific

All are available on Lulu.com

PREFACE

California Split: Racing through the Sixties is a sequel to my book, *Berkeley Daze: Memoir of a Frat Boy*. ***California Split*** covers the years from 1963 through 1968. The mid-sixties were a wild and crazy time in the San Francisco Bay Area and in Europe. As will be seen, in addition to my various adventures, I was often a witness to many historic events of the decade. Many names have been changed in this memoir, others arbitrarily assigned. Dialogue has been reconstructed with the goal of conveying the spirit of the conversation, if not the exact words.

I hope you enjoy reading ***California Split.***

CHAPTERS

BOOK ONE 1963—1965 1
PROLOGUE 3
1. PEACE CORPS 5
2. COLUMBIA 18
3. HOMEWARD 27
4. LIMBO 33
5. U.S. ARMY 38
6. KENNEDY 49
7. FORD ORD 53
8. WARRIOR 66
9. PRESIDIO 72
10. OFF-BASE 88
11. SURVEYOR 100
12. LIM'S LAUNDRY 110
13. DON'S NUPTIALS 120
14. THE SPLIT 130
15. NEW YORK 134
16. BERDAU & CO. 148
17. PARIS 158
18. LE SCÈNE I 168
19. LE SCÈNE II 175
20. NÜRNBERG 185
21. ARMY HOTEL 195
22. NAZI GHOSTS 200
23. NEW YEAR '65 206
24. FRÄULEINS 214
25. BROKE 222
26. VADUZ 227
27. FLY ME 234
28. HELLO AMERICA 240

BOOK TWO 1965—1968 ... 247

1. THE APARTMENT ... 249
2. HOSTEL ... 258
3. THE CONTESSA ... 263
4. ZEITGEIST '65 ... 269
5. THE DOLE ... 275
6. BY-THE-SEA ... 280
7. MOVIES ... 284
8. HOLLYWOOD ... 292
9. SASHA ... 301
10. TENDERLOIN ... 309
11. THE HAIGHT ... 313
12. KEMP ... 322
13. FILMIC ... 328
14. SASHA II ... 335
15. TV LAND ... 341
16. BERKELEY REDUX ... 346
17. MEXICO ... 355
18. TOURISTA ... 361
19. YUCATAN ... 369
20. PACIFICO ... 377
21. BEING ... 383
22. YVONNE ... 386
23. DIRECTOR ... 400
24. WAR ... 414
25. NOCE ... 429
26. HOOKED ... 440
27. THE KNOT ... 447
28. BIG SUR ... 453
29. GRIND ... 458
30. KRON-TV ... 466
31. NEWS STORM ... 477
32. FLIGHT ... 485

BOOK ONE
1963—1965

PROLOGUE

Nothing had worked out as planned.

With wine in hand, I sat on the patio of my parents' home in Martinez, California getting pleasantly bombed while I watched the shadows lengthen down the brown hills behind our house. In August, the hills are always the driest, primed for a grass fire but so far, they have escaped that fate this summer. By contrast, there was no escaping my fate. The central fact of my life was that I had been "de-selected" out of the Peace Corp with no clear plan except to deal with the Army.

Mom and Dad had met me at the San Francisco Airport with little to say except, "What are you going to do about the draft, Allan?"

"I don't know," I replied. "Check out the reserves, I guess. Maybe see if I can go to graduate school."

"Don't count on us to finance that, Allan," said my father, noticeably balder and grayer since I saw him last.

"I'm not, Dad. I thought I might be able to work and go to school at the same time," I said.

"That's a tough road to hoe, son. Why don't you just do your duty and serve your country?"

Serve my country? I didn't feel any obligation to serve my country in the military. That's what the Peace Corps had been all about, alternative service to my country. The military was about coercion. Most people served because they had to, not because they wanted to. However, my father was of the World War II generation when men went off to fight fascism to save democracy without questioning their leaders.

"Now, what are you going to do about work?" Dad asked later during a

Sunday meal of roast beef and mashed potatoes. "You need some money coming in. Maybe I can help you out with a temporary job at the county although it is late in the season."

"Thanks, Dad, but don't worry about it," I replied already itching to move back to Berkeley. "I can probably find something temporary through the Cal Placement Office."

Of course, all the time I was thinking if I had kept my mouth shut and followed the prescribed program, I might be teaching in a classroom upcountry in Nigeria right now.

How did I fuck up so badly? It seemed such a sure thing. I thought I had everything the Peace Corps wanted—good educational background, athletic skills and near fluency in French. I decided my downfall might have begun with the so-called "survival trek" deep in the jungles of Puerto Rico.

1. PEACE CORPS

June 6, 1963

An ocean of lush green envelops me, vital and alive. Yet dying and rotting in the humid trade winds. Deep, deep in the chlorophyll veil, light is diffused by a lace of vegetation, an eternal twilight at midday. A sweat that belongs not only to the body but mixes with the leaf mold, the air and the mosquitoes.

I scribbled this out in my journal while on a three-day survival trek in the mountainous interior of Puerto Rico. I was hot, sweaty and itchy from cutting my way through the jungle.

I and seventy other trainees had been dumped into the wilds and instructed to live off the land. I was taken by boat across a lake in a wilderness area of Lago Dos Bocas and put ashore at the edge of the jungle.

"I'll be back Tuesday," said Jack, my Peace Corps trainer. "There are plenty of bananas and roots around here to help you get through this, Al. You might get hungry, but you won't starve."

Jack stood in the boat in his khaki shorts, bush shirt and deep tan, like the king of the jungle. Nothing fazed him. However, I was not as sure about my situation as I eyed the thick vegetation in front of me. "Sure thing Jack, whatever you say."

"Just remember, Al, your machete is your best friend. Make a clearing and pitch your tent."

And with that, Jack started up his little outboard motor and putted off, hardly leaving a wake.

This whole operation struck me as absurd. Of course, I could survive by eating bananas, but I was sick of bananas. I had been sampling different varieties of bananas for days on short little educational hikes from our base camp. If I ate another banana, I might throw up.

I chopped back into the jungle a few yards until I came to a clearing. I pitched my tent, unrolled my sleeping bag and flopped down. I tried to read a paperback that I had brought along but after a few minutes, I was bored. It was humid and despite the repellent, the mosquitoes were biting. I checked the little map they had given me. According to it, a road was about a hundred yards up the hill. I started to blaze a trail.

I was having second thoughts about the Peace Corps. Six months ago, it seemed the perfect solution to my post-graduate future after UC Berkeley. A chance to travel the world, serve in some exotic location, do some good for mankind while avoiding the draft and save up enough money for graduate school. Sure, it was a hassle getting in what with all the questionnaires, the background investigation, the meetings, and the physical. But after I got through that, I thought it would be clear sailing. Now I was confronted with a Peace Corps staff with the mentality of high school teachers. The staff treated us as if we were little freshmen. It was getting under my skin.

***

As I trekked along, I wondered what Lori was up to. She had told me that she planned to use the survival trek as a dieting opportunity and to read and sleep a lot. I met Lori on the flight from New York to San Juan. We were waiting in line to use the bathroom. Lori was a well-shaped blonde of medium height, blue eyes with a slight Asian slant and a pout. She later told me it was the Scandinavian-Mongol blood in her. As we waited, I struck up a conversation.

"Well, how do you like it so far?" I asked.

"Like what?" she said looking up at me, puzzled.

"The crash training in New York." (We had spent ten hours the previous day listening to lectures on the culture, customs and lifestyle of Puerto Rico.)

"A bit much for just a training camp," she said.

"Yes, three weeks of fun and games in the jungle," I said. "I hope you brought your mosquito repellent."

Lori was from Minnesota and had wide experience with mosquitoes. She had graduated from Smith College in French and had joined the Peace

Corps to teach the language. She had hoped that she would be assigned to a French-speaking West African country such as Senegal or the Ivory Coast, but like me, she settled for Nigeria. The Peace Corps promised she could teach French there. I started conversing in my junior-year-abroad French with her and she seemed pleased. She had only spent a semester in France and was afraid her French was deficient. Actually, she spoke it rather well. So, we hung out together speaking French, even though the emphasis in the training camp was on Spanish.

A few days after our arrival we had the weekend off so Lori and I decided to travel to San Juan together. We took a ramshackle bus down the mountain to Arecibo on the coast and then a taxi over to San Juan. We wandered around for a few hours, checking out El Morro, the 16th-century Spanish fort, and the old section of town. Then we had a couple of daiquiris at the Caribe Hilton Hotel. Now we needed to find a place to stay. I was wondering what the arrangements would be.

As if reading mind, Lori said, "Allan, two rooms are silly and expensive. Let's find one room with two beds. If you can put up with me, I can put up with you."

"Fine by me," I replied.

A quick glance around at Hilton's beautiful open-air lobby with its palm trees and gurgling fountains told us it was too expensive.

The hotel clerk at the front desk pointed out a much cheaper hotel down the street. "Rather modest, but the La Dora is quite pleasant. Lots of atmosphere," said the clerk eyeing Lori.

We walked over and sure enough, it was a quaint colonial type hotel with a courtyard and a fountain. The clerk at the front desk informed us he had room but with only one bed. "It's a very, nice double bed," he smiled.

I took a breath and looked at Lori. She shrugged and said, "Sure, OK."

The room was furnished in heavy Spanish colonial furniture and looked out on the courtyard. Lori nonchalantly plopped her suitcase down on the bed and pulled out a dress for dinner. She went into the bathroom and changed. I put on a pair of white pants and a Hawaiian shirt that I had brought along.

Soon we were wandering around old town looking for a place to eat. We noticed a long line of people at one little joint and decided it must be good because so many people were waiting. Three men joined the line behind us. Two appeared to be African and the third, a slick looking Puerto Rican in a tailored suit. I asked the Puerto Rican if the wait was worth it for this restaurant.

"Well worth it," he said in unaccented English. "For the price, it's the best in San Juan. As you can see, mostly locals eat here. That's why I'm here—to show these gentlemen authentic Puerto Rican cuisine."

Carlos said he worked for the U.S. State Department and was escorting two African diplomats around the country to show them how a third-world country like Puerto Rico was prospering and developing. When he found out we were Peace Corps trainees, he insisted on treating us to dinner, courtesy of the U. S. State Department. Eventually, we were seated at a large table in the courtyard and had a pleasant, lively meal with Carlos and his companions ordering the local specialties washed down with San Miguel beer.

During the meal, one African remarked, "You live well here. But then it's so easy to prosper in Puerto Rico when you are under the umbrella of the U.S. government."

Carlos responded, "It has its advantages but there is much here that any country can do. And of course, there is the question of aid. Kennedy has vowed to increase foreign aid to your country."

"Of course, for which we would be most grateful," nodded the African, holding his San Miguel up as a toast.

After the meal, Carlos took us all to a nightclub where we danced and had a few drinks. Lori was enjoying herself. Quite a good dancer, she even made me look good. Of course, Carlos was the best and danced with her several times. I had the feeling if I went to the bathroom, he would make a move on her. However, Carlos was a perfect gentleman, as were the older middle-aged Africans who also took turns dancing with Lori.

That night after a chaste kiss on our balcony, Lori and I slept apart in our big double bed like an old married couple.

***

Coming back to the training camp late the next afternoon, we got a few knowing looks from other volunteers and a scowl from Jack. Apparently, we had been noticed as an item. Later, Jack spoke to me alone.

"You know, Al, you and Lori going off like that alone is not a good idea. Especially so early in this training."

I tried to hide my irritation. This was Jack's Boy Scout mentality showing up.

"Why not?" I replied. "Lots of trainees went off to San Juan this weekend,"

"Yes, they did but they went in groups, not in pairs"

"So what? We're grown-ups," I said. "They probably split into pairs later."

"Maybe but it's the image thing. You know people are watching, taking note of behaviors. A word to the wise, be discreet."

I told Lori about this encounter. She said one of the women Peace Corps counselors talked to her too. She thought it was all bullshit as well but did say it might be good not to be so obvious around camp. "We could still see each other, Allan, out of range of the others."

And lo, one clear, warm starry night with the gentle trade winds blowing, Lori and I snuck off from camp and found a giant banana leaf upon which to lounge. The air was sweet and filled with the fecundity of the earth. Lori laughed and giggled as I nestled down beside her, the massive leaf protecting us from the bugs and crawly things. Her eyes reflected the starstruck night in the small clearing in the jungle in which we lay. Then all was at peace. All was hidden.

***

Lori faded from my mind as I broke through the last few yards of jungle and came out on the dirt road. I walked along the road a half-mile until I came to a ramshackle little store or *tienda* as they called it here. Inside, the store was chock full of beer, cheese, vegetables and chickens, fresh, plucked and hanging on hooks. The lady behind the counter acted as if she had been expecting me.

Damn, I was hungry! I went to war with myself. This was supposed to be a survival trek. Live off the land. Roots, bugs, maybe a small bird brought down with a slingshot. Most likely bananas though. Two days of bananas. I was in a quandary. Finally, I decided I didn't want to live on bananas like Lori. I wanted a beer and some bread and cheese. That was living off the land too, I rationalized. You explore your terrain and gather what is edible. Well in my terrain, there happened to be a tienda stocked full of goodies. Wasn't that what an explorer would do if he came upon a store in the middle of the wilderness? Stock up when he could. Who would know anyway?

The beer and bread with cheese tasted good. I consumed most of it right there in the store. Then I brought some back to my little camp along with a half-chicken that I cooked for dinner over an open fire. It was tough and plain tasting with no seasoning but it did the job of nourishing me.

I crawled into my tent around eight and read for an hour by flashlight.

Then I dozed off, awakening hours later to a gray, damp dawn, feeling stiff and bitten. This outdoor stuff in the tropics sucked. They should have given us mosquito netting.

I spent a lot of time looking at the lake that morning, half-hoping to see the boat but knowing it was not due until noon the next day. I hiked back up to the tienda for coffee and rolls for breakfast. As I came back into camp, I spotted Jack climbing out of his boat down on the lakeshore. Shit! What was he doing here? He was a day early.

I dumped the food into the brush and kicked dirt and leaves over the fire and the remains of the last night's chicken. A minute later, Jack came walking up.

"What's up, Jack?"

"Change of plans, Al. We have to shorten this training exercise by a day. We're going to have a special visitor at the base camp tomorrow. Everybody has to be there. I'm here to take you back," he said glancing around, noticing the remains of the fire covered by leaves.

"So how did you get along, Al?"

"Fine, just fine, Jack. I ate a lot of bananas."

"Good. Had a little fire, did you? Gets cold at night up here."

I wondered if he could smell the coffee on my breath.

I packed up and climbed into Jack's boat with my gear and we motored off. Survival camp was over and done with.

That special visitor to the Peace Corps Camp turned out to be Vice President Lyndon Johnson. I didn't see Johnson because the Peace Corps officials decided to make it look like a regular day of training for the Vice President. So I was off with some others on a rock climbing training session.

Those who were in camp described Johnson as a friendly, folksy man. He simply walked through the main camp nodding and smiling, shaking hands and saying hello to those who were around. Still, he was in a hurry and didn't have time to check out the training exercises that were taking place out of the camp area. Nevertheless, the word was Peace Corps funding was assured for another year

***

At the main camp, we slept in bunkhouses with an outhouse and a washhouse. Meals were taken in a large open-air dining hall with a tin roof. Amenities were few except for a large swimming pool down the road and a library. Overall, the Peace Corps camp reminded me of a Boy Scout operation—rustic, run by gung-ho counselors, mostly former teachers.

Many of my fellow volunteers were from the East Coast, although Alex, a hip English major was from Duke in North Carolina. He liked literature and writing and was fascinated with Lawrence Durrell and the concept of "negritude."

"Look at the first chapter in *Justine,* in Durrell's *Alexandria Quartet,*" said Alex. "Dust tormented streets. Beggars and flies. Five races, five languages, five sexes. Lemon scented skies. Doesn't that put you right into the place?"

"It sure does," I replied, "but people I know who have been there say Alexandria is a shithole now and probably wasn't much better back in the 1930s when Durrell was there."

"Of course Al, but what a wonderful shithole. Anyway, it doesn't matter what it's really like. It's what's in the writer's imagination."

"I prefer Henry Miller's description of 1930's Paris during his down and out days," I said. "He was a bum and a freeloader but he had the right spirit about the place."

"Yes, but Durrell is much more appropriate to our situation now," countered Alex. "He describes Alexandria as the culmination of Africa—a mélange of all the continent's people including the black races of central Africa. Just think of it, Al. Hundreds of miles south, across the wind-swept Sahara lies the groin of the continent. Abidjan, Lagos, Accra--a fecund humidity in which strange growths thrive," said Alex waxing poetic.

"I hope not too strange," I responded. "At least I hope they are curable. All this Peace Corps talk about bilharzia, sleeping sickness, malaria and god knows what else."

"Don't worry about it, man. The important thing is to groove on the blackness of it all. Ever read Aimé Césaire on negritude? Or Sartre's *Black Orpheus?* Or perhaps negritude's more popular expression by James Baldwin?"

"Yeah, I read Baldwin's *The Fire Next Time.* I even saw him once at Berkeley. He certainly delves into the black experience but it's focused on America and France."

"Doesn't matter. It's all the same thing. Africa is the starting point," Alex insisted. "That's where it's at."

***

A typical day in camp began at 5:30 a.m. "Rise and shine," Jack would shout, already in his khaki shorts and T-shirt at the barrack entrance. You could see he was itching for another day of enlightened harassment. It was still dark outside, the tropical dawn not due for another half hour. Muttering and bitching, we rose, pulled on our shorts and T-shirts, took a piss and splashed some cold water on our faces in the washhouse and were ready to go.

We usually began the training day with a mile run on a dirt road through the jungle. The first half was a pleasant downhill jog through the cool dawn. The second half was a killer, up the hill at a more rapid pace with Jack leading the way. The run was followed by calisthenics ending with the dreaded rope climb. This was a 2 ½ inch thick rope dangling down twenty feet from a sturdy tree branch. Every day we were expected to make progress up it hand over hand. No hooking of feet allowed. At 6'3" and two-hundred pounds and in good shape, I thought I could ace the rope climbing. However, a body that served me well in most sports was not designed for rope climbing. It was a struggle. It took me several tries a day for several days to make it all the way to the top. In the beginning, only light little girls could make it to the top. At the end of the three-week camp session, still only half of the men could do it.

The exercise period was followed by a large breakfast of eggs cooked to order, hash browns, sausage, ham, bacon, pancakes, French toast, and a wide variety of tropical fruits—papaya, mango, pineapple, paw-paw, melon and bananas. You could have as much as you wanted. Everybody stuffed themselves. Following breakfast, we listened to lectures about the Peace Corps and our mission in Nigeria. This was followed by an hour of Spanish lessons so we could communicate with the Puerto Ricans when we went off on our treks. Often we went on a midday hike to examine the local flora and fauna in this mountainous section of the island. It was during these treks we were instructed on how to live off the land.

After an hour rest in the afternoon, we hiked down to the swimming pool for training in basic lifesaving techniques and open water survival. Then several times during the three weeks, we were trained in rudimentary rock climbing and repelling. Overall, it was a healthy Tarzan existence.

***

Our third and final week of the training session was highlighted by a three-day cross-country trek designed to meet the local people. Unlike, the survival trek, we could officially buy food along the way. All we carried were our sleeping bags, toiletries, canteens and our machetes. I was with three other volunteers, two of them obviously intent on following the rules of the trek to the letter.

We began the trek by hiking a mile or two down the mountain road from the Peace Corps camp until we came to a large lake (Lago Caonillas) in the Rio Abajo National Forest. Hot and sweaty from our hike, we bought cokes from a nearby tienda and relaxed in the shade. Two large canoes sat on the lakeshore waiting for us. According to the trek instructions, we were to use the canoes to paddle several miles across the lake, two people per canoe.

One of the volunteers, George, looked at the canoes and then at the long expanse of water and announced, "Shit, I'm not going to get in one of those things and cramp my knees up. I'm going to hitch around to the other side. You guys can paddle by yourself."

The other two volunteers were alarmed that our expedition was already falling apart. "Hey, you can't do that George. We are supposed to canoe together."

"No way," said George. "I'm not going to wreck my knees anymore. I screwed them up playing football. That's enough. I'm hitching around. I'll be other side waiting for you." With that, he walked off down the road.

I too looked at the long expanse of water. It was early afternoon. The heat and humidity were at its most intense. I too was in no mood to canoe across the lake. All I wanted was a beer and a siesta. Plus, I had noticed a cute little Puerto Rican girl in the tienda working behind the counter and thought, "Hey, are we not supposed to meet people? She's a people."

As George lumbered off down the road to hitch a ride, I approached the two remaining volunteers. "You guys go ahead. I want to hang here and rest up some more. If I don't catch up with you in two hours, just continue. I have a map of the route we are supposed to take. I'll catch up sooner or later."

"Brown, you're as bad as George. You're not going by the established procedure," said one.

"Worry not. See ya," I said.

The two volunteers shrugged and loaded up one of the canoes and paddled off. I waved goodbye from the shore.

The girl had been watching all of this and listening. I suspected she understood English. I went back to the store and bought a beer from her. Her name was Olga and she did speak English. I explained I was in the Peace Corps. She knew all about it.

"Yes, I know. You are on a hike to meet people. You stay here tonight and be with real Puerto Rican family."

"*Muy bueno, gracias,*" I said all the while gazing at her bright black eyes, at once shining and smiling. She took me to her house next door, a ramshackle affair that looked as if it might collapse any second. However, inside it was quite comfortable and one bedroom had a large queen size bed with fine linen on it. This was to be my bed.

"I couldn't," I protested. "I have a sleeping bag. I'll sleep in the hammock on the porch."

The porch looked out on the lake and seemed inviting.

"No, no." she insisted. "You are our guest."

"OK."

I met the mother, a pleasant, placid lady who was sitting at a sewing machine. Later, the father came home in a pickup. He did construction somewhere. Olga ran the store. Both parents went into the house and discreetly disappeared. Olga and I sat on the front porch. I was drinking another beer, now lounging in the hammock while little Olga with her bright black eyes chattered in English, saying she did not often have a chance to speak English with Americans. She brought out snacks and fruit, papaya, bananas, melon. We ate and looked out to the lake. It was peaceful. She sat for a while humming quietly, then pulled out an English romance novel and started reading. The large hammock swung gently on the porch. I was nodding off, having had one beer too many.

"That's OK. You take a siesta, that's what Puerto Ricans do. Take life easy on a hot day," she said.

I closed my eyes, and fell asleep,

When I woke up an hour or so later, it was nearly dark and Olga had gone back to the tienda to sell more food and beer to the locals now coming home from work. Inside the house, her mother was fixing dinner, while the father was watching a small black and white TV in the corner. The smells of cooking beans and chicken wafted through the dwelling. Soon we were dining on a delicious meal of rice and beans and succulent roasted chicken, washed down with San Miguel beer. Later, it was back on the porch for Olga and me. I told her I had to leave early the next day.

"That's OK but I want you to write me from New York. I want to know about your life. Maybe when I graduate from high school, I can visit you."

I looked at her. Olga, a small dark universe with her dark shining eyes, a little fairy queen flitting about that wretched tienda. All dressed up now in a Chinese silk dress with slits on the side. Radiant beyond words, an innocent waiting for the arms of a stranger. An airy-fairy fluttering in the tropic air.

I slept alone in the beautiful double bed that night listening to the sounds of the jungle and wondered if it would be possible to see Olga down the road. The next morning, as I bade her and her parents farewell, I promised Olga I would write and I did over the next several months. Then she wrote me that she had a job in San Juan where she would finish her schooling and make some money. After that, I never heard from her again. She had probably met some guy and was now happily married in the jungle.

***

It took me three hours to paddle across the lake and hike to the rendezvous point. I saw no sign of the others so I walked along a dirt road hoping I might run into them somewhere. Still no sign of my fellow trekkers. Finally, I checked my map and figured it was about a twenty-mile hike to the next rendezvous point near the village of Maraquez. No way was I going to hike that in this heat so I hitched a ride in a pickup truck to Maraguez. The Peace Corps directives had been vague about our mode of transportation. We had initially assumed it was to be on foot but they did not specifically forbid a lift now and then from the locals.

Maraquez turned out to be nothing but a tienda and a few ramshackle houses. I looked around a bit but no sign of my fellow trekkers. Onward.

According to the trek map, I had to hike to the peak of a nearby mountain, Pico Pinto, which was another five-hundred feet in elevation. After a short rest and a coke, I followed the road up near the crest of the mountain. By that time, the road had dissolved into a trail. I passed many broken down huts inhabited mostly by women and dirty little babies. Sloe-eyed mothers peered out from their miserable huts. One offered me some water which I desperately needed since I had forgotten to fill my canteen. I dissolved my water purification tablets into a tin cup, took a sip and continued. Finally, the jungle was so thick I could barely make headway even with my machete. I decided to forget the summit. I descended to the road again and hitched a ride around to the other side of the mountain, still wondering where my group was.

The other side of Pico Pinto turned out to be in an upscale neighborhood of haciendas on the outskirts of the coastal town of Ponce. Now walking on paved roads near the top, I had a panoramic view of the countryside. Low clouds brushed the mountaintops, cutting off all but a ribbon of the blue Caribbean in the distance. On the arid flat below lay sprawling Ponce dripping into the sea. At my back, a humid sun penetrated my shirt but a soft wind cooled me off. I sat down on the curb and took it all in.

Across the road, a series of small waterfalls tumbled down a rock cliff hewn out of the mountainside. Each rivulet dripped into vine-entangled pools of various depths, producing a water symphony of sound. I got up, crossed the road and dunked my head into one of these pools and felt the refreshing flow of the water down my neck and shoulders. As I was drying off, the winds suddenly increased and the clouds drew nearer, darkening the sky to the south. I started walking fast down the hill, then running for a nearby tienda as the heavens opened up into a tropical downpour.

***

After a beer on the tienda's veranda, the storm dissipated. I caught a ride to Ponce and checked into a budget hotel. Later, I enjoyed a good meal, feeling no guilt whatsoever for living off the land in my own particular style.

Strolling back to my hotel, I encountered a husky, outdoorsy looking woman wearing a Peace Corps T-shirt.

"A Peace Corps trainee?" she inquired, looking me over.

"Ah...yeah." I replied.

"I'm with the staff here in Puerto Rico," she said as if that was important for me to know.

"Do tell."

"So where's your group?" she asked looking up and down the street. "You're not alone are you?"

I had never seen this babe before and concluded she was not involved in my training camp session so I made up a story. "Uh, they're around somewhere. We're relaxing in Ponce before hitting the bush again."

"Is that part of the game plan?" she asked accusingly. "Aren't you are supposed to stick to the jungle and meet the real folk, not these city types who all speak English."

"Well, you do what you can. We've had plenty of jungle," I explained. "We go back in tomorrow."

She shook her head and walked off down the street.

"Mind your own business bitch," I muttered to myself. I went back to my comfortable hotel room with a big double bed and slept.

The next morning, I hitched a ride to the final rendez-vous point where the Peace Corps truck was supposed to pick us up. I waited two hours and still no truck. Then I started to hitchhike back to the Peace Corps training camp, now worried what Jack would say if I came in alone without my group. Between hitched rides, the Peace Corps truck finally came lumbering along. I waved it down. On board were my fellow trekkers, dirty, tired and disgusted. They had gotten lost and spent two wet nights camping in the bush. They looked me over enviously. I, who was clean, rested and happy, said, "Well you should have stayed with me at Olga's tienda meeting the natives."

Later back at camp, I heard through the grapevine that the two straight-arrow trekkers had ratted me out and that my errant behavior had been noted. I imagined it being recorded in some Peace Corps log as "not a team player" and forwarded it to Columbia University where we were to undergo the next phase of our training.

The third week ended with exams which included rappelling down a two-hundred-foot dam, climbing cliffs and bobbing in the ocean for a half-hour with hands and feet tied. This latter exercise was part of the open-water survival course. After we were done with that little bit of insanity, we snorkeled for an hour in a pristine cove and I examined my first coral reef with all the bright fish swimming about. I resolved someday to learn how to scuba dive and see it up close.

***

At the end of our training session, we bussed it back to San Juan to spend the night before flying back to New York. This time, courtesy of the U.S. government, the whole group checked into the luxurious Caribe Hilton with its great beach, pools and tons of tropical splendor.

After checking in, I told my roommate, Bob, that I was expecting a guest and hinted that he might want to disappear which he did. Soon Lori knocked at the door and a few minutes later, we started getting it on. However, right in the middle of the proceedings, the door opened and Bob barged in, saying he had forgotten his bathing suit. I sat up and Lori pulled the covers over her head, hiding. Mouth agape, Bob apologized for disturbing us and disappeared immediately.

Lori, now dressing, chided me for not using the bolt lock on the door. "You should think of those things, Allan. Jeez, what an embarrassment!"

I sensed our amour was in peril. When I saw Bob again, he gave me a funny look.

"Say Bob, be a pal," I said trying to act nonchalant. "Don't mention what happened in the room. We don't want to start rumors."

"Sure, Brown. I understand."

But I wondered if he really did.

Later, Lori and I had another great meal out at our favorite restaurant in the old section. This time other volunteers joined us. I noticed that Lori was distant. Nevertheless, we all ate and sipped margaritas to excess and then went dancing for our last night in Puerto Rico.

The next day we flew to New York.

2. COLUMBIA

It turned out that the dorms at Columbia University were hotter and more humid than the jungles of Puerto Rico. The air-conditioning had been turned off for the summer. Large fans blew air through the common rooms and the hallways in a futile effort to keep things cool. Fans in the dorm rooms were at the volunteer's expense. My room was small, cramped and stifling. I forced opened the window to get some air and later ran out to buy a fan.

My roommate was Chris, a tall, skinny fellow with a goatee and a beret. He told me he was a music major from Lawrence College in Wisconsin and wanted to spread the word. "Like it's music that's the international language! That's what is going to bring people together!"

I agreed.

Chris said he wanted study African music and teach the western variety to budding young African musicians and develop some mix of the two.

"Sounds like a program," I replied.

The Peace Corps group was much larger now, some two hundred volunteers versus the seventy or so who trained in Puerto Rico. The Puerto Rican contingent was feeling smug. We were tanned, tough and hip to the Peace Corps gig. We felt we were the stars of the show and on the fast track to overseas. Only later did we realize that Puerto Rican sojourn meant little in the grand scheme of formal Peace Corps training at Columbia.

The next day I filled out forms, took a physical and got shots for a myriad of diseases I didn't know existed. I spent the afternoon taking an annoying battery of interest and psychology tests.

On the psychology test, I was confronted with such questions as: *What does a black tarry bowel movement make you think of?*

"Shit, man, shit," I whispered, shaking my head.

After an hour of this crazed test-taking, my positive mental attitude was disintegrating fast, so I started answering the multiple choice questions willy-nilly, treating the whole thing as a joke. As I was to learn later, this was a serious mistake.

The classroom training included lectures on Nigerian politics, culture, and language—all taught by assistant professor types from state colleges around the nation. Most preached the superiority of the U.S. democracy and its suitability for emerging African nations. At the same time, they disparaged the socialist and communist trends in Africa.

"You know that they train many sons of the African elites at Moscow University," stated one crew-cut professor. "The best influence we can have on them is to demonstrate the power of democracy and we can do that through our culture. In addition to teaching English, history or French, we can teach them basketball."

The class blinked. "Basketball?"

"Yes, it's a great game," he enthused. "Cheap to set up and best of all, it's purely an American game. The Nigerians have their cricket, soccer and so on but basketball perfectly expresses our American way of life—loose, free-flowing, spontaneous, yet coordinated and winning. That's what American democracy is all about."

"Huh?"

Returnee Peace Corps volunteers came to our classes and extolled the glories of Nigeria but told us to watch out for the British colonials who viewed the Americans as naive and the Peace Corps as President Kennedy's kiddy corps doing diplomacy on the cheap. As one returnee put it, "The Brits are fun to be around but rather cynical about the whole idea of the Peace Corps. They will always point out how it was the British who brought the Nigerians into the 20th century."

We were also warned never to be to open in our criticism of Nigerian society. Two years earlier a Peace Corps volunteer, 23-year-old Marjorie Michelmore, had written a postcard describing the miserable conditions in Ibadan, Nigeria:

> With all the training we had, we were absolutely not prepared
> for the squalor and absolutely primitive living conditions rampant
> both in the city and in the bush...

It was a rather mild criticism but somehow, she lost the postcard and it was found by a Nigerian college student who had copies made and distributed it. Peace Corps volunteers were then denounced as "agents of imperialism and members of America's international spy ring." This made front-page news in Nigeria and for a while sparked an international protest but eventually, things cooled down and the volunteers went on to serve in Nigeria without further incident.

***

One day a visiting psychologist bluntly posed the following question to the men in the class: "How do you plan to deal with sex in Nigeria?"

Most men had a variety of answers including, "I'm married...," "I plan to become a priest...," "Self-gratification."

The females in class giggled.

"The willing daughter of the chief," I joked.

"No, not the correct answer," the psychologist sniffed. "The correct answer is you will fraternize only with other Peace Corps workers and expatriates."

A flash image in my mind:

I am off in a grass hut somewhere upcountry miles away from the nearest white woman. I'm supposed to be teaching French but I wind up teaching everything to grade school kids and organizing basketball games. The days are long and boring and the beer is warm. My maid is 13-years-old but a full-grown woman. Black as ebony, skin glistening in the sun, she turns a wide eye to me. We go off to the hut for a siesta where I personally explore the meaning of negritude.

In fact, such a scenario was highly unlikely. They told us most teachers in our group would be assigned to well-established schools in major towns and villages where there were plenty of other expatriates and fellow volunteers. However, great emphasis was still put on relating to Africans and learning their ways.

I took this lesson to heart and started going to the West End Bar where many Africans attending Columbia hung out. This was a scruffy, cavernous bar/restaurant on Broadway where the beer and food were cheap and the talk lively. Most Africans at Columbia were socialists and some even proclaimed to be communists.

"See it this way, Allan," said Amari, a well-dressed Yoruba from Nigeria. "The Peace Corps is a nice idea but to many Africans, it's just another face of imperialism. The more extreme suspect it is full of spies and saboteurs."

Amari readily admitted he had done time in Moscow but he said it was too boring and the women not too appealing. He vastly preferred New York and Columbia with the nightlife. "One cannot live by ideology alone," he said with a twinkle in his eye.

The Africans were great fun and good dancers. A few of us volunteers went to parties with them where we learned to dance the "highlife." One of my companions was Jean, a free spirit from Colby College in Maine. We were having a great time but after a few parties, Alex warned us that he was getting bad vibes.

"I heard through the grapevine the Peace Corps brass prefer we attend their sponsored parties with designated Africans."

"No way" I protested. "I'm not going to those boring little soirees with the sons and daughters of establishment African diplomats at the U.N."

"Yeah, I know they suck but what are you going to do?" Alex shrugged.

"Man, these socialist cats are where it's at," I said. "This is the real Africa."

I'm not arguing with you, Allan," said Alex. "It's just that these dudes are too radical for the Corps and it doesn't do any of us any good being seen with them."

Still, Jean and I continued to hang with them anyway and to have a great time dancing the "highlife."

***

We also got a glimpse into the local black power movement in New York. At Alex's urging, Jean, I and several others went to a rally staged by Malcolm X in Harlem a few blocks east of Columbia.

As Alex put it, "Africans are fine but we can't ignore the voice of their black brothers in America."

In the summer of 1963, Malcolm X was considered the most radical black man around. He was a convicted criminal and possibly a murderer. Yet, Alex thought he was cool. He said Malcolm X's militancy was the way to make the white establishment sit up and take notice.

The streets were jammed for blocks. Police helicopters whirled overhead while cops staked out rooftops, their riot guns at the ready. No doubt, plain-clothes policemen and FBI agents milled about in the crowd, some taking photos. Malcolm, impeccable in a dark suit and tie, spoke in a calm but penetrating voice telling his black audience to never turn the other cheek when it came to white man.

"Right on man, tell whitey how it is," shouted one black next to me.

Malcolm told the crowd that blacks needed nothing from the white man except to be left alone because the white man was the devil and could bring no good. After all, it was the white man who had kidnapped the black man from Africa.

Despite the militant rhetoric, most blacks just smiled and nodded at us as we joined them in the cheering. For some strange reason, we felt completely safe in this restless crowd. And Malcolm, the black man of the moment, seemed like a God. Few could imagine that he would be murdered by his own people a couple of years later.

***

By this time, my relationship with Lori had definitely cooled, although she did invite me to a party with some of her Ivy League friends working in New York for the summer. We sat around in a hot, suffocating little apartment on the East Side and drank beer from a keg. I found them a square bunch, overly worried about their careers.

The women talked about their little jobs as editorial assistants at various publishing houses and the men about mailroom life at the ad agencies and brokerage firms. I thought the low point of the evening came when a Harvard MBA student, sweating in a white shirt and tie, held forth on his great new job with S & L Green Stamps.

"This is where the markets are headed," he claimed. "Coupon discounts on everything from gas to bread. Of course, what the consumer doesn't know is that the overall price is jacked up for everyone whether they use the stamps or not."

Later, on the crosstown bus back to Columbia, Lori was quiet, looking out the window. Finally, she said, "You seemed bored at the party, Allan."

"Oh no, not bored," I replied. "I simply can't relate to people who have their life all planned out in the service of corporate America."

"Well, at least they know where they are going. They're directed. You might take a hint."

"Not me. I'm happy-go-lucky. You know that."

"Sure, I know that." She paused and looked at me with her clear blue eyes and then said. "Allan, this can't go anywhere. What happened in Puerto Rico was Puerto Rico. Now we are living in a fishbowl. I want to make it through the training and go to Africa. I've dreamed about it ever since Kennedy created the Peace Corps. I can't get distracted"

"Distracted?" I said puzzled. "Lori, we both have the same dream. I want to go to Nigeria too but I still want to see you. I mean it's not mutually exclusive, is it?"

Looking out the window, she didn't answer.

I didn't see Lori much after that. Frankly, her friends did bore me. I kept hanging out with Jean and the Africans. Jean was wide-open chick, with a big smile and an athletic body. She excelled in volleyball and lacrosse and wanted to teach both in Nigeria. She had brown hair and well-shaped limbs and a great curved back. Her favorite song was "Chantilly Lace."

> *Chantilly Lace and a pretty face and a ponytail*
> *hanging' down. A wiggle in the walk and a giggle*
> *in the talk...Makes the world go'round.*

She would sing it as we made the long, hot walk from the gym to field-hockey fields in the park on Riverside Drive. The late afternoon sun shining through the haze of humidity cast blue shadows on the sidewalk. Almost like Africa. We could taste it. We could feel it. Jean with her lacrosse stick loping along the field, graceful, fast and full of skill, snatching that little ball up and whirling into the net for a score. I could imagine us being off somewhere in upcountry Nigeria, far from the naggings of the Peace Corps.

***

Meanwhile, Peace Corps training at Columbia marched on, now focusing on teacher training. Since I had spent a year abroad in Aix-en-Provence, France, followed by a minor in French at Berkeley, I was assigned to teach French. For two weeks, I taught a beginning French class at a high school in the Bronx. This was my first experience with inner-city education. The school was a scruffy complex of large brick buildings in a slummy area of the Bronx. Mostly blacks and Hispanics, the high school juniors looked twenty-five going on thirty. The males seemed one step removed from state prison. The women, while smart, appeared to be more interested in nailing a guy and getting married than studying French. The irony was that this group represented the motivated kids who needed at least one year of French or some other foreign language to graduate from high school and possibly go on to college. I thought I did rather well but the observer, a little man with a wimpy mustache, noted that I made a couple of mistakes in gender agreement. Eventually, I got into the swing of teaching French and felt I was connecting. Indeed, another observer told me I had the magic touch in communicating with the kids.

Our Peace Corps training also included various sports. We were instructed in rugby, soccer and cricket. I was familiar with rugby and soccer but cricket left me baffled. I played as well as the other volunteers but when the games dragged on for hours, I began to yearn for old-fashion American baseball. However, most of the emphasis was on basketball, the American sport the Peace Corps wanted desperately to export. I had played varsity basketball in high school and on an intramural basis in college. I was good at both playing and teaching the sport. I figured this would be a plus with the Peace Corps.

***

In mid-August, the big day came for the final selection of volunteers. The Peace Corps brass had already told us that about a quarter of us would not be going to Nigeria because they had more volunteers than needed for this particular tour. Everyone from Puerto Rico contingent felt sure he or she would be selected to go.

The morning of the final cut, a slip of paper in my mail box told me to report Assembly Hall "B" and later to a counselor's office. I checked with some other volunteers. Most were headed to Assembly Hall "A" This did not bode well. I and about fifty others (many from the Puerto Rico gang) filed into Hall "B" and sat down. One of the underlings eventually came out and informed us that we would not be going to Nigeria.

"This is no reflection for the most part on your skills as a volunteer," he explained in a high whiny voice. "It's just an unfortunate development in matching manpower to the needs and wants of the host country. We thank you profusely for your time and effort in this Peace Corps training phase. And we encourage you to apply again for other terms of service overseas. You will receive full consideration."

Stunned silence in the audience. Then a low murmur and shaking of heads as we filed out the auditorium.

Later, while waiting for our appointment with the counselors, we joked trying to make light of the situation. The general attitude was, "Well at least we had a great time in New York and Puerto Rico at government expense."

However, this was a pathetic attempt to cover up our deep disappointment and shock at not being considered fit enough to join the "A" team. Alex, Lori and Chris made the cut but Jean did not. She was in tears.

"What did I do wrong?" she sobbed.

"Nothing. You did nothing wrong. You would have been perfect." I consoled her wondering if it was her association with me and the Africans that was the kiss of death.

I finally went in to see the counselor. A heavyset, balding man in a rumpled gray business suit sat behind the desk. With sweat popping out on his brow, he told me again what I had already heard: the Peace Corps could not use my services this time but to re-apply, perhaps next for a more appropriate slot.

"I see here you have experience in land surveying," he noted, "Surveying skills are something we can use, road building and the like"

"Yes, I do have experience surveying. My father is a civil engineer. Surveying is a family tradition. But what was my problem here with this group? How come I was selected out?"

Leaning back in his cheap government swivel chair, he said, "The observers told us that you had the makings of a good teacher, but were not skilled enough in French, plus there was the matter of your psychological testing. The analyzers felt that you did not take the tests seriously enough. Either that or you are seriously unbalanced."

"That was a joke. It means nothing." I replied.

"We realize that but the psychologists say it shows hostility to authority. We can't take a chance in these touchy times."

"What about basketball? My record must show I did rather well coaching the sport," I responded.

"Yes, all of that was duly noted," he said, "However, we feel that you might be better off signing up for another tour down the road if you wish. We simply have too many volunteers for this one. It was partly our oversight. We apologize."

He handed me a wad of cash for airfare and expenses back to California and told me I was expected to clear out by end of day. "Oh by the way, Mr. Brown," he said escorting me to the door, "we are going to have to notify your draft board that you are no longer with the Peace Corps, so you might want to do something about that."

"Thanks. I certainly will," I said stunned, now realizing that my grand master plan for the next two years was wrecked and in all probability, it was Hello, Uncle Sam.

***

I hung around the dorm for a couple of hours, then packed and said goodbye to Lori.

"You were too much to handle for the Peace Corps," she said, as we walked out the dorm together.

"You know what this means don't you?" I said.

"No, not really," she replied.

"The Army."

"Might do you some good," she said, giving me a little kiss on the cheek.

Little Lorie, so conventional after all. Well, fuck'em all.

I briefly considered staying in New York and working. I had enough money for a few weeks until I found a job. However, I was not in the mood to job hunt during a hot, muggy New York summer. In addition, staying here did nothing to solve my draft problem. So I took a cab to Idlewild Airport (later renamed Kennedy Airport) and boarded the first flight back to California via Chicago. It was over and out for the Peace Corps.

3. HOMEWARD

So why was I going to Chicago instead of flying non-stop to California? It was a long, complicated story. I was going to visit Bobbie, an old girlfriend from my junior-year-abroad in France. We had planned to go into the Peace Corps together, but fate intervened and I had gone in on my own. Still, I wanted to see her.

I had brought along my favorite snapshot of Bobbie at Sts.-Maries-de-la-Mer in the Camargue in the South of France. The photo showed her moments after running around a small *corrida* with a little bull chasing her. Her face was streaked with dust, but she was smiling with her wholesome blonde, Midwestern looks.

When I phoned her from New York, Bobbie couldn't believe that I had been ejected from the Peace Corps.

"What did you do?"

"Let's don't go into that."

"You must have done something. Probably it was your rebellious attitude or something with some woman."

"No. Well, maybe, I replied. "Anyway, my basic problem was you weren't there."

"Let's not go into that."

Initially, Bobby and I had gone around together as "friends" while attending the American Institute in Aix-En-Provence. However, after we traveled off alone to Greece for a month, things got intense and we started talking about a future together. One scenario was to join the Peace Corps together. However, a chance encounter in Paris with a neighborhood boyfriend had thrown our relationship into a tizzy. Bobbie confessed she was still madly in love with Tom. Tom, who was at the Naval Academy, hadn't given her the time of day. However, after a five-day sojourn in Paris in which it was obvious that Bobbie and I were staying in the same hotel room, Tom's interest seemed to perk up. Of course, he was shacking up with Bobbie's best friend, Jackie who was traveling with us. After London, I had to fly home because my money had run out. Bobby, Jackie and Tom traveled on throughout England and Scotland. That fall Tom dropped out of the Naval Academy, enrolled in Northwestern University, and began dating Bobbie.

Bobbie met me at O'Hare Airport and was as nice and charming as usual, but a bit distant. We did the usual routine of the Field Museum, the Art Institute, and Roth's Blackhawk Restaurant. However, after a day, I could tell the fire was gone. Two days later, I bid her goodbye with a kiss on the cheek and was on my way to the airport where I made a last minute change of plans and booked a flight to Los Angeles. I wanted to see Darrah, yet another old girlfriend. I gave her a call from O'Hare, half-expecting to be told to buzz off. Instead, I got an earful of sympathy at my Peace Corps demise and an invitation to see her.

***

At LAX, Darrah was waiting, sharply dressed in an aqua-blue tailored suit with a blinding white blouse. She was very L.A. looking, tanned and slim, her long black hair glistening.

"Bubba," she said and gave me a big fat kiss. Our little departure scene last May seemed to have been forgotten. We had had a fling last spring semester before I went off to the Peace Corps. It ended badly when Darrah discovered I was leaving a few days early for Peace Corps because I was going to see Bobbie in Chicago. "That blonde bitch," as she put it. "That's who you really care about." But now, all seemed to be forgiven.

As Darrah drove me to her parent's house in West Los Angeles, she told me she was going to summer school at UCLA taking courses in music appreciation and film. I related the Peace Corps fiasco.

"I never thought you could put up with that kiddy corps stuff for long," she said pulling up in front a modest two-story stucco bungalow. I retrieved my suitcase from the trunk and was starting up the steps to the front door when Darrah pulled my sleeve.

"This way Allan. We live down here," she said as she led me through a basement door into a downstairs apartment. While large and well-appointed, it was dark and gloomy.

"My mother is in real estate and she rents the upstairs to another family," Darrah explained. "We're crammed into this basement for the time being. We're supposed to move to a bigger house soon with no apartments for renters."

Her parents were not home but her tomboy sister Tomi was. Tomi, a striking, sun-streaked blonde, showed me her surfboard, "It's one of the shorter boards. Fiberglass. Really, rad. It catches the waves just right. Almost thinks by itself."

Tomi surfed at Malibu and that was an embarrassment to the family. Darrah later told me according to her mother, "Jews don't surf."

"Tomi is a terrible student," Darrah continued. "She couldn't even make it into UCLA. She goes to junior college but is threatening to drop out."

"I guess you're the brains of the family?" I observed.

"I'm not that smart. I just work hard. I know good grades are essential. Good grades I nearly blew because of you last semester."

She came at me with her fist in a mock battle. I playfully held her off, knowing she was probably horny but we could do nothing about it right then.

I dutifully met Darrah's mother and father. She was a tall imposing woman, the father, a small, meek-looking little man who did not say much. He gave me a perfunctory hello and made a beeline for the couch to read his newspaper. Darrah told me her father rented downtown office space. Her mother provided the real income with her real estate.

We had a congenial dinner talking about Berkeley and the Peace Corps. It was known that I wasn't Jewish but nobody seemed concerned about that. As Darrah explained, her family was not religious. That night, I slept in Tomi's room. Tomi had decamped to a friend's house.

I was half-asleep when I heard the door creep open. It was Darrah in her nightgown.

"Darrah, what are you doing here?"

"Shh... I am just visiting. I want to be with you for a while."

"OK. But we can't do anything. Not here in your house. Your mother would kill us."

"Shh... don't worry about it."

She crawled in and snuggled down but did not sleep. She said her body was on fire. And before we knew it, it was old times again. Then she quietly slipped away before dawn. I hoped that nobody was the wiser.

***

The next day, we drove to Beverly Hills to visit one of Darrah's friends, Annette. On the way, Darrah explained that in Los Angeles, there were Jews of modest means like her family and of course, the rich Jews, many of whom had moved to Beverly Hills. She knew both because in her lifetime many of the poor Jews she knew became rich through one enterprise or another.

As she explained this, I was admiring the plush landscaping of Beverley Hills—the thin, towering palm trees, the perfectly trimmed hedges and lawns interspersed with flowering bushes. Other mansions set back, often obscured by stonewalls, elaborate wooden fences and vegetation. Mansions ranging from the quaint gingerbread Tudor, to the castle in Spain variety to the low-lying sleek glass and steel structures.

Annette lived in an updated Tudor. The driveway was packed with a Jaguar XKE, a Mercedes sedan, a bright yellow Volkswagen bug and a Ford pickup truck. Annette, tall and dark with a perfectly bobbed nose, answered the door. She hugged Darrah as if they hadn't seen each other for months when it had been only a week. She led us into the house. The front interior was traditional Tudor with the appropriate early California furniture but as we made our way to the back, the house opened up into an ultra-modern kitchen and a South Seas decor dining area and family room. This looked out on an expansive flagstone patio which gave way to a large kidney-shaped pool and a landscaped yard of grass, rocks and gardens.

Annette introduced me to her mother and father who were puttering around the pool and garden. Mom was spraying some plants; dad was listening to a ball game on the radio while he fished around with a pool net trying to capture the one or two errant leaves that had drifted down from a nearby tree.

The parents took a break from their backyard duties and offered us some cokes and sandwiches.

"Or maybe you'd like a beer," said the Mr. Aaron, as he settled his bulky frame into a recliner.

"Ah, coke will be fine," I said, wanting to stay sharp.

"Good, enough. Well, I'm having a brew. Good old Budweiser. Of course, nothing like the Budweiser from Czechoslovakia that I used to drink."

He didn't strike me as particularly Jewish. He seemed like a regular blue-collar guy, heavyset, thick muscled arms and grizzled gray hair. A working class man who had clawed his way up. Darrah had told me that Mr. Aaron had been a young man in the Nazi work camps during World War II, but managed to escape with some other kids and hid in the forests. After the war and a spell in the displaced person camps, he avoided being sent to Israel and through the intervention of a relative, arrived in L.A. in the late 1940's.

"L.A. was booming." Mr. Aaron explained after a beer. "I arrived at the right time. I apprenticed under my uncle who ran a garage. I became a car mechanic. I noticed that people practically lived in their cars here. They went to drive-in churches, drive-in banks and drive-in cleaners. Never out of their cars if they could help it. So, I thought why not a drive-in car wash? Nobody gets wet or dirty. You simply drive through a whirl of water, brushes and soft rags assembly line style."

"That sounds complicated," I said.

"Yes, it was. At the time, L.A. had a few drive-in car washes around but nobody had exploited or perfected the idea on a grand scale. So I got to work and set up an automatic car wash at my uncle's shop. Before I knew it, I had a whole chain of them throughout L.A."

While this tale was being told, Mrs. Aaron was talking quietly with Darrah and Annette, now and then glancing over to me. I figured they were talking about the last minute preparations for Annette's big wedding coming up with her fiancé, Ned.

Ned was the son of a well-known L.A. land developer. As Darrah told the story, Ned's father escaped from Germany in the late 30s with the family jewels. He settled in Shanghai until the war ended and then made a fortune by buying up land in Hiroshima right after the atomic bomb leveled the city. He resold the land within year or two at great profit and with his new found riches, he made his way to Los Angeles and bought land at the start of a major building boom. Son Ned was now going to Boalt Law School at Cal, had a great apartment in the Berkeley hills and was living with Annette who was now a senior at UC.

After lunch, we slipped into our bathing suits and swam around for a while. Both Annette and Darrah looked fine in their black, one-piece bathing suits. One with dough, the other not. I mused on how easy it seemed to be for some like Annette and how hard for others, like Darrah and her folks—Jews who had not made it big in L.A. The afternoon waned, and after a tasty margarita or two prepared Mrs. Aaron, we collected ourselves and said goodbye to Aarons.

As Darrah drove back to her place, she said, "Mrs. Aaron thought you were cute."

"Cute?"

"Well built, actually."

"Yeah, just a big dumb goy." I replied.

"Well, she was disappointed that you weren't Jewish. According to her,

Jewish girls should never get involved with goys but I pointed out that there aren't many Jewish guys like you."

"I feel like mush now after all that hassle with the Peace Corps." I said.

"Do, tell. Well you are back now and for the moment, we're together," she said squeezing my hand. She then pulled down the sun visor of her car as we headed west on Sunset Boulevard into the late afternoon sun. "Let's enjoy it."

***

The following day I went with Darrah to her summer classes at UCLA. She was making up units that she missed after spending a semester in Italy. One of her classes was on film history. The class was full of budding young filmmakers into film classics, especially the films of the Russian filmmaker Sergei Eisenstein. That day we saw his masterpiece, *The Battleship Potemkin*. The instructor pointed out the famous massacre sequence on the steps of Odessa. As he put it: "This is the ultimate in montage editing, creating tension and a point of view merely through the juxtaposition of selected shots. All of it creating tension and terror."

Later, I asked Darrah why she, an English major, was taking a film class.

"Well, many reasons," she said as we walked along the Santa Monica pier. "First of all, it's an easy course. We watch films and then discuss them. I have to do a couple of papers and believe me, there are no geniuses in that class. No competition. Still, it's interesting. Who knows, someday I might write a film script."

We leaned over the rail and watched a flock of seagulls swoop down on the bait a luckless fisherman had thrown in the water.

"If you ever get act your together Allan, maybe you could film it. You know they have a very good film school at UCLA and more importantly, they have great connections to the Hollywood studios. "

"Really?"

"Yes, the kids who go through the course there get jobs with the studios."

"Probably, fetching coffee for the director."

"That too, but some become readers. They read scripts, make recommendations and go on to bigger things"

"Something to think about but right now I have to deal with the Army." I said.

"Ugh," said Darrah wrinkling her nose. "Usually, I wish I were a man but when it comes to the military, I'm glad I'm a woman."

"Me too." I said.

4. LIMBO

My days of sitting on the patio in Martinez, sipping wine and watching sunsets soon ended. I had tried to find work surveying at the local engineering firms but no one was hiring. In addition, home life was becoming a drag. At age twenty-three, I felt I was too old to live at home. My father kept bugging me about the draft and the Army. By early September, I had had enough and went to the Cal Placement Office and promptly found a part-time job as a warehouseman in the university book warehouse. It didn't pay much but it was enough to cover a modest rent and feed myself. Next, I found a room on the Southside of campus, three blocks from Telegraph.

My room was one of four bedrooms in a large apartment-like set up with a common lounge, laundry room and kitchen. My three fellow renters were two guys and a woman, all supposedly graduate students at Berkeley. I passed myself off as one too. I still felt that I was a student at Berkeley, albeit a student-at-large, like some independent medieval scholar.

The room itself was light and airy and a nice breeze blew through it if I left the door and the window open. It was furnished in cheap Danish modern with a narrow twin bed, a desk, a dresser and a make-up stand with a mirror. My sheets were lavender and flower pasties were on the wall, making me think that this was once a girl's room. However, I soon got used to the decor and color and later discovered the lavender sheets didn't get dirty so fast.

Sitting at my desk at the window, I could see out through the trees to the quiet street and the Oakland hills in the distance. On my days off from the warehouse, I would read and daydream looking out the window. Sometimes I wrote letters to friends in Europe or scribbled what I thought were profound observations in my journal:

> *Perhaps the modern tragedy is there is no tragedy. The great as well as the small are struck down indifferently. Fate relieves us of the responsibility to account for ourselves. Like the mindless amoeba, we grope and form ourselves through a series of biological acts. Since the spark of creation was the result of probability, what we are is also the result of chance.*

Or:

> *Between the two darkness of birth and death, we live in mindless electric agitation until the fuses blow. Still, in spite of our impotence, we have an instinct to make order out of chaos. Bergson called this ordering instinct "reason" and considered it a mechanism for survival.*

Or maybe this:

> *Life becomes so boring that you want to scream. In its extreme, living becomes an imposition on your being—a bleak, tedious affair terminated by the relief of death.*

Whoa! My journal entries may have been all gloom and doom and a reflection on the general chaos in the universe, but my day-to-day mood was sunny, mellow and almost dreamlike. Here I was living in Berkeley, a student-at-large, sampling only those intellectual fruits that I chose. I read and re-read some of the classics like *Le Rouge et le Noir*, *Madame Bovary* and *Moby Dick*.

It was the first time that I had tackled Melville's *Moby Dick*. I had the luxury of a very slow read—line by line, paragraph by paragraph, page by page, chapter by chapter, all the time checking out the obscure references sprinkled throughout the novel. In a literature course, I would have had to rush through the work in a week or so. I took three weeks, several hours a day and when I was through, I was convinced *Moby Dick* was the Great American Novel, and that Herman Melville was a literary genius. Here he had mixed philosophy, metaphysics, poetry, whaling and sailing lore with the chase of a lifetime. Of course, it all ends badly. The great white whale destroys the ship and the crew, including Captain Ahab, and then goes on its merry way. Only Ishmael survives, left clinging to a coffin in the middle of an infinite ocean.

Darrah had recommended *Moby Dick* and envied me for having the leisure to read it carefully. Yes, Darrah was back at Berkeley and coming to see me now and then in my little room where we read selections aloud from the book while lying in my narrow little bed.

***

Darrah was living in a two-bedroom apartment with two roommates a few blocks away. They had managed to make the apartment cozy with cast-off furniture, floor pillows, Impressionist art posters, decorative lamps, and a couple of Japanese screens for room dividers. Trish, one of the roommates, was an excellent cook and she liked to practice on her roommates and friends. I was invited over a few times and partook of the goodies. I also got a close look at the lives and loves of the JAPs (Jewish American Princesses.)

Trish had light brown hair, a short but shapely body with slightly crossed eyes. Overall, she had a motherly air. She gave the sense that she always wanted to take care of somebody, preferably male. Right now, she was getting over a summer fling with an Israeli tank driver that she had met on a kibbutz in the Promised Land.

"I never knew Jewish guys could be so manly," she remarked. "These guys do everything— drive trucks, drive tanks, shoot guns, build things, get into fist fights and have great bodies. Nothing like the Jewish men we see here at Berkeley."

"Yes, but do they have a brain in their head?" Darrah asked.

"Some do, many don't but who cares," laughed Trish. "Like I said they all have great bodies."

"I like a brain in a great body," Darrah laughed, glancing over to me.

All of Trish's pining came to an abrupt halt one day when she got a phone call from her Israeli lover boy who had landed unexpectedly at San Francisco Airport and was ready to claim her.

"Oh, shit," said Trish covering her mouth after she hung up.

"Oh, shit?" mocked Darrah. "This is what you wanted, right?"

Wail. Sob. "I don't know," said a near hysterical Trish. "He was really neat in Israel. I'm just not sure how it will work out here."

"You invited him over, didn't you?"

"I had to, what else could I do?"

A few hours later, the Israeli showed up on the apartment's doorstep. He was a tall, muscular fellow with a scruffy beard and bright blue eyes. In broken English, he explained he was on leave from the Israeli Army and had come here to take Trish back to Israel where she had been so happy.

Well, that didn't happen. I don't know how he took the news that he was only a summer fling and after his departure, Trish moped around feeling guilty. A week later, she was back to her old outgoing, happy, caring self and now seeing an old friend from L.A.

That friend was Joe Schwartz. A tall, cocky, frighteningly bright guy from Beverley Hills. Joe was a senior at Cal majoring in English. He claimed he was going to be a famous writer someday. Joe was in my French Reading class two years ago. He was a showoff then often interrupting a tedious reading Jean-Paul Sartre's novel, *Les Jeux Sont Faits* and offering a literary interpretation in French. In the two years since he had only gotten worse. He essentially thought he was god's gift to the literary world. Yet, he did have his insights, especially when it came to the three Jewish girls in the apartment.

His analysis was the following: There was Darrah who showed promise as a writer and journalist and who was applying to the Columbia School of Journalism. (Darrah was on the staff of the campus newspaper, the Daily Californian.) There was Trish whom he thought was kind and motherly and would no doubt marry a successful Jewish doctor or lawyer. Finally, there was Keri—a blue eye, blonde beauty that one would never think of as being Jewish. In fact, she was descended from Russian nobility. Now, she was sleeping with her English TA, a Brit from Oxford, replete with tweeds and a pipe. He lived in a groovy, hillside apartment with a view.

"All bright, great, beautiful Jewish Princesses," Joe would say while sitting at the dinner table devouring some feast or other prepared by Trish.

"Really, the girls with the 'golden cunts.' Available to the highest bidder."

Smiles but no comment from Keri or Trish. However, Darrah told him to stuff it. She was going to be her own person and have a career in journalism.

"Like I said, Darrah," replied Joe. "Career or not, you are still one of the 'golden girls' even if you are a brunette. You'll find your money bags."

"Ha, fat chance," said Darrah and then, "Joe, you know what?"

"What?"

"You're an asshole."

***

My warehouse job soon became spotty. My days were cut from three days a week to two days, to simply being on call for work as needed. On the workdays, my supervisor Nick would pick me up in his beat-up Volkswagen bus, and off we would go to Richmond where the University of California Press warehouse was located. My job was to retrieve the books that had been ordered, pack the books up and ship them off.

The warehouse housed the entire output of the University of California Press. Often when work was slow, I would disappear into the back of the warehouse and peruse the shelves of thousands of books. It was a veritable treasure trove of academic esoterica—arty short stories in Berkeley literary reviews, journals of old California pioneers, learned treatises on the mating habits of Polynesians as well as the cannibalistic practices of spiders. It was all here, so much printed fodder to bundle up, ship out or throw out if it was deemed too dated.

Nick, a latter-day Beatnik, considered himself the ultimate literary critic. He knew what was hot. He had his finger on the academic pulse. His goal, as he once told me over some cheap red wine at his bungalow, was to out Kerouac, Kerouac. He claimed he knew him. Nick said he was writing some major tome that would make *On the Road* look like a boy scout outing. I took Nick seriously because he was in his thirties and obviously committed to this Bohemian lifestyle even though he said he had a Master's in English Lit and could teach if he wanted.

So that was my scene in September of 1963. I was leading a lazy, independent student life in Berkeley, lounging around and having a good time, but knowing that it could all come to a screeching halt thanks to the U.S. Army.

5. U.S. ARMY

Early October, my father received a query from the Martinez draft board as to my whereabouts. The board also wanted to know if I were enrolled in school. It seemed the Peace Corps had indeed notified them that I had been released. Dad passed the letter on saying only, "You better take care of this, Allan."

Take care of it. Yes. Certainly. But how was I going to take care of it? One option was to enroll full-time in graduate school. That would give me a student deferment. I considered going San Francisco State because I knew that Berkeley would never admit me to its graduate school because of my mediocre grades. But the main hang up was, I had no money to go to school full-time and Dad was not about to foot the bill.

As he put it: "We did our bit for you at Berkeley and Europe. Your brother Don has to finish his engineering degree."

"OK. OK. I get the message."

Also, I didn't want to sponge off them anymore. I wanted to entertain the illusion that I was independent. Still, independence had its price. And that price appeared to be no money for graduate school and the Army.

I began to reconsider another more drastic option that was the current rage in Berkeley for avoiding the draft—getting married. A while back, I had run into Clarissa on the Terrace Restaurant at the Student Union. Clarissa was an on-and-off girlfriend from my senior year. She was now a senior herself and with her curly blonde locks, iceberg blue eyes, she was as lovely as ever, although a little on the thin side. Her patrician looks belayed her offbeat character. She was bright, funny, sardonic, hip but also virginal and wanted to remain that way until Mr. Right came along. I liked her basically as a friend. She was fun and we went out occasionally.

One afternoon at La Vals Beer Garden, Clarissa updated me on what was going on with her. She didn't know what to do after graduation with her degree in history. She was considering graduate school but was restless and wanted to see the world so she thought she might become a Pan Am stewardess.

"Oh, a 'fly me' girl," I joked.

"Well, it's a way to get around," she pouted.

"I hear the stews are a fast lot. Sort of flying concubines."

"What do you know? There are all kinds. They want bright, attractive, college girls like me. I guess they want somebody for the international business types to talk to."

"I sense you have shaken off your catholic education," I teased.

"Not entirely. This would be a short-term job, I think. I still want to settle down and go to graduate school. Who knows, maybe even marry."

"Marry?"

"Yes, why not. Isn't that the fate of most women?"

"You would hate it. You are too much of a free spirit."

"Well, someday I want to marry, Al. You know, I see these senior girls around me and they are absolutely panicking that they haven't found a husband yet.

"They're stupid," I said. "Too much indoctrination at their mother's knee."

"On the other hand, maybe they aren't that stupid," countered Clarissa. "It's a statistical fact that a woman's best chance of finding a suitable mate occurs in college. Just, think about Al, especially here at Berkeley, a pool of bright, healthy people with good career prospects, good genes and maybe good looks."

"Stop it. You're making me want to gag."

"Yes, it is nauseating," she laughed. "Let's have another beer."

I talked about the Army and my quandary over the draft.

"Tough choice but there is a way out," she said. "Do you have a current girlfriend?"

"Not really."

"What about Darrah?"

"Darrah?"

"Yes, I saw you two on the Terrace recently. I didn't bother to say hello since you were so engrossed."

"We're just friends. I don't see her that much."

"Well, what I was about to say was if you had a cooperative girlfriend you could get married, or married at least in the eyes of Uncle Sam and avoid the Army."

"Marriage?"

"Haven't you heard? Kennedy is exempting married men from the draft," she declared.

"Oh, yeah, I know that. But that would be like jumping from the frying pan into the fire. The draft is only two years, marriage could be a lifetime."

"Yes, that's true but still. It's an idea and it would get you out of the draft."

Suddenly I realized what she was hinting at. She stared at me with her beautiful blue eyes, now slightly moist as if she was about to tear up. I leaned across the table and kissed lightly her on her sweet salty lips.

She pulled away and continued as if talking to herself. "I mean it's not like we can't get along. We both joke around and like intellectual tomfoolery. I've been to your house. You've been to my house. We both come from modest middle-class families. We have a lot in common and despite my refusal to go to bed with you last year, I'm attracted to you and I think you are to me. We look good together. We could have a future together."

She took another sip of beer and then laughed. "Oh listen to me, I sound like one of those pushy marriage hungry women."

"No, you're not. You make a lot of sense, Clarissa. Still, marrying to avoid the draft, that's heavy. Also, I would want to marry the person for herself, not to escape the Army. I'm touched though and you're still one of my favorite people, Clarissa. We should pick up where we left off last year."

"You mean until Darrah came along," she countered.

"No comment."

We cracked some peanuts and drank the rest of beer in silence, and then I said. "I don't know what I'm going to do about the Army. In the meantime, stay single until I figure it out."

We drank to that.

***

Resigned to my fate, I notified the draft board of my whereabouts and two weeks later, I received a notice to report for an Army physical down at the Oakland Induction Center at 6 a.m. sharp.

I showed up at the appointed hour along with some fifty other Army prospects and waited in a dingy waiting room. A scruffy sergeant who looked as if he had just rolled out of bed handed out a batch of forms including a medical history form. It asked questions such as "Was I attracted to other men?" Or, more specifically, did I have any homosexual experiences or was I suffering from any venereal diseases? The Army appeared overly interested in our sex lives. If you really wanted to get out of the whole business, you could put down you were queer and after a short interview with an Army psychologist, you would be declared unfit for service. I had heard of several Berkeley students who had done that. Of course, I wondered if such a sexual orientation would be noted somewhere on an official file and follow you the rest of your life.

After filling out the forms, we filed into the examination room where several doctors and their medical assistants were waiting for us to begin the physical. No private rooms for this. It was like an open-air cattle call. We had to strip down to our shorts, leaving our clothes on the hooks and benches that lined one wall. We were ordered to keep wearing our glasses if needed and to hold our wallets in our hands.

First, we were weighed and measured for height. Then our blood pressure was taken, blood was drawn, chest thumped on, heart listened to, head examined for lice, eyes examined and so on. This was all done assembly line style. The grand finale came when the doctors snapped on their rubber gloves and told us to drop our shorts.

There we stood, bare ass in the cold room, genitals hanging down or shriveling up as the case may be as each doctor poked and manipulated them to determine if we had a hernia or venereal disease. Once that little task was completed, we were told to turn around facing the wall and to bend over. Out of the corner of my eye, I could see my particular doctor dipping one gloved index finger into a jar of Vaseline that was sitting on a little stand. The next thing I knew said finger was slipping up my ass, feeling around.

I felt like I had to take an immediate shit. A second or two later, the finger was gone and I was handed some tissue to wipe myself and told to pull up my shorts, put on my clothes, and return to the waiting room to wait for an interview with an Army psychologist.

I was interviewed by a buzz-cut officer wearing tiny steel frame glasses who spoke with a slight German accent. Images of Nazi interrogations from old black and white movies flashed through my mind. He glanced over my medical history and then turned to me and said, "So Mr. Brown, why do you want to join the U.S. Army?"

"I don't want to join the Army but what choice do I have?"

"None, of course, but we would like to know how you feel about it."

I was tempted to say, "I want to kill and get away with it." Such an utterance might have also gotten me out of serving. I had heard through the Berkeley grapevine that next to saying you were queer, having stated a desire to kill would disqualify you from service. The Army did not want psychopathic killers. They wanted to teach you how to kill indifferently, not passionately.

I simply said, "Ah, I guess I want to serve my country if I have to."

"Fine, fine." He stamped my papers with a 1-A classification and said, "Good day, Mr. Brown...Next."

Once everyone had reassembled in the waiting room, we were told our draft boards would send us our official classification in the mail within two weeks. We were then dismissed.

This Army processing had taken only two hours but my whole world had changed. I felt that I been reduced to a piece of meat, a violated one at that. That was probably how the Army considered us, fresh meat to be trained to kill other fresh meat. We were not individuals, simply collective units to be sacrificed for some larger Army cause.

I got back on a Muni bus to Berkeley, stopping at an International House of Pancakes on Telegraph. After a big pancake breakfast, I went back to my room and crashed on the bed, wondering what I had gotten myself into.

***

The next weekend, I went to a post-football game party at my old fraternity house, Alpha Kappa Lambda. There I ran into two alums, Redmond and Johansson who were currently in the Army Reserves. Redmond had served three years in Army Intelligence and Johansson six months in a civil affairs unit. I told them about my Army predicament.

"If you have to go Army, Al, do it in style," said Redmond. "The intelligence gig is great. You wear no uniform. You usually work nine to five and you can get a direct commission. The work is interesting, kind of cloak and dagger. Often there is travel involved. I spent two years in Germany and a year at the Oakland Army Depot."

I thought that sounded interesting. The only catch was you had to enlist for a three-year tour. But, as Redmond put. "Look at it this way, Al. When you're out, you're out. No reserve meetings to go to. Yes, I'm in the reserves, but it's inactive reserves, unlike my friend Johansson here who has to attend weekly meetings for nearly six years. "

"Wait a minute," said Johansson. "That's all very well, three years at a cushy job in Army Intelligence but believe me, Al, if you have something else to do with your life, join the reserves right off, the meetings and all. I didn't waste three years of my life on active duty. I went to law school and now I'm about to take the Bar."

Johansson then told me about the civil affairs reserve unit he belonged in Sunnyvale on the Peninsula and said if I were interested, he would give me a recommendation.

Redmond countered, "Not so fast, Al. If you go the three-year route in Army Intelligence, with your French you could easily wind up in France as a military attaché."

Redmond gave me the name of an Army recruiter who specialized in Intelligence recruits.

I took this all under advisement and plotted my course. Initially, the idea of going overseas as an Intelligence Officer working in civilian clothes was tempting. It would be a way to live and further experience Europe. With any luck, I could be assigned to Paris as a military attaché. Also, the thought of going to reserve meetings for six years was appalling. So with my heart pounding, I went to see Redmond's recruiter down on University Avenue.

"Smart idea, son. Don't let the bastards draft you and serve as a grunt," said the skinhead sergeant major with stripes galore as he toyed with a dummy grenade. "And don't even think about the reserves. That's six years of bullshit meetings. Mickey Mouse stuff. Sign up for a three-year stint and with your academic background, you can pick what you want to specialize in and where you want to serve. Make the Army a positive experience that can help you in whatever career you later chose. Hell, you probably could get a direct commission without going to Officer's Candidate School."

"Ah, I was thinking about Army Intelligence. I have a friend who did that work in the Army," I explained.

"Good choice," he nodded. "You appear to have the background for it, speaking a foreign language and all. Play your cards right and you could wind up as a military attaché at some embassy in a French speaking country, maybe even France."

"That would be great."

"Yeah, well it's possible. Tell you what, if you're interested in pursuing Army Intelligence, why don't we set up an interview down at the Oakland Army Depot where the have an office. See what they say."

After a few minutes on the phone, the sergeant major had an appointment set up for the next day. I thanked him for his efforts and walked out on a cloud. Running through my mind: *Army Intelligence, serve in*

Europe, maybe Paris. Live the Continental life. Maybe have a hot sports car to zip around in. I would be twenty-six when I got out. Still time to go to law school or maybe into the Foreign Service. I bet I would have some bucks saved up by then.

***

The next day I showed up at the Oakland Army Depot and was directed to the Office of Army Security located in a rabbit warren of offices in the back of a warehouse. There, I shook hands with a Major Colby, a squat muscular guy in a short sleeve white shirt with a tie and a buzz cut. Despite his civilian garb, he definitely looked military.

"So you're interested in Army Security?"

"Ah, Army Intelligence," I corrected.

"Same thing. We secure the U.S. Army whether it is men or material. Says here you spent time in France and speak French. What were you doing in France?"

"Oh, I was a student at Aix-en-Provence learning French and soaking up the culture, studying history my major."

"Are you willing to undergo a background check? The Army has to make sure you're not a Commie. Berkeley and all that. A little pinko up there, ha, ha."

"Sure. I have nothing to hide."

"Now how well you speak French?"

"Pretty well."

He eyed me and sighed, "OK, we'll see." He pressed a buzzer and in came a tall skinny officer in a white shirt and tie that was too loose around the neck.

"This is Captain Benjamin. He spent several years serving in French-speaking countries. Fluent. Ben, go next door and give Mr. Brown a workout."

We went next door and sat down. Captain Benjamin looked at me as if I were a dubious prospect and then in French started rattling off his experiences in France and South Vietnam. I hardly got a French word in. I guess he was showing off. His accent wasn't too good but he definitely knew the language. He asked me to tell him about my year in France in French. Luckily, this was one spiel I had down pat and I spoke for about ten minutes describing Aix, my courses and some of my travels. He nodded as I spoke and then engaged me in a dialogue about the Army and pointed out that if I signed up, I would most likely be sent to Saigon. The Army was in desperate need of French speakers there.

I feigned enthusiasm for such an assignment, wondering what happened to the possibility of a European posting. I asked him about military attaché duty. Captain Ben explained, this time in English, "Oh, that's considered prime duty. It's usually reserved for soldiers who re-enlist after their first three-year stint. Almost impossible to get the first time around. No, we need French speakers like you over in Vietnam. It's considered good duty."

I told him I would think it over and said goodbye to the major and the captain, my ambition to be an Army Intelligence officer dimming. I didn't want to serve in Vietnam. I thought that the place was on the verge of all-out war.

Redmond urged me to take the plunge. "Go on Brown, it'll be the time of your life. Just think sitting in those Saigon cafes chasing those sweet Vietnamese chicks. You'll be in hog heaven."

"Yeah, but what if it blows?"

"Well, it's a roll of the dice. With the Army, you never know where you will wind up."

Hmm, I thought. Redmond is right. Once, I sign up the Army will do with me whatever it wants. I had heard the stories about guys signing up to serve in Europe and then they are shipped off to Asia, or stationed in some hellhole base in the Midwest. I decided to look into the reserve option.

***

The next day I phoned the civil affairs reserve unit that Johansson belonged to and inquired about joining up. The sergeant I talked to was noncommittal except to say the unit was had only a few slots open. I mentioned that I was Lt. Peter Johansson's fraternity brother and he could vouch for me. The sergeant told me to show up at next Monday's meeting and he would introduce me to the company commander to see what was available.

The civil affairs reserve unit met in an armory in an industrial section of Sunnyvale. I could see all the tanks and jeeps in the yard as I drove up. I casually wondered what a civil affairs unit did. All Johansson ever said was that they set up and ran governments of towns that the U.S. forces occupy. That sounded interesting to me. Move in after all the fighting was done and set up shop. Nylons and Hershey bars to the locals, maybe even make a few bucks on the black market. Most of what I knew about occupation forces came from movies and from reading *Catch 22* by Joseph Heller. While the book was obviously a satiric exaggeration, it probably had an element of truth to it.

I arrived just in time for company formation. I noticed the parking lot was full of MGs, Austin-Healys and Jaguar sport cars. The Civil Affair troops were clean cut, professional looking. Young men on the make in civilian life, probably working for large corporations like IBM or Bank of America. I saw Johansson in full uniform march into the main room with a clipboard under his arm as if he were the inspector general.

I stood around on the edge of the formation while the company commander went through some announcements and then dismissed the company for various classes and exercises. Johansson passed by, nodding to me, but said nothing as he went about his business. Very officious. The company commander came over, shook my hand and led me into his office.

"So you want to join our civil affairs unit, Mr. Brown."

"Ah, yes. I heard from my fraternity brother Lt. Johansson that you do interesting work and since it appears I have to spend time in the military, I want it to be rewarding. I think I have a lot to offer."

"Well, yes. Here, why don't you fill out this application and we will see what's what." The captain left for about twenty minutes to attend to some business, then came back to his office, and looked over my application.

"OK, I see. Berkeley graduate, History major. We have quite a few Berkeley and Stanford graduates in the unit." He continued, "A year in France. Speak French?"

"I do OK, thinking he was going to test me.

"That's a handy language to know since we seem to be getting more and more involved in Vietnam."

"Yes, I've heard that," I said thinking back to my encounter with Army Intelligence.

"You know, of course, when you join the Army Reserves there is always a chance we will be called up. A slim chance at this moment, but you never know."

"I understand."

The captain leaned back and pulled out a folder from a file cabinet, opened it and flipped through some pages. "Hmm, looks like you might be in luck. We have a few clerk-typist positions open but with your background maybe you would be more interested in a Public Affairs slot."

"Public Affairs?"

"Yes, a public information specialist. When we take over a municipal government, we have to mind our public relations with the locals. We have to get vital information out to them. That's what a public information officer does. He deals with the local press or radio stations if they are still up and running. The problem with my unit is that I have too many lawyers or wanna-be lawyers going to law school in this unit or business types who have to get back to their jobs. Not enough people with a broad liberal arts and international background like yours.

A light bulb went off in my head. I smelled opportunity. I had toyed with going to journalism school since graduation. Now here, I could possibly gain some journalistic experience with the Army free.

"Ah, is there some training involved in this, you know the particulars of the field?" I asked.

"Yes, very good training," he replied. "The Army runs an information school at Fort Slocum in New York. With my recommendation, you would be a natural for it. There is one catch, though."

"What's that?"

"This specialty requires a seven-month active duty commitment, not a four-month one like clerk typists. That's why it's hard to fill. Most soldiers in the reserves want to keep their active duty time to a minimum."

Thinking fast, I quickly calculated that I had no pressing business that required me to be off active duty in four months. I had no employment obligation nor did I have a deadline for returning to school. Plus, I thought the experience might be worth it. So I said, "No problem."

"Good now, why don't you fill out some paper work for me."

***

A week later, I was sworn into the Army Reserves. The administrative sergeant told me that it appeared that I would go on active duty for Basic Training at Fort Ord, Monterey sometime in late November. Everything appeared on course. Except that at the second meeting, after I was all signed sealed and delivered, the company commander called me into his office to say there had to be a slight adjustment in my military occupational specialty (MOS). I thought, "Oh, here it goes, I'm going to be a clerk typist. This other gig was too good to be true.'

"Actually, you might like this even better," he smiled. "How about a Broadcast Specialist instead of a general public information specialist."

"Broadcast?"

"Yes. The higher-ups feel that this unit needs a Broadcast Information

Specialist more than just a general information specialist. Stay up to date and in tune with the times, so to speak."

"Hmm... so what would this involve?"

"Radio, maybe television work. The Army is part of the Armed Forces Radio and Television Network. You would be trained in the technical aspects of radio and television as well as media relations with local media. Sound interesting?"

I was stunned. Broadcaster. Images of Edward R. Murrow. The *Huntley-Brinkley Report*. News Anchor. Documentary producer. "It sure does," I answered.

"Good then, it's all settled," said the captain. "In the meantime, before your tour of basic training starts, just keep coming to meetings. I know you haven't been issued a uniform yet but we still like our troops to look presentable. So get a short haircut soldier."

"Yes, sir!" I stood up, saluted the captain, turned on my heel and marched out of the room.

I was in the Army now.

6. KENNEDY

A few days later, I moved back to Martinez. I had paid my room rent for October but with my impending orders to report for basic training, I figured that living the life of a Berkeley bum was too expensive since I had no real income. Luckily, my father managed to get me a temporary job working on a County landscaping crew for a month. I said goodbye to Darrah who was now so deeply engrossed in her studies and college life in general that I sensed she was relieved to see me go.

"The Army might do you some good," she said.

"I suppose," I replied laconically now that the initial enthusiasm had worn off.

"Look, Allan, you'll be getting some valuable training as a Broadcast Information Specialist, something that you could develop a career out of in radio or television," said ever-practical Darrah.

"I know but right now all I have to look forward to is eight weeks of grunt training at Fort Ord in the middle of winter."

"You can do it. Look at you, a big, strong, guy," she said punching my arm.

"I know. It's the mental trip."

"Poor, bubba." She said hugging me and then whispered in my year. "By the way, Columbia School of Journalism has accepted me. I'm off to New York next year."

"Really? Congratulations," I said. I was happy for her but at the same time sad because I sensed it was goodbye to Darrah. It was over. Not that it could have led anywhere, anyway. She was going to be a career journalist and I was going to be....what? I didn't know.

***

The landscaping job was a bore but it did provide some money and gave me something to do until Basic Training began. Contra Costa County had hundreds of miles of landscaped roadways to maintain and they had the money to do it, thanks to a booming economy. The landscaping along the freeways was taken care of by state crews but the county did the approaches and the secondary roads.

I was on a crew of three that drove around in a pickup truck with a big tank of DDT in the back. Our job at this time of year was to spray the bushes the county had planted and to do weed control. This necessitated donning a mask, gloves and goggles to protect us from the DDT. It brought back memories of my days at Dow Chemical when I had to clean giant concrete electrolysis cells that often spewed forth chlorine gas and dripped hydrochloric acid. However, this DDT spraying was less intense and we took turns doing it. One person would do a few hundred feet and then take a break while the other sprayed. Lunch breaks often ran to two hours with time for personal errands. We usually knocked off around three-thirty and drove slowly back to the maintenance garage in Martinez. Quitting time was 4:30.

My workmates were an Okie drop-out and Joe, an overweight supervisor who sat in the truck, drinking coffee, reading his newspaper and listening to the radio. I had to contend with questions like, "You went to Berkeley. How come you're doing a job like this?"

"I'm just marking time until I go into the Army."

"Oh, that figures," Joe would say. "I did time in the Army myself. Back in 1951. Korean War you know."

"Yeah, I know. You already told me."

Joe would continue as if he hadn't heard me, "Yeah, it was a bitch. Even though I was in Supply and away from the fighting, I still froze my ass off. Vowed never to be cold again. California winters are cold enough for me."

Yawn. I had heard this story many times over. I thought if I had to do this job for a living I would have shot myself long ago. Look at Joe—fat, stupid and happy sitting in his truck listening to radio.

The weather stayed beautiful throughout late October and into November. It was a rare New England fall in California. The leaves were turning bright yellow and red, the sun was warm, but the air crisp. Days slowly drifted by until one day I had an attack of hay fever that caused a splitting headache. I had to go home early and when I arrived, my mother handed me an envelope from the Army. I was to report to Fort Ord on Sunday, November 24 by 4 p.m., Thanksgiving week. I was relieved because I had thought the Army had forgotten me. I was eager to get this over with.

Two more weeks crawled by and finally, I reached my last day of work, Friday, November 22. The Okie and I were trimming some shrubbery along a county roadside when Joe shouted from the truck, "Hey, boys. Some asshole shot the President."

"Kennedy? Shot?"

"That's right. The president. Get in and take a listen."

We got in the truck and listened to the announcer intone that President Kennedy had indeed been shot while riding in a motorcade in Dallas Texas. Texas Governor John Connolly had been shot too. There was no word on their conditions. We listened for a while and then Joe decided that he better check in with maintenance. He thought that maybe there would be an attack by Russia now that Kennedy was dead and he had civil defense duties to attend to. Joe radioed in and the big boss told him to return to the maintenance barn. Work was over for the day.

My first thought on hearing all of this was, "Shit!" This probably meant my induction into the Army would be delayed because of all the confusion.

When I got home, my mother was crying and my father looked grim. He had come home from work early too. We sat down and watched Walter Cronkite on television with the rest of the nation as the story of Kennedy's assassination unfolded.

I had mixed feelings about Kennedy. He looked good on television and he was witty and well-spoken even with his strange Boston accent. I felt as my father did, that he was essentially a rich kid who was in over his head as President. I also knew from my work at Cal-Neva Lodge at Lake Tahoe in the summer of 1960 that he used it as a hideaway when porking Marilyn Monroe among others. Yet, he had done a few good things like setting up the Peace Corps and announcing a deadline for putting a man on the moon. His major screw-ups had been the Bay of Pigs fiasco which precipitated the October Missile Crisis. That nearly got us into a nuclear war with Russia. Also, he was sending more and more military advisors to South Vietnam in an undeclared war with the Viet Cong and North Vietnam. This had all the makings of another fiasco.

Still, an assassination. That was so nineteenth century. That was Abraham Lincoln stuff. The commentators noted that this was the fourth assassination of a U.S. President. Besides Lincoln and Kennedy, there was

McKinley and Garfield. Truman was almost assassinated by Puerto Rican terrorists in 1950.

Then there was the question of Kennedy's secret service protection or lack of it. Where were they? Why didn't they check the parade route out, especially that warehouse on Dealy Plaza? We learned that Lee Harvey Oswald was apparently a crack shot. He had been trained by the Marines and spent time in Russia.

Two days later, on Sunday, Oswald was gunned down by Jack Ruby right in the Dallas police station. How did that happen? Many people smelled a rat. Some said it smelled of a coup. Vice President Lyndon Johnson was now president. The assassination happened in Texas where Johnson was from and where Kennedy was unpopular. In fact, Kennedy had been warned not to go down there.

Still, I was sorry for Kennedy's family. Blood splattered Jackie, beautiful and anguished. Later, John-John and Caroline standing at attention at the funeral. John-John saluting. The horse-drawn caisson with the casket going by. The riderless horse with the boots backward in the stirrups. The mournful wail of the Irish bag pipes. It was all very moving and all very unreal.

Monday, November 25 had been declared a National Day of Mourning. Still, my entrance into Basic Training went off on schedule. As the sergeant told me on the phone Saturday, "No change, son. This is the Army. Your cycle begins tomorrow, the 24th. Be there by 1600 hours or you will be considered AWOL."

"Yes, sir!"

"Recruit, you don't 'Sir' a sergeant."

7. FORD ORD

Dad drove me down to Fort Ord Sunday afternoon only hours after Oswald had been shot. The bizarre horror of that moment faded as we made our way south on a beautiful day to the Monterey Peninsula. We cut through the Coast Range Mountains and came out at Santa Cruz and the sparkling Pacific. Then it was down Highway One, past cabbage fields and sand dunes, past the small town of Marina until we came to the Fort Ord turnoff.

On the way, my father talked about how close he had come to serving in the U.S. Navy Seabees during World War II.

"They needed civil engineers in the Pacific and I was ready to go. I had enlisted in the Navy Reserves, but they kept delaying my active duty."

"How come?"

"A variety of reasons, Allan. The Navy had a policy that married men with children would be the last to go. Also, I was doing what was considered vital wartime work designing bridges for Kaiser in the Bay Area. By the time the Navy decided that I could go, it was mid-1945 and all the air bases and military infrastructure had been built in the Pacific, so there was no longer any need for my services."

"So, I bet you were happy."

"Well, your mother was happy that I wasn't going. To be frank, I had mixed feelings. On one hand, I was relieved that I didn't have to leave her and you kids. On the other hand, I had a nagging feeling that I hadn't done my part in the war. I had many civil engineer friends who had served overseas. They could have escaped active service but they plunged ahead and served. A couple of them never came back," said Dad wistfully.

"At least you had a choice," I said. "With the draft, I don't have any choice. What a waste of time."

"Serving your country is never a waste of time, son. It's your duty. Make the best of it."

"I'm not sure if it is my duty," I replied. "Still, seven months active duty is better than two years as a draftee."

"I don't think it'll be a bad deal," said Dad. "Look, that specialty they gave you. It could be right up your alley. What was it, a broadcaster or something?"

"Yeah, something like that. But you know with the Army, nothing is a sure thing."

"So true."

By and by, we arrived at the entrance gate of Ford Ord and the guard waved us on in as if he was expecting us.

***

At first, it wasn't too bad. The U.S. Army didn't pay much attention to us recruits that first week because of Kennedy's funeral and Thanksgiving. Most officers were either on leave or off planning for the next Soviet missile crisis since nobody believed that the Kennedy assassination was the work of a lone gunman. It had to be part of an international plot. Thus, we recruits were in a holding mode.

We sat around in barracks and hung out at the PX cafeteria, the movie theater and the bowling alley for the entire week. Other than an initial set of Army fatigues, no one had issued us our uniforms or given us the infamous Army buzz cut. Fort Ord was like summer camp with a lot of free time and the food wasn't bad. Thanksgiving dinner was especially good with fresh roasted turkey and all the trimmings. We even got an Army bus tour of Carmel-By-The-Sea, the day after Thanksgiving. Quite a few recruits came back drunk.

Our week of relative inactivity gave us time to stroll around Fort Ord and soak up the atmosphere. In 1963, Fort Ord was considered the most beautiful, luxurious Army training base in the nation. Most training bases were located in various hellholes on the East Coast, in the Midwest or the South. Fort Ord was situated on twenty-eight thousand acres of ocean front property. From its low rolling hills, there were magnificent views of the Pacific. I used to sit out back of the mess hall on a patio and marvel at the pristine blue of the infinite ocean, feeling very beatific. That was the spirit and the irony of the place—soldiers surrounded by natural beauty while learning the arts of killing.

One day in the post library, I flipped through a little booklet which outlined the history of the fort. Founded in 1846 during the Mexican-American War, it was named after Major General Edward Ord, an Indian fighter who had served under the military explorer John C. Freemont. Fort Ord officially became a training base in 1917 and has served as the primary training center for West Coast Army recruits ever since. After World War II, under the command of General Joseph Stilwell, Ford Ord became known as the most progressive Army training center in the nation. Stillwell was committed to seeing that the enlisted man had opportunities for relaxation and recreation so he constructed tennis courts, baseball diamonds, gymnasiums, libraries, movie theaters, bowling alleys and service clubs—all for the use and enjoyment of the lowly enlisted man.

***

After our initial week of leisure at the base, we grunts didn't see much of these facilities. No, the Monday after Thanksgiving weekend, we were plunged into Army reality. We moved from the relatively modern barracks near the reception center of the base to older rickety wooden barracks in the back. These featured large drafty sleeping rooms with rows and rows of bunk beds and a massive latrine with open stalls. So essentially you took a crap in full view of everyone. While the days were sunny and warm at Fort Ord, the nights were cold and damp. All this night air circulated freely throughout the barracks because the windows were kept wide open. Our company sergeant claimed the fresh air would prevent disease. That was a joke, as I later found out.

The first couple of days were spent setting up for Army life. First, we were issued piles of uniforms and underwear. Next, we were measured for a dress uniform. This was followed by inoculations of one sort or another with some recruits getting sick and throwing up in reaction. And finally, the hair cut. I had rather long hair, not beatnik length but shaggy enough. Off it came, down to the scalp. I had worn crew cuts in high school and didn't look too bad in them but this was ridiculous. I looked as if I had stepped out of space ship from another planet where all the men were bald.

I noted the barbers took sadistic delight in shaving the heads of long hairs, frequently gouging scalps with their clippers. A couple of smart-ass recruits had reported in with short buzz cuts thinking they could avoid the Army haircut. No such luck. It was still right down to the skin with them too.

Other than looking like hell, the worst part of my skinhead haircut was the chill on my scalp. My long hair had kept my head warm on the long chilly nights in the barracks. I now began to wear my fatigue cap night and day.

Test taking followed the housekeeping. The U.S. Army wanted to know how smart you were. It wasn't enough to know that you had graduated from college; they wanted to know about your basic IQ. I suppose it made sense since the recruits came from varied backgrounds. Many were high school dropouts, others functional illiterates but perhaps smart anyway, others simply morons who would be discharged because they were too stupid for even the Army. The reservists formed the brightest group which was not surprising because they had been smart enough to enlist in the reserves instead of waiting to be drafted.

I sat down with thirty other recruits one day in a classroom and took an IQ test which did not require much literacy, just the ability to deal with shapes and mentally rotate cubes and triangles. We were also tested on some simple logic and arithmetic. It was the type of test that I had taken in elementary school. Following the test which was graded immediately, I sat down with the Test Sergeant who noted that I had scored high and that with my college education, encouraged me to go to Officer Candidate School.

"No, thank you," I said. "I'm here just to serve my active duty time and reserve obligation. I'm not interested in any longer enlistment."

"I understand," he countered, "but we always try to encourage men like you to serve longer to make a real contribution to the Army. In turn, you will find that you will profit immensely later from your officer experience."

"Yes, I've heard that but I just want to do my reserve thing."

"Well, yes. Let's see here. They have you down as a Broadcast Information Specialist," he smiled. "That's a good one. Who did you know to get that MOS?"

"Nobody. I was just at the right place at the right time."

"I see. Well, it's considered a plum assignment. You're lucky. And based on your test scores and education, you should be well qualified for it. Had any broadcast experience?"

"No, not at all."

"Well, the Army will no doubt train you," he said putting my folder into a file.

"By the way, I would like you to talk to a Master Sgt. Duncan in the next room before you return to barracks."

"Master Sgt. Duncan?"

"Yes, he's a Green Beret. And the Green Berets always want to interview people with high scores and good educational background."

"Do I have a choice?"

"No, private, it's Army SOP that at least you listen to their pitch. You have the late President Kennedy to thank for that."

"Yes, Sergeant." I got up, went into the next room and sat down at a classroom desk with about ten other recruits.

A short, husky soldier with bulging neck muscles and arms as big as trunks, all contained within his smartly tailored khaki shirt, came into the room. He perched on the edge of a desk, carefully removing his forest-green beret with the Special Forces pin and setting it on the desk. Before introducing himself, he motioned with his thumb out through an open window to a brand-new, fire engine red Austin Healy sitting at the curb.

"Take a look at my new runabout, fellows. I have the U.S. Army and the Green Berets to thank for that."

We all took note of his flashy sports car and nodded. He seemed like a cool guy in spite of his military bearing.

"Enough about my car. Let's talk about the Green Berets. My name is Master Sergeant Donald Duncan. I've been in the Army for about nine years. I'm currently in the U.S. Army Special Forces unit, commonly known at the Green Berets. You can find us in any of the hot spots around the world. Right now, the Green Berets are advising the South Vietnamese Army on how to deal with the Viet Cong. This is not gung-ho, muscleman work. It requires specialized skills, intelligence, ingenuity and independence. You are often on your own, making it up as you go along. One reason you recruits are here in this room is because you have scored well on your tests and because most of you have some college education. And a few of you look in good physical shape," he said scanning the room.

A couple of the hunk recruits smiled and nodded. Some just shuffled their feet. More than a few were reservists which Sgt. Duncan acknowledged.

"We get some of our best men from the reserves. We know you troops just want to get in and out of the Army because you think it is a waste of time. Well for most recruits it is a waste of time, but for those who choose to extend and go the Green Beret route, it's an experience that will pay big dividends down the road. Plus, as has been pointed out, there will be none of those boring, time-consuming reserve meetings to go to."

A couple of reservists nodded.

"OK, here's the deal if you're interested," said Duncan pacing around. "It's a three-year enlistment. When you finish basic, you go on to advanced infantry school, then airborne school. When that's completed, if you haven't washed out, you undergo Special Forces Training. It's a tough, rigorous course focusing on counter-insurgency. It will definitely make men out of you. Long range night reconnaissance, silent weapon use, explosives and so on. In the latter part of the training, you are instructed in specialized skills such as radio operations, language, intelligence gathering, more explosives and medical care. A typical Green Beret team consists of five men; each specialized in one of these skill sets. The team often operates in remote areas, dealing with indigenous people or as in the case of South Vietnam as counterinsurgency advisors to the South Vietnamese troops." Pause.

Duncan surveyed the room looking for reaction and then, not finding much, he concluded, "All in all, it's a great life and it sure beats being a clerk typist."

Following his pitch, Duncan handed out some promotional material on the Green Berets and told us to think about it. "I'll be around here for a week if you want to get back to me. Just let your sergeant know. If I'm not in my office, you can probably find me tooling around base in my sports car. If you sign up, maybe, I'll let you drive it."

After this, my head was spinning. Green Beret. Jeeze. So gung ho. Glamour. Direction. Kill the Commies. Was I tempted? I didn't know. Sgt. Duncan made it seem so appealing. I filed his pitch for future consideration.

***

The first two weeks of basic training were outrageously dull. It wasn't hard, just boring and stupid. The Army called it Phase One. Here was the drill: Up at 5:30 a.m. to the bark of the company sergeant who shouted something like "Drop your cocks and grab your socks. It's time to pay your dues to Uncle Sam." So we were up like jack-in-the-boxes and outside in less than five minutes falling in formation for calisthenics in the pitch-black dawn lit only by a single street lamp.

One-two. One-two. One-two-three. Jumping jacks, squats, push-ups. Sometimes the drill sergeant participated and other times he just strolled around poking a troop or two in the ribs with his riding crop as they exercised. The half-hour session would usually finish with chin-ups, three recruits at a time on the bar with everyone watching. Some could only do two or three to start. Others, seven or eight. By the end of Basic Training, most were up to twelve.

Following calisthenics was breakfast and here I must say the Army did a good job. Scrambled eggs, bacon, pancakes, hot oatmeal, cold cereal, coffee, various juices, milk, even grits (the cooks were from the South). The food was doled out cafeteria style and we sat at tables of four. All very civilized.

After breakfast, we cleaned up the barracks and stood for inspection while the company sergeant went up and down the rows, often finding fault with the way you made your bunk, folded your clothes or shined your shoes and in general acting chickenshit. Nobody took a shower in the morning because the day was to be spent sweating and getting dirty going through the various training activities.

The first two weeks were spent learning how to march in formation and learning the manual of arms with the M-14 rifle we had been issued. All of this was interspersed with various cleanup duties, "policing the area" as they called it and KP which I will get to later.

The most boring part of Basic was the marching—*Left, right, left, right. No troop your other right. Right turn, left turn, to the rear march, to the rear march. Port arms, double time march.*

This was all bullshit that I had endured from Cal ROTC and it went on forever. Since most of the marching drills occurred in the morning, we initially we froze in our thin field jackets until it warmed up and then everyone shed their field jackets.

Following a light lunch of sandwiches (now I understood why the Army stuffed you in the morning), we would have a class on General Orders, Army Chain of Command and protocol and history. Then we would often double-time to one obstacle course or another or to areas of hand-to-hand combat where we learned the basic moves in jujitsu, wrestling and boxing.

Still, there was some downtime. Sometimes the sergeant would just march us off to the backcountry in the afternoon and tell us to take a break. The break would last an hour or so, and we would lay around in the warm sunshine and gaze at the far-off Pacific.

By 4:00 p.m. or so, we would be back at the barracks and be dismissed. We had an hour or so of free time before dinner to clean up and shower. Dinner varied from hearty meat and potato meals to leftovers from the previous day. Everybody ate quickly because we all wanted to get away from the barracks for the evening. If you hung around the barracks during the evening, the sergeant would often find some shit detail for you to perform, like cleaning the bathroom.

Some went to the enlisted men's club which was technically off-limits but rarely enforced. Others took in a movie or went to the bowling alley. My favorite spot was the library. Nobody ever thought of looking for a recruit there. It was a pleasant, well-stocked library with comfortable chairs, a screening room for old movies and listening rooms for recordings. There were also scores of magazines and newspapers from the around the world. I got to know the librarian, a pleasant middle-aged woman. She told me she had been a civilian employee of the U.S. Army for twenty years and had served at various Army bases around the world. That was an idea—serve with the military as a civilian. None of the military bullshit, just the goodies, nice pay and travel. See the world on the government dime.

***

Drill got so boring and repetitive that I was desperate to get out of it. Going on sick call with a fake illness was too obvious, although plenty of troops were coming down with the flu. No, my escape was having my glasses fixed. A couple of L.A. recruits clued me into this. The procedure was this: Complain that your prescription glasses are too weak to perform Army training activities; make an appointment with the Army optometrist; spend half a day just to be seen; after your eyes are examined, drop out for the rest of the day at the Service Club. A week later, you're back to pick out new glasses and have them fitted. That's another half-day day. Following the fitting, go to a base movie. This ploy worked for getting out of two days of drill for each pair of glasses. Some of L.A. dudes managed to go through three pairs of glasses, ("Oh gee Sarge, they fell off and were crushed") with a net avoidance of six days of drill. Other scams included having a dentist appointment to have your teeth cleaned. Not filled. After all, these were Army dentists. Or, one could kiss ass with the company commander, be his gofer, fetch his laundry, make coffee, and do his typing. These were usually wimpy little guys who would be nothing more than clerk typists anyway.

Our company commander, Captain Long, was a remote figure. A West Point graduate with a haughty demeanor, he didn't dirty his hands much with us lowly troops. He left that to his lieutenants and platoon sergeants.

There was an unwritten rule somewhere in the Army that there must be at least one little prick in power in every Army unit of note especially when it comes to training the troops. I had noticed this in Army ROTC at Cal. It was often a little guy who had not done much in athletics, no matter how much he tried, who rose to the level of prickdom when he gained authority. These little pricks especially loved to exercise this authority when it came to big guys.

Our little prick was our Second Lieutenant Mallory. A little red-haired guy, about five foot five. Always spit and polish, always on my case. He would come up and give my person and my rifle an extra look during inspection and always seemed to be standing over me during calisthenics to see that I performed each exercise correctly. Part of the problem was that I had rebuffed his attempt to make me a squad leader since I had had ROTC in college and knew a bit more about the Army drill than most other recruits.

"We need squad leaders, Private Brown. Squad leaders are the most important leaders on the frontline," he said.

"Sir, that may very well be true, Sir, but I'm a short timer. I am in and out of here in a few months. I would suggest you find somebody who's a draftee who's going to spend a while in the Army."

"Private Brown, in this man's Army you never know. You could be extended tomorrow, indefinitely. Look at me," said Mallory puffing up. "I thought I was done with the Army after my first two-year hitch but for a variety of reasons, I re-upped, went to Officer Candidate School and now have my bars. I'll probably make it a career."

The word was Mallory was a fuck-up in civilian life. After being fired from a few sales jobs and a stab at teaching, he re-upped for three square meals and a place to sleep.

Following that little interview, Mallory leaned on me for a while, then gave up and moved on to more fertile pastures. My general slacker attitude was common among the reservists, especially among the crew from Los Angeles. The six or seven L.A. guys had all joined the same reserve unit. They were the cool dudes with ace cars parked on base. Often their girlfriends visited them on the weekends and brought in plenty of cash for wild stays in Carmel. Generally an older group, around twenty-five, they seemed to have a line on everything and managed to escape most of the dirty details. They even managed to escape the skinhead military haircuts after the first go-around. They slipped extra cash to the military barber to cut it short to military length but also to do it with style.

By contrast, the other group of interest was the eight or nine recruits from Alaska. These were all draftees and all spent the first few weeks walking around base in a daze with silly smiles on their faces. "This is fucking paradise," said one. "The only place that beats it is Hawaii." They thought the Army food was great and the training a lark compared to their life in Alaska which consisted of crabbing, fishing and logging. All were big, muscular fellows with frostbite scars on their face and blotches from too much booze. "Nothing to do in the winter but drink and chase squaws," they would explain. "Boy does that get old."

If they thought Fort Ord was paradise, they practically fainted when they saw the L.A. women visiting their boyfriends on base. Rolling up in sports cars, getting out in tight skirts or shorts and tight sweaters, hair in bandannas. The Alaskans drooled, explaining," In Alaska, there's only one white woman for every fifty guys and usually she's a whore." Of course, the Alaskans were insanely jealous of the L.A. guys with their women. With white women still scarce for the Alaskans, they managed to discover a Mexican enclave nearby with many cute señoritas who were ready to take them on and maybe even convince them to marry so they could get their green card. Most were daughters of braceros who picked the crops in nearby Salinas and Watsonville.

"Not white, but cute enough and certainly a lot better than the Eskimo or Indian squaws we have to put with in Alaska," was the consensus. Generally, though the Alaskans were as much interested in drinking as anything else and often went to the off-limits enlisted man's beer hall for midweek drinking for which they were routinely gigged and assigned to extra KP duty.

Oh yes, the "Kitchen Police." I had to endure this nasty duty four times during Basic; once because I loitered around the barracks too long on a Sunday. The sergeant was looking for an extra body because somebody had gone on sick call. This was a bitter pill indeed because I had planned to hop on the Army bus and spend the day lolling around Carmel with its cafes, cozy pubs and scenic walks along the beachfront. As compensation, the sergeant gave me dining room orderly duty. This was considered light KP duty. I was responsible for cleaning up the tables after a meal, bussing the dishes, setting up the tables, mopping the floor and making sure there was enough milk in the milk dispensing machines for the next meal. The rest of the time, I would peel potatoes on the back veranda, tossing the spuds into a big pot while listening to music on a portable radio and gazing out to sea.

Other times on scheduled KP, I worked in the dishwashing section of the kitchen. I had to scrape the aluminum eating trays, stack them into the dishwasher, put the utensils into baskets and then start the steam dishwasher. Fifteen minutes later, I had to take it all out, sort the silverware and re-stack the trays for future use. This was hot, sweaty work, but still not as bad as being a pot washer.

Pot washing was the worst. It often had to be done by hand to remove the crud left over from cooking. It usually required a lot of elbow grease. Wearing thick rubber gloves and dealing with strong detergents and hot steaming water, one did nothing but scrub the pots clean of the major crud. Once that was done, into the steamer washer they went for the final cleaning.

Then the assistant mess sergeant would inspect our handy work (He was invariably another little Southern prick) and tell us pot washers to go over about a third of the pots again. "Can't have the troops come down with the shits because of some lazy pot washers."

On and on this went from five in the morning until seven at night at which point you would collapse on your bunk and pass out. Luckily, I only had the pot washing detail once during my basic training. Usually, it went to troops who had fucked up badly or had pissed off some sergeant.

***

By the third week of training, things became more intense, more focused on learning how to kill the enemy and avoid being killed yourself. Although we had yet to fire live rounds with our M-14, we had learned how to strip the weapon, identify its parts, and reassemble it all within a matter minutes. We also learned how to attach bayonets and how to do a bayonet attack. First, we practiced with padded pugil sticks, learning the parry and thrust maneuvers with a partner and then we used the rifle with the actual bayonet, charging and sticking a stuffed dummy, all the while yelling, "Kill." This was rather fun. At least it vented pent up aggression and anger at the Army.

Probably the least liked exercise was the chemical warfare course. Here we learned about the various nasty gasses and biological agents that some unscrupulous enemy might use on us troops even though they had been outlawed by the Geneva Convention. None of these gasses or agents was used on us during training but we did have gas mask drill. It involved putting the gas mask on and running around in it during various exercises. The grand finale of the chemical warfare course was entering a tear gas chamber unmasked and then spending several minutes breathing in tear gas fumes before the order was given to put on our masks. This was nasty business with everybody coughing, sneezing, gagging and gasping for breath. Some even throwing up.

However, just as we were getting into high gear with our basic training, the Army brass decided to suspend basic training for two weeks over Christmas. Initially, I was in a funk. Here we had wasted the first week because of the Kennedy assassination and Thanksgiving so the actual training cycle didn't begin until the following week. The Christmas break would begin Friday, December 20 and end Sunday, January 5. When we returned from the break, we would still have five more weeks to go. That meant we would not be finished until the second week of February. This cycle of Basic Training would be taking twelve weeks instead of eight weeks. In addition, as the Brass loved to point out, if you didn't pass each phase of basic training or got terribly ill, you might have to recycle the entire eight weeks. A certain percentage of troops always did. No matter if you had completed all but one week of basic training, you would still start over from scratch.

One reason they decided on the break was that half the troops had the flu and a few had come down with pneumonia. They didn't want to recycle the whole company. I had a touch of flu myself and couldn't get rid of it. Snot was flying and coughing was all over the place. At times, I thought I was running a fever. The open windows in the barracks with all the fresh air were supposed to keep sickness at bay but it proved useless. Many recruits thought the open windows were the problem because it got cold and damp inside the barracks. I think the real problem was the cramped quarters in which we lived, the skimpy clothing in which we exercised and the broken sleep patterns.

Every other night, I had to serve on fire watch, a two-hour stretch in the middle of the night. This was a pain but it served a real purpose since the barracks were old, constructed of wood and occasionally did catch fire. The result was my flu kept getting worse. I felt I was on the verge of pneumonia myself. Of course, the Army doctors would not prescribe antibiotics unless you were on your deathbed. Thus, by the time December 20 rolled around, I was ready to go home to my sickbed.

***

Half-dead, I climbed aboard a Ford Ord Greyhound Bus which dropped me off in San Francisco. I took the Muni transit over to Berkeley to my brother Don's apartment and crashed there a couple of days. The first thing Don said when he saw me was, "Jeez, you look like shit." The second thing he said was, "That's really a bad haircut on you."

"You should talk," I wheezed. "You didn't look so good when you came home from the Air Force Academy either."

"Touché. At least the Academy focused my attention on a practical major," he replied. "Not history like you majored in."

Don was a year younger than me and we had a rivalry of sorts. He had left the Air Force Academy after only a summer and a semester, figuring it was too chickenshit for him.

He immediately enrolled in the school of engineering at Berkeley where he was doing rather well. I always felt that Don was much smarter than I was. Not only that, he was taller around 6'5" but I still weighed more than he did. Despite the rivalry, we were friends and got along pretty well. He was there in a crunch for me when I needed him.

After a couple of days at Don's with no improvement in sight, I had my mom come pick me up. She took one look at me and made an emergency appointment with Dr. Bradshaw in Martinez. After an exam, Dr. Bradshaw said I was on the verge of pneumonia and prescribed some antibiotics. So I spent four days in bed in Martinez, eating well, and slurping down vanilla milkshakes until I felt almost human.

Eventually, I felt well enough to go skiing after Christmas with Don and two of his frat brothers. The skiing at Squaw Valley was mediocre, the snow thin and slushy. I mostly sat around the lodge drinking cheap red wine and playing chess. Before I knew it, Christmas break was over. I had gotten a little face tan skiing, and had been well fed and tended by my mother. I felt ready to resume the rest of my basic training.

8. WARRIOR

Week four of the Basic Training Cycle and I was loaded for bear. I was back in good health and warm thanks to a pair of ultra-thin long johns my Mother had bought me. I was ready to become a warrior. From here on, basic training would focus on marksmanship with live ammunition, grenade throwing, simulated war games, and long marches. However, it should be noted that not everyone was so enthusiastic. A couple of the L.A. dudes failed to return. They had somehow finagled medical discharges and three Alaska guys had gone AWOL because it was crabbing season up there and they didn't want to miss the big money. Their remaining buddies explained that the deserters would return in about four weeks, as if they had a choice and were merely spending time at a summer camp. Word was they would be spending time in a brig when they came back and then would have to go through the whole basic training cycle again.

We now spent hours on the rifle range learning how to zero in our sights and shoot at human form silhouette targets from thirty to two-hundred yards away. The first few shots with an M-14 were always a learning experience. First, lying in the prone position, trying to hold the rifle steady and snug against your cheek, the rifle would buck and you would miss the target by a mile.

"Squeeze the trigger, you morons. Don't jerk it," the gunnery sergeant would yell. By the end of the session, quite a few troops had bruises on their cheekbones from the kick of the rifle. After a kick or two myself, I got the hang of it, held that baby tight against my cheekbone, and managed to hit the target a few times.

Over the next couple of weeks, we fired hundreds of rounds in various positions—prone, squatting and standing. I was doing well, usually hitting the targets in the kill zone, often in a tight grouping. (The Army was big on grouping, i.e. keeping your shots in a tight bunch.) I was hoping for at least a Sharpshooter designation. The highest designation was Expert. Only the Okies from the Central Valley seemed to achieve that since they were brought up on guns and hunting. Most had a deadly aim from shooting at squirrels.

The acid test came one day on a simulated combat range where one soldier at a time walked over a hilly course as if on patrol. Enemy target silhouettes would pop up at various ranges in various camouflaged positions from behind a tree or in a bush and the soldier had only seconds to shoot at it before it disappeared. This was the most challenging and fun shooting exercise. I did rather well hitting the majority of the targets, finally achieving my Sharpshooter designation.

Still, when I thought about it later, here I was, proud of my skill in killing potential human beings. Although they were only silhouette targets in human shape, it was still a kill shot. I felt weird. It was so impersonal, so distant. Yet, for a real human target, it would be a very personal experience—the experience of a bullet tearing through your flesh, possibly your head, maybe feeling it or not. Quite possibly, the human target might utter "Shit," before dropping dead or into unconsciousness. Perhaps he might be saved by a medic, perhaps not. For the shooter, there was the distant hollow feeling that he had killed someone in cold blood who may not have even been shooting at him or even known what had hit him.

***

Around week six, there was another hair-raising exercise. The live-fire exercises at night. For days, we were instructed and practiced crawling along the ground with a pack and our rifle. This was messy business, especially, after a rain which often occurred in January. Finally, the day of reckoning came when we had to crawl fifty yards under a mesh of barbed wire and under a hail of live machine gun fire. The drill sergeant told us the machine gun fire would be directed three feet over the ground, so if we kept our butt down, we would have no problem. Then in a somber tone, he related a story about some dip-shit recruit from a past cycle who had panicked, stood up and was cooked.

"Of course the Army was very sorry, but could not be held responsible for the soldier's action who had been well trained in what to do. We call it a 'training accident.' Quite common," said the sergeant coolly. "We do make sure the soldiers' families are compensated for their loss."

Swell, I thought, vowing to sink into the ground even further during the live fire exercise. Of course, the L.A. guys laughed it off, claiming that the machine guns were firing blanks. Ho, ho. I didn't want to test that proposition and flattened down further on the ground. Actually, it wasn't so bad. The red tracer bullets whizzed overhead like fireworks on the Fourth of July but it appeared to me looking up they were at least four feet off the ground. I crawled along, grunting under my forty-pound pack with my rifle cradled in my arms and before I knew it, I had made to the other side of the course.

Everyone in our platoon made it across in good style much to the relief of our drill sergeant who was patting everyone on the back. He directed us over to a large cooler of beer, saying that we had all done well. "This exercise was the acid test. It will stand you in good stead when you get into real combat. Keeping a cool head when all the shit is going down."

I'm thinking, "What combat? It sounds like we are going to war tomorrow. What does this sergeant know that we don't?"

Later, one of the Okies who knew firearms and ammunition had an ashen look on his face. He had picked up one of the machine gun shells and claimed that it indeed was once a live round, not a blank. "Fuckin eh, these guys don't fool around," he said tossing the shell on the ground.

The other exciting exercise was tossing hand grenades. Unlike, the live-fire exercise, this was done safely from behind a sandbag bunker. The only risk was holding the grenade too long after you pulled the pin or accidentally dropping it on the ground. A sergeant standing nearby made sure that grenade was thrown within seconds after the pin was pulled. The blast wasn't too great, but big enough to injure you should you screw up tossing these low powered training grenades. So we happily tossed the grenades at make-believe targets and into fake enemy foxholes for several mornings. It was an easy exercise requiring little of the precision of rifle marksmanship.

Another chore was completing the basic training obstacle course within a certain time limit. This was your basic Tarzan stuff involving hurdles of various sorts, climbing cargo nets, scaling walls, balancing on logs across ponds, crawling through tunnels and hanging from a pulley while flying along a cable between trees. Almost everybody passed the time test. However, a few stragglers had to run it several times before they could pass.

Throughout these last several weeks, we went on ten-mile hikes, fifteen-mile hikes and the granddaddy of them all, the twenty-five mile hike. All of this with fifty-pound packs on our backs. The worst part of these hikes was that they were boring. Trudge, trudge, trudge, sometimes double time, sometimes singing Army cadence songs:

> *I know a girl from Kansa City*
> *She's got a mole on her left titty.*
> *Sound off,*
> *Sound off.. (response)*
> *One, two, three, four."*

The scenery was dull in the backcountry of Fort Ord, just rolling sandy hills with scrub oaks, and no view of the ocean. We were given breaks about every hour and a thirty-minute lunch break for the longer hikes. Many troops wondered aloud why so much hiking. "Shit, I know for a fact that most of the time, troops go into battle in trucks or armored troop carriers or helicopters," noted one L.A. dude. The drill sergeant would nod and say that would most often be the case, but that marching was good conditioning and discipline and that troops could not always count on motorized transportation.

The twenty-five mile hike was not too bad. We took all day doing it, covering about three miles an hour. We left before dawn and were at back the barracks around 3 p.m. Only a few of us had blisters. The Army knew how to make us take care of our feet with proper sweat socks and powder. Army boots may look goofy and clumsy, but they work for sustained walking or marching.

Our basic training was capped by a three-day, two-night bivouac that included two-night infiltration courses. This was supposed to be the culmination of our training. This is where we put all our newly learned combat skills to practical use in a vast, non-stop war game.

First, we hiked about five miles to the bivouac area, set up camp, and settled down for the night. Sometime around 11 p.m., all hell broke loose with gunfire, explosions and flares going off. The enemy was approaching. We rapidly formed into squads and set out to meet our foes. We advanced a hundred yards or so and then hunkered down in pre-dug foxholes and waited. Our M-14's now set on automatic were loaded with blanks. The expert marksmen had telescopic night sights on their rifles in order to pick off the enemy. Somewhere in the shadows lurked not only the enemy but also a referee who would determine who had shot whom. How this was determined was a mystery to me. Still, we got into a firefight with shadows and somehow we were declared winners. (This has all changed today. Now with night vision goggles and pinpoint, non-lethal laser targeting, such simulated firefights are much more accurate and realistic.) The night exercise over, we returned to our base camp and tried to get some sleep.

The next day, we went out on patrol again, hung out in foxholes, briefly encountered another enemy squad, and had another simulated firefight and then it was back to camp. The second night, we became the aggressors and went out to make contact with the enemy at their base camp. We shot at each other with blanks and were declared the losers. Back to our camp. The third day, a morning patrol, we tossed hand grenades at fake enemy strongholds. We also practiced elementary squad maneuvers with covering fire. Before we knew it, the exercise was over, and aside from losing many hours of sleep, it wasn't too bad. We broke camp and hiked back to the barracks, feeling like full-time warriors.

So what had happened here? In a word, "transformation." I had gone from being an indifferent recruit just trying to get through basic training with the least sweat to a soldier with a sense of accomplishment about my warrior skills and a fascination with killing. The Army had instilled in me a sense of shared responsibility for my squad's well-being. They called this "battlefield cohesion," which meant taking care of your buddy, your squad and by extension, your platoon and your company. We fought not only to conquer the enemy but also to protect our buddies. From its point of view, the Army had done its job.

***

For graduation, we marched smartly on the parade ground in full dress uniform before the generals and the battalion and company commanders. We looked sharp and felt sharp as we went through our manual of arms. Awards were given to units and individuals who had excelled and general certificates of completion to those who passed all the basic training tests.

We also received our orders for the next training phase of our active duty. Nearly all of the draftees were going on to advance infantry training. Most of the reservists were going off to clerk typist school, many right at Fort Ord. Only a few oddball MOS types like me were going to different bases in the Sixth Army Area.

My assignment was the Presidio 6th Army Headquarters in San Francisco for my Broadcast Specialist duties. I had already been told that I would not be going to Fort Slocum in New York for the Information School. That was reserved for three-year enlisted personnel. I was mildly disappointed but it was hard to argue when the Presidio was considered such a plum assignment.

Early the next morning, I climbed aboard the Army Transport bus with my duffle bag and said goodbye to my new-found Army friends and goodbye to Fort Ord.

9. PRESIDIO

Several hours later and half asleep, I found myself stepping off the Army Transport bus onto the lush grounds of the Presidio. I blinked in the sunlight, bedazzled by the tall, swaying date palms, the emerald green grass, and the white-stucco Spanish Mission style buildings with red tiled roofs. Here and there, officers and enlisted men in full dress uniform strolled about leisurely, some carrying briefcases others not. The fog had burned off the Golden Gate in the distance and even though it was mid-February, the day was warming up fast making it uncomfortable in my dress uniform.

I swung my duffle bag over my shoulder and made my way up the street to a row of red brick barrack buildings, looking for one marked "Headquarters Company Sixth Army." As I walked, I noted a squad of troops chopping weeds in the parking strip with the word "Stockade" stenciled on the back of their fatigue shirts. What was that all about?

I found the Headquarters barrack and climbed the stairs to a wide veranda with wicker rocking chairs and wicker coffee tables scattered about. This was the Army? It seemed more like a southern plantation. In one of the chairs rocked the Company First Sergeant, a distinguished looking, grey-haired black gentleman reading a newspaper.

"Can I help you, son," he said looking up.

"Yes, Sergeant," I said trying hard not to call him "Sir" even as I checked out his impressive First Sergeant insignia, his rows of campaign ribbons, and a sleeve full hash marks. All of this indicated that he had been in the service a long time. He too was in full dress uniform. As I later learned, everyone wore a dress uniform around here all the time because it was a headquarters base.

"Private Brown reporting to Headquarters Company."

"Here, let me see your papers," he said taking my orders. "Come on into my office." He got up and led me into his cubbyhole office, off the main entrance. First, he picked up a fly swatter and swatted a bothersome fly that was buzzing around his desk. Then settling down in an old leather chair, he looked over my papers, nodding. "Broadcast Information Specialist, not bad. The Army PIO around here is pretty active. Let me show you your sleeping quarters."

He led me up a flight of stairs to a large second-floor room that looked over the parade ground. Smartly made up bunks with footlockers and metal armoires lined the room. In the center, was a big conference table loaded with board games, newspapers and magazines—all neatly stacked. The room was deserted. The First Sergeant explained the troops were out on morning duty and would be returning shortly for lunch.

"Here, this bunk and locker are yours," he said pointing to a bed in the corner of the room. "Stash your stuff, have some lunch with the troops and then I'll take you over to the Broadcast Center where you can check in."

After I stowed my gear, I went down to the mess hall on the first floor. The big swinging doors were still locked, so I waited on the porch which was now filling up with hungry troops coming in for lunch. I struck up a conversation and learned that most were reservists assigned to the main administrative building across the way as clerk typists. Although, one of them, Ladd, a tall, smooth looking cat, intoned that he was an "awards writer."

"What does an awards writer do?" I asked.

"Essentially, I'm a scribe for the Generals. I write the copy that goes with awarding some troop or unit one medal or another. I also write the letters informing some unlucky parent that their son has died in the line of duty."

"Died in the line of duty? Wow! Where would that be?"

"Nowhere officially, but between our unofficial involvement in Laos, Vietnam and training or friendly fire accidents, somebody is always dying somewhere."

"So how did you get into that?" I asked amazed by all the nooks and crannies of Army specialization.

"I don't know. I was an assistant magazine editor for a while in Philadelphia so the Army thought I could write. Not a bad way to spend my two years." He smiled.

"So you were drafted? How come?"

"Yes, I guess I was lazy, passive. Really, I didn't want to go the reserve route with all their meetings. Anyway, I'm up for a direct commission—second lieutenant. So it won't be too bad."

About this time, the doors opened and we filed in and sat down at tables covered with plastic white table clothes set with polished silverware and a little artificial flower in the middle.

"Table clothes and flowers in the Army. Not bad," I remarked.

"It's always like this at lunch. Best meal of the day," said Ladd looking over the menu. "The Headquarters Company mess hall is the showplace for visiting Brass. Dinner is not as elaborate. By the way, how do you like your steak?"

"Medium," I said, impressed that the Army was about to feed me steak.

"Try it rare. They always cook it medium rare," he said filling out a card which handed to a kitchen orderly.

We then got up and filled our plate with fresh salad goodies at the salad bar. Ten minutes later, we were served nicely done filet mignon with crisp, tasty French fries and vegetables. To drink, we had our choice of pop, milk or water.

"The only downside with this meal is no beer or wine is allowed," said Ladd. "They're afraid the troops might not report to duty after lunch."

Two other new arrivals at our table were as amazed as I was about the lunch. "Almost civilized. It's like the Polo Lounge," said one who had introduced himself as Joel, a dark, Italian looking guy. His companion was Bruce, a deep-voiced fellow with perfect chiseled features.

"Polo Lounge?"

"Yeah, at the Beverly Hills Hotel where we take lunch sometimes doing deals and such," said Joel. "Bruce and I are from the same Hollywood reserve unit. We're in show business."

Joel claimed he was a film director but when I asked him what he had directed, he said simply, "Oh, I doubt you would have seen them in any movie theater. Maybe at a Frat Party."

Joel said his bread-and-butter was shooting porno films but he was trying to go legit and had some projects ready to go as soon as he got off active duty. Bruce, on the other hand, looked rather familiar but he didn't say much.

"Ever watch *Bonanza*?" asked Joel. "Bruce here appeared in several episodes as a teenager but he's been written out," he said glancing over to Bruce who winced. "Now he's just a bit actor and part-time disc jockey in L.A."

Bruce also had a Broadcast Specialist MOS and judging by his voice, it was obvious he was destined for on-air work.

All the time I'm thinking, how different this was from the Army of grunts at Fort Ord destined to hump through dusty Army bases around the world. There were truly two Armies in "this man's Army."

***

After lunch, the First Sergeant accompanied me across the parade ground to the main administration building. On the way over, I started saluting every officer that I saw but there were so many. Most of them didn't salute back; they simply nodded and smiled.

"Don't bother, Private," said the First Sergeant. "On base during working hours, we don't salute officers. You would spend all day doing it since the place is overflowing with officers. Nothing would get done."

The administration building was a flurry of activity. Officers and WACs charged up and down the stairs as if they were on some important mission. Maybe they were. However, I noticed that most of the WACs were beauties. I later learned that most had been hand-picked by the Brass for their looks and not necessarily their intelligence. Few could type, let alone spell. Most were receptionists and gofers or had other unspecified duties.

We went down a flight of stairs to the Broadcast Center, a rabbit warren of offices and broadcast studios. I was introduced to the civilian who ran the place, a Mr. Mason, a short, chubby little man who spoke with a lisp. The First Sergeant excused himself, as Mr. Mason looked me and my papers over.

"Broadcast Information Specialist. Hmm. Have any experience in broadcasting?"

"Ah…not at all but I think it would be a fascinating field to be trained in," I replied.

"Yes, well, we do much more here than broadcast duties. We are in essence a production and distribution center of radio programs for the Armed Forces Network in the Sixth Army area. We also distribute Army programs such as the *Big Picture* to television outlets on the West Coast. From time to time we produce radio and TV public service shows for the local media on the Sixth Army activities and history."

"Sounds good to me."

"Yes, well you would be considered a trainee and while you will be trained in radio and broadcasting operations, your primary responsibility will be to take over distribution duties of the tapes and film. I see here you are from the Bay Area. You know your way around San Francisco?

"Pretty well."

"Do you have a current driver's license?"

"Yes."

"Good, because one of your duties will be to function as a driver and escort for important visitors and Public Information Officers (PIO) who come by to visit our facility. This duty is not as dull as it sounds. You will have passes to all San Francisco cultural attractions—theater, film, symphony, opera, anything that your charges wish to see or do."

"Wow." My head was spinning.

"Yes, you'll be a busy trooper indeed. Now let me introduce you to Arlene who is in charge of distribution."

Arlene was an attractive woman in her mid-thirties who sat at a desk in the film-editing center. She shook my hand and smiled as I was introduced.

"Oh...good, finally somebody to send these tapes out." She motioned to a stack of audio tapes on a table next to an Ampex dubbing machine.

We chatted a while. She told me she had been a civilian employee of the Army for over ten years and loved it because she could travel the world on the Army dime. Her last tour of overseas duty had been in Japan where she was in Public Information. Now her passion was film editing for Army documentaries. Still, she was responsible for the distribution operation here.

"We make over a hundred copies of various radio broadcasts we send out each week. It's a lot to keep up with. But if you're organized, you can do in a few hours a day."

She showed me how to make the audio dubs, explaining that the hi-speed Ampex dubbing machine took only a few minutes to copy a fifteen-minute radio show. "It's fast but spot-check each tape to make sure you have a clean copy," she warned.

Arlene then showed me the shipping cartons, the shipping labels and a book listing the shipping addresses of various Armed Forces Radio outlets in the Sixth Army.

She also pointed out a storage rack of film cans marked *Big Picture*. She explained that while these half-hour films were produced around the world by Army Documentary teams, the Presidio was the distribution center for West Coast TV Stations.

"Shipping these films is a relatively easy job," she explained. "All it requires is slipping the film can into a shipping box and slapping on a label and sending it out. About a dozen of these films go out every week."

I was getting the picture now. Most of my time would be spent doing dubbing and shipping duties. What happened to my broadcasting duties?

As if reading my mind, Arlene said, "Now let's take a look at the glamor part of the operation. She led me to one of the radio studios where a program of country music was in progress. A slick looking sergeant in a glassed-in studio was making clever commentary like, "bringing you a bushel basketful of good times with the latest country hits."

Arlene showed me the radio board in an adjacent studio with its myriad of dials, knobs, and mixers. "You might get to operate one of these for the talent if someone takes the time to train you."

"What about being on air?"

"Ah…that's something for Mr. Mason to decide. You would have to do an audition. The Army doesn't let just anybody on the air."

"What about doing news?"

"News? We don't do news here," she replied. "All the radio shows are musical, country, pop, jazz and so on. About the closest we come to news are the little local documentaries we do on the Presidio and the Sixth Army. That's what I am involved in. I do some editing for that."

"Really?" I said, my interest peaked.

We went back to the editing center and Arlene showed me her set up. She had an editing bench with rewinds, a viewer and an editing block. On one side was a bin in which to hang her filmstrips.

"I often go out with a cameraman and we shoot the historical sights around the Presidio," she explained. "And then I edit the film into little three to five-minute packages that are aired on a weekly Armed Forces show hosted by Sergeant Kirk. He narrates the film live on TV. He's a regular walking encyclopedia on the Sixth Army."

This duty struck me as something that I would like to do so I said, "Maybe I could help you out here."

"Oh, sure no doubt," she replied. "There's plenty of work. I'm going on vacation for two weeks to Hawaii. You can probably go out with Sam the cameraman on a few shoots and write up a shot sheet. But save the film editing for me," she winked.

I had the feeling she was flirting with me. She wasn't bad. Nice shape, a little short. Who knew?

"Of course," I nodded.

***

Back at Headquarters Company, I discovered how easy-going serving at the Presidio could be. It being Friday afternoon, I noticed the barracks emptying. Soldiers were leaving in their civvies with little tote bags. I, still in my dress uniform, wondered what was up. The First Sergeant motioned to me to come over. "Private Brown, it's the weekend. You can take off."

"Take off?"

"Yeah, unless I tell you differently, you are on leave every weekend. You don't need a special pass. Just be back here Monday morning in time for formation."

I took advantage of my freedom and immediately went over to Berkeley for the weekend.

As I soon discovered, Headquarters Company had no reveille, no more jumping out of my bunk at 5:30 a.m. Only formation at 7:30 a.m. Nobody cared where you spent the night as long as you were at formation. Even getting out of formation was easy. Since I was a designated driver, I didn't have to fall out with the rest of the troops. My early morning duty was to pick up a car from the motor pool. About the only requirement was that I had to be at work by 8:30 a.m. and to look sharp in my dress uniform which was a chore because I had only one. The enlistees all had two dress uniforms, two pairs of dress shoes and many Army dress shirts so they could trade off. Still, I managed to keep my uniform pressed and cleaned and was generally presentable. Formal inspections were rarely held.

The motor pool was run by Raz, a gruff old master sergeant who appeared to be in his fifties. The first day he met me, he looked me up and down, and sniffed, "Short timer, I bet. I can smell them a mile away."

"I'm afraid so. Private Brown here to pick up a vehicle for the PIO Office."

With a frown, he turned to a book listing his available cars and pointed out a big black Buick sedan down at the end of the row. "That should do you. It's presentable enough for taking the Brass around town. That's what you PR boys do, isn't it?"

"So I hear."

"Winning the hearts and minds of the public. All bullshit as far as I'm concerned," he sneered. "The only thing that counts is bullets."

Over the next few weeks, I learned bits and pieces of Raz's story. "Been in this man's Army going on thirty years. Missed the First World War, but I've been in all the rest, Europe, the Pacific, Korea. Haven't made Vietnam yet but I'm trying. A chance to serve. That's all I'm asking. Three squares and bed, that's all I require." Then gazing off across Crissy Field towards the Golden Gate, he would say, "I'll probably die in this place but I'll go with my boots on. No retirement for me. They'll have to carry me out."

***

My daily routine went like this: After picking up the car and parking outside the Broadcast Center, I would start working on my dubs of the radio shows. I soon streamlined the process. First, I had a batch of labels printed with the addresses of all the Armed Forces Radio outlets in the Sixth Army area so I wouldn't waste time writing them out myself. Then I got an assembly line going for the high-speed dubs and worked at a rhythm. I pushed the Ampex to the max and kept it up hour after hour, spinning off one dub after another with only a few seconds to change tapes in between. I did spot check but not often. I was confident of my machinery. Sometimes in order to get the week's dubbing over as fast as possible, I would come back after dinner and dub away in the Broadcast Center until ten or so. After all the dubbing was complete, each audio tape went into a little shipping box. I slapped on an address label and off it went to the intended address.

Big Picture shipments were simple and took only a couple of hours to complete, except when I stopped and watched an entire program for my own amusement. They were well-done documentaries, not overtly gung-ho. Because they aired on commercial TV stations, they were aimed at a general audience and most left a positive impression about the U.S. Army on the viewer.

***

With Arlene gone, I was able to go out on several shoots with Sam, the cameraman and the Sixth Army history expert, Master Sergeant Kirk. A twenty-year Army veteran, Kirk was a minor celebrity on the base. As one of the PIO liaisons with the local media, he appeared regularly on local television extolling the historic glory of the Presidio and the Sixth Army. As he put it, "This Army base is unique. It's called the Garden Spot of the Pacific Command. I've been to Army bases around the Pacific including Hawaii and none of them can compare."

Sgt. Kirk knew what he was talking about. The history of the Presidio went back to the days of Spanish control of California. The fort was established in 1776 by the Spanish, partly in reaction to the Yankee American Revolution. In 1822, after becoming independent of Spain, the Mexicans took possession of the Presidio. During the Mexican-American War of 1846, the U.S. seized control of the Presidio and eventually developed the fort into a full-scale Army base by the time of the Civil War. From then on, the Presidio served as the base of operations for action in the Far Pacific, including the Philippines during the Spanish-American War in 1899. It was also a training base for World War I officers. During World War II, it was the U.S. Western Defense Command Headquarters for the Pacific Theater and later for the Korean War. Now in 1964, the Sixth Army Headquarters' main mission was to keep a close eye on the action in Southeast Asia.

I drove Kirk and Sam around for shoots at various historic spots such as Fort Point, an old civil war fort right under the Golden Gate Bridge. Fort Point was famous for having never fired a shot at an enemy during its long existence. Its purpose, of course, was to protect the Golden Gate, the only entrance to San Francisco Bay and therefore of immense strategic value.

Sitting as it did in the shadow of the bridge and often shrouded in fog, Fort Point was a specter from the past. You could easily imagine the Civil War era troops waiting in the cold and in the fog for an attack by a Confederate ship that never came. A brooding, hulking structure of brick, several stories tall, it was loaded with cannon and gun ports facing out to the Golden Gate.

My job was to take notes on what was filmed while Sgt. Kirk and Sam explored the long empty hallways and the gun ports. Overhead, we could hear the *thuck, thuck, thuck* of traffic going across the Golden Gate Bridge.

Outside, I noticed a retaining wall with stairs going down to the sea. I recalled that movie star Kim Novak jumped from these stairs trying to commit suicide in the Alfred Hitchcock movie *Vertigo*, only to be rescued by Jimmy Stewart.

The Presidio Sixth Army also included a complex of minor forts and gun emplacements nestled in the Marin headlands north of the Golden Gate. One fort, Fort Baker, was tucked into a little enclave on the bay just across the bridge. Over on the ocean side of the headlands, the hills were honeycombed with old fortifications and bunkers from World War Two. Perched on the highest hill was a Nike missile site. Below in a little valley and steps from a beach was Fort Cronkite where more troops were stationed. This was all off-limits to the public.

We wandered around these fortifications with the 16 mm silent film camera rolling. At one point we entered a dank concrete bunker. Gazing out through the observation slits, one could easily imagine being an observer here during World War II, spending day after day looking for Japanese warships or possibly subs. Occasionally, the big artillery guns were brought into play and started shelling simply for target practice. Now, of course, attack was most likely from the air and that was the purpose of the Nike missile site.

Other days we would simply drive around the Presidio proper filming the grounds and the byways lined with forests of blue gum eucalyptus, cypress and Monterey pines. Traveling along Infantry Terrace and MacArthur Avenue, we shot the stately homes of the senior officers. These were large white Victorian and Queen Anne mansions perched on the heights overlooking San Francisco Bay. Sometimes we would descend to Crissy Field near the waterfront and shoot the little prop airplanes landing and taking off as they ferried the Brass up and down the coast. Nearby was the infamous Presidio Stockade, a two-story Italianate building, surrounded by a tall, electrified fence. Word was the place was a chamber of horrors. The stockade was off limits for filming.

Then it was on to Letterman Hospital near the Lombard Street entrance of the Presidio. This was the largest Army Hospital west of the Mississippi, a mammoth complex, noted for its excellent care. We prowled the hallways, peeped into the wards, and observed the doctors and nurses walking briskly about. Sgt. Kirk noted that an increasing number of patients were arriving from Vietnam and Laos with weird tropical diseases and strange infections caused by punji sticks and other booby traps found in the jungle.

We did notice that not even being a patient got you out of housekeeping duties. We often saw the less ill or injured sweeping the hallways and emptying trash.

***

Once all this footage was shot, Sgt. Kirk would take it back the Broadcast Center and start figuring out how to assemble it. With my shot sheet notes, he would sketch out a rough script and then start editing the film. I often watched him do it. I wrote out a few rough scripts myself based on some the historical material Kirk had, but aside from a few splices, he wouldn't let me physically edit the film. Everybody was so protective of the editing function.

"We have only one copy of this film," I heard constantly. "This is not Hollywood. No duplicates. If this film gets screwed up, we are out of luck. So if you don't mind," he would say after watching me fumble around with the splicing block and move in himself to continue the edit. Of course, after Arlene returned, I didn't get near the editing bench and had to content myself with the rough scripts which Kirk did appreciate and use.

Once the three to five-minute pieces were edited, Kirk would go off to

California Split

the photo library and retrieve stills that further illustrated the historical points he was trying to make in an upcoming show. He also used various artifacts—shell casings, old rifles, grenades, an odd cannonball. Once a week, we would haul all this stuff off to the studios of KGO-TV on Golden Gate Avenue to produce the show, *The Presidio*. This was a half-hour public service show that featured Sgt. Kirk and his special guests who would discuss the history and current activities of the Presidio. This was also my first look at the inner workings live television.

As I soon discovered sitting in the control room, "live" television was a chaotic crapshoot, to say the least. The on-air director had to coordinate three studio cameras with film, slide and videotape sources. One studio camera was on Sergeant Kirk who sat in a chair on a set with a photomural of the Presidio in the background. The second camera had a two-shot of Kirk and a guest. The third camera focused on a particular artifact that Kirk was describing or on a studio card that had one of the old Presidio photographs pasted on it.

As Sgt. Kirk adlibbed, referring to various artifacts and film clips, the on-air director snapped cues to a technician who punched various buttons on a large switching console which resulted in a cut or a dissolve from one camera to another or from one video source to another. The selected image would then go out on the air.

All the time the on-air director would be watching the clock, making sure the program segments came off on time. A couple of times he would cut to a commercial that were usually public service spots. And in the final last minutes of the show, the studio floor manager would count down Sgt. Kirk for his closing ad-lib. The show would be over at precisely 28:50 after the hour.

After witnessing this the first time, my head was spinning. I couldn't believe anyone could coordinate such a split second effort and make it look like anything on the air. Yet the on-air director told me it was all part of a day's work. "That's the nature of the beast, trooper. Live television. It can drive you nuts or be a real high. Think what those New York TV directors went through when they did a live drama. This little public service show is a piece of cake."

"Piece of cake?" I replied shaking my head. "It was moving so fast, I couldn't keep track of what was going on."

"Sergeant, clue in the Private," laughed the on-air-director. "He's supposed to be a trainee in this stuff. He should volunteer down here to find out about the real television world."

I must admit I was fascinated yet repulsed. It seemed too slap-dash to me to produce anything of quality. Yet it was exciting.

***

Radio production, by contrast, was a much more leisurely affair. Since the radio formats at the Presidio were all taped, one could start and stop an on-going show if need be although, the three disc jockeys I knew were loath to do that. They claimed it took away the spontaneity. Even though there was only a small Army audience for their work, they took it very seriously.

Specialist Jens, a blond-haired fellow about my age who specialized in Country and Western music. He would assume a phony country accent and spin the latest hits featuring Johnny Cash and June Carter.

Marine Sgt. Hughes did middle-of-the-road pop, sometimes dipping into rock and roll and lately featuring a group from England called the "Beatles" just out with "I Want to Hold Your Hand," a song that struck me as rather lame.

The Jazz show disc jockey was Sgt. Katz, and as his name implied, he was a cool cat indeed. Despite Army regulations, he sported a well-trimmed goatee. He specialized in the jazz of Thelonious Monk, Miles Davis and Charlie Parker. Sgt. Katz was the oldest of the group, already a twenty-five year veteran. He was also a jazz musician that played Army gigs. Katz had served in World War II and stayed on during the occupation in Vienna. He was full of stories about the good times he had there, "Shit, we had it all going on. The black market, the jazz gigs. We played everywhere. Of course, the women. I'd give my left nut to get back to Europe."

"So why don't you?" I asked.

"Well, I had to come back to the Bay Area sometime. My aging folks live here. I'm thinking about retiring. This peacetime Army isn't what it used to be. You can't get rank. I've been a staff sergeant for ten years now. I'm going nowhere. I've had some good assignments, Europe, the Far East, Hawaii, now here. For stateside, the Presidio is about as good as it gets but I'm still getting out."

Sgt. Hughes would chime in, "I hear you Katz, I'd get out too but I haven't got my twenty in. Plus, I still have the itch. I have to get over to Saigon. I hear it's "boom-boom G.I." all over the place. That aside, I need that tax-free overseas pay."

Sgt. Jens was the most skeptical of the lot. "You're crazy Hughes. Vietnam is going to blow. You'll be fighting gooks before you know it. As for me, when my enlistment is up next year, I am out of here. I'm going to find me a nice little Country & Western station in the South and talk my old man into helping me buy it. I want to own a string of them. And I'm telling you, despite this rock and roll stuff, country is here to stay and there'll be big bucks in it."

Of course, none of the disc jockeys was in a big hurry to leave the Presidio. There was too much going on in the showbiz world of radio. Nearly every week some celebrity singer would come by for an interview. While I was there, I met Nancy Wilson, Vicki Carr, Jack Jones and Mel Torme I would hover nearby, fetch them fresh coffee, listen to their stories and laugh at their jokes.

Then there were the freebies. Record promoters would come by and drop off the top hit records in all musical genres hoping for a play. The Army troops were the ideal demographic for them — young men between eighteen and thirty-five. And finally, there were the parties and the receptions and believe or not, even Army groupies, lonely young Army wives or daughters who listened to the Armed Forces Radio network and hung around. The jocks were living large.

Occasionally, I was able to work the radio board for Sgt. Jens. He showed me how to cue records, how to segue into tunes, how to fade in and fade out. How to play with some effects, how to splice audio tape, etc. Jens also encouraged me to give it a try as an on-air disc jockey with him working the board.

I did an audition tape for traditional pop but it was terrible. I simply didn't know what to say. I wasn't knowledgeable about the music, although I knew a few things about Elvis and the Beach Boys. I sounded stupid and contrived on the air and my voice was too irregular.

"Don't sweat it, Al." Jens said. "It comes with practice. You have to do your musical homework and develop a spiel. Work on it with a tape recorder."

"Hmm. I think I would be more comfortable with a newscast, I said. "At least I would have a script to read."

"Yeah, but it's not ad-lib radio. That's where it's at," Jens replied.

Needless to say, I was not put on the air at the Presidio. However, the other broadcast trainee, Bruce, the bit actor from Hollywood was immediately on-air doing middle of the road music. He had a good broadcast voice and knew what he was doing at a board.

However, after a few weeks at the Presidio, Bruce was shunted off to Desert Strike, an Army desert exercise at Fort Irwin in the Mojave Desert near Needles, California. His job was to be the local disc jockey for the Armed Forces Network down there. I wasn't too envious. Everyone said Fort Irwin was a hole and the two-month Desert Strike exercise a nightmare to be avoided. I contented myself with working with Sgt. Kirk on the TV shows and going about my shipping and driving duties.

***

As Mr. Mason implied, being a chauffeur for bigwigs at the Presidio was not dull. One of my more frequent passengers was a Colonel Yates, the head of the Public Information Office. He was Mr. Chamber of Commerce for the Sixth Army, constantly attending civic meetings and receptions downtown, most often at the Fairmont Hotel and the Mark Hopkins. He was constantly promoting the Presidio and its civic contributions to San Francisco. He was also on the verge of a forced retirement after twenty years in the Army. (The Army had too many colonels.) Yet, as he said, "I'll be back as a civilian employee." In fact, he was slated to be the top civilian liaison between the Presidio and the San Francisco community. I guess he loved the hors d'oeuvres and the rubber chicken served at these events. I would often go in and partake myself while checking out the San Francisco Society set with its rail thin women and portly, well-groomed power brokers.

Sometimes the assignment was to drive returning officers from Vietnam around to the nightspots and wait while they drank it up, listened to jazz and ogled the strippers. One Green Beret officer stuck in my mind. After a night of hard partying, he was in a confessional mood. "Don't believe what they tell you about Vietnam here," he said slouched in the back seat. "It's all-out friggin war. We are in up to our eyeballs. I've seen action in not only South Vietnam but Cambodia and Laos too. Laos is a pip. The whole fuckin' thing is run by the CIA. These South Vietnamese fuckers can't fight worth a shit. We show them how but eventually, we have to go in and do the job ourselves. All long-range recon, dead of night stuff. Lots of knife work. Got to watch it though, booby-traps all over the place. Lost a buddy to an infection from a punji stick."

"No kidding," was all I could say.

Another passenger was a major who headed the Army PIO office in Saigon. When he discovered that I knew French pretty well, we chatted for a while in French and he told me what a great gig it was. Saigon was full of beautiful women, great parties. The danger was far away. He said all they did was write press releases about what a great job the Army was doing and escort big shots around.

"Yeah, it's a good life," he said. "I'm probably going to extend my tour."

"I keep hearing there's a lot of action in the jungle," I said.

"Yeah, well, sometimes. Occasionally, we have to chopper out and document the aftermath of another "victorious" battle by our friends the South Vietnamese. Part of the propaganda campaign. But even that's exciting."

"I'll bet."

"Yeah, I could use a French speaker like you over there. Most of my PIO troops can barely say *bon jour*. Why don't you extend?

"Extend?"

"Yeah, it's only it's only a nine-month tour. I'll make sure you get the PIO assignment. And at the end of your tour, you'll be in the inactive reserves. No meetings or summer camp. Think it over Private Brown."

"Ah, I will," I said seriously.

"By the way, direct commissions are easy to come by. Just another perk you could have," he said as he handed me his card.

***

A few days later, I went to see the base recruiter, known as the "re-up" sergeant.

"If you can guarantee my MOS and where I will serve, I might be interested in extending," I explained to him.

The burly sergeant looked me over and shrugged. "Why not? We get a lot of guys like you. Reservists who see the light," he said shoving a bunch of papers at me. "Remember, while the Army will try to honor your request and the request of the PIO major, this is still the Army and we will use you where we see fit. Take these papers with you and think it over."

I did think it over. I didn't have a clue about what I was going to do once I was done with my active duty. Maybe go back to school. Maybe try to go into broadcasting. Maybe re-join the Peace Corps. Maybe just make some money land surveying and then go to Europe. I didn't know. In some weird way, I thought extending for a year in the Army might be the answer. I dreaded going to reserve meetings and summer camp for five and a half years. Plus, I wanted some adventure.

I knew a fellow reservist, Frank who had been a lowly clerk typist for a general. Frank had become so gung-ho, he re-enlisted for a full three years in order to become a helicopter pilot. As he put it, "I always wanted to fly. This is a great opportunity. With the general's backing, it's a cinch I'll be able to get into flight school."

"Yeah," I said. "But three more years."

"Where's your patriotism, Brown?" he replied. "They need helicopter pilots over there in Vietnam to ferry the South Vietnamese troops around. I'll even get a Warrant Officer's rank."

"Whatever, Frank. I wish you well."

In the end, I put my extension papers in an envelope in my footlocker and decided to delay my decision for a while.

10. OFF-BASE

In addition to my on-base duties, I led an active off-base life. The enlisted men's service club had a line on part-time jobs to supplement a private's meager income. One job was serving as a movie usher at a nearby neighborhood movie theater. Hollywood Joel had latched on to this job and he told me they needed another usher. So I worked two nights a week at the theater for a month.

The main movie for that month was Stanley Kubrick's black satire *Doctor Strangelove or: How I Learned to Stop Worrying and Love the Bomb* which was playing to rave reviews. I must have seen it a dozen times over the next few weeks. I had the dialogue memorized. The film was a great antidote to Army life. The other major film playing was *The Victors* directed by Carl Foreman with George Hamilton, Vince Edwards and Albert Finney. This anti-war movie was so controversial that it was banned from the base theater; so of course, the neighborhood theater was packed with Army enlisted men and officers. *The Victors* focused on the rampant corruption of the U.S. forces in occupied Germany in 1945. I thought it was mild compared to the satire of Dr. Strangelove which was much more subversive, yet was allowed at the base theater. (I figured it was the Air Force angle the Army Brass enjoyed.)

When I wasn't working at the movie theater during the evenings, Joel, Bruce and I would go to a pub on Lombard Street. One night Joel met some women staying in a residence hall on Pacific Heights. This was a popular place for singles and a treasure drove for us. We hung out there many evenings, playing cards, shooting pool or going out. All very congenial and light.

At the time, I was adrift woman wise. Bobbie had recently married Tom in Chicago. I had been invited to the wedding but declined to go using the Army as an excuse. Darrah was immersed in her Berkeley scene. And my lovely Clarissa had lined up a stewardess job with Pan American Airlines and was all excited about that. All talk of getting together after she graduated had apparently been forgotten.

***

While hanging out with Joel and Bruce, I learned something of their Hollywood ways. Bruce was the serious one. Not too flamboyant. He struck me as very level headed for a bit actor and part-time disc jockey but Joel was a weird cat. He had hooked up with Rita, a fat chick who lived at the boarding house. I wondered why? He could have had his pick of women up there. After all, he was a good-looking guy, very smooth with women, a trait he no doubt developed from his porno directing days. He said his girlfriend Rita was a hoot and she would try anything.

I had my suspicions about Joel. By his own account, he had been a wayward youth. At fifteen, he quit high school in St. Louis and lit out for New York to become a teenage song-and-dance man. Apparently, he had some talent because he did appear in a few off-Broadway productions. At the same time, he lived with various older showbiz producers. He didn't say what the relationship was but I could guess. Five years ago, he moved to Hollywood where he landed bit parts here and there in film musicals, until he decided he wanted to direct. He calculated the quickest way to get real directorial experience was doing skin flicks.

"The trick is to keep a clear head when all the action is going on. You have to be able to concentrate on those money shots."

"That must take a lot of concentration," I joked.

"Believe it or not it does take a lot of concentration. I can remember sometimes sitting on the camera dolly, going in tight on some guy porking the sex star, and me being blown at the same time. I never missed the shot. And it was all so slam bam. It had to be done in one take. But now I feel I'm ready to move on. When I get back to Hollywood, I'm going legit."

"Yeah, if anybody remembers us after being gone for six months," said a worried-looking Bruce.

"Shit, Bruce it's only six months," said Joel.

"You know as well as I do, Joel that it's out of sight, it's out of mind in Hollywood. It's as if you don't exist," said Bruce. "You have to be on the scene right there in someone's face to get any work."

"Ah, don't worry about it, Bruce."

"Well, I do. And now in a week, I have to deal with this Desert Strike exercise. Being a disc jockey in the middle of the Mojave Desert."

"Poor baby," said Joel patting Bruce's cheek.

"Well, at least, I'll be within striking distance of L.A. on the weekends," said Bruce trying to cheer himself up. "I'll be able to show my face around at the parties."

"There, you see," said Joel. "It won't be so bad. But we have to get cracking on that script idea."

"What script idea?" I asked.

"Bruce and I have an idea for a script but we need a place to work on it. You know the scene here in the Bay Area, Al. You know anybody with an apartment around here?"

I mentioned my brother Don's apartment in Berkeley. They thought that was a great idea. I phoned Don. He said he and his roommate were going home for the weekend, so the place was ours.

***

Thus it was, we took the Muni over to Berkeley one Saturday afternoon and set up writer's camp in Don's Northside apartment. Joel moved the dining room table to the center of the living room and Bruce broke out his portable Olympia typewriter and laid out a stack of fresh white typing paper with four or five carbons. Joel pulled out an old movie script from his pack that he had ripped off from some studio. As Joel explained, the scripts would serve as formatting guides.

All this preparation was done solemnly, ritualistically, almost religiously. I expected Joel to give an incantation, calling on the Muse of Script Writing. The only detail missing was a specific story idea. So we spent the next couple of hours brainstorming. Joel and Bruce knew they wanted to write about Army life but which aspect?

"OK. There's this sergeant," said Joel pacing around the living room. "Highly decorated. Eighteen-year veteran. Caught the end of World War II. Served in Korea. Let's make him a master drill sergeant. Now stationed at Fort Ord."

"That's fine," said Bruce, furiously typing out a rough draft story treatment. "It's good background but what happens. What's the story line?"

"I have an idea," I chimed in. "Let's make him a father with two kids and a philandering wife. He's strapped for cash. He needs more rank. He wants to go to Vietnam for the combat pay."

"That's good, Al, but we have to push it further," said Joel. "Also we have to remember that this will be a budget movie. We can't actually film Vietnam. Maybe some jungle in Mexico. We could use Asian looking Mexicans as Vietnamese. But I think this should be an interior movie. There has to be some sort of internal, personal crisis."

"Like what?" I asked.

"Like maybe why does he tolerate his unfaithful wife," said Joel tentatively. "Like maybe he is not in love with her. He's in love with the Army. He's in love with his troops. He loves being around men. Like maybe, he's a repressed homosexual. And the crisis of the story comes when he realizes it and makes a move on some handsome troop after a night of drinking. Of course, the troop recoils and beats up the sergeant. The movie could end with shots of the sergeant hanging out at the gay bars in San Francisco, giving up his family, the whole bit."

"Wow," said Bruce. "Who have you been reading? Gore Vidal? John Rechy?"

"Yeah, I have dipped into their works. What do you think, you guys?" said Joel still pacing, pleased with himself.

"It would never fly. Too advanced for Hollywood," said Bruce. "It would have to be so toned down and subtle that an audience wouldn't get it. Also it needs more action."

"I think Bruce is right," I said. "I think you would have a better story if the Sergeant was a straight ahead, gung-ho warrior. He wants not only to go to Vietnam to get rank and combat pay but also to fight communism. Let's make him a Green Beret. Special Forces type, trained to infiltrate behind enemy lines, gather intelligence, set off explosives, etc. The conflict could come when he realizes how corrupt the South Vietnam regime has become and how they are killing off innocent villagers. Maybe he thinks about resigning from the Army but there is one last mission that requires him to personally kill suspected Viet Cong whom he thinks are innocent villagers. He can't do it so another Special Forces team does. He returns to the States under a cloud. He resigns from the Army and becomes an anti-war protester. The last shot could be him marching with the protesters right outside the Presidio gates."

"Good story line, Al. But I don't think Hollywood is ready for an obvious anti-war movie, especially one so current with the time. Kubrick could get away with it with *Strangelove* because it was a satire and so far-fetched as not to be taken seriously."

"Yeah. Hollywood is still patriotic," concurred Bruce. "Let's stick to the first version. But like Al said, the Sarge has to be straight. Let's have him go to Vietnam, doing his job and then returning and in a fit of violence, he kills his wife's lover and his wife. The last scene is the poor Sergeant going off to Fort Leavenworth, half-insane. Something like that."

"Sounds good to me," said Joel. "Let's break it down into scenes."

At this point, I ordered a pizza for everyone from La Vals down the street. When I returned with the pizza, the sun was setting behind the Golden Gate casting a golden glow over the living room but Joel and Bruce never noticed because they were so deeply immersed in script writing.

As it turned out, they kept it up all night. When I asked why they had to write it one session, the answer was, "That's the way we do it in movieland, Al. Strike while the iron is hot. Brainstorm, write, write, write. Get it done," said Joel pacing around while Bruce typed. "I mean a script is not a novel. It's only an 80-page document, a blueprint for the director and the stars. We'll have this baby done by tomorrow afternoon."

"Do say," I yawned. "I'm going to bed."

And true to their word, by noon Sunday, a sleepless Joel and Bruce had produced a finished script with a carbon copy which Joel said he would submit to a producer he knew. Entitled, *The Sergeant*, the story line was a compromise. The sergeant is gay but latent, also a war hero, but doesn't resign. In fact, he is promoted to sergeant major. In other words, a typical Hollywood ending. Joel said this might be his break-through movie and he hoped to interest Rock Hudson in playing the sergeant. Failing that perhaps, George Nader.

***

Bruce soon took off for Fort Irwin to be a disc jockey for the Army during its Desert Strike exercise. Joel was still around but he was becoming a drag with his Hollywood persona and exhortations of weird sexual practices. So I started going out on my own, wandering around downtown.

One foggy night while riding the cable car along California Street, an angel-faced young lady sitting across from me asked the way to Fisherman's Wharf.

"You're on the wrong cable car," I replied. "You have to transfer to the Powell-Mason Street cable car at Powell."

"Oh," she said pouting. "Darn."

Well, feeling like a gentleman in my full dress Army uniform, I offered to escort the young lady whose name was Susan. On the way, I learned that Susan was from Kansas City and that she had a job at a personnel agency. She was a counselor for people looking for entry-level management jobs.

Hmm...I thought a serious, practical person. However, Susan wasn't in a serious mood that night.

"Kansas City? Kansas," I said. "Miles of wheat fields, right?"

"No, Private Brown," she mocked. (I had introduced myself as Private Brown.)

Kansas City, Missouri. Kansas City is in Missouri, right on the border of Kansas."

"Do tell. I've heard of Kansas City beef and Kansas City jazz. What else is going on there?" I asked.

"Well, it's a very cosmopolitan town with museums, symphonies, art galleries and beautiful leafy suburbs, very unlike the rest of Missouri. It's also the home of Hallmark Cards."

"Oh, that's very hip," I said teasingly. "So what brought you out to San Francisco?"

"Ah, I needed a change of scenery. This is sort of my Graduate Year Abroad. I never went to Europe when I was an undergraduate at the University of Missouri. My parents didn't trust Europeans. They thought it would be too much for their innocent daughter."

"I see."

I later learned that Susan had, in fact, followed a European boyfriend out to San Francisco. He was a physics major now doing graduate work at Berkeley. But apparently, things had not worked out, so Susan was free as a bird. She was looking to move out of the modest hotel where she was staying. I mentioned the boarding house that Joel, Bruce and I had discovered up the hill from the Presidio.

"It seems like a nice place. Cute rooms. The food is not bad and it is full of young single men and women like yourself." I offered to take her over there the next day.

Susan reminded me of Bobby. Wholesome Midwestern good looks. Friendly, not complicated. Trusting, actually. Susan later told me she was attracted to me because I was in uniform and had a fuzzy haircut. I looked like a harmless Midwestern boy, but being from this area, I still represented something of an adventure.

And so it went. Susan moved into the boarding house and we ran around the city together, going to cheap restaurants, free movies, and free plays courtesy of the servicemen's club. Since neither of us had a car, we took the Muni bus or the cable car wherever we went. Eventually, I began spending the nights at the boarding house and when it was discovered, the house manager had a shit fit, threatening to either charge me or throw Susan out.

Susan stepped up and announced that she was done with the boarding house and its fattening meals. She was moving to a furnished apartment on the Marina where we could have some peace and decent food. I had mixed fillings about this. On one hand, the convenience of an off-base apartment was appealing. The Army didn't care as long as I was on the job at 8:30 a.m. with my vehicle. The disc jockey, Specialist Jens who had met Susan envied me, saying, "Y'all found yourself a great little sweetheart, Brown. Be good to her."

On the other hand, this arrangement smelled of playing house with lurking commitment. Susan laughed it off, saying she understood that this wasn't serious. However, I felt bad exploiting the situation because while she was a nice person and very attractive, she didn't have the fire of Darrah or the bubbly personality of Bobbie. Maybe it was her conservative Midwest upbringing.

"My parents are right out the novels of Evan S. Connell," she explained. "They're essentially Mr. and Mrs. Bridge. Dad comes home from his Insurance Company, settles down in his easy chair to read the *Kansas City Star*. At 6:30, Mom serves her sensible meat and potatoes dinner with Brussels sprouts. Later Mom knits as they listen to the radio or watch TV. They go to bed at ten-thirty right after the news. It's all very boring."

"That doesn't sound much different from what my parents do," I replied.

Susan continued, "My sister and I were taught our table manners and good posture. We had dance lessons and piano lessons. Iris and I were very well behaved and good students. We went to the Episcopal Church every Sunday. So my parents were appalled that I had a foreign boyfriend at college and nearly died when I left to follow Fritz to the Bay Area."

Very nice, very sensible Susan appeared to have a streak of rebellion. Still, I thought Susan would make a good mother and run a tight household. She was already a good businesswoman. She would be a wonderful wife for some Midwestern dude. For a while, I acted like that Midwestern dude. I would put in my workday at the Presidio and then take a bus over to her apartment. It was a studio apartment right out of the 1930's with steam heat radiators, a puke-green sofa, a wobbly coffee table and a fold-down double bed.

I was beginning to feel like a character in one of the Mr. and Mrs. Bridge books. Susan would come home, lugging groceries for the evening meal, cook it in her Midwestern style with occasional forays into international cuisine and spices. I would watch the news on a fuzzy, second-hand black and white television set with rabbit ears. After, dinner we would go out for a walk along the Marina waterfront park. Susan noted more than once that all that was missing was a dog to complete the domestic scene.

After a month of this, I was looking for a way out. I started making excuses that I had to sleep at Headquarters Company in order to make formation. I began showing up only two nights a week. Susan complained that the apartment was too lonely when I wasn't around. So after renting the apartment for only two months, she moved in with another single woman who had a larger apartment off Union Street near Laguna.

I was relieved. The pressure was off and the girlfriend's apartment was a groovy Victorian with charming nooks and crannies, a fireplace, and a great sound system which we made use of by playing Prokofiev's Lt. Kije's Suite over and over while drinking Chenin Blanc wine. The new apartment gave renewed energy to our relationship.

***

Late March, Susan and I went off for a weekend of skiing. We rode up with brother Don and his girlfriend Nancy to a luxurious ski cabin near Squaw Valley that belonged to one of his fraternity brothers, Jerry. Jerry and his girlfriend were going to join us up there.

Susan had skied only once but she was eager to take lessons and learn. She had bought all the clothes and was a cute ski bunny indeed. We had a fine day of spring skiing at Squaw. Susan dutifully took a lesson in the morning and picked up the basics rather fast. "All that dance training," she said. In the afternoon, we skied together on the easy slopes.

As we were getting ready to go over to the cabin, Don pulled me aside. "Allan, we are going to have some extra company."

"Extra Company? Who?"

"Darrah."

"Darrah!"

"Yeah, she wormed her way into an invite. She bugged Jerry. And she's bringing a friend."

"No shit."

At this point, I should probably explain that Darrah knew Don as well.

In fact, she had gone out with him a couple of times before she met me. As Don once said, "she had good hands." She had apparently kept in contact.

When we got to the cabin, Darrah was already there with her "friend," Rab.

They had skied that day at nearby Alpine, an easy beginner resort. Rab was a skinny little guy. Handsome though, probably Jewish and he looked younger that Darrah. I nodded, shook his hand when introduced. I introduced Susan who didn't have a clue about Darrah. Darrah said a tight hello and then turned away.

I didn't know whether to be amused or pissed off. Darrah had said nothing about a Rab, although I knew she was going out with other guys. After introductions, we ignored each other.

Following a spaghetti meal washed down with cheap red Pisano wine, we retired to the large living room with the roaring fire. We listened to music, played cards, danced, and drank some scotch. Later, sitting on the floor in front of the fire, Darrah dreamily played with curly locks of Rab.

That was too much, so I led Susan to our bedroom with a king-size bed. The revenge footnote to all of this was Darrah and Rab had to sleep in the living room because all the three bedrooms had been allotted. They left early the next day and I didn't see them after that.

***

If being with Susan and attending to the duties of a Broadcast specialist was the bright side of my time at the Presidio, I gradually became aware of the underbelly of the place. For instance, Vietnam was a sensitive issue. For many regular Army troops stationed at the Presidio in the spring of 1964, Vietnam was the place to go for rank and overseas combat pay if only for a mere nine months. Already there were some 15-thousand American advisers over there, based mostly in and around Saigon or on some fortified base like Cam Rahn Bay. As noted before, a few gung-ho types such as the Green Berets actually went on missions into North Vietnam and Laos and stirred up trouble. Others seeing action were the Army helicopter pilots ferrying South Vietnamese troops in and out of various battle zones.

Cold War and military logic went something like this: Starting a war with the Soviets in Europe was unthinkable as well as tangling with China. Vietnam was a safe little war, way off in South East Asia. It was a place where we could fight the Commies in peace with little threat of Soviet intervention. It was also a place where Regular Army troops could gain rank and increase their financial security at little risk. Or so they thought.

Already in the spring of 1964, our safe little war in Vietnam was inspiring anti-war protests. Nearly every weekend, fifteen or twenty protesters with signs reading, *Peace not war, Get out of Vietnam*, demonstrated outside the main gate of the Presidio. Sometimes movie star Sterling Hayden joined them. We used to see the protesters as we came and went on our weekend rounds in our civvies. Sometimes we would sit on a retaining wall across the street, drink beer and watch the protests. Men in dark suits with sunglasses and cameras also observed the protesters from nearby.

The protesters seemed like a harmless group to me but they absolutely inspired terror and anger among the Army regulars who mumbled, "Traitors, communists, peaceniks, send them over to Hanoi."

In reaction to the anti-war protests, we had to attend a special series of noontime lectures on how vital Vietnam was to U.S. interests. It was the key domino of all the dominos in that part of the world. If South Vietnam fell to the Commies, all of Southeast Asia would follow was the mantra.

We were further warned to have nothing to do with the protesters. "Do not taunt them or talk to them. Just ignore them and go about your business," the lecturing officer admonished us. "Above all, do not join them even as a joke. Otherwise, you could wind up in the stockade."

Of course, all of these lectures were hush-hush, almost top secret. We were advised not to discuss them with civilians. We had to sign a release to that effect.

I met Specialist Johnson at these lectures who later told me what a crock this all was. "Army Intelligence has its head up its ass. It doesn't have a clue what is going on either in Vietnam or here with the anti-war protests," he stated flatly.

Johnson apparently knew what he was talking about. A bright, intense guy, he had been bounced out of the Army Intelligence School in Maryland for a variety of reasons. This was the school I would have gone to had I signed up for Army Intelligence.

"I aced all their exams and exercises but it was determined that I had a bad attitude," he explained. "It was essentially a brain-washing operation. So here I am serving the rest of my three-year enlistment in the Maintenance Company, the absolute dregs of the Army."

I often saw these maintenance troops driving aimlessly around in pickup trucks performing various chores. One of Johnson' duties was to supervise the stockade prisoners as they weeded the base and maintained the lawns. "These guys are a sorry bunch," he said. "A lot of them are in here because of some minor dumb-shit infraction like maybe falling asleep on guard duty or being AWOL for a girl."

"Or having a bad attitude," I teased.

"Yeah, you name it," he continued. "You should see their cells, cages really, not fit for animals. The prisoners have to put up with overflowing toilets, cold ass showers and hardly any light. Of, course no heating at all. The Army thinks it's the fucking tropics here. When that fog comes rolling in, you feel wet to the bone and chilled. To top it off, the guards are goons. All of them are on power trips. They also have itchy trigger fingers. Those weapons they tote around are all loaded. One of these days, someone is going to get shot."

All of this started me thinking. Service in the Army was a chancy business. The slightest infraction with a wrong prick officer or sergeant could mean endless KP or even the brig. Yet, there were attractions. Some interesting duty like mine. The security of three square meals and a bed. The chance to see the world. I checked myself. This was all recruiting poster bullshit.

That night I tore up my extension papers. I had decided to forego that PIO opportunity in Saigon. It sounded interesting on the surface but with my luck, full-scale war would break out, and I would find myself extended over there. Worse yet, I might find myself out on the frontlines getting shot at while trying to save the hearts and minds of terrified villagers.

No, I decided I would quietly serve the few remaining weeks of my active duty and return to civilian life. I was eager to make some money over the summer and go to graduate school next fall. I had spoken to Mr. Mason about San Francisco State where he taught part-time in the Radio, TV and Film department.

"If you're interested in pursuing this radio/TV business, Private Brown, I would highly recommend SF State. They do a good job in this. State-of-the-art facilities and instructors who have years of experience in the real world of film, TV and radio."

"I might be interested down the road. But right now, I have to earn some money to go back to school. I'm on my own."

"I understand. If you need a recommendation, don't hesitate to call me."

"Thanks, I will."

***

Before I knew it, my active duty days at the Presidio were over. One clear, crisp morning in late June, with my discharge orders in hand, I said goodbye to Arlene, the disc jockeys, Mr. Mason and Sgt. Kirk. I slung my duffel bag over my shoulder and walked out to the parking lot where my Dad was waiting in his car and waved adieu to the Presidio with its lush landscaping, its winding lanes and its spectacular views of the bay and the Golden Gate.

11. SURVEYOR

After a few days of sitting at home in Martinez and hearing, "What are you going to do now, Son?" I started going around to the local surveying firms and filling out job applications. My dad was somewhat bemused that his son with a history degree from Berkeley was still in the surveying game.

"I don't plan to make it a career, Dad. It's just good money for the time being until I can save enough to go back to school," I explained.

"Well, it's honorable work," he replied. "As you know, that's how I started in this civil engineering business."

Right he was. Land surveying was a Brown family tradition. When my father was seventeen in 1929, with only a high school education, he landed a job with the state of California as a chainman (surveying assistant.) He was good at mathematics, especially trigonometry which was essential to surveying. Soon he was promoted to instrument man, the person who made the calculations, established lines and turned the angles. In short order, he was the brains of the survey party. Dad worked all over the state—the Mojave Desert, the Sierras, the Pacific Coast and the Bay Area where he surveyed the bridge approaches to the San Francisco Bay Bridge then under construction. It was also in the Bay Area where he met and married my mother in 1935. Eventually, he was based at headquarters in Sacramento. There, by dint of night courses and hard studying, he became a licensed civil engineer.

In addition to his regular engineering job at Contra Costa County, Dad did surveying side-jobs. When my brother Don and I were little, Dad sometimes took us along on the weekends if it was a simple job such as locating the property lines for a rancher in the foothills of Mt. Diablo.

Typically, we would show up early on a Saturday morning with all the surveying gear—the transit, the measuring tapes, the stakes and the sledge hammer. Dad would warn us to stay out of the poison oak and then set up his transit and start surveying. As we grew older, Dad showed us how the transit was used to determine angles. He let us help him measure distances with the chain, a long steel measuring tape. Sometimes, he calculated the distances by turning angles with the transit and using a table of logarithms.

Dad enjoyed surveying. He enjoyed being outdoors in the hills, in the weeds and yes, even around poison oak. I don't know how much we helped our dad but Don and I always had a good time tromping around, climbing trees, running through pastures while our dad surveyed. He often said he should return to surveying full-time because he would have half the headaches of his county job and make more money. But he never did. He was a true public servant wanting only to improve the roads and bridges of fast growing Contra Costa County.

However, his surveying lessons stuck and I managed to work summers during college at various engineering firms in the county as a chainman, making good money, most of which I saved for college expenses. Now it appeared that surveying was about to become my default profession in my post-graduate years.

Soon, I got a call from Wilson & Company asking me to come to work as a chainman on a survey party. This was a surprise to me because Wilson & Company was based in Oakland in Alameda County but as the chief engineer explained, they were doing a lot of work around Moraga and Orinda in Contra Costa County. So the next morning, I drove over to Oakland for an interview.

Wilson & Company was an old-line engineering firm located downtown in a four-story building off Broadway Avenue. Founded in the 1920s when Oakland was undergoing rapid expansion, Wilson & Company was still a major player in the area.

"Here's the deal, Al," said Stan, the chief engineer. "We have five crews and are putting on three more for the rest of the season. You'll be on one of them as head chainman, working mostly in Moraga on a big subdivision going in there."

"Sounds good," I said.

"I have just one question. I looked over your application and it appears that you have a fair amount of experience in this field for a non-engineer. How come you never majored in civil engineering up at Berkeley?"

"Too stupid, I guess. I like history."

"Well, stranger things have happened," said Stan. "I have one guy here, Mike, who's from Oregon. He majored in marine biology. But he's an instrument man now, so you never know. Now go check out your equipment."

I made my way through the drafting room with its rows of drafting tables. The draftsmen were hunched over their drafting tables, engrossed in their work. They were the ones who produced the blueprints for the jobs we were to lay out in the field. It was vital work but very tedious detail work. Eight hours a day at that drafting board. I was glad I was field man.

In the equipment room, I picked up a web belt with a plumb bob holster, a sixteen-ounce plum bob and a leather pouch for miscellaneous items. All the major surveying equipment such as the transit, chains, and stakes would be drawn on the day of work or was already in the survey vans.

"I put you on the payroll today, Al," said Stan. "We pay union wages here, about $4.50 an hour for a head chainman. I assume you're in the union."

"Oh, yes. Here's my card," I said handing it over proudly. "Operating Engineers, Local Three."

"Good, good," said Stan glancing at my card. "By the way, can you work this afternoon? Your party chief Bert is coming in for some more blueprints. We're on a rush job out there at the subdivision. You'll be paid overtime of course."

Did I have a choice? No. I had no choice. I had to be ready to hump and make money. I was back in the surveying game again.

"Sure, no problem," I answered, glad I had had the foresight to wear Levis and my old surveying boots.

A few minutes later Bert came charging in. He was a wiry, little man who walked with a limp and a permanent squint in one eye. He told me later that one leg was shorter than the other because of years standing on hillsides. Same for the squint. That was from years of peering through the transit sight with one eye open and the other eye closed.

Bert looked me over as Stan explained that I was to be his head chainman. "Well, you look big and strong enough, Al. How fast are you?"

"Fast?"

"Yeah, how fast can you move down the line pounding in stakes every fifty feet and not vary more than a hundredth off the line?

"Fast enough, I guess," I said wondering what had I gotten myself into. I hadn't done subdivision surveying for a couple of years and this guy struck me as a maniac. I wondered what had happened to his regular chainman.

"Well, it doesn't matter," he said. "I'll put you through my own special training course and you'll become Speedy Gonzales out there."

I looked at Stan. He shrugged and said, "Don't worry about Bert. He's a pussycat once you work with him a while."

Bert smiled, grabbed his blueprints, and ran down the stairs to the parking lot where we jumped into his survey wagon and barreled ass through the Caldecott Tunnel to the subdivision he was working on in Moraga. Bert said he had a curb-and-gutter line of some five hundred feet that he wanted to set so the contractor could pour cement tomorrow.

"We only need two guys for this," Bert said setting up his transit. He quickly established the line and then picked up the rear of the chain. I took the head end of the chain and hiked down the freshly carved road for fifty feet and set a stake on line.

"That's good Al, now drive that baby in," yelled Bert.

I knelt down with my little five-pound sledgehammer and began tapping the stake into the ground. Bert got impatient and came over with an eight-pound sledgehammer. "Shit, Al, get rid of that little sledge and stand back. I'll show you how to do it."

Three large swings and Bert drove that squat stake right into hard, clay ground. "You see Al, it's all about the weight of the sledge and the momentum of the swing. If your grip and distance is right, you'll knock those silly-ass stakes in with just a few swings."

"Got it," I said setting a tack into the top of the stake, pinpointing the line. I drove in a long, thin guard stake right next to it and tied a red plastic ribbon around it so the bulldozer operators would see it. Then I continued down the line driving stakes in every fifty feet, improving my swing each time.

After three hours of this, Bert called it quits. "Shit that's enough for those curb and gutter guys tomorrow. Good work, Al. Follow my directions and you'll become an ace at this chaining business."

Bert was right. I worked with him at breakneck speed over the next several weeks. We were a three-man crew. Bert was the combination party chief and instrument man. I was the head chainman and Jose, a little Hispanic who did most of the grunt work like hauling stakes, cutting brush and occasionally pounding stakes, the rear chainman. Unlike most party chiefs who loaded themselves down with field surveying reference books, mechanical calculators, protractors and drawing paper, Bert traveled light. He had a thin volume of trigonometry tables (logarithms, tangents, cotangents, sines, cosines, etc.) in one back pocket of his Levis and in the other back pocket, a little notebook in which he printed his notes on elevations, angles and drew little maps.

Bert knew all the tricks and the shortcuts in the field such as laying out the curb radiuses at the intersection of two streets. No setting up and turning angles with the transit for Bert. He would eyeball it, swinging radius arcs by hand with the chain. "This is easy shit, once you know the trick, Al and it saves a hell of a lot of time."

Bert's other special skill was determining the cuts and the fills for lots and streets on an incline. This subdivision, like most others around Moraga, was situated on a hillside. The streets were always built on a cut of the hill where the ground was stable. However, a house lot was often created by cutting out part of the hill to level it and then filling in the rest of the lot with the loose bulldozed dirt and compacting it. Bert's job was to indicate to the earthmover where to cut into the hillside and how much to fill up to elevation. This was usually done on the fly with only a hand level and an elevation rod while all the heavy equipment was zooming around us.

My job was to hold the elevation rod at the various points on the lot or street in question so that Bert could determine the cuts. Of course, unlike most party chiefs who made voluminous notes and calculations in the notebook, Bert did nearly all of this in his head or scribbled it out on scratch paper on his knee.

Other chores in laying out a subdivision included situating the streets, the sewer lines and the all-important property lines for the lots. Street and lot layout had to be exact within hundredths;[1] curbs and gutters, within a few hundredths; sewers within a tenth in line but only a hundredth in elevation. As Bert and other surveyors often said, "The shit must always flow down hill." However, working on hills like these, a sewer gradient was easy to achieve.

Bert usually quit around 3:30 p.m. instead of 4:30 unless overtime was involved. However, as he noted, he produced twice as much as the other crews did so it was no big deal. One reason Bert quit early was he was taking night classes to become a licensed surveyor. He wanted to get his state license so, as he said, "I can work for myself and be free of prick bosses." Thus, I often found myself off work and on board a Muni bus back to my room at Berkeley by 4:30. (I had moved out of Martinez and now had room in Berkeley.)

Midsummer, Bert had to go into the hospital for a hernia operation and

---

[1] In 1960s surveying, a foot was divided into tenths instead of 12 inches; the tenths were then divided into hundredths. There were then ten hundredths to a tenth.

he was out for two weeks after that. I was put on another crew and the difference was like night and day. My party chief was Hattendorf, a big, loud mouth redhead who spent most of the year at a drafting board. He only went out in the summers. He had also married one of the Wilson daughters, so he enjoyed special privileges such as never having to worry about a layoff. Despite his bluster, Hattendorf was as slow as Bert was fast. We did mostly preliminary work for another subdivision that was about to go in. This involved finding old property markers from other nearby subdivisions and running a baseline to the planned subdivision. All the streets, lots and sewers would be determined off this baseline.

I was working with a scrawny East Indian guy as my rear chainman. Raji had just graduated from Berkeley in civil engineering. He explained he had taken this lowly job as a rear chainman because nobody would hire him as a full-fledged engineer and also because he wanted field experience in surveying before he returned to India. He was also putting his wife through school.

Raji was always bugging Hattendorf to let him run the instrument. Hattendorf would tell him to fuck off and to stick with his brush cutting and ferreting out the old property markers. Behind his back, Hattendorf would call Raji either a "nigger" or a "wog." Then he would bemoan the fact to me that he had to work with a "wog."

"I only have this guy on my crew because the boss wants it. Something about maintaining good relations with his alma mater, the engineering school at Berkeley. All bullshit if you ask me." Thus spake Hattendorf with only his little associate degree in drafting from Alameda Community College to back him up.

Raji, on the other hand confided to me that he thought Hattendorf was the stupidest surveyor he had ever encountered. I clued him in. "He's married into the Wilson family," I explained. "He's a lifer here."

"That's a shame. Wilson is probably losing money with this man. He's laying out critical baselines and I don't think he knows field operations very well. These lines could be feet off."

"Maybe, but hey, as long as it pays," I said. "I'll stick with head chaining."

A few weeks later, Raji was ousted from the crew by Hattendorf. He claimed Raji was too slow cutting brush and couldn't find his ass, let alone a property marker. Stan quietly put Raji on another crew he was forming. In short order, Raji became an excellent instrument man and Hattendorf went back into the office.

Bert was now back but he was re-united with his old head chainman whom he apparently preferred to me. That was OK. I was relieved. I was tired of working at top speed all day. However, I was grateful to Bert for teaching me all the tricks in the field. I knew that would stand me in good stead for future employment. Stan assigned Jose and me to yet another crew.

My new crew chief was Mike, a tall, slender, sensitive looking guy with a full beard. Sort of a bohemian, woodsy type. He seemed out of place in the rough and tumble world of subdivision land surveying. But Mike was very bright and knew his stuff. He had worked as a surveyor on contract for the federal government in Oregon. "Geodesic work," he said, "locating mountains and rivers for maps and so on."

As Stan had said, Mike's background was not in engineering but marine biology from the University of Oregon. As Mike put it, "This surveying business is not a career thing for me. It pays the bills and puts food on the table for my family, but I'm saving up to go back to school and get a doctorate in marine biology."

"Me too," I said.

"Yeah, I was wondering about you," said Mike with a quizzical look. "How come a Berkeley graduate is doing this grunt work?"

"Just like you. A buck is a buck. But you know, I'd like to get some experience running the transit now and then. Maybe you'll give me a shot."

"We'll see. One mistake in determining an angle or an elevation and we're screwed."

I immediately liked Mike. He was my kind of guy and he was a good surveyor too. He didn't push you. He took his time establishing angle, line and elevation, but he was efficient and we managed to get a lot of work done, work that did not have to be re-done, as so often was the case in surveying. Mike made use of the latest technology. He used the Curta Calculator, a small, hand-held mechanical German calculator to determine angles and distances. We called it the "pepper grinder" because of the noise it made when you cranked the little handle on top to perform the calculation. It was tricky to use. You had to set the various dials correctly but once mastered it saved hours of calculating time. "This baby cost me two hundred dollars but it's worth every penny," Mike said, as he carefully put the calculator back into its case.

Despite his surveying skills, Mike confided to me that he had second thoughts about this subdivision surveying business. "Look, Al, what are we doing here?" he asked one day as we sat on a grassy hillside looking out over Moraga Valley for our lunch break.

"As far as I can see, we are laying out subdivisions in Moraga," I answered while munching on my sandwich.

"That's right, Al. We're carving up these beautiful rolling hills so the lawyers and bankers from San Francisco can build their sprawling ranch houses on hilltops and burn up gas in long rush hour commutes."

"I guess you're right."

"Damn straight, I'm right. We're turning California into a suburban sprawl. In essence, we're raping the landscape. And the kicker is more than a few of these houses will wind up sliding down the hill once a heavy rainy season sets in."

"You think?"

"Sure do. They're sitting on fill lots. Loose soil. These contractors fake it on the compaction. They do a few heavily compacted lots and then have the inspector take his soil compaction tests on those lots. I've seen it with my own eyes. There's no random testing. Somebody is paying somebody off. Someday those sprawling ranch houses will slide down the hill."

"Boy, are you cynical," I replied. "Anyway what can we do about it?"

"Nothing. We're just cogs in the wheel."

"Well, why don't you quit?" I asked.

"I will, hopefully soon. But as I said I have a wife and two young mouths to feed."

"Oh, yeah I forgot," I said. "Well, at least you're exempt from the draft."

"That's right I'm exempt from the draft because I'm married and have kids but I wouldn't serve anyway."

"Oh?"

It turned out Mike was a peace activist. On weekends, he and other Bay Area activists protested our involvement in Vietnam. He said he even demonstrated once or twice outside the Presidio.

"No, shit. I used to watch you guys when I was doing my active duty there a few months ago," I said.

"No kidding?" he replied, surprised.

"Yeah, maybe you saw me and other troops in our civvies sitting on that retaining wall, drinking beer."

"I never noticed."

This sparked a long discussion about our involvement in Vietnam. Mike launched into the history of the French Colonial rule in Vietnam and how the Vietnamese had been fighting invaders for centuries.

"First the Chinese, then the French, then the Japanese, then the French again until the battle of Dien Ben Phu in 1954. Did you ever take a good look

California Split

at the newsreels of that battle?"

"Yeah, I've seen them," I replied.

"Did you notice that the French troops are all wearing American-style uniforms and using American weapons?"

"Now that you mention it, I did," I said. "If you didn't know the history, you would have thought it was Americans fighting."

"Well it was really a proxy war," continued Mike. "The French wanted us to fight it for them. And now we are, all in the name of fighting communism."

"Yeah, I heard plenty of that," I said. "The domino theory."

"Right, Al. That's a crock. It's essentially a local movement for independence and reunification of their country. After Dien Ben Phu, the big powers split the country into North and South Vietnam. Now we have this mess on our hands. Mark my words: this is going to blow up into a full-scale war."

"I'm with you there, Mike. I've seen it first hand. Except my take is that it's not ideology that is driving up our presence there. It's military bureaucratic momentum. It's the only war the U.S. military has. I know many regular Army types who were itching to go over there to get rank and combat pay."

"Yeah, that's probably a factor as well, Al. Never underestimate bureaucracy."

Despite, these long, involved discussions about Vietnam, Mike and I took time out to sit back and enjoy nature. The bees were buzzing around. Ripened apricots in the orchards dropped to the ground with a plunk. The heady fermented smell of rotting fruit permeated the air in the warm, sleepy afternoons. Sometimes we took a cue from Jose and nodded off under a tree for a twenty-minute catnap. Then it was up with a start and after a few gulps of strong black coffee, back to surveying.

Mike started letting Jose act as head chainman and me as instrument man. He believed in training his crew to improve their skills. I would man the transit to determine elevation cross-sections and I also turned angles. (Mike would check). "Not bad, Al. I'll make you into an instrument man yet."

"Well, it's nice to know, but as you said, if you fuck up the angles, the whole subdivision could be off."

"That's right. That's why I always double check."

Despite the constant double-checking, after a few weeks, the law of averages caught up with us. Mike discovered that a baseline that we were working from in one subdivision was off by over two feet. He checked and re-checked. We wasted a whole day trying to locate the error. Finally, Mike discovered that the problem was the baseline had been derived from a marker that Hattendorf had set at the entrance to the subdivision. But as Mike later told me, Hattendorf would not admit the error. He claimed that his marker had been derived from an old corner monument which itself was off by a few tenths and that turning the angle had multiplied the error into several feet. Since correcting this mistake would cost Wilson & Co. thousands of dollars in lost time and wages, somebody had to pay. Not Hattendorf because he was the son-in-law. It was Mike that paid. He was demoted back to instrument man and put on another crew.

As Mike put it: "They told me that they knew I wasn't responsible for the baseline error, but that I should have caught it immediately when I started working off that baseline. That was a crock but I'm relieved. Being a party chief is too much responsibility. Who needs it?"

Before I knew it, it was September and I kept on surveying for Wilson & Company. I worked on various crews, even with Bert again. I couldn't quit. The money was too good. With the overtime, it was piling up fast. By living cheap, I had saved some two thousand dollars in my Bank of America savings account. My goal was four thousand dollars by the end of the November when the season ended. Still, I tried to regain my student status by enrolling in night classes at San Francisco State, thinking I could do both—work in the day and be a student at night. As it turned out, this fantasy soon bumped into reality.

12. LIM'S LAUNDRY

One reason I was saving so much money was that I was living cheap. A week after being hired at Wilson & Company, I moved to Berkeley and rented a furnished room over a Chinese laundry on Dwight Avenue for forty dollars a month. My days of living at home were over. Although I was now without a car, it was an easy commute by public transportation to Wilson & Company from Berkeley. All I had to do was hop on a Muni bus which took me to downtown Oakland in less than a half-hour.

The other reason I moved out was I wanted to be on the Berkeley scene again. I wanted to hang out on Telegraph, sit in the local cafes, eat at Larry Blake's steak house, have breakfast at the Pancake House, see my friends, some of whom were still at Berkeley, and possibly meet ladies on the Terrace on the weekends.

My room over Lim's Laundry reminded me of my room in Aix-En-Provence. It was large and had an alcove with French windows that opened out on Dwight. The bed was comfortable and the desk, table and chairs, while old, were decent. It also had a basin and a medicine cabinet. The bathroom was down the hall and featured a huge, old-fashioned bear-claw tub that was great for a cool soak after a dusty day surveying. The building, owned by a Dr. Ward, had six or seven such rooms with a grungy communal kitchen where I could heat up my meager meals when I didn't eat out. Usually, a meal in my room consisted of a Swanson's TV dinner with a beer.

My fellow residents were an assorted bunch, including a couple of middle-eastern types, an English grad student and a rummy older guy with a beard who looked as if he spent a lot of time in bars. We barely acknowledged each other's existence when we crossed paths.

Downstairs, Lim, a wizened old Chinaman with a scraggly goatee, did all my laundry and mending. He often told me I should get married and have a wife to keep house.

"No good man live alone when so many women around here. Beautiful college girls. Many make a good wife," he said picking through my filthy clothes.

"Thanks for the tip," I said.

I was content in my room. But Susan, whom I still saw, was horrified. "How could you live in such a place, Allan? It's a dump."

"It works for me now," I said. "I need to save money."

In fact, Susan was having a hard time dealing with my job as a surveyor. "I mean it's so blue collar, even though it pays well," she said more than once.

"That's right. It pays well," I replied. "That's why I do it and also to be outdoors, not cooped up in some stuffy office."

"Little did I think I would be going out with a surveyor when I met you," she countered but squeezing my now well-muscled arm from swinging a sledgehammer, she continued, "but there are benefits."

Susan thought that I should have rented a place in San Francisco and looked for a job in broadcasting or at least gone to San Francisco State for a teaching certificate. She had it fixed in her mind that I would be a good teacher.

"Teaching is a possibility down the road," I said. "I might take a few night courses at San Francisco State this fall but I have to keep working if I want enough money to go full-time."

"Well, what about television?" she asked. "You seemed to like that in the Army."

"Yes, it was interesting. I enjoyed putting together those Army public service shows. Still, commercial broadcasting doesn't pay well to start. In fact, all I heard about when I was at KGO-TV was how you had to volunteer as a gofer if you wanted to get into the TV biz. I thought they were cheap pricks."

"Don't be so crude, Allan. You're better educated than that. I don't want to see you become simply a blue-collar guy."

"Maybe that's what I am," I taunted.

I could see Susan was having second thoughts about me. Everything was OK as long as I was on the San Francisco scene in my dress uniform. She could imagine the possibilities despite her claim that it was all just a fling. However, now that reality intruded, she saw that I was just a lug from a modest middle-class family satisfied to make a blue collar buck, wasting his college degree, on a career track to nowhere. She, with her upper-class

Midwest upbringing, had a hard time dealing with that.

***

When I said some friends were still around Berkeley, it was wishful thinking. Hardly anyone was around. My good friends and fraternity brothers Gerard and Jean-Paul from my undergraduate days were studying in France. Darrah had graduated and gone home for the summer. She would be off to the Columbia Graduate School of Journalism in the fall. Only Clarissa was around, working as a waitress in an upscale Berkeley restaurant but she was due to leave for flight attendant training for Pan Am in a few weeks. Also, as I learned, she had had a fling with a married grad student named Charlie. As she related to me one teary night while sitting on my bed, her fling with Charlie had ended in disaster.

"How could I have gotten involved," sobbed Clarissa. "I knew he was married but he told me it was over. Now he's back with his little wifey in Boston."

"Jeeze, take it easy Clarissa," I said offering her a shot of Johnny Walker from a bottle I had sitting on my dresser. "You never know about married men. You should stick with single guys like me," I said moving in closer to her on the bed.

"Oh, Al, I think of you as a friend now," she said softly.

All the time I'm thinking to myself "what a flake." Just last fall she was practically proposing to me to keep me from being drafted. Now here she had thrown her virginity out the window for some married jerk.

"I even chased him to Boston and confronted his wife and family," she said in a tight little voice.

"Boston!"

"Yes, I was so stupid. My father had to fly out to Boston to retrieve me."

"And you wanted to get involved with a two-timer. Whatever happened to Pan Am?"

"Ah, I put them on hold but now since the break-up, I'm planning to go into training in a month or so."

Finally, Clarissa dried her tears, looked at me with her pure blue eyes, gave me a little kiss on the cheek and waltzed out of my room. I would not see her again for a year. Women, what a trip!

***

Early August, I received a letter from Bobbie in Chicago. Guess what? Hubby Tom had been accepted into graduate school at Berkeley to study for a doctorate in English. He had just graduated from Northwestern University. To quote from the letter: "We need a place to stay in Berkeley, so I naturally thought of you. Could you find us a nice apartment that is reasonable and near campus?"

I was stunned. Bobbie and Tom coming to live in Berkeley? Talk about coincidence. Last fall, when I saw Bobbie in Chicago, it was apparent that she was committed to Tom even though he was slow on the uptake. However, with a determined Bobbie going through machinations that I didn't want to imagine, the two were engaged last fall and married in March at Holy Name Cathedral in Chicago.

As she described it, it was a big catholic wedding with several hundred guests and extended family. Her dream was fulfilled—married to her childhood sweetheart in a lavish wedding. Her other vision for a husband was that he be a university professor, preferably an English professor discoursing on *Beowulf* in a tweed jacket and pipe. It appeared that Tom was on track for that. Finally, being a good catholic, she envisioned a family of four or five kids.

I didn't know how to reply. Apparently, my role was to be the magnanimous ex-boyfriend helping them set up in Berkeley. However, I wasn't quite sure I wanted to play that role. I was busy with my work and my life in Berkeley. I would have to take time out to find them a decent apartment which was no easy task in Berkeley only weeks before the fall semester began.

Luckily, I ran into old Dr. Ward collecting his rent. I had heard he was one of the largest landlords in this area of Berkeley with scores of apartments and houses. I explained the situation: Young married couple, new to Berkeley, close to campus, reasonable rent. He said that he might have something.

"It is not fancy but it's large," he wheezed. "The bottom apartment in a house with its own entrance around the corner on Blake Street.

"OK, let's take a look."

I went with Dr. Ward over to the house on Blake. It didn't look too bad, kind of an old craftsman bungalow. Inside, it was spacious with a closed-in porch, a living room, dining room, kitchen, bath and two bedrooms.

"One bedroom could be used as an office or a guest room," the good doctor explained.

"How much?"

"Oh, if they sign a one-year lease, one-hundred-fifty a month."

I knew that was a good price for the area, so I said OK and I wrote out a check for a month's rent as a security deposit.

A few days later, I met Bobbie and Tom at the Oakland train station. They had had a romantic, cross-country train ride out from Chicago, a second honeymoon. The first honeymoon had been to the Bahamas for a week. Both were beaming, still with the glow of newlyweds and curiously, I was not jealous. I was happy for them and somewhat relieved for myself. Maybe being their friend would not be too bad. After the initial hugs and greetings, I loaded their two large suitcases and a trunk into my Dad's station wagon and drove them to Berkeley to their new apartment.

I had a key and let them in. Bobbie glanced around, smiling, saying "It's so big, Allan. It's like a house. It's rather nice too. A few little things and it could be a real home while we are here at Berkeley. Thank you so much for finding this for us."

Tom seemed to like it too, especially the second bedroom where he could set up a study. We ate out at that night at Larry Blakes and then I left them to their domestic bliss and returned to my bachelor room alone.

Later, sitting in my alcove staring out at the nighttime street, sipping scotch, my goodwill dissipated. I was annoyed that they would now be on the Berkeley scene with their obligations, possibly cramping my style. I had the feeling deep down that Tom going to graduate school at Berkeley was no accident. I felt it was all part of a big taunt on the part of Bobbie. I was sure Tom could have gone to other top graduate schools in English.

A few weeks after they were settled, Bobbie mentioned that she had been roaming around the Northside. "That's such a scenic area with views and such. And it's so peaceful and quiet. Near to the campus too. We might move there when this lease is up."

"Yes, it is nice, but a two bedroom apartment on the Northside will be much more expensive than this," I said while sitting in a rocking chair on their closed-in porch with Heineken in hand.

"I know. But I love the area," said Bobbie. "Maybe we can cram into a one-bedroom."

"Whatever," I said feeling under-appreciated for the apartment that I did find them, an apartment that would now be abandoned at the first good opportunity.

***

Despite the presence of Bobbie and Tom, I did manage to carry on as usual. Having an espresso at the Mediterraneum now and then, checking out

Moe's Bookstore across the street, eating at the various Chinese, Indian and Near Eastern restaurants as well as at Larry Blakes. Occasionally, I would venture over to La Vals on the Northside for pizza and beer, sometimes with Tom and Bobbie, sometimes alone.

As the fall semester of 1964 got underway, I realized that Berkeley was changing. The Greek ambiance of the late 50s and early 60s had all but disappeared. Gone was the carefree prankster flavor that filtered through campus especially on big football weekends. Greek life was not as popular. Rushing was down. The students now seemed more intense, more serious and certainly more politically active. Many were involved in anti-war protests, protests that had intensified in the wake of the Gulf of Tonkin Resolution in August.

Earlier in July, the same protesters had demonstrated at the Fairmont Hotel and the Cow Palace during the Republican Convention in San Francisco. A convention that saw the nomination of "bomb happy" Senator Barry Goldwater for president. During the Fairmont Hotel protest, police moved in, knocked a few heads and arrested many others.

Currently, the student activists were protesting the eviction of off-campus groups that had set up tables on the sidewalk at Bancroft and Telegraph, the main entrance to campus. No longer would groups such as *Fair Play for Cuba, Young Socialist Alliance* and *SLATE* be able to pass out leaflets, put up posters or collect money for various causes at that location.

There also seemed to be more non-students hanging around Telegraph, many with long stringy hair, beards, sandals, beads, sometimes with weird Indian headbands. A few of them had set up little stands along Telegraph selling handmade jewelry, little bells, gongs, and colorful T-shirts with swirling colors. And everywhere, the scent of pot and incense. It was a colorful mess that I enjoyed perusing but had no idea that it was the start of a counter-culture movement that would shape the last half of the 1960s in the Bay Area.

At one point, I got a closer look at this lifestyle when I accompanied Mike on a visit to his sister's house in Berkeley. She was a cute blonde version of Mike but her house was a pigsty, dirty to the point of being infectious with crusty goop all over and what appeared to be mouse droppings on the floor. Dirty dishes were piled in the sink. Flies buzzed about. A cute but filthy little kid crawled through it all. On the cluttered coffee table sat a bag of pot with roach forks and other pot paraphernalia. The smell of incense filled the house along with the soft music of East Indian ragas.

The husband, a painter with long greasy hair, smelled of turpentine and body odor. He painted weird contorted Berkeley scenes many of which were hanging on the walls. Interspersed among the paintings were photomurals of Big Sur where they hung out on weekends.

"So Mike," said the sister as she took a drag on a joint. "When are you going to kiss off that surveying job and go back to school? That's where you belong. Not carving up California for the man."

"It pays the bills," said Mike defensively. "I'll get back by and by. I'm saving up."

"Speaking of bills," she said, tilting her head back, inhaling, "could you help us brother, dear? We are a little tight this month. Tips are down at the health food restaurant."

"Ah, I guess," said Mike reaching for his wallet. Would twenty do?"

"How about forty. I see two twenties in there," she said now standing up and peering over his shoulder and into his wallet. "I'll pay you back next month."

"Right. Let's get out of her Al, before Sis bleeds me dry," said Mike handing over the twenties.

I followed close behind, happy to be back in the fresh air. However hip and artistic this life was, it was too toxic for me. I wasn't a fussy housekeeper but I did bathe, my clothes were clean except when I surveyed and I washed my dishes. I didn't think being a slob precluded being an artist or writer.

***

Overall, I was content with my lot at this point. I realized there were worse ways to make a living than surveying. One scenario I envisioned was working six months surveying; the other six months writing, traveling or going to school.

It was the going to school part that I dealt with late August. That was my original rationale for this surveying gig. Save up enough money to go to school full-time. But now, I began to think I could do this part-time at San Francisco State. Since it was essentially a commuter school, they offered a vast array of night courses. I figured I could handle at least a couple of courses but which ones? I was torn. On one hand, there was film and broadcasting but a glance at course offerings indicated that they required a lot of group project work dealing with film equipment, shoots, TV or radio studios. I didn't have that kind of time. That was something I had to do full-time.

I finally settled on two English courses which required only reading, a paper, a midterm and final—19th Century American Literature and The Plays of Shakespeare. I also chose a Public Relations course on how to play the media and get the message out. Based on my Army experience, I thought this knowledge might come in handy. It was a full load for a part-time student.

Enrolling in SF State as a graduate student was a cinch. Any Berkeley graduate was an automatic admit, no matter the grade point. All it took to enroll was one trip over at night, handing in my Berkeley transcript, filling out some paperwork and writing a check for the registration fee of $100.00. And now that my father had finally bought a new car, a Buick, I acquired ownership of the family 1955 Chevy station wagon and thus had wheels to transport myself over to San Francisco State after work.

The campus itself was quite a contrast to Berkeley. Located on the outer fringes of San Francisco near Lake Merced on 19th Avenue, SF State appeared to me like an overgrown high school. This campus, built in the early 1950s, featured a boxy modern style with a lot of glass imparting an industrial feel. However, it was somewhat softened by the landscaping of lush lawns, bushes and punctuated here and there by a redwood tree or a Monterey pine. The night students poured off the 19th Avenue Muni tram, many still in suits with briefcases, serious in demeanor, on the make in San Francisco. In contrast, a few daytime students strolled about in their beards and sandals, mellow, laid-back, looking for truth. As I said, not quite Berkeley but there it was and it was good enough for me.

The first week or two of classes went well. I was glad to be back in the academic saddle. I enjoyed reading selections from Hawthorne, Irving, Emerson, Melville, Whitman, Twain, James etc. The whole cast of American 19th-century literary greats. Shakespeare was even do-able. We concentrated on three plays— *Macbeth*, *King Lear*, and *Othello* with the idea of analyzing them in-depth. I became convinced the best way to appreciate Shakespeare was to concentrate on the text and not be distracted by rigmarole of a theatrical production.

The PR course was a revelation as well. We read Daniel Boorstin's *The Image: A Guide to Pseudo Events in America*, a brilliant book about the contrivances of the public relations machine and the phoniness of most news events. The teacher also instructed us in writing news releases, making media contacts, etc. With these courses and my work, I was busy, busy, busy but I still had to make time for Army Reserve meetings.

***

It was with a mixture of dread and anticipation that I began chipping away at my five-and-a-half year of reserve obligation of weekly meetings. A week after I was released from active duty at the Presidio, I reported to the civil affairs unit in Sunnyvale. As I suspected it was a terrible commute from either Martinez or Berkeley in rush hour traffic. The reserve meetings started at 7 p.m. so I had to set out by 5:30 to make it, crossing the Bay Bridge and inching my way down US 101, past Burlingame, San Mateo, Redwood City, Palo Alto and finally Sunnyvale. Sometimes I tried a different route, going down the East Bay Freeway, past San Leandro, Hayward and over the Dunbarton Bridge. But it made no difference, it was a long tiring, traffic-choked trek and by the time I arrived at the Army Reserve Center, I was exhausted.

At first, the company commander was happy to see me, happy to have a broadcast specialist in his midst. I completed his roster of civil affairs personnel but after an initial greeting, I was ignored and treated as just another E-2 Private, a lowly grunt subject to clean up chores such as putting chairs away, sweeping the hallways and picking up trash from the classroom

In addition, the lectures were dull with officers droning on and on about the proper bureaucratic structure of German towns and villages during the occupation. I wondered why they lectured about Germany. That was a done deal. What about the governmental structure of Vietnamese villages? I found it curious that Vietnam was never mentioned.

As far as I could determine from the occasional lecture, a Broadcast PIO specialist duties included broadcasting the good tidings of the U.S. Army occupation force and informing the local populace on such matters as hours of electricity, procurement of water supplies, food distribution, etc. Sometimes this had to be done from a jerry-rigged sound truck if no radio station was in operation. It all sounded out of date to me.

The portion of reserve meetings devoted to military formations and drill was rather lackadaisical with only token efforts at executing smartly. As long as our uniforms were decent and we had a shave and a haircut, inspections were rare.

Because I had just gotten off active duty, I was excused from the two-week summer camp at Camp Roberts down near Paso Robles. Tired of the long commute to Sunnyvale, I took advantage of this time by telephoning around to reserve units nearer to Berkeley that used Broadcast PIO specialists. Eventually, I found one right under my nose— a Psychological Warfare Unit that met at the Presidio. They had openings for my MOS and I arranged for a transfer.

"Psy-war Ops." That phrase had a nice ring to it. I had visions of engaging in devious, under-handed mind games on the enemy, encouraging him to come over to the side of the right and true. The Psy-War unit made extensive use of broadcast specialists since much of their psy-warfare was done over the airwaves. The Army would use existing facilities or set up their own radio stations to broadcast insidious messages to the enemy designed to destroy his morale.

The guys in this unit were a varied lot, much more interesting than the businessmen and lawyers in my civil affairs unit. There were several advertising types, a couple of real-life broadcasters in the San Francisco radio market, assorted artists, grad students and a bohemian or two who somehow skirted the not very well enforced haircut edicts. All had had the same goal: to avoid the draft and combat.

As one of the ad types, Zack, exclaimed, "We are the original rear echelon mother-fuckers. We fight with your brains, not our bodies."

Surprisingly, the lectures were interesting. We explored mob psychology, the nature of the true believer, the basic principals of propaganda and persuasion techniques. We heard lectures on how to demonize the enemy, how to promote atrocity stories, even how to use so-called witchcraft, sorcery and magic to influence the enemy.

We examined some of the leaflets being dropped on North Vietnam such as a photo of a B-52 on a bombing mission with the caption in Vietnamese, "This is the mighty B-52," implying that the North Vietnamese could not escape its path of destruction. Another item was a playing card showing a skull with the ace of spades on it. Below it was a photo of a dead Viet Cong with the caption: "This is the sign of death." This card was left near the bodies of Viet Cong victims. It was said to be very effective.

I even studied the official Army Manual on Psy-War techniques which derived the present-day Psy-War principles from the writings of Joseph Goebbels, the Nazi Minister of Information. I also reread one of my favorite books, *The True Believer* by Eric Hoffer for insight into mob psychology and mass movements. Hoffer felt that mass movements were spurred by individual feelings of self-hatred, self-doubt, and insecurity. He also believed mas3s movements were interchangeable. He noted that in the postwar years fanatical Nazis often became fanatical Communists, later fanatical anti-communists, even fanatical capitalists. This was fascinating stuff for me.

So with my surveying job, my three-night classes and my weekly Army Reserve meetings, I felt engaged and productive as I sat in my alcove with my French windows open, overlooking Dwight Avenue, cozy in my room above Lim's Laundry.

13. DON'S NUPTIALS

In the midst of my busy life of job, school, and Army, I had to deal with my brother Don getting married at the tender age of twenty-two. Twenty-two! He would be twenty-three in October, but still, I thought that it was too young to marry. Here I was twenty-four and the way I was going, marriage was light-years away. I felt Don was still a babe in the woods as far as women were concerned. His only real girlfriend had been Nancy whom he had met at sorority-fraternity exchange two years ago. Oh, he had gone out with a few girls, including Darrah, but despite that, I felt he was still an innocent when he met Nancy.

After their initial encounter at the party, Nancy practically abducted him. She, at 5' 10" and a college freshman, had instantly decided that he, at 6'5" and a sophomore, was the man for her and that they were going to marry. Nancy was quite a package. Tall, slim but well-built, athletic, almost a tomboy, a cute face with a pageboy haircut. I went shopping with her once at an exclusive women's store in Oakland. She was shopping for an outfit in order to surprise Don and she wanted my opinion. She came out in a skin-tight jumpsuit and I about fell off my chair. The body of a young goddess. But alas, she was Don's property so I played the good guy, future brother-in-law and protector.

Nancy was from a well-off San Jose family. Her father was a vice president of a fortune 500 hundred company in charge of operations on the West Coast. She spent money freely and was apparently convinced that Don with his recent mechanical engineering degree would conquer the world and become rich. And it was the world that they were setting out to conquer. Right after the marriage, they planned to fly off to Australia where Don had a job with Food Machinery Corporation waiting for him in Melbourne.

"There is nothing but opportunity down there, Allan," he explained.

"Yeah, the Outback, flies and kangaroos," I replied.

"Sure, that too. But from what I can make out, there's rapid industrial expansion underway and a need for the products of FMC. Also, as you know, we have our way paid down there because the Aussies need engineers."

"Sounds like a lark, Don. Be sure to see a lot down there because I bet you'll be back here within a couple of years."

"Who knows but I'm going to give it a shot, Allan. At least I'm carrying on the engineering tradition of the Brown family."

"What's that supposed to mean?" I said. "I'm a land surveyor just like dad was."

"Yeah, but that's not really you. You're a history major and you don't know what the fuck you're going to do. At least I'm directed."

"Touché."

"Also," he continued, "I've been stuck in the U.S. all my life. Except for a few quickie trips to Mexico, I haven't been anywhere."

"Do tell," I said

"Yeah, you had your good times in Europe. Now Nancy and I are going to have fun Down Under."

So Don was set. He was going to Australia with Nancy. Still, there was the wedding gauntlet to through before they could split. Small detail. Actually, it was a humongous detail. This wedding was to be a blowout extravaganza in August thanks to Nancy's dad who was, of course, footing the bill. First, there was the actual wedding in an affluent church, then an elaborate reception at the exclusive San Jose Country Club. Hundreds were invited. I was to be Best Man, although I dreaded the prospect. I would have to make a little speech and a toast wishing them well.

***

However, before the nuptials could get under way, the two families had to meet. Mr. Landry graciously invited the entire Brown family to dinner at Trader Vics in Oakland. That sounded good to me. I loved those tropical rum drinks in a coconut shell with a little hat. However, I made a mental note to have only one. It would do Don no good to have his older brother bombed at the "meet and greet."

So one weekday night after work, I suited up and drove down to Trader

Vics on San Pablo Avenue. The Landrys were already in the lounge along with Don and Nancy. Mom, Dad, and my kid brother Kenny arrived a few minutes later. Everybody introduced themselves and immediately we were ushered into the restaurant proper and seated in an alcove engulfed in tropical vegetation with a little waterfall dribbling nearby.

Mr. Landry struck me as a no-nonsense business executive in his Brooks Brothers suit with an impeccable button-down white-collar shirt and subdued silk tie. A gentleman of medium height, wavy blond hair and a take-charge demeanor. It was obvious he was running the show here. His wife Betty was an attractive, slender woman with a charming personality and winning smile.

My dad who had just gotten off work looked rumpled in his everyday suit, although, there were signs that he was freshly shaven for the event. Mom was cool looking in her colorful silk summer dress with white pumps. Thirteen-year-old Kenny was already tugging at his tie and the collar of his dress shirt that I was sure he was forced to wear. Don had on his old fraternity charcoal suit that looked too short for him. (Was he still growing even in college?) Nancy wore an Asian looking silk dress with a slit up the side and an orchid behind her hair. She said she wanted to be in the spirit of the place.

So here we all were, charming, polite, on our best manners. Mr. Landry suggested we order a round of drinks.

"I would recommend the Navy Grog here," he said. It's a spectacular drink. Not too fruity or sweet, just a solid rum punch that you could imagine the sailors drinking."

I said I would try that. So did dad and Don. The women decided on the traditional Mai-Tai. Kenny had a coke.

After perusing the menu, Mr. Landry announced that it might make sense to order the supreme Polynesian buffet for eight that included a bit of everything. That sounded fine to us. Meal ordered, drinks on hand, we settled down and had polite conversation which involved me having to explain what I did to justify my existence and being greeted with "Oh, that's nice." Then Mr. Landry toasted Don's bright future in the mechanical engineering game.

"Always a demand for good engineers," he said. Then turning to Dad, Mr. Landry continued, "Engineering seems to run into the Brown family."

"Apparently it does," said Dad. "But I didn't push them in that direction."

And so the conversation went. Yawn. After a sumptuous buffet of pork, fish, pineapple, coconut and taro goodies and a liquor-laden coffee drink, I felt sleepy, dreamy what with the drip of the waterfall, and the seductive strains of recorded Polynesian music and chants. I had visions of young wahine nymphs running around topless with me lounging on the beach eating lotus, somewhat like a latter-day Paul Gauguin. Should I split to Tahiti? Become a beachcomber? Write in paradise? Nancy looked good. No, off-limits. Should I go over to see Susan? No, I needed someone more exotic. Plus obligation. I had to get out of there. I had done my duty. I had shown up and hopefully passed muster. But who cared? I was free. I wasn't tied down like brother Don. Only twenty-two and already a ring through his nose.

I suddenly stood up and said, "I have to be at work early. Please excuse me," and I left.

***

A couple of weeks later— the big wedding day. It was a well-organized drill with almost military precision. We all drove down to San Jose two nights before the wedding and checked into a Holiday Inn, courtesy of Mr. Landry. Three rooms. One for my parents, one for Kenny and me and one for Don to host his frat brothers and other guests. The next day, three rental cars were at our disposal. Don and I picked up our tuxedos at a local rental store, all prearranged. That afternoon we trekked over to the church and went through a wedding rehearsal. Nancy was there in jeans, looking disheveled, along with a flock of bride's maids, one of whom was a dark, sultry looker. She seemed familiar me. But I had no time to talk. I had to pay attention to my Best Man duties. Afterwards, a big pizza bash at the local Shakey's Pizza. The sultry looker was there briefly but with so many people and too much beer, I couldn't get close.

The next day, up bright and early. Sunday. Nothing to do in the plastic motel room so I went swimming in the pool. The wedding was at two. I read the Sunday papers and before I knew it, it was time to suit up in my tux. Not a bad fit. Almost Cary Grant suave. Something to this dressing up. Maybe I missed my calling as a movie star or failing that as a gigolo. I helped Don dress in his tux, not that he needed it. He was Mr. Cool, oblivious I think to what he was getting into.

One p.m. we climbed into our respective rental cars. Dad insisted on driving his new Buick. I didn't blame him. We drove to the church located near the San Jose Country Club. The church—modern, stylized stain glass windows with a vaulted ceiling. Lots of triangles, here. Light beaming in. Massive wood beams. Very comfortable pews with cushions. Definitely upscale worshipping. A mainline Congregational church. Funny though, because the Landrys were originally Mormons. But now fallen away, like so many California Mormons.

The church was jammed. So many friends and family. Some had flown in from the East Coast, others from Idaho and Utah. Many young ladies. I recalled other weddings I attended back in my fraternity days. It was common knowledge among the frat brothers that the best opportunity to score was in the aftermath of a sorority wedding. Did that still hold true? Yet, some of them looked so young. No sign of the sultry bridesmaid.

Finally, the big moment. The processional music began. All of us in the wedding took our place and performed our assigned roles. Down the aisle, came a beautiful Nancy in a designer white wedding gown escorted by her father. Don waiting at the head of the church, handsome in his tux. I to the side. Soon the ceremony was under way conducted by the portly minister in a dark suit. I passed the ring to Don at the appropriate moment.

The vows completed, the kiss. A passionate, deep throat-rattling kiss. I glanced over to the sultry bridesmaid who smiled demurely with only a slight hint of wickedness.

Soon, but not soon enough for me, it was over. The bride and groom marched out of the church and into a limo covered in chalk, shaving cream, balloons, trailing cans, and just married signs. Then whisked away to the San Jose Country Club for the reception.

The country club east of town—cool, green, well-watered fairways in the midst of scorched brown hills. An ultra sleek, low-slung, rambling clubhouse. A money place for the business elite of San Jose to play golf and do deals. The clubhouse was immediately flooded with wedding guests. Food piled high on buffet tables, waterfalls of Champagne, and again Trader Vic goodies galore. Waiters in white tux jackets and white gloves made their way through the crowd with platters of hors d'oeuvres. Music—a combination of rock-and-roll and easy listening from the fifties.

Before I knew it, I had three glasses of Champagne and it was time for a toast to the bride and groom. Feeling a little light-headed, I advanced to the dais where Don and Nancy were now posing for pictures. I, now master of ceremonies, looked at the expectant audience, smiled and raised my glass and said something stupid which ended with the toast: "Here's to their children, may they all be giants." All clap. Relief. It was over. Now I could settle down and enjoy the reception.

"Nice toast," said a voice behind me. I turned and was greeted by the sight of the sultry one. "Remember me?"

"Ah, you look familiar," I said as I scanned her low-cut Italian silk dress, swelling breasts, eyes wide and dark, generous mouth, white flashing teeth, hair cut in the messed up Italian fashion. A hot Sicilian afternoon.

"Yeah, I bet. I'm Tami. A friend of Nancy. I met you last year at a party but you probably forgot because I was with my now ex-boyfriend.

"Sure, sure," now I remember, I said, remembering vaguely.

"Nice wedding," she said nodding to Don and Nancy still posing for pictures.

"Yeah, quite a blow out."

"Don is a lucky guy. Nancy is great."

"Great gal," I agreed. "You plan to catch the bouquet?"

"Oh no, I'm staying well away from that," she laughed.

"So where have you been?" I asked. "How come I haven't seen you around?"

"I just got back from a year in France from my junior-year-abroad."

"No kidding. Where?"

"Montpellier."

"Great town. I did a year in Aix-en-Provence myself three years ago."

We talked about the South of France and Europe. She seemed hip, liberated. Tami and Nancy were from the same San Jose high school and had gone to Cal together but unlike Nancy, she hadn't joined a sorority. "Those Sallies were too uptight for me," she said at one point. "I like the luxury of having an apartment."

We both had another champagne and suddenly the rest of the room wasn't there and we were dancing. Slow: Johnny Mathias: "Chances Are." Fast: Chubby Checker, "Let's Twist Again."

Before we knew it, the reception was breaking up and I offered to drive Tami home.

"Thanks but I have my own car. I have to drive down to Pebble Beach where my family lives now."

"Pebble Beach?"

"Oh, we're not rich or anything like that," she said. "My dad's a contractor. He builds homes for the rich. So we get a house at cost."

"Look, I'd like to see you again soon," I said

"Well, why don't you drive down next Saturday and we can make a day out of it, One of the last days of summer," she smiled.

"Sounds good." And that's how we left it, me with a tingle in the groin.

Somewhere in all of this, Don and Nancy had escaped in the limo to a Hilton suite near the San Francisco Airport, exhausted from the wedding. They were to fly off to Australia the next day, stopping off at Samoa and Auckland, New Zealand before hitting Melbourne. We threw the usual confetti and rice, yelled, banged cowbells and then returned to the party.

***

The next Saturday, I drove down to Tami's Pebble Beach house with eager anticipation. Tami, in shorts and a lacy blouse, answered the door and invited me in. She introduced me to her father, a tall, dark swarthy guy with big contractor hands and her mother, a petite dark-eyed woman. I could see where Tami came from. Somewhere, a little brother was running about. They lived in a nice but rather modest house for the area which was set in a forest of Monterey pines a mile or so from the golf course.

Tami had packed a lunch and we took off for Big Sur in her VW convertible bug. About twenty miles down Highway One, we stopped at the turn-off to Pfeiffer Beach and hiked down the trail to the beach. This was Henry Miller country. Big sky, big mountains and a big glittering sea. All there for beatific contemplation. The day was clear and warm for the coast, in the low seventies. Tami was running around the beach in her bare feet, getting her shorts and blouse wet in the surf. Clingy. Nature girl. After a sandwich of some local smoked fish and a few hits of Riesling from a bota bag, we stretched out on the blanket in a secluded spot and gazed out to sea using a small log of driftwood as a headrest. Soon we were clutching in the sand.

"Allan, let's slow down," she murmured. "I just met you."

"Yes, but I feel like I have known you for a long time."

"I know," she said stroking my heated brow.

We pulled apart, and stared at the sea. Then we got into a seaweed fight, pretending the long strands of seaweed were whips. She told me she wished she had an older brother. Maybe I would fulfill that role, I thought.

That night, I was invited to stay over in the guestroom. We played monopoly with her younger brother and mother while Dad watched TV. All very homey, all very family. The next morning, Mom fixed a large pancake breakfast as I explained my life. How I was planning to go back to school. How I had to survey to save up some money.

"That's good," said the Dad. "It'll make you appreciate it more when you go back. It's good to get your hands dirty. I worked all the way through college myself, San Jose State."

I could sense that he liked me and was impressed with the fact that I was in the surveying game.

After breakfast, Tami and I drove leisurely through the Pebble Beach Golf Course still cool and green with the aquamarine surf lapping at its shores. We then drove down to Point Lobos a few miles south of Carmel and climbed around the rocks, the coves and among the cypress trees. Later, we strolled about in Carmel itself, checking out the overpriced shops. Finally, I announced that I had to return to Berkeley before the traffic became too bad. I drove Tami back to her house and with a hug, I said goodbye and was on my way. Tami would be back in Berkeley in two weeks and I would be waiting.

***

The real reason I had to get back the Bay Area was that I remembered I had a picnic date with Susan that we had set up a week ago. I had completely forgotten about it. I drove directly to her apartment in San Francisco arriving around six. And there I was met with a very pissed-off Susan.

"You were supposed to be here at noon. Remember. We were going to have a picnic in Golden Gate Park."

"I know," I answered sheepishly. "I got hung up in San Jose with the Landrys. A mandatory family-in-law thing," I lied.

Susan sensed something was up, but she knew nothing about Tami. "Well, you could have phoned," she pouted.

"We can still have the picnic, right on the Marina," I said lamely.

No, it's too cold now. The fog is rolling in. We'll eat in the dining room and listen to Prokofiev. You can make a fire. I fixed your favorite chicken. It'll be cozy."

I felt like a shit. Susan was such a good person. But she didn't set me on fire. She was comfortable, safe, and predictable. All great qualities for a wife down the road but not right now. I spent the night with images of Tami on the beach still firing my brain.

***

A couple of weeks later, Tami moved into her Berkeley apartment on College Avenue with her roommate. I went over to help lug stuff in and lo, I met ex-boyfriend Bill who was also helping. He was an overweight, passive looking guy. I wondered what Tami ever saw in him. He seemed nice enough though and not too surprised to see me. It turned out Bill was getting an MBA at Berkeley in finance. Tami bossed him about saying put this here, put this there. Of course, she bossed me about too. Finally, the job was done and Bill left. I stayed on for a while and had a beer with her and her roommate. I suggested we go out to a movie but she said she had too much to do. She looked tired and had put on some weight since I last saw her. But she still had the sultry, smoldering look. Seeing I was getting nowhere, I split saying I would telephone her in a few days about going out the next weekend.

In the interim, Bobbie phoned me up and announced that she and Tom wanted to go on the town in San Francisco and dine at Fisherman's Warf and asked if I want to come along and bring somebody. They had yet to go to the city and they had no car. I would provide the wheels. Be tour-master in effect.

"Uh, OK," I said thinking how it was just a year-and-a-half ago that Bobbie and I had done the San Francisco thing when she was out here for a visit. On the other hand, I thought this would be the ideal invite for Tami which as it turned out it was. She was eager for a good fish dinner and curious about meeting Bobbie whom I had briefed her on.

"Oh, so it's an old girlfriend, huh, Allan? Serious was it?" she teased.

"Well, yes. But we are just friends now. I'm basically their tour guide for the Bay Area."

"I look forward to meeting this Bobbie."

And so it went. All the time I was thinking women are a trip. If they go out with you, they are always interested in past girlfriends. They are like dogs sniffing each other out.

On the appointed night, I picked up Tom and Bobbie first and then we went over to Tami's for a glass of wine while she put the finishing touches on herself. She was stunning. Tan and slimmer than I had seen her last, apparently spending time at the apartment pool. The same messed up Italian haircut, but in a low-cut red dress that set off her chest, her dark features and dark hair. Tom did a double take. And charming Bobbie, after a brief glance, said all the appropriate things, "Love your hair, love your dress." Of course, Bobbie looked great too, in an outfit that matched her blue eyes and set off her reddish blonde hair.

Over we went to Alioto's on Fisherman's Warf. Bobbie had chosen the place. This is where we had dined before. We had the seafood works—

platters of lobster, flounder, shrimp, etc. washed down with two bottles of Chenin Blanc. Conversation was light. We compared notes about the South of France. Bobbie mentioned our trip to Greece. Tom squirmed. Tami smiled. Both wanted to know about Monterey, Carmel and Big Sur because they were planning a trip down there.

Afterwards, we hit a jazz club on Broadway, strolled through Chinatown and then had a coffee at Enrico's Cafe while watching the denizens of San Francisco nightlife go by. Finally, it was up to the Top-of-the-Mark for a nightcap and some slow dancing to live music. Tami melted into my arms and moved right along with my every move. A light bulb went off. Hey, I thought tonight could be the night.

It turned out I wasn't wrong. We dropped Bobbie and Tom off at their place and I said, "It would be a shame to end the evening right now." She agreed with a little kiss.

"My place is not fancy." I said. "I try to maintain the illusion that it is somewhere in the South of France."

"Great. I'll try to keep the illusion alive as well. Let's check it out."

And check it out we did. I opened the French windows to the warm night air. Traffic was light on Dwight. I put on some Miles Davis on my little portable record player and we relaxed on the bed sipping scotch on ice from the two water glasses I had on the dresser. Soon we were under the sheets.

At this point, I must digress on Tami in the nude. She was stunning, full breasted, a little wide in the hips but she had the sheen and the mantling of a Polynesian—creamy dusky skin suffused with a rosy hue emanating from under the surface of her skin. I could imagine the hormones coursing through her body. Also, she was well-practiced in the bedroom arts

The next morning, I could barely drag my ass out of bed. Groggily, we got up and dressed and then stumbled out into the street into the cold light of dawn, I in my grungy surveyor jeans and she still in her little red dress. I drove Tami to her apartment. She said little. I felt that somehow she was having regrets.

"Will I see you soon?" I asked.

"Of course," she said.

"I'll call you in a couple of days."

She smiled and skipped up the stairs into her apartment.

14. THE SPLIT

Monday, October 19, 1964:

Let's see. Airline reservations made. Passport located. Three-thousand dollars in traveler's checks. My old Samsonite suitcase packed. The rest of my belongings stuffed into my trunk. Ready to vacate my room over Lim's Laundry. I had given Dr. Ward notice that I was leaving. Since I had no lease, there was no problem. I notified Wilson & Company that I was quitting. They were pissed, complaining that I was leaving them in the lurch. I didn't care. They would have laid me off in a few weeks anyway. I also informed my reserve unit that I was moving to New York City and would join a reserve unit there. They gave me a month to accomplish that little chore. Finally, I sent a letter to San Francisco State stating that I was withdrawing.

My flight: the 11 p.m. Red Eye to New York City.

What was going on here? Why was I pulling the plug on my life in the Bay Area? Let's backtrack to see how it came all came about.

I might as well start with San Francisco State. The night courses were fine but as the deadline for withdrawal drew near, around week four, I realized that I couldn't deal with the workload. I needed to do this full-time. Further, I discovered I wasn't ready to be a student again. I needed to get out in the real world and find a real job. The surveying life wasn't doing it. The money was good, too good. If I continued, I could see myself being trapped in surveying for life.

I was interested in a career type job, possibly in advertising, public relations or television. And what better place for such a job than in New York? Darrah, now enrolled in the Columbia School of Journalism and her ex-boyfriend Rab apparently forgotten, had written me extolling the opportunities for a young man on the make in Manhattan. I knew this from my prior New York stay when I was in Peace Corps training. I had scorned this "on the make" life style then, but I thought perhaps that I was ready for it now

Then there was the woman issue. The thing with Tami had cooled right after that night. We went out again but alas, with no repeat performance. I discovered that at heart, Tami was a conventional girl looking for a Mr. Right, somebody who would take care of her. Hence, her interest in men like Bill going for an MBA. Also, I think part of our big night was inspired by a competitive female instinct to prove she was a better woman than Bobbie.

When I told her, I was going to New York to find a job in advertising or media of some sort. She said that was a great idea. "Maybe after a couple of years, you'll come back here and be a big advertising hotshot in San Francisco."

"Maybe" I said.

Susan had left San Francisco a couple of weeks after our picnic fiasco. Since I wasn't around much and since she was tired of San Francisco, ever-practical Susan decided to return to Kansas City where she had taken a marketing/public relations job. I helped her pack and saw her off at the Oakland train station. She was all dressed up like a perfect San Francisco lady, wearing white gloves and a hat. She gave me a little kiss, wiped a tear from her eye, and said goodbye, promising to write. I felt sad too. She really was a good person. I felt like a shit but this was right in the middle of the Tami heat so my mind was clouded.

Other factors for leaving were at play as well. The Berkeley scene was becoming old. I was tired of Telegraph Avenue and Sproul Plaza. I was tired of La Vals. Plus, Cal was in an uproar. Students were protesting what they viewed as restrictions on free speech on campus. Early October, Jack Weinberg, a former grad student and political activist was arrested. The students surrounded a police car on Sproul Plaza in order to prevent the officers from taking Weinberg away. His ally and friend, Mario Savio addressed the crowd from the stairs of Sproul Hall urging the student to protest what Savio called the "odious machine." The next day University President Clark Kerr met with the students and agreed to drop the charges against Weinberg. Over the next week, a movement was born which the students called, "The Free Speech Movement."

Where was I in all of this? Nowhere. I couldn't relate to this more activist crowd. As I made my way one night through the debris and the aftermath of a protest that still littered the plaza, I felt old and detached.

Then there were those letters from Gerard and Jean-Paul describing all the great times they were having Paris. All the women. How well set up they were. Their adventures traveling to Spain, Majorca, the Canaries, even North Africa. I had an itch to get back to Europe if New York didn't work out. Perhaps I could find a job there. Work in Europe. That appealed to me. Now that I was flush, I had that option.

Behind all this lurked another siren call. West Africa. I was still pissed at being thrown out of the Peace Corps. I felt it was unjust. So I screwed up a little bit. So I wasn't the best French teacher around. So what? As I learned from letters from my old Peace Corps training buddy, Alex, standards in Nigerian schools were not that tough; plus, he said there were plenty of non-Peace Corps teachers around that had come on other programs, even on their own. The Nigerian school system was hiring. Alex mentioned that he knew some independent volunteers who taught English in nearby French-speaking countries such as Dahomey and the Ivory Coast. That's what I had wanted to do in the first place. Teach English in a French speaking country. So I filed that in the back of my mind. Europe was on the way to Africa. I figured should the spirit move me, it would be an easy hop from France.

Topping it all was the truck crash on Interstate 280 in which I was almost involved. I was driving over to San Francisco State one night in the slow lane of the three-lane freeway minding my business, when this hulking semi came up fast behind me, right up on my tail, only a few feet away. What an asshole I thought. I then sped up suddenly, leaving him in the dust. What happened next seem so unreal that I didn't believe it had really occurred. The driver swerved onto the shoulder. Then his semi went out of control, jackknifed and slammed into a concrete bridge abutment. I observed it all as an ever-diminishing image in my rearview mirror. The last thing I saw was his cab bursting into flames. I didn't slow down. I kept going. I wasn't part of it. I didn't cause it, I told myself. I felt detached, as if I were watching a movie.

The next day I read the truck had gone off the road for no apparent reason killing the driver. However, the police said he had probably fallen asleep or was impaired. This set me to thinking how chancy life was. How it could end in a second. And how I had better take advantage of my freedom while I was still alive to enjoy it.

So that's how it was. I woke up one morning in my room above Lim's Laundry and decided that October 19 was the day to split. A split inspired by a mixture of motives, confused motives maybe, but all underlined by a burning desire to get out of the Bay Area. A split made possible by cash burning a hole in my pocket.

After a flurry of activity including making airline reservations for a $300 one-way ticket on American Airlines to New York and a trip to Wilson & Co. to pick up my final check, I loaded up the Chevy station wagon and drove to Martinez. There, I announced to Mom that I was flying to New York. She was in shock and immediately phoned Dad who came home early to wish me bon voyage even though he couldn't fathom why I was taking off.

"I don't get it, Allan. But you're an adult now and can do what you want as long as you are willing to pay the price," he lectured.

During my last hours at home, I played catch with Kenny on the front lawn while Mom fixed a tasty pork roast dinner. Afterwards, Dad drove me over to San Francisco Airport where I waited in the lounge until my flight was called. A few hours later, I was in the air flying through a star-spangled night with the Bay Area lights receding far behind me. I was gone!

15. NEW YORK

Nov. 2, 1964:

The morning light barely penetrates my humble abode as I peer out through the bars covering the lone window of my "garden" apartment on West 94th Street. The sound and the sight of early morning feet shuffling by is the only signal that it is time to get up. Once again, my junky alarm clock has failed to go off. Such is life, living on the cheap in Manhattan.

***

My cramped apartment of 400-square feet of living space featured a gloomy living room/bedroom, a tiny, decrepit kitchen and an even smaller bathroom that could barely accommodate a basin, a toilet and a shower stall. Two-hundred-fifty dollars a month for this, plus another $250 for a security deposit. This was week two of substandard apartment living and I was ready to scream. I looked back fondly on my spacious, sunlit room over Lim's Laundry for a sixth of this price. Still, my presence here was all part of the big plan—making it in New York.

How did I get to this point? Me. Mr. Rebel trying to make it in the New York corporate world. After two weeks in New York, about all I had accomplished was to seriously deplete my stash of cash. I had spent $300 for the airfare; $500 for the first and last month's rent of my hovel; another $400 for business clothes and the rest for general living expenses including a lot of eating out. Out of my stash of $3,000 only $1,400 remained.

When I left Berkeley, little did I dream that I would be living such a meager life here in the Big Apple. I had arrived tanned and buffed, glowing with California health. Now I was pale, sallow and rapidly losing muscle tone. Darrah made note of that the last time I saw her.

"What's happening to my California boy? You're as pale as I am."

"I guess it's New York living." I said.

I had encountered Darrah just hours after I landed sleepless at Kennedy Airport. I took the airport bus to Port Authority Terminal and then lugging my Samsonite suitcase down the stairs, hopped on the MTA up to Columbia University where I located a cheap hotel on West 112th near Morningside Drive. I was feeling proud of myself. Landing in New York and knowing all the transportation tricks. This, the result of my stay last summer in Peace Corp training.

After I dumped my suitcase, I hiked up Broadway a few blocks to Columbia University. I checked the university directory and located the Journalism Building. It was one of the older buildings on campus with a statue of Thomas Jefferson out front. Inside, on the first landing, I paused before a pair of swinging doors of what appeared to be a city newsroom. The doors flew open and out came the journalism students. Right in the middle of the rush was Darrah, hustling along. As she rushed by, I called out her name. She turned startled.

"What! Allan!"

"Hi. It's me."

"I can see that. What are you doing here?" she said coming over. I noticed her sallow skin and weight gain. Her thick tangled hair was slightly greasy. The glow of Southern Californian living long gone.

"Nice greeting, Darrah. I'm here in New York to see what is what. Job hunting."

"Job hunting?"

"Yeah, like you said I should be doing."

"Well, you don't look like a New York job hunter in your jeans and T-shirt. You still look like a California boy," she coolly noted.

"So let's discuss it. When are you free?"

"Ha, I'm never free. They keep us running day and night around here, chasing stories. Here's my address and phone number. Give me a call later this afternoon." Darrah scribbled out the address on a piece of notebook paper.

"Will do," I said folding the paper. "See you later."

I watched as she scurried off down the stairs joining the flood of budding young journalists. Wow, I thought. What a hustle.

After my fleeting encounter with Darrah, I walked around campus, checking out the Teacher's College building where I had undergone my ill-fated Peace Corps training over a year ago. It looked the same. Except there was no stifling summer heat. It was the peak of fall here with the leaves brilliant yellow, red and orange. However, despite the bright sun, there was a chill in the air. I shivered in my thin T-shirt and light windbreaker. Then hunger pangs struck. I realized it was about 10 a.m., New York time and I had yet to eat breakfast. I found a coffee shop nearby and had the steak and eggs special. Then with a full stomach, feeling slightly queasy from the grease, I returned to my hotel room and crashed until late afternoon.

Once I was fully awake, I called Darrah who had just gotten back from school after covering a children's art exhibit in Harlem. She said she was thirsting for a beer and would meet me and some other friends at the West End Bar.

***

The West End Bar was a scruffy as ever with its dim light and beat up wooden booths. The floor was a disgusting mess of spilled beer, popcorn and peanuts. I had spent many hours here with the Africans before I was thrown out of the Peace Corps. I spotted Darrah sitting in a booth with two other students. I went over and slid in next to her. She introduced me to the pair, Alvin and Steve, both classmates in the journalism graduate program. All three were working on a cool pitcher of beer.

"Jeeze that tastes good," said Alvin. "Right you are," said Steve. Darrah just drank. The conversation consisted of them complaining about how hard they were working, how the teachers ran them ragged chasing stories around town.

As they explained it, each one had a specific beat to cover such as education, politics or crime. In addition, they were also expected to cover breaking news such as transit crashes, harbor fires, race riots, whatever. Once the story was covered, they had to run back to the Columbia newsroom and type up it up. The story would then be critiqued by a teacher/editor and rewritten on the spot, on deadline. The best stories would be transmitted on the Columbia wire services. Often, these stories were picked up by other local news organizations which apparently valued the efforts of these budding journalists.

The Columbia Graduate School of Journalism was strictly a meat and potatoes journalistic operation. No theory courses were offered. That was for the fuzzy-headed professors of mass communication who populated the state universities. The Columbia program also had the added attraction of employing on a part-time basis some of the top reporters and writers in New York City. It was a place where the students could network with the best and make contacts for the future job prospects.

After expounding at length on how great it all was, Alvin and Steve wanted to know what my scene was. Darrah had already introduced me as a friend from Berkeley.

"Allan is job hunting in New York," she explained.

"True, but I might also split for Europe. It all depends," I corrected.

The pair eyed me and then glanced at Darrah who was at this point feeling no pain as she consumed a third stein of beer.

"So, you really have no plans, huh?" said Steve. "It must be nice to be so footloose."

"Hardly," I said. "I don't know what I'm doing from one day to the next."

"Direction is fine but you have to be flexible," said Alvin. "Take me for example. I was supposed to go to law school like a good little Jewish boy but I got involved in my school newspaper and couldn't stay away from it. So now, I'm going to be a journalist much to the chagrin of my mom. I've already lined up an internship at the *New York Times*. They looked at my clippings and said they were pretty good."

Darrah abruptly announced she had to go. "I have to write a movie review for tomorrow on top of everything else."

I slid out of the booth and walked her back to her apartment. Darrah didn't say much on way. Worn out from the day. I sensed the last thing she needed was me hanging around when she was so busy.

When she reached her apartment building, she turned to me and verified my suspicions. "Look, Allan, I can't spend much time with you. You see how it is. They run you ragged here. And I have to do well. I can't blow this opportunity."

"I understand. I just wanted to say hello," I said trying to act nonchalant. "I know how to take care of myself in New York. You don't need to babysit me."

"Oh, I didn't mean that," she replied. "I feel so tired and I have so much to do. Give me a call in a few days, maybe we can go out to a play. I'm supposed to see *Raisin in the Sun*, this weekend. I have a pass. If you want to come, I can get you a student ticket."

"Sounds good," I said. Without further ado, not even a little peck, she turned and went up the stairs, a sad sack and very different from the feisty Darrah I used to know.

***

So here it was the middle of the week, and I was essentially at loose ends. Initially, I didn't know what to do. Stay in New York and job hunt as I had originally planned, or just spend a few days and fly off to Europe. I decided to stay at least through the weekend to see what was what. I returned to my hotel and crashed again, still not over my jet lag and time change.

The next morning, I awoke with a clear head and suddenly a clear vision of purpose. I decided I had to give New York a try. I got up, had a big breakfast while scanning the *New York Times* want ads. God, what a lot of job ads and this was only for a Wednesday. Workers wanted in every category— Advertising, Import-Export, Public Relations, even jobs for radio and television production assistants. I knew the Sunday job ads would promise even greater abundance. I was eager to strike out to gauge my marketability.

However, I first had to get organized for the job hunt. I had to concoct a resume and I had to buy some job hunting attire—a new suit, shoes, dress shirts, etc. But most of all, if I were really committed to staying in New York for a while, I had to rent an apartment either on a sublet or a month-to-month lease. Staying in this dump of hotel with its moldy bathroom down the hall would not do.

I knew from my earlier stay in New York that the cheaper apartments were on the Upper Westside. The Eastside apartments were out of my price range. Most were over-priced little boxes hardly larger than a master closet.

I focused my search on the West 90s. This was sort of a Greenwich Village north. Sure enough, when I checked the *New York Times* classified, there it was, all laid out. Studio and one-bedroom apartments ranging from $200 per month to $600 per month. I marched up and down the West 90s until I managed to find a furnished "garden" studio on West 94th renting for $250 a month. The catch was I had to sign a one-year lease and give the landlord a month's rent in advance for a security deposit.

"You leave earlier, I keep the security deposit," said a Mr. Finkelstein lounging in his bathrobe in his luxurious apartment on West End Avenue right around the corner from my apartment.

"If I have to leave, can I sublet it?'

"That's OK, but I have to approve of the tenant," said Finkelstein.

"Do I get my security deposit back?'

"That remains to be seen. It's all there in the lease," he answered as he ushered me out the door.

The "garden" apartment, as already explained, was a dimly lit dump. Paint was peeling on the walls in the kitchen and in the tiny bathroom. It had a faint, damp odor of recent flood damage at the best, or a backed-up sewer at worst. The so-called furniture consisted of a studio couch that also functioned as a bed with a thin mattress and sagging springs, a cast-off dresser from some defunct hotel, a smelly easy chair that I was afraid to sit for fear of catching a disease. Also in evidence, a rickety coffee table and a chipped Formica table near the kitchen with two rusty metal chairs. The only natural light in the place was from the grated window facing the street. Of course, there was no garden in sight. However, it was all I could afford at the moment and still have some cash left, so I made do. I had a telephone installed. I bought a cheap, second-hand TV for company and supplemented the scanty kitchenware with a good frying pan and a coffee pot.

Gee. I suddenly realized I was really on my own. I couldn't escape to my parents' home in Martinez for a decent meal. I couldn't hang out and mooch off my friends in Berkeley, especially Bobbie and Tom who had fed me many meals. I had to do it on my own.

Aside from my dingy quarters, the building wasn't too bad. Two flights up the apartments were roomy with good light. I found this out a few nights later when I met a young lady loaded down with groceries. I offered to help her lug them up two flights of stairs to the apartment she was sharing with a roommate. For my trouble, she invited me to dinner. Her name was Nan and she was a social worker for the City of New York. She was a heavyset, large breasted Jewish girl, but very pleasant. Her roommate, Carole, was a nurse at a nearby hospital. Just down to earth New York girls.

I introduced myself as their downstairs neighbor and explained a little bit about my scene. They nodded as if they had heard it all before.

"We've been living here for a couple of years now. It's a great place. A great building. Your apartment excepted," said Nan. "Once you are settled maybe you can find a roommate and move upstairs."

"Yeah, we'll see. I don't know how long I'll be here. I have to find a job pretty quick before my money runs out," I replied as I devoured my spaghetti with an occasional slug of red wine.

"Don't worry, Allan. You'll find something soon. There are many jobs here," said Nan.

Nan was a Columbia University graduate in sociology. She went on to say she could find a much better job in Manhattan but she felt a call to serve the poor.

"And besides," she continued, "the pay is good for being a civil servant. It's just the bureaucracy that gets you down. If you can't find anything you like, you might give it a try."

"Who knows?" I replied.

I thanked them for the meal and returned to my apartment, marveling at how friendly New Yorkers could be. They didn't know me from Adam. I could have been an ax murderer for all they knew but they took me in and fed me.

In the days that followed, I spent a lot of time in their apartment, eating meals, watching TV, and playing with their cats. (I chipped in for food.)

It was all so homey. They had fixed up their large one bedroom apartment nicely with curtains and frills, comfortable furniture and a view out on West 94th Street. I whiled away many happy hours here. I also found Nan increasingly attractive. She was low-key and mild, none of that abrasive New York aggressiveness.

One Saturday night, Nan and her roommate threw a rent party and an odd assortment of people showed up. As Nan explained, the purpose of a rent party was to charge admission, provide the beer and wine, and music and collect enough to cover the rent. Four hundred bucks a month for her one-bedroom. It was a raucous affair, with participants ranging from the button-down junior executive to the bohemian, beatnik artist. Many girls were dressed in black with heavy makeup. Even a couple of cool blacks in colorful dashikis beating on conga drums. Also the whiff of marijuana. A party scene right out of *Breakfast at Tiffany's*. But all relatively behaved. At least no one called the police.

***

So that was the apartment scene in my building. I was pleased with myself that I had plugged into it so quickly. The job-hunting project was something else. First, I had to look the part of a junior executive on the make. I went down to Rockefeller Center to an upscale men's store and bought a Botany 500 suit for $90.00. A dark blue suit with vest, narrow lapels and a snug conservative cut. Not exactly Brooks Brothers but it would do. Along with the suit, I bought two white oxford cloth button-down dress shirts, a narrow silk tie, belt and black, calf-length socks.

The salesman fluttered around me with his measuring tape, measuring my neck, arms, my waist (34 inches) the length of my legs, inseam, close to my crotch. He was probably queer but I didn't care; he knew his job. "How tall are you, Mr. Brown?"

"Six-three."

"Weight?"

"Two hundred pounds," I answered. "Say, why do you need all that information?"

"Oh, we like to keep your vital statistics on record so we can be of service to you in the future. And I'm sure you are going to have a wonderful future here in New York. You'll be looking sharp once we have you decked out. My nice tan. Where did you acquire that? Bermuda?'

"Ah, no California. I worked outdoors."

"I can tell. You look very fit," he said buzzing about. "Say, could I interest you in another suit. We have special going on for the second suit, 50% off. You really do need two suits to job hunt in New York. How about a gray pinstripe?"

"Ah, I would like to but right now I'm short on cash."

"Well, why don't we open a charge account and you can take it home with you today?" said the salesman smoothly.

I yielded, knowing that I would need at least two suits. "Sounds good," I said.

After being fitted for the gray pinstripe, also a Botany, I started looking at shoes.

Here the salesman chimed in, "I would recommend a pair of black dress loafers, perhaps Bally. Tie shoes are so ordinary. Many young New York execs wear the dress loafers now, especially in the advertising field."

"OK." I said looking down at my rather old tie dress shoes that I thought I could get away with wearing.

The salesman took my foot measurements (13 narrow) and came back with a sleek pair of Bally loafers. When he slipped them on, they fit like a glove. I was impressed as I walked around the store. Walking on air. I felt it would be a shame to wear them out on the street. As if reading my mind, he said. "Here's a pair of rubber overshoes to wear when the weather turns bad. You know, rain, snow or sleet. They're on the house."

"Thanks, ah..."

"Arnold, Mr. Brown. Always at your service. Now, while we are on the subject of weather, let's step over here and look at topcoats.

"Topcoats?"

"Yes, of course. You can't walk about New York in winter without a proper topcoat over your suit."

"Gee, I hadn't thought of that," I said. Indeed, I had not thought of it at all. No one in California wore a topcoat. They were rare in San Francisco even with the fog rolling in. At most, one wore a London Fog raincoat.

"What about a cotton twill raincoat?" I asked. "London Fog or something like that."

"Oh that'll be necessary too. But for right now for chilly November weather, you'll need a wool topcoat. It looks so smart over a suit. Raincoats are all right when it's raining but to wear them on a cold day with no precipitation is rather cheap looking."

Sigh. "O.K, show me a topcoat."

And so it went. Arnold talked me into a dark wool topcoat that looked thin to me but one that he claimed would keep me warm. In any case, it went well with my suit.

When all the damage was done, I walked out that store about four-hundred dollars poorer, but at least now, I was dressed for success. However later, I was to learn about discount houses, here and there in the corners of Manhattan where I could have gotten all this stuff all at half price. But what did I know? I was a retail moron.

***

My next step was conjuring up a resume. I needed a typewriter to do that so I went over to the Sloane House YMCA on West 34th Street. The Y had a library where it rented typewriters by the hour; plus, it had scores of reference works and directories on hand for job hunters.

I spent most of the day there honing my meager resume. I listed my educational background: B.A. History, Univ. Of California, Berkeley. 1963, Certificate of French Studies, Aix-en-Provence, 1962. My most relevant job experience: U.S. Army: Broadcast Information Specialist dealing with radio, TV and public relations at the Sixth Army Headquarters. And then I listed my experience as a surveyor which dwarfed all my other work history. I thought at least that would show that I could hold a job.

After many drafts, I felt I had a decent resume, clean of typos. The next step was to have copies of made up. I took my resume to a nearby print shop and waited for a stack of fifty to be printed up.

Now with resumes in hand, I launched my job-hunting campaign focusing on the major ad agencies. Based on the ads in the Sunday *New York*

Times, I phoned around and talked to either an employment agency representing an employer or the personnel department of a particular employer. All the responses were the same. "Send us your resume and we will get back to you if we are interested." This I did but I also realized that it might be better to show my face around as well. I suited up and hit the street, my resumes neatly tucked into a slim, black leather valise that I had bought.

First, I made the rounds of Doyle Dane Bernbach, Ogilvy & Mather and J. Walter Thompson (JWT), the ad agencies that I knew were looking for so-called management trainees. But without an appointment, I never got past the entrances of their headquarters. I had to content myself with dropping my resume off at the reception desks, often staffed by very hot receptionists. I always made it a point to spend a few minutes with the receptionists engaging in charming chitchat because I knew from reading the job-hunting books that making a good impression on a receptionist was often the key to getting an interview.

Sure enough, the next day I got a call from the JWT personnel office asking me to come by for an interview. They were indeed looking for management trainees and said I had a background that interested them. I suited up once again and made my way over to their headquarters on Lexington Avenue. At the appointed time, I found myself seated across the desk from a slick young dude who looked no older than I. He introduced himself as Todd.

"So, Al. Can I call you Al?" Todd said eagerly.

"By all means," I said.

"So, what brings you to New York, Al? I see by your resume, you're from California."

"That's right, Todd. I left California to try break into advertising here in New York because this is where the action is. I know JWT recruits at Berkeley but I thought I would come here direct."

"I see. But why advertising? You're a history major. I would have thought you would be more interested in government work or possibly teaching."

"No, not really," I answered in my best job hunting mode. "I thought history would give me a good liberal arts education but I also liked writing and as I noted on my resume, I do have some exposure to the media, radio, TV and public relations thanks to the Army."

"Oh yes, the good old Army. I was in PIO myself," said Todd.

I thought, "Good. Now we have something in common. Maybe we can deal."

"OK, Al, let me describe the situation here at JWT for those starting out," said Todd now pacing behind his desk. "We believe that a potential career employee must learn the business from the ground up. He must know who is who and he must know their way around the agency. Later, once that is accomplished, we assign him to various departments, such as creative services which include copywriting, graphics, art, TV, film production and so on. Or he might be assigned to media services which select the particular media most suitable for the dissemination of the advertising product. Down the road after a few years' experience in one department or other, we evaluate the individual to see if they have account executive potential. That's the Holy Grail around here—becoming an account executive. He's the person who deals with the clients, keeps them happy and finds more clients. He's the bread and butter of advertising. That's about it. Any questions?"

"Uh, no not at this point."

"Good, now let's take a look at where someone like yourself would be starting," said Todd heading for the door.

"Where would that be?" I asked, following him out.

"Ah, the mailroom."

"The mailroom?"

"Yes. As I said, we expect our beginners to know who is who in the company and to be very familiar with the layout of the company," Todd said as he led me down the hallway. "Six months to a year in the mailroom will give you that knowledge. Of course, starting salary is modest, about seventy dollars a week."

I was stunned. Seventy dollars a week as mail boy! Me, a college graduate who was used to making two hundred dollars a week in surveying. I bit my tongue as Todd hit the down button of the elevator to the basement mailroom. We entered a large, brightly lit room lined with mail bins and sorting tables. And there they were, working like little beavers, the mail boys, all dressed up in suit and tie, furiously sorting mail into the various pouches of their mail carts. Carts that they would soon wheel through the hallways of JWT and distribute to their intended recipients. A couple of guys grinned sheepishly at me as they went through their mailboy routines.

Todd introduced me to the manager, a fat guy in a tight white shirt with clip-on tie. An obvious high school graduate, I thought. Most likely on a power trip since he got to boss around the college graduates.

A few minutes in the mailroom were enough for me. I was conflicted. On one hand, I thought if this is what you have to do to get started in advertising, maybe you have to do it. On the other hand, it was so demeaning. Such a waste of talent. In any case, as soon as we returned to the reception area, Todd shook my hand and said he would be contacting me shortly about a possible position as a starting trainee. I thanked him and said I looked forward to hearing from him.

As soon as I hit the street, I took a deep breath. Did I want to do this? Be a mailroom gofer? I ducked into a bar off on a side street for a noon time beer and to think this mail boy thing over.

I discovered that the softly lit bar was a hangout for advertising types. The guy sitting next to me sipping a double martini turned out to be a junior ad executive at one of the other agencies. We struck up a conversation and I told him about my experience.

"Shit, that's the way it's done in the ad world here in New York, fellow. I have a degree in English from Dartmouth. I'm a good copywriter, but I was still stuck in the mailroom for six months when I started out. I wrote copy on my own time, showed it around and kissed ass. That's what you have to do to get out of the mailroom. Show talent and kiss ass."

"No kidding."

"Well, it worked for me." He continued, "I know guys who have never gotten out of the mailroom. Boy, do they become bitter. Most of them quit. Or they're fired for some minor fuck up. It's survival of the fittest. As a general rule, if you're in the mailroom for more than a year, and haven't got some nibbles from upstairs, you better be moving on."

"Good advice," I said sipping my beer.

"Yeah. By the way, what area of advertising are you interested in?" he said looking me over.

"Oh, I like to write but I also like film and I did some TV production in the Army."

"That's good. Those are two growth areas. Be sure to check out the TV commercials now running on the networks. That'll give you a frame of reference when you're bullshitting on a job hustle."

"Thanks. I'll keep that in mind."

After a good night's sleep, I decided to forego the mailroom option at JWT for the time being. I sensed advertising was too ephemeral for me, too political. And judging by most of the commercials that filled the airwaves, it wasn't all that creative. I needed something more concrete, something more directly creative and exciting. Perhaps something like television or television news. I thought back to my time hustling around KGO-TV studios helping Sergeant Kirk put together his TV shows. Although frantic, I liked that. I felt I could do that for network news.

California Split

I didn't watch the network news much but when I did, my favorite show was the *Huntley-Brinkley Report* on NBC. I thought their shows were informative and entertaining. And the writing was sharp, especially Brinkley's stories. Their film reports always featured great footage, especially from overseas. I didn't see why I couldn't work for the network news in some capacity. I felt I already had an insight into how television and film worked based on my Army experience. And I figured with my history major, language and literature background, I could handle the journalistic chores.

Of course, I was terribly naïve. One simply didn't pound on the door of a network news operation and ask for a job. As I was to learn, you generally needed contacts and prior TV news experience. But at the time, I thought why not? I didn't have anything to lose.

The next morning, I took the subway over to Rockefeller Center and prowled the Art Deco lobby and hallways of NBC looking for the network news operation. I discovered that the upper floors where the network news was located was closed off to the public except for the reception area. A stunning redhead behind the reception desk told me I had to have an appointment if I wanted to see any news personnel. She did say that I could drop my resume off and she would forward it. NBC News would contact me if it were interested. I asked her how many resumes come in off the street.

"Hundreds upon hundreds," she smiled. "But we do go through them. Somebody upstairs screens them so that only serious resumes get through."

Charm time. I smiled at her. It wasn't hard because she was a very comely with a New England accent. "Would you mind taking a look at my resume and tell me if you think it would make the cut?"

"Not at all. But it would only be a guess," she said giving it the once over. A few seconds later, she handed it back, saying, "Sure this works. You have a degree from a good college, overseas experience, fluency in French and some practical experience in broadcasting through the Army. Not bad at all. It should get some attention."

"Thanks."

"The only thing I would recommend in the future is including a photo of yourself so they can see what you look like. After all television is a visual medium," she said smiling.

"Good idea, I said

"Also, why don't you talk to Hank? He's a page here at NBC. He can clue you in as to what it's like to work here. He should be hovering around on the first floor near the main studio."

"Thanks again," I said heading down the Art Deco stairway to the first-floor studio. I found Hank sitting on a gold braided chair reading a newspaper. I knew him from the name tag on his blue blazer under the emblem of the multi-colored peacock.

I introduced myself and we began chatting.

"Oh, yeah, it's a trip working here. I meet all the stars, Johnny Carson who is going to tape this afternoon. Bob Hope, Bing Crosby, Frank Sinatra. Everybody who's anybody. Of course, this is just a temporary gig. I do comedy script writing. I'm hoping to get on Carson's show as a writer. I've gotten some positive feedback."

It turned out Hank had a degree from NYU in television and film production and had landed this job as a page through an alum who worked here.

"It's all about connections and visibility if you want to work at the network, Al. Forget about working in the boondocks. It's better to be on the scene here at the network working at some low-level job. Even the mailroom."

"I've heard that before," I replied. "That's the spiel they give at ad agencies."

"Screw ad agencies. Stick with the network. That's where it's happening what with the entertainment shows and the news. Look, the presidential election is only days away. NBC is going to be covering that big time. Wouldn't you want to be in on news like that? Working in the mailroom could give you an entrée. I know guys who have made it into news starting out in the mailroom."

"Well, we'll see," I said. "I left my resume with the receptionist. Maybe I'll get a nibble."

"Here, give me your name, address, and telephone number," said Hank. "Maybe I can give you a plug for the mailroom. I know some guys down there."

"Thanks, Hank. Hope to hear from you, "I said as I strolled off, thinking no matter how I tried to dodge it—a mailroom appeared to be my future.

16. BERDAU & CO.

Mailroom or not, I had to find a paying job quick. As I scanned the *New York Times*, I noticed many ads for management trainees in the import-export business for immediate employment. The average starting pay was not great, about $100 per week but more than the mailroom. Still, this import-export business piqued my curiosity. A straight selling job marketing services and products did not interest me but this did. Import/export had a hint of the exotic and the prospect of travel. I could see myself going overseas to foreign markets and bringing back ivory tusks, rhino horns, African masks, pearls, colorful textiles, priceless herbs, spices, and of course, a lot of rattan furniture. I noticed one ad in particular for Berdau & Company that stipulated the applicant should have a speaking knowledge of French. I thought why not? Why not give them a call? It turned out the telephone number was for an employment agency that was screening applicants.

The recruiter answered my call directly. When I told him I might be interested in applying for the Berdau job, he asked me a long list of questions, and then apparently deciding I was a worthy prospect told me to come down to his office with my resume. The next day I did. His office was a scruffy place down near the Battery—a maze of streets that constituted Lower Manhattan and the financial district. The recruiter introduced himself as Sid. He was a gruff, no-nonsense guy, rumpled and sweating in the humid, overheated office. Sid leaned back in his creaky swivel chair and looked over my resume while puffing on a cigarette.

"OK, the resume looks good. The French bit is great. Can you really speak frog?"

"Not bad for an American," I answered. "Want to try me out?"

"Nah, all I know is English and some Yiddish. I'll take your word for it. In any case, old Berdau will test you out. Now as to the rest. You don't have any real business experience but they're not looking for that. They'll train you as to exactly what is needed. The important thing is you look the part. Nice suit, by the way. It all helps. Tell you what, I'll phone Berdau and send you over. Go wait in the hallway while I set this up."

I went out in the hallway and stared out a grimy window for a few minutes while Sid made the call. Finally, he poked his head out the door, saying "Go on over to Berdau. It's only a few blocks from here. Here's the address. Good luck and remember the first week's pay is mine."

Leech, I thought. But hey. A job is a job. I needed income.

I made my way through the labyrinth of streets until I came to the address. On the way, I began to wonder what the hell I was doing. This could be for real. If I didn't watch out, I would have myself a job. A career-type job, requiring commitment, hard work. I would be expected to exhibit all the Horatio Alger bullshit that I had heard about.

**

The Bureau Building looked as if it had been there for at least a hundred years. A dark, old dirty brownstone, four stories high. Quite a contrast to the sleek new office towers nearby. I walked into the main entrance and was greeted by a geezer in a doorman's uniform who appeared as old as the building. A closer look revealed he was of some vague Asian origin, maybe Filipino.

"I'm here to see Mr. Berdau. My name is Allan Brown. I have an appointment."

He looked down at his appointment list. "Oh, yes. Here it is. I just wrote it down. Go on up to the second floor and into the first door on the right. You can't miss it."

I dutifully trudged up a wide flight of stairs, pausing on the landing to look at a large, mural map of the world. It had scores of red dots on it indicating the scope of the Berdau import/export trading empire. I noted many dots in the South Pacific—Tahiti, Fiji, the Cooks, the Philippines and Southeast Asia. Wow! I was impressed. This outfit was truly global.

I turned right and went through a pair of leather-padded swinging doors into what looked like an old trading room right out of *Lord Jim* with rows of desks and maps and blackboards on the walls. The blackboards were filled with schedules of ships, airplanes and lists of products to be shipped or received. A row clocks above the blackboards indicated the time in the major time zones of the world. There was a musty, spicy smell about the place that seemed to emanate from the mahogany paneled walls and the scuffed and scarred hardwood floors. Young men, some foreign looking in dress shirt sleeves, walked back and forth, writing up on the boards; others hunched over their desks reading various shipping manuals; still others, on the phones chattering away in English, French, Spanish and German. In the center of the room, a stock ticker and a news teletype spewed out the latest news.

A gorgeous Eurasian woman in a slinky silk dress came up to me. "You must be Mr. Brown. I'm Lorraine, Mr. Berdau's secretary. He is expecting you. Go right in."

She pointed to a glassed-in office up a short flight of stairs on a balcony that reminded me of the bridge of a cruise ship, not doubt allowing Mr. Berdau a bird's eye view of the trading floor.

"Mr. Brown, come on in," said a booming voice through the open door. The voice belonged to a tall, impeccably groomed gentleman with steel gray hair and a wide smile of perfectly capped teeth. His suit was tailored in Continental style with two side vents instead of the American one—a style that I had seen often in France. If it weren't for his unmistakable New England accent, I would have thought him a French diplomat.

"Sit down, sit down. Sid gave you a glowing report. He said you might be the person I'm looking for. God knows, I have been looking a long time. So tell me about yourself. *En français, s'il vous plaît.*"

Gulp. OK, here goes, I thought to myself, worried that my French had gotten rusty since the Peace Corps. I began rattling off my background, my education, my time in France. I must have talked for three or four minutes before he cut me off.

"OK, not bad for an American. I was brought up bilingual. My grandfather from France founded this firm. I spent a few years in France going to school. Still. I know it's hard for an American to learn another language. You could use some grammatical polishing but you have your conversational skills down pretty well. Good enough for business. I assume you can write and read at a decent level in French. If not, there are plenty of people here to help you. Native speakers. We do extensive business with French-speaking countries in South East Asia, French West Africa and of course the South Pacific. Let me give you a little history of our firm."

Mr. Berdau went on to describe how his grandfather, from an old trading family in Marseille, immigrated to New York in the late 19th century to import furniture from Southeast Asia and pearls from the French controlled Tuamotu Archipelago.

"My father concentrated on the black pearl trade and we did quite well with that. All those New York society ladies had to have a black pearl necklace. I used to go with him on some of those trips. It took months by ship. Now we fly. When I grew up, I took over the pearl trade from Dad and spent much of my young adulthood in French Polynesia," he said with a dreamy smile that quickly disappeared. "Of course it wasn't all wahines and gorgeous sunsets. I had to be sharp on the pricing of pearls that fluctuated day-to-day on the world market. One false move and I could lose thousands of dollars."

"Alas, reality eventually intruded and I had to come back to New York to take over the family business. My father had died unexpectedly from a heart attack. He was only his early 50s. Well, pearls were profitable, but I knew we had to expand. The postwar was a different time. We now have hundreds of lines of import/export items ranging from the old Tiki tourist items to Asian household goods to the latest in chemical and pharmaceutical products.

"Right now, we are trying to market a special disinfectant for use in tropical zone hospitals and health facilities. It's been in use in the Philippines and has been a tremendous success there. Infection rates are way down from the old norms. Now, we plan to launch it here in the Southern United States. That's where you might come in. We need a sales force to peddle this disinfectant to Southern hospitals. But at the same time, we need a management trainee to stay here and maybe do some overseas travel to gain a big picture point of view of our operation."

As he was talking, I took this all in. Big picture. Some overseas travel but focusing on disinfectant. Sell to the South. I didn't know what to think.

Finally, he finished his spiel, paused and looked me over. "Yes. I think you might be the type of lad we need. Tall, clean-cut American but has been around. Knows some French. Make a note to improve. In essence, I like the cut of your jib, if I may use a nautical metaphor, Mr. Brown. So without further ado, I'm offering you the job. It will pay $110 a week to start but promotions come rapidly in my company. And if you go out as a salesman, we have a rather generous commission program. But that's all down the road. The first month will be training in all aspects of the business. What do you say?"

"Ah, sure. I mean yes. I think I'd like working here. I also think I can make a real contribution here," I said trying to appear upbeat.

California Split

"Great. Can you start Monday?"

"Yes, I can." I said, now thinking what was I getting into? I didn't know if I could handle this job. In addition, how could I live on $110 a week? I would be spending over half of my monthly income on rent. But I still said "Yes."

"Good, good," nodded Berdau. Our official starting time is 9 a.m. but everybody is usually here by eight. One hour for lunch. Quitting time unless there is some crash project is 5 p.m. I want everybody home with their families at night. A good family man is a good employee. Are you married?

"Ah no."

"Of course not. A young man like you on the make. I suspect you have lots of female company. I have two daughters myself. Both in college. One is a senior this year at Vassar. Both will be home in a few weeks for Thanksgiving. Maybe we'll have you out to our country house in Connecticut for Thanksgiving. You being a California boy probably don't have any family here in the East."

"No, not at all."

"As I thought. Footloose. Not afraid to leave the known for the unknown. Not afraid to leave beautiful, warm California for the cold, heartless East," he mused. "Shows gumption. That's what we need at Berdau & Company. See you Monday, Mr. Brown."

Boom-sha-boom. That was it. I had the job. I walked out of the office and down the stairs in a daze but proud that at least someone thought I was worth something in the New York world of business.

***

So the grind began. Up at 6:30. Shower. Dress. Breakfast. Either a bowl of cold cereal or a quick bacon-and-eggs breakfast at the corner coffee shop. Up Broadway to the 96th Street subway stop. Strap hang for a half-hour in a crowded subway car with the *New York Times* folded under arm or stuffed into my little valise. Sometimes sweating in my topcoat. Emerge from the subway in Lower Manhattan and trudge the few blocks over to Berdau & Co. On the job by 8 a.m.

The first week went well. I was instructed on filling out the various forms one used to arrange for the importation or exportation of goods. All the legal documents—the export declarations, bills of lading, letters of credit, export licenses, etc. Vince, a fellow worker who dressed in Italian style suits, led me through the paperwork. At lunch one day, he began cluing me in on what was what.

"It's not a bad place to begin in import/export. Old-line firm. I've been here a year and learned a lot. But it's still an old fuddy-duddy firm. I mean all this rattan, Tiki crap they still import. That's old school. There's much bigger game out there. I know they are trying to modernize what with this disinfectant stuff, but the geezers who run this place don't have clue?"

"Don't have a clue?" I asked. "What do you mean?"

"Like it's stone age, man. By the way, watch out for the kraut VP, Stoltz. He's the hammer in the company. Old Berdau plays nice guy. You get your marching orders from Stoltz."

"Oh, do say?" I nodded, filing that piece of information away.

I was introduced to John, the top Asian buyer who had just returned from Japan on a hunt for the best cultured pearls. He explained Berdau was expanding its pearl base from the natural to the artificial. While he was there, he also looked at the latest in miniature transistor radio products that Berdau was thinking about importing. "Clever, these Japanese. They basically rip off American technology and then refine it. They're doing it with cars and now are moving into electronics."

The best part of the week was hanging out in the shipping department and touring the warehouse down by the East Side docks. It was a dark, cavernous, wondrous place, filled with aromas and trade artifacts from around the world—china, batik fabrics, glass wear, spice candles, candleholders, brass lamps and teak, mahogany and rattan furniture.

By the end of the week, I was feeling confident that I could do the job. It was an interesting place to work. I could see myself eventually going overseas on buying trips, but first I wanted to stay in New York and become expert in the bureaucratic minutia of import/export.

Week two changed everything. First thing Monday morning I was called into Stoltz's office. I had seen him around but had not formally met him. It was as if they were keeping him in a closet in order not to scare away new employees. He was a short, heavyset man, in a tight suit with slicked down hair and old-fashioned rimless glasses. Mr. Stoltz motioned for me to sit down and began talking with a slight German accent.

"So, Mr. Brown. Now you have taken our little tour of Berdau & Company and learned some of its ways, what do you think?"

"Fascinating company. Fascinating work. I'm eager to learn more."

"Yes. It is instructive to gain an overall view. Learning how to deal with the paperwork is essential but now it is time to go to work and start making money for the company."

"Oh yes. You mean, going out into the field. On buying trips, maybe."

"Not exactly. Buying trips are for those of long experience here. The reason you were hired was to be part of our new sales force. I believe, Mr. Berdau mentioned that."

"Ah, yes, he did."

"Certainly he did and as he no doubt told you, we are about to market a new disinfectant to medical institutions in the South. Overall, filthy institutions. Very lax hygiene. The specially formulated disinfectant we are marketing will bring them into the 20th century. What you will be doing is traveling the South and calling on those institutions, developing contacts and making sales. More than likely, your base will be in Atlanta.

"Atlanta?"

"Yes, not a bad town for the South. Quite cosmopolitan. Centrally located. You will have an expense account and a leased car at your disposal. The travel department will arrange all the details. We expect you to spend this week here going over materials related to this disinfectant, to become an expert on it. We will drill you on this. You will practice your presentations and they will be critiqued." Stoltz said pointing to a pile of thick binders on his conference table. "I assume you have had some basic chemistry at your college. If not, I can help with some of the technical material. You can use our conference room to study these materials this week. Next week, we expect you to fly off and start setting up your base of operations in Atlanta."

I was stunned. I didn't know what to say. I was about to be deported to the South to peddle some disinfectant about which I didn't have a clue. I had a sinking feeling in my gut. This was for real. Was this how a career was supposed to be? Be a good soldier and go where ordered. I feigned pleasure at the prospect of my new duties and took the binders to the conference room where I read through them, but not absorbing much. The basic gist of the materials was that hospital patients in the South had a high rate of secondary infections that could be directly traced to poor sanitation and lack of sterilization. Some of the infections referred to included *Pseudomonas Aeruginosa* and *Acinetobacter*. All Greek to me, but terms I had to speak knowledgeably about.

After four hours of mind-numbing reading and a long lunch with Vince who commiserated with me over being sent to a southern Siberia, I went home early, saying I didn't feel well.

The next day I spent the entire eight hours in the conference room, taking notes and referring to textbooks on pharmaceuticals trying to gain an understanding of this crap. Day three, Stoltz came into the conference room and lectured me on how to make a sales presentation.

"Visual aids are important, Mr. Brown. We have some made up here," he said putting up a chart on an easel board which showed the superiority of this disinfectant, listing how many bugs it would vanquish compared to other products.

As if to ease my mind, Stoltz noted that my initial contact in the hospital setting would no doubt be an administrator, not necessarily an expert on disinfectants, so I shouldn't be too technical.

"No worry, there. I barely understand this stuff myself," I responded.

"Ah yes," he sighed. "Well if we wanted an expert, we would have hired a chemistry major or somebody out of pharmacy school. No, Mr. Berdau believes a smart generalist salesman is the best. We will see."

Toward the end of the week after sweating through more manuals and ginning up some sales aids, I realized that I couldn't go through with this. The technical aspects of the disinfectant were beyond me. I couldn't give a credible sales pitch on this. Plus, I didn't want to move to Atlanta. No to the hot, sticky South with all its problems and turmoil. I tried to stall for time, telling Stoltz I was not ready to launch this product.

"Nonsense, Mr. Brown. You are as ready as can be expected. You will learn on the road, talking to the experts. Be a learning student. Charm them with your curiosity. You will pick up the jargon and the facts that you need to know. We are patient. We do not expect immediate results. At this stage establishing a personal rapport is paramount."

I was not mollified. I felt sick to my stomach all day Saturday. Also, I was pissed. I saw my chance at a glamorous international life in import/export slipping away by being confined to the South. Finally, Sunday, I sat down at a rented typewriter at Sloane House and wrote Mr. Berdau a letter of resignation, explaining I had to return to California unexpectedly because of a family crisis which, of course, was a lie.

The next thing I did was make airline reservations on Icelandic Airlines for Luxembourg on Tuesday. The one-way plane ticket cost me two-hundred dollars, a bargain low season rate. Now I had only eight-hundred dollars left of my stash, although I was owed two weeks' pay by Berdau. Sid would probably get his hands on that when he learned of my resignation. I didn't expect to see it.

While I was at it, I wrote a letter to the Army Reserve Coordinator of the Sixth Army explaining that I was moving to Europe and that I would locate a reserve unit there. (I still hadn't joined a reserve unit in New York.) Of course, I knew that the odds were I would be put in a control group for reserve members who move around all the time. This was a paper reserve unit. Once in, you did not have to go to meetings or summer camp but you were first on the list if it ever came to activation, a remote prospect in the fall of 1964. But this was all a minor consideration to me.

***

Let's back up here. There were other reasons for leaving New York so abruptly. Although barely here a month, I was already tired of hectic, claustrophobic living. It was exhilarating at first but soon became a drag. All that nervous energy spent in just day-to-day living. That was not my style. I was a laid-back Californian used to wide-open spaces where deserted beaches and remote mountains were only a few hours away. Here, everywhere you turned it was people and traffic jams.

Then there was the expense. New York was the most expensive city in the nation in which to live. Another month here, I would be broke, job or not. I wanted to get out while I still had some cash. Eight-hundred dollars would see me through two months in Europe if I stayed in cheap hotels and ate out at student restaurants. Somehow, I felt confident I could find employment over there. I recalled all those jobs advertised in the *International Herald Tribune* when I was a student at Aix-En-Provence three years ago. Jobs galore were listed; jobs connected to the U.S. military, jobs in sales of American products, even jobs in the news media as freelance stringers for news organizations.

And finally, I had not met anybody of interest here. I was effectively living a solitary life outside of work. Yes, I saw many beautiful women, beautifully dressed, but they were so remote, so far out of my league. Most were on the make looking for Mr. Moneybags. I was the poor boy. Yes, there was Nan, the Jewish girl upstairs, the social worker. She was good company but not a romantic prospect. And Darrah was long gone. Not that I wanted to restart anything with her but she would have provided an entrée into new social situations.

The last time I saw her was when we went to see an off-Broadway version of *Raisin in the Sun*. Darrah had to write a review of the play and she spent the whole time scribbling down notes in the dim light of the theater. Afterwards, she had to rush back to her apartment to bang out the review. Darrah, always on the job playing junior journalist.

When I phoned her a week later, she said she was happy to hear that I had a job. "Import/export. Who would have thought," she said. "It sounds like a real opportunity, Allan. Much better than those mailroom jobs you told me about."

"I guess," I said thinking about my future peddling disinfectant. When I broached the subject of seeing her again, she was evasive at first, saying she had an interview the next day lined up with LeRoi Jones, the black playwright. It was to be a real scoop.

Finally, she said, "Look, Allan. As you can see, I'm very busy with my work and you're a distraction. You have to get out on your own here in New York. Don't rely on me."

"OK, OK. Relax. I'm out of your life," I said defensively, feeling rather hurt.

I still remembered the days when she was desperate to be around me. But those days were long gone.

"See you around," I said

"See you around," she answered.

Click.

I hung up and stared at my barred windows, my spotty walls, my decrepit kitchen and my broken down furniture. It was indeed time to split.

On the day of my departure, I packed my suitcase and vacated my apartment, sacrificing my security deposit. I was last seen lugging my Samsonite suitcase along West 94th Street to the nearest subway stop en route to the airport.

***

At Kennedy Airport, I made a quick call to my parents to let them know that I was leaving for Europe. My mother answered the phone. Dad wasn't home yet from work. When I told her, all I heard was a sob from the other end and words to the effect, "Allan, I don't think you know what you are doing. Please come back to California."

"Sorry, mom. I can't. I'll be all right. I feel I have to go and explore opportunities over there. I'll probably have this chance only once in my life. Don't worry. I'll be all right. I love you. Give my love to Dad, Don and Kenny. Bye."

I failed to mention to Mom that if Europe didn't work out, I might try to go on to French West Africa to teach on my own personal Peace Corps mission.

An hour later, my flight was called and I boarded the Icelandic Airline jet. The New York chapter of my life was over. I took off from Kennedy Airport to Europe on a one-way ticket with barely eight-hundred dollars in my pocket.

17. PARIS

Sunday, November 22, 1964:

Five days in Paris and already the blue fuzz of some forgotten sweater is at the foot of my bed. Five days in Paris and the yawning gray days will turn into weeks and then months. One silhouetted tree replaces another on the banks of the Seine while Notre Dame stands mute—a witness to the centuries of passing hours. Time becomes a drifting leaf, wandering aimlessly in the eddies of the Seine until it dissolves into the liquid gray.

I closed my journal, put down my pen and gazed out over the rooftops of Île St. Louis and the Seine beyond. Time indeed was passing but things were not as gloomy as my first few days in Paris.

***

Upon landing at Luxembourg, I boarded an airport express bus bound for Paris. I arrived at the City of Light mid-afternoon near the Champs-Elysées. It was all so easy, the Icelandic Air flight and the Paris bus. Like catching a subway.

I lugged my Samsonite suitcase through a cold drizzle over to a cafe on the Champs-Elysées and took stock of my situation. I had a little less than eight hundred dollars left. I had blown twenty on odds and ends getting over here. Again, eight hundred dollars was not much but it might see me though a couple of months of Paris before I found a job.

As I mulled this over, I noticed several young American girls hawking the *International Herald Tribune* up and down the Champs-Elysées. It was a scene right out of Godard's *Breathless*. I looked for Jean Seberg. No Jean Seberg. I thought if nothing else, I could sell newspapers. I bought a paper from one of the hawkers and thumbed through it as I gnawed on a *sandwich jambon* (ham sandwich) and sipped on a beer.

Excellent newspaper, I thought. All the top world stories with an emphasis on what was going on in Europe. Of special interest to me was the want ad section in the back of the paper:

> *Wanted: Buyer for the European Exchange System.*
> *Wanted: International merchandising executive.*
> *Wanted: Schoolteachers for U.S. military bases in Europe and Asia.*
> *Wanted: Accountants for international corporations.*
> *Wanted: Mutual fund salesmen to sell to US military personnel.*

I folded up the paper thinking time enough later for serious job pursuits. First, I had to find a hotel and then find Jean-Paul and Gerard. I had an old address but both had said they were moving to new, separate quarters. I figured they had gotten tired of living together.

I took the Metro over to Blvd. St. Michel in the heart of the Latin Quarter. I remembered several cheap hotels from my brief stay in Paris in 1962 and headed in that direction. I chose one at random for 25-francs or about four bucks a night and checked in. It was the standard French fleabag—one lumpy double bed, an armoire, a basin with only cold running water and heat that came on for a few hours in the late afternoon. Of course, the toilet down the hall was one of those squat down jobs that the French claimed was the most natural position to take a crap in.

I crashed immediately. After all, I had barely slept on the plane and with the time change, I was severely jet-lagged. I fell into a deep, unconscious sleep for about six hours. Then, boing! I was wide away at 2 a.m., ready for the day except there was no day. I looked out the window into the dead of night. Nothing. Only empty streets. My stomach growled. I was hungry. Where to eat at this hour? I thought about it for a second and then remembered Les Halles, the early morning markets of Paris. I knew the place would be a beehive of activity at this hour. I could find something to eat there. I checked my little Michelin map guide of Paris. Les Halles wasn't far. Across the Seine, just beyond the Louvre. A little over a mile.

I got up, dressed, grabbed my umbrella and went out into the nighttime streets of the Latin Quarter. I crossed the Seine on the Pont Neuf and headed straight into a maze of streets on the Right Bank. After a few false turns, I stumbled onto Les Halles Market, a vast produce, fish and meat market, all housed under a massive wrought-iron shed. It was a netherworld of trucks coming and going and of farmers and merchants haggling in the ghostly halogen lights with the cries of *"Allez, allez, allez."* I found an all-night cafe and ordered a big bowl of onion soup with a half-baguette and proceeded to stuff myself, all the time marveling at the carnival of night people going by.

Afterwards, I walked back to the Left Bank, pausing on the Pont Neuf to gaze at the Seine shimmering in the night light. The silhouette of Notre Dame hovered off in the distance. On an impulse, I descended some stairs to the Quai, the river walk along the banks of the Seine. As I strolled along it occurred to me that this might be a dangerous thing to do. Nah, this is Paris, not New York. I saw bums sleeping in the cold mist, huddled up under the bridge. A lucky few slept over warm subway grates.

Back at my hotel, I slept a few more hours, waking up around 8 a.m. I thought about taking a shower but the nearest bathhouse was several blocks away so I made do washing myself at the basin and shaving with cold water.

Now somewhat refreshed but hungry again, I went back on the streets and found a cafe on Blvd. St. Michele where I had a café-au-lait and croissants. Not finding that filling enough, I begged the waiter to bring me a ham omelet.

"But Monsieur, it is too early," he sniffed. "We do not serve the omelet until after eleven."

"*S'il vous plaît*. I'm starving."

"Humph. I'll see what I can do." he said as he shuffled off.

Fifteen minutes later, he was back with the omelet and a half-baguette. It wasn't bad but certainly not worth the fifteen francs he charged plus the tip (*service compris*).

Finally, filled and refreshed, I focused on my task for the day—locating Jean-Paul and Gerard. At first, I was naïve enough to expect that I would simply bump into them around the Sorbonne. I knew Gerard was enrolled in the Foreign Institute so I hiked up Blvd. St. Michel a few blocks to the Sorbonne and entered its elegant 17th-century courtyard. Wandering through the Grand Hall, I was struck by the variety of students. Africans, Asians, Polynesians, a few scattered Americans and of course the French. I noted whatever their national origin most of the women were dressed in the chic French style. Blouses, sweaters, skirts, high heels, no pants. Cute little jackets or coats with scarves. All carefully coiffed, some made up. Intent. None of casual leisure one saw at the California schools. On the make in their very own French way.

The guys were in suit coats, sport jackets, slacks, a few jeans, wool scarves, a beret or two. Many wore piercing, little rimless glasses. I more or less fit in with my khakis and my old Harris Tweed jacket that I had lugged from California. At the very least, maybe I could pass for British or Canadian.

A clerk in the registrar's office for the Foreign Institute could only tell me that a Gerard Dubois was registered there but he had no idea of what courses he was taking or what his class schedule was. Typically French. You enroll. Pay your fee. And they don't care what you do. Either you earn a certificate of French studies or you don't. Plus, the clerk didn't have his current address, only the old one that I had.

I glanced into a Foreign Institute class that was in session. Most of the students looked bored as a French language professor explained the finer points of the subjunctive tense. No Gerard, so I wandered around the Sorbonne, up and down its elegant hallways and peered into its historic salons, many now filled with eager students. These were only a fraction of the classes being offered at the Sorbonne which had several facilities scattered around the Latin Quarter. The Sorbonne itself was part of the much larger University of Paris with over a hundred thousand students.

After exploring the Sorbonne for an hour or so, I headed over to the University of Paris Medical School to look for Jean-Paul. The school, located a few blocks away, was housed in a run-down, fortress-like building from the thirties. Inside medical students from around the world were scurrying hither and yon, trying to get to class on time. You could feel the tension in the air.

Jean-Paul had written that the competition was tremendous with major "make-or-break" exams along the way. Most medical students either quit or flunk out. However, like all of higher education in France, the cost was nominal. That had been the big attraction for Jean-Paul. "*Mon Dieu*," he used to say, "The medical schools in the U.S. are a rip-off. Imagine paying four or five thousand a year in tuition when I can go for free in Paris."

Unlike, the registrar's office at the Foreign Institute, the medical school registrar did have the class schedule for Jean-Paul. According to the schedule, he was supposed to be at an anatomy lecture due to begin in a few minutes. I trooped up the stairs with the mass of students to the indicated classroom and sat in the back. No one checked for a student I.D. Any student looking type off the street could attend. I scanned the classroom looking for Jean-Paul. A student or two gave me a quizzical glance and then returned to their text. After 15 minutes, still no Jean-Paul. Finally, as the teacher was droning on, I scooted out the door past him. He shrugged, probably thinking I was just another failing premed student.

Out in the hallway, I reconnoitered. Shit! Now, what do I do? No Jean-Paul. No Gerard. Only an old address in Montmartre. Needles in a haystack. I was swearing at myself for my lack of foresight. I should have telephoned Gerard's parents from New York for his new address. Of course, I could still do that from Paris. Maybe as a last resort. But they must be around here somewhere. I had to think. I retired to a nearby cafe, bought a *Herald Tribune* and had another *sandwich jambon* for lunch. I was getting sick of these ham sandwiches but they were cheaper than most items on the menu.

It was only 2 p.m. I was tired of people hunting but I had the rest of the day to kill. So I wandered down Blvd. St. Michel to the riverfront along the Seine and browsed the open-air bookstalls protected by tarps from a light drizzle that had begun. The offerings were eclectic, ranging from first editions to pornographic novels, from prints to posters, from ancient, esoteric maps to the popular magazines of the day.

Across the street was the Shakespeare & Company Bookstore, the famous English bookstore that in earlier incarnations at other locations promoted Hemingway, James Joyce, Henry Miller, Lawrence Durrell and a host of other literary greats. I went in and wandered through a labyrinth of bookshelves jammed full of new and used books from ceiling to floor. It was a comfortable, quirky place where one could sit at a table or in easy chairs and spend hours going through the finest in Anglo-American literature. I found a used paperback copy of Henry Miller's *Tropic of Cancer* and thumbed through it. I had read it before but I always found fresh insights such as this one on Paris:

Paris is like a whore. From a distance, she seems ravishing. You cannot wait until you have her in your arms. And five minutes later you feel empty, disgusted with yourself. You feel tricked.

I felt like that. Paris was a whore. So far, it had promised much but delivered little. It remained remote, impersonal—a gray, postcard world. Still, the bohemian life beckoned. Chase French girls, eat cheap, live cheap. Read the great works at Shakespeare's. Maybe write. Why worry about a job and career? Just bum around in Paris or Europe for that matter. Work now and then to earn a few bucks to survive. America was fading fast from my consciousness. Who needed it with all its hustle and artifice and its ever-present military obligation? Stay in Europe.

I bought the *Tropic of Cancer* paperback and returned to my hotel room to retire early and maybe spend another early morning at Les Halles.

***

Luckily, I managed to sleep through the night, waking at 7 a.m. Maybe jet lag was over. I felt great, except I felt grungy and I stank. A cold-water rinse at the washbasin would not do. I had to hit the bathhouse located a few blocks away. I gathered up my shampoo, my washcloth, a bar of soap and hiked over to the place.

I paused before a basement door marked *Bains Public* in a rundown building. I entered and found myself in a Dante's Inferno of steam, heat and humidity. A bored concierge at a desk pushed a locker key and a grey-white towel my way as I paid her four francs. She pointed to men's shower and locker room, a room with a wet concrete floor and a moist slim covering everything.

I gingerly stripped, put on my flip-flops to avoid a fungal infection and stored my clothes in a locker secured only by a flimsy lock. Towel around my waste, I stepped into a tiled shower stall, closed the door and turned on the water.

Behold—hot, full force water coming out the showerhead. I adjusted the pressure and the temperature and stepped into Nirvana. I must have spent a half hour in there soaking, occasionally scrubbing with the various implements hanging from the wall, washing my hair with my own shampoo until I felt squeaky clean—the grime and dirt of travel washed way.

Back out on the street an hour later, feeling like a prune, but still warm from the shower despite a chill mist in the air. I settled in at my cafe on the Boul Mich. and ordered a café-au-lait and a ham omelet from the same waiter as yesterday. This time he only raised an eyebrow. In the meantime, I looked at my Metro map to figure out a way to get over to the American Express Office near the Opera House. I thought I might have a letter waiting for me from my parents after they had recovered from the shock of me splitting to Europe. Maybe they had sent me some money.

***

The main American Express Office in Paris at 11, Rue Scribe, was a venerable institution harking back the days of telegraphs and steamer trunks. It was here one could arrange money transfers, buy traveler's checks, exchange money into francs, send telegrams and most important of all, pick up mail. In their post office section, the pigeonhole mail slots dated from the turn of the century. For no charge, American Express would not only receive and store your mail but also, upon request, forward it to other American Express offices around the world. You could travel the world, and still have your mail catch up to you. But alas, after a ten-minute wait in line, I discovered that this day there was no mail for me, let alone money. Still, my trip was not wasted. I exchanged two hundred dollars of my ever-dwindling cash supply into francs and hit the street.

As I stuffed my francs into my wallet, who should I see coming across the street? None other than little Jean-Paul hustling intently along, apparently headed for American Express as well. One of the needles in a haystack had been located.

I stood on the curb waiting for him to catch sight of me. He almost passed me by when I called out, "Hey, *petit cochon*."

He wheeled around, startled, and then saw that it was me. "*Mon Dieu*, Allan. What are you doing here!?"

"Looking for you and Gerard. What else?"

"*Quelle surprise!*" Jean-Paul said trying to act pleasantly surprised but I sensed he might have been annoyed by my greeting which meant "little pig."

"Yes. Small world. I arrived a couple of days ago but I didn't have your new address, so I went around to the medical school and the Foreign Institute trying to find you guys."

"Yes, yes. Well you see, we both moved. Gerard is in a hotel on Île St. Louis, and I have another place in Montmartre. We decided that a year together was enough. We needed some space. Wait for me and we'll talk."

I waited while Jean-Paul picked up his mail and then we walked over to Harry's New York Bar nearby. We found a table in the back and ordered two pints of Bass Ale.

"So tell me again, Allan. What you are doing here?" asked a puzzled Jean-Paul.

"Ah... I don't know," I said, "other than to get out of the U.S. and see you two."

"Are you going to go to school or something?"

"No. I don't think so," I said. "I'm done with school for now. I thought I might look for work in Europe. There seem to be a lot of want ads for Americans in the Herald Tribune."

"That is true. Europe is starting to boom. And they are open to

American know-how," nodded Jean-Paul.

I then launched into an account of my time in New York, my job at Berdau & Co. and my impending banishment to Atlanta, Georgia.

"Yes. It is good that you left," nodded Jean-Paul. "Who would want to live in the South? If you are able to find work with an American company, Paris is a great place to live. I don't think I'll ever go back to the United States. After all, France is my home."

"Hear, hear," I said raising my glass.

Jean-Paul then explained his scene in Paris. "The reason you didn't find me at the faculty of medicine is that I have abandoned my medical studies."

"But why?" I asked, shocked. "You were so intent on becoming a doctor. In fact, you told me, you came to Paris specifically to study medicine."

"That is true. But I received minimal credit for my years at Berkeley. So that meant I would have to endure five more years of medical school. I couldn't do that. Maybe I was fooling myself that I wanted to become a doctor. In any case, I am now more interested in comparative literature, especially German lit. I'm doing some important research work in that already."

"What about Gerard? What's he doing?"

"I don't know I haven't seen him for a couple of weeks. I don't think he's doing much at the Institute. He's mostly screwing around. He has been having quite a lot of success with the women. They are attracted to him. A tall, thin, blond guy who looks French but is American. Even though his spoken French is weak, the ladies seem to dig it."

"Meow." I replied.

"Your accent is better than his."

"Perhaps but that's not saying much."

"Never fear, *mon vieux*. Hang out here for a few months and you'll be talking like a Frenchman. Say, I must be going," he said glancing at his watch. "I have a class at the Sorbonne."

"When will I see you again?" I asked, sensing that Jean-Paul was likely to remain scarce during my time in Paris.

"Uh, this Saturday, Gerard and I are going over to an Alsatian restaurant on Île St. Louis with some friends. The beer is supposed to be great. We could meet there."

"A beer joint?"

"Yes, I'm still a beer guzzling frat rat, albeit a French one."

"Once a frat rat, always a frat rat," I said, giving him a pat on the back.

Jean-Paul nodded and scribbled out Gerard's address on a piece of notepaper, drained his beer and left.

I lingered at Harry's Bar, taking in the atmosphere of the place that once was the haunt of Hemingway and Fitzgerald along with many other literary greats. Pictures of writers, actors, sports stars and other celebrities lined the paneled walls—ghosts from the past. However, today Harry's Bar was filled with English tourists, apparently the kind who loved to travel in dreary, drizzly weather. I vaguely wondered if the French ever set foot in here.

***

After Harry's Bar, I took the Metro to the St. Michel stop and hiked over to Île St. Louis. This was a little island in the middle of the Seine, one bridge over from the larger Île de la Cité, the location of the Notre Dame Cathedral. Île St. Louis was one of the oldest parts of Paris, with narrow streets, overhanging apartments, and chic restaurants, boutiques and hotels. It was to one of these hotels that I was headed, Hotel Adelphi, the current home of Gerard.

The reception desk in the small lobby was manned by an American who introduced himself as Ben. I wondered what his scene was. I thought it unusual to find an American running a reception desk in a French hotel.

"Is there a Gerard Dubois registered here?" I asked.

"Sure is and I think he is in. Third floor. Room 300. Only two rooms up there. The roof garden room. Go on up and knock on his door."

I trudged up a flight of narrow stairs, wondering what kind of firetrap this place was. On the third floor landing, I knocked at Room 300. I heard a shuffle and Gerard's voice. "Who's there?"

"Al Brown."

"Brown!" he said, unlocking the door.

"Yeah, none other."

"Wow, this is a surprise," said Gerard, looking thinner and more Euro than I saw him last. "Come on in."

"Howdy bro," I said shaking his hand. I stepped into a large, charming attic room with the sloping ceiling and French doors that opened out onto a little roof garden with a great view of the rooftops of Île St. Louis and the Seine.

"Welcome to my humble abode," said Gerard proudly. "It's about time you came to Paris."

"Better late than never," I said continuing to look around. "Say, how did you find this place?"

"I met desk clerk, Ben, at a cafe one night and I told him I was looking for a place since Jean-Paul and I had decided to split up. We talked. He said he was working at various hotels in Europe as part of some graduate hotel management program at the University of Michigan. He's a cool guy. He has red Austin Healy sports car still with Michigan plates. He's a hit with the French chicks."

"Lucky guy."

"Yeah, fucker always has his wick wet. But I digress. Ben told me there was great, top floor room opening up at his hotel. And for a long-term stay, the rent was reasonable. I bit. Just dumb luck. But this place is great. I even have a full bath right outside the hall. I share it with the other room. However, the guy is never there. So, it's like it's all mine. A lot of privacy here and the dollies love it."

"I'll bet."

Gerard indeed had a sweet set-up. He had made the place very homey with Art Deco posters on the wall, some decent furniture, a large queen size bed that did not sag and a portable stereo with a good collection of jazz and classical records.

And again, the view. I sighed. Finally, feeling relaxed. I knew I had found my Paris connection. I knew the good times would roll now. I had a beer and fell asleep on his bed while Gerard sat at his desk, plowing through the intricacies of the advanced French grammar.

18. LE SCÈNE I

The good times did indeed roll. First, Gerard said he knew of a great little hotel a few blocks away that was much better than the one I was staying at and not much more expensive. We hiked over to Hotel Madrid and checked it out. An old lady at the desk looked me over before committing herself to renting a room.

"*Oui, Monsieur.* We have a room. It is the low season. A nice room on the third floor with a view. I will give you a special discount if you stay for several weeks. "

"That I plan to do," I said.

After a quick look around the room, I decided it would do nicely. It wasn't as elaborate as Gerard's room but it did have a view of the rooftops, a firm double bed and a full bath right down the hall. No more public bathhouses for me. The price, a reasonable two hundred francs a week ($35.00).

New housing taken care of, we went over to a student cafe near the Sorbonne. There, I met Gerard's friends from the Foreign Institute and a few from the Sorbonne itself. It was a varied bunch including two Jewish Americans, one Southern gal, an Icelandic blonde, one German dude, a Lebanese fellow, three Frenchmen and one very cute French girl, Anne-Marie. It was a lively group and the conversation was in French and English. I happened to be sitting next to the young lady from Nashville studying at the Institute. Denise, a carefully groomed ash-blonde, spoke excellent French and had barely a southern accent when she spoke English. She also dressed in the chic French style.

The Icelandic girl, Anna, looked young but she was a beauty. As soon as we arrived, she made a beeline to sit next to Gerard. He told me later that

Anna was the daughter of an Icelandic diplomat to the United Nations. Gerard claimed that they had nothing going on but she kept hanging around him saying she felt safe with him. He was her protector from the more blatant male advances. Of course, Gerard was interested in more amorous action; still, he kept Anna around, almost like a pet.

We sipped beer and talked about this and that, about what I was doing in Paris and about my plans. The major topic of discussion was the outing to an Alsatian restaurant Saturday night. Tonight, though, most were going to dine at the Cité, the main student restaurant. I asked Gerard if they would let a non-student in.

"Sure. They don't check very closely," he said. "You just need a ticket, although technically you need a student ID as well. I can give you a ticket."

"Thanks."

We finished our beers and cafes and hiked over to the Cité. I filed in with the rest of the group, handing my ticket to the man at the door. A few flashed their student IDs. Others did not.

We stood in line at the cafeteria-style setup, waiting to fill our trays. I noticed that the offerings had not changed much from my student time in Aix-en-Provence. Thin slices of non-descript meat, piles of French fries, watery, overcooked vegetables and bowls of salad greens the French ate at the end of the meal. None of this was great but it was cheap. Each ticket cost five francs or about a dollar. However, as I learned from Gerard, in order to purchase tickets you definitely had to show your student ID.

"Shit, Al," said Gerard. "Why don't you enroll at the Institute? They'll take you on any time of the year. You'll get a student ID card and be able to access all the goodies like eating at the Cité."

"Ah, I don't know if I'll be around long enough to make much use of it," I said. "I can probably fake it for a while. I'll just buy tickets off you."

"Uh, yeah, that'll be OK for a while," said Gerard not too enthused.

"Or you could try the Israeli student restaurant, said Seth, one of the Jewish guys. They never check. Nobody eats there unless they have to. It's all that Israeli kosher crap."

"Thanks, I'll keep that in mind," I replied.

As I was to learn, Seth was a real character. A feisty, little red-haired dude with a goatee, he looked like a cross between a beatnik and a revolutionary. Seth was originally from Brooklyn but had been in Paris for two years and was thinking about going overland to Asia with the eventual goal of freelance reporting from Saigon. He admitted he was living hand to mouth. He found odd jobs ranging from selling newspapers to writing freelance articles for hometown newspapers, to acting as a paid extra in movies. Sometimes he did English dubs for French movies. His latest gig was an extra part in *What's New Pussy Cat* which had just been filmed in Paris with Woody Allen, Peter Sellers, Ursula Andress and Peter O'Toole. Even Gerard had appeared as an extra the film. As he explained. "It wasn't much. A bunch of us sitting in a classroom and stomping our feet."

But back to Seth.

"Why do you want to go to Saigon?" I asked Seth.

"Opportunity, man. Opportunity. Fame, fortune. Become a war correspondent like Peter Arnett."

"You know that war is heating up don't you?"

"So what? It's places like Saigon where you make your spurs as an international journalist in a war zone."

"Do tell," I replied.

"Yeah, and I have a buddy over there. Sean Flynn, the son of movie star Errol Flynn. He's making out as a free-lance photographer. He was here in Paris a few months ago."

"OK, whatever," I said. "But I just spent seven months in the Army. I'm not getting near Vietnam if I can help it."

The other Jew was Charlie from the University of Chicago. Whereas Seth was full of adventure, Charlie was essentially a "stay-at-home" type. He could barely tolerate Paris.

"I'm only in this fuckin' place because my college advisor told me as a history major, I should do time in Europe. I chose Paris because I knew some French. But the Institute sucks, the French suck. The only thing this place gives me is time to write."

Although his parents were hounding him to go to law school, Charlie had decided he was going to write the great American novel and he was always referring to Saul Bellow or Philip Roth as his idols. By his own admission, Charlie spent most of his time in his hotel room reading *Playboy* and beating-off since he had failed to score with any French girls and couldn't bear the thought of hustling American girls. This was all strange and self-defeating to me. Here he was a good-looking guy, lying in bed and drooling over some plastic Playboy Bunny. Anyway, let's leave Charlie for the moment and move on to some others in our entourage.

André, the German with a French name, was a cool looking fellow, reputedly smooth with women even though he had a beautiful fiancée who was a stewardess on Lufthansa Airlines. André was an econ/political science major but didn't seem to sweat his studies much. His major claim to fame was he was the son of the current mayor of Bonn, Germany, a fact to which he was indifferent. Indeed one reason he was studying at the Sorbonne was to get away from his notoriety in Germany. Also, he felt more at home in France than Germany. "The Germans are too stiff for me. Too bourgeois. I need more light, song and laughter."

Dede, a Lebanese from Beirut was a suave, charming fellow who enjoyed hanging out with Americans. In fact, he was planning to study at Berkeley for a master's degree in electrical engineering. He was generous of spirit, always inviting Gerard and me over to his apartment for scotch, cool jazz and the latest blonde girlie pics. Dede was enamored with blondes, especially Marilyn Monroe type blondes. Europeans women did not seem to interest him. He currently had his eye set on Denise.

Dede's American orientation came partly from his father who taught at the American University in Beirut. And, as he would always point out, his family was Christian, not Muslim. "Beirut is a carefully balanced town between the Christians and the Muslims and yes, even some Jews We get along for the moment but it could all degenerate into civil war at any time." Dede said he was always looking over his shoulder when he went home. He had already made up his mind he would live abroad either in Paris or in the States.

Then there was little Anne-Marie sitting several chairs away. A bright little gal with a cute face, big brown eyes, and a southern cast to her skin. She said she was half-Spanish. She was from Montpellier and always wore a pillbox fur hat with her long dark hair flowing out. Although short, about 5' 3", she was well filled out in the right places. Not fat. Just ripe. I noted that she was very outgoing for a French girl and when I sat next to her on another cafe outing, she spoke pleasantly in slow, clear French that was easily understood. She spoke some English but wanted to learn more.

"Hey, this could work out," I calculated.

As for the others, the three French guys, not much can be said. They were typical French, slightly snooty, deigning to hang out with Americans primarily to improve their English. I think Anne-Marie was friends with one and that's why she was here, although she told me later, she just enjoyed being around Americans. But enough of the personality profiles. Back to my dining problems.

Sustenance and cost were of the utmost importance to me at this point. I decided to try out the Israeli Restaurant. This turned out to be a ramshackle affair in a temporary building on a small plaza a few blocks away. However, it had a happy, carefree atmosphere with blaring Israeli music and cafe tables and chairs outside even though the weather was lousy. Posters and signs both Hebrew and French were plastered on the walls and bulletin boards. Newspapers clippings recounted the latest Israeli-Arab news. Handouts in English solicited for volunteers (both Jews and non-Jews) to come and work for a few months in Israel on a kibbutz or failing that simply come and visit. I took a handout for further study.

No one checked IDs at this restaurant and you could pay cash for a meal. The food was a mix of Jewish kosher and Middle Eastern—rice, couscous, falafel, fish, lamb and beef kabobs, various soups, yogurt, fruit, Israeli bread. This was definitely a healthier diet than that offered at the Cité. And dirt-cheap. Only four francs a meal. I decided that this would do for a main meal place.

Looking over my handout on the kibbutz, another light bulb went off. If I ran out of money and could find nothing in Europe, why not work on a kibbutz? After all, it would be free room and board in exchange for labor on a collective farm and I heard they even gave you spending money. I could travel around the Middle East after.

In 1964, Israel was considered the new Zion. The new Promised Land. My impression of Israel was in line with the images portrayed by Leon Uris in his book, *Exodus,* as well as what I had heard from Darrah's friends. That of heroic Jewish settlers, surrounded by Arab armies, battling for their lives in a conflict that evolved into the 1948 War. The Arab-Israeli conflict had been a festering sore ever since. Still, working on a kibbutz was an alluring prospect for a gentile who was broke. I filed that possibility away for future reference.

***

Come Saturday night, we all gathered for dinner and beer at the Brasserie de l'Île St. Louis. This was a curious joint with a décor more likely to be found in Germany than in France. With its stuffed animal heads, hanging antlers, antique brass fixtures and folk art paintings, it was unique to Paris. It had been around since 1870, when its chefs fled to Paris after Germany took over Alsace-Lorraine.

The food was the typical German/Alsatian fare, plenty of sauerkraut, ham, fowl and pork loin with various cheeses and white wines. But the real attraction for us was the beer—delicious homemade Alsatian beer served in liter steins. Good beer was hard to find in Paris. Most places served only mediocre French beer.

It was cozy inside this restaurant with the low lights refracting off the brass and the glass. The music was folksy Alsatian mingled with laughter and the clink of glasses and mugs. Outside—a black misty drizzle, another Parisian late fall night. We ate, drank and conversed. Gerard and Jean-Paul chatted with the two other French girls at the next table while Anna made goo-goo eyes at Gerard. Dede had Denise in his sights. She was pleasant but I could tell not interested in him that way. I made it a point to sit next to Anne-Marie with her little pillbox hat. She spoke in her languid French.

"Ooh. This beer is so good. I am afraid I will become tipsy," she said taking a draught.

"Here, be sure you eat a lot to it soak up. Try these potatoes," I said holding my fork out full of roasted potatoes.

"Oh yes, that is good," she side taking a bite. But I must be careful or I will become too fat."

"Nonsense. If I may say, you are perfect," I said.

She smiled. And returned the favor with a fork full of sausage from which I carefully took a bite.

"Just like Tom Jones," I remarked. "Have you seen that movie?"

"*Mais oui*, it was a very sexy movie."

"Say," I said after we finished eating, "why don't we go over to a booth by ourselves where it's not so noisy and you can tell me more about yourself? You can practice your English."

"*Bonne idée*"

We removed ourselves to a small booth off in the corner and I ordered another round of beer.

"Monsieur Allan. I cannot drink all this. I am already tipsy but it is so good."

"You must be part German."

"I don't think so. But I am a mélange. I am part Spanish, part French and some Italian. And who knows what else. As you know, since you lived in the South of France, there are many races there," she said looking over at me with lips half open as if waiting for something.

"Yes, I know," I said leaning over and giving her a light kiss on the lips.

She clapped her hand on her mouth right after the kiss and suppressed a little burp. "Oh, my, I am not polite."

"Nonsense, you are a perfect lady. Let's get out of here."

She nodded. We got up put our coats on and stepped out into the drizzly night.

She shuddered and leaned against my shoulder. I offered to take her back to her place on the Left Bank but she said she could make it on her own.

"Nonsense. We'll take a cab. But first, why don't we stop by my place to let that beer wear off."

"OK," she said in a little voice. "But take care of me. I am tipsy."

"I promise," I said. She smiled and followed me to my nearby hotel.

I really did mean it. I was going to take care of her. I was going to behave. In fact, I was the perfect gentleman, fetching two espressos from the next-door cafe that I took up to my room. We sat by the window looking out over Île St. Louis in the silent night. I had no music. I dearly wished I had a stereo set up like Gerard. But no. Instead, Anne-Marie hummed a little tune. By and by, she turned to me and said. "I am so tired."

"Well, lie down on the bed."

"Come let's lie together," she answered.

Well, one thing led to another and before I knew it, she was kissing me hard and soon both of us were under the covers. She had a very nice little body, full, strong. Olive skin. She bore down, moving expertly. We kept it up most of the night.

***

The next morning Anne-Marie had a beer hangover and felt remorseful about what we had done. It turned out she had a boyfriend from Martinique who was off in military service in French Polynesia and she was feeling bad that she had been unfaithful. I assured her that stuff happens and she herself admitted that he was probably making it with some bimbo hula girl.

"Even though I like you," she said getting dressed. "I must have time away from you. I must think."

"Think? What is there to think about? Why don't you stay? We can spend the day together."

"No, I must go. I have to study. The Sorbonne is a very hard school for me. I must study to pass my exams."

"OK, I'll see you tomorrow at the cafe."

I led Anne-Marie downstairs, and just as we were going through the front door, the crone who ran the hotel stuck her head out of her downstairs apartment, smirked and then withdrew saying nothing. But when I returned, she accosted me, saying that I could not have any overnight guests since she had to report each and every hotel guest staying to the Paris police. Any unregistered guests staying in my room could lead to a fine. She warned me that should it occur again, I would have to leave. The police wanted to know where every tourist or visitor was every night. Looking out for Algerian terrorists, I suppose. So it was with the French police state.

19. LE SCÈNE II

Monday, November 23:

The weather remained drizzly and dark. The days growing short. What to do this week? Maybe sit in on Gerard's French classes as a visitor if they would let me. I glanced at my French calendar. There was no indication that Thursday, the 26th was a day out of the ordinary. But back home it was Thanksgiving. I liked Thanksgiving. It seemed right to give thanks for North American abundance. Still, I was prepared to ignore the holiday since I was in France. Then Gerard mentioned that the American Cultural Center on Blvd. Raspail served a traditional Thanksgiving dinner for American expatriates

"It's turkey with all the trimmings at a nominal cost," he said. "All we have to do is show our passports to get in although you are allowed to have a French guest."

"Let's do it," I said. "Turkey would taste great."

"Right on," nodded Gerard.

Jean-Paul was not interested. "Yes, it is a nice holiday but it is not French. I have had enough Thanksgivings in America to last me a lifetime. Besides the turkey here is not good. All frozen. The French do not generally eat turkey."

"OK, whatever, Mr. Frenchman," I said as we discussed this at our cafe hangout. I thought about inviting Anne-Marie, but I had not seen her since our encounter Saturday. She hadn't shown up at the cafe so Gerard, Charlie, Seth and I trooped over to the American Center, an elegant building out of the 1920's, designed in a vaguely southwestern style. This was where homesick Americans gathered and the French showed up to enjoy American culture in the form of film, dance and jazz.

The place was jammed. Long tables had been set up in the main reception room. We were served cafeteria style from a hot food table with volunteers ladling out turkey (white meat or dark) mashed potatoes, sweet potatoes, vegetables, cranberry sauce, some semblance of stuffing. Coffee, milk and juice to drink. For extra cost, wine or beer. We chowed down with gusto.

Surprisingly, there were few American students here. I guessed that most were happy to get out of Thanksgiving for a year. The Americans here were an older, varied bunch who had been in Paris a while. Most were not too prosperous looking. With their beards and sandals, they appeared to be starving artist types although there was one table full of happy, black American jazz musicians who apparently made a good living in Paris.

Gerard mentioned that the center was also a gathering place for American writers in Paris, both unknown and well-known including James Jones, the author of *From Here to Eternity*.

"James Jones? He lives in Paris?" I said, surprised.

"He sure does," said Gerard. "I've seen him here now and then. He likes to talk to young writers."

James Jones did not strike me as the type of writer who would live in Paris. I thought of him as a meat and potatoes writer who had depicted the lives of grunts in World War II. I knew he had written other books like *Some Came Running* but I didn't consider him a serious literary writer. I had once read a hundred pages of *From Here to Eternity* from a copy that my mother had. She had worshiped the book. From what I had read, I thought it was simply a romantic potboiler although I did like one of the main characters, Private Prewitt. Still, I thought it would be interesting to hear from James Jones. According to the Cultural Center calendar, Jones would be at the center next week to talk about writing and his latest novel, *The Thin Red Line*.

On the appointed evening, I showed up with about fifty others jammed into the library to hear Jones speak or as it turned out to hear him ramble. He strolled in looking casual in Levis and a tweed coat with an open collar dress shirt. He was a short, brawny thick-necked guy with a broken nose on a massive head. He looked like a prizefighter. But when he spoke in his southern Illinois southern drawl, he was very gentle and warm. He didn't have much to say about writing in general except to say that he wrote about what he knew and he knew a lot about the Army in time of war and small town living in the Midwest.

Someone asked him why he lived in Paris. He said he did so because he was tired of the American hustle for writers and the pressure to publish. Also, he lived in Paris because it was cheap and inspiring. He said he was thinking about doing a novel on the new "lost generation" in Paris. Still, I had the impression that despite his enormous success, he took nothing for granted. Although his latest book *The Thin Red Line* was a commercial and critical success, he viewed each project as starting from scratch. He parting words were, "Never give up or give in to the bastards. Find your own voice, your own vision."

All duly inspired, I sipped some punch, eyeing Jones from afar, telling myself, if he could do it, so could I. But truly, I didn't have a clue when it came to novel writing. About the only "creative writing" I had done was the drivel in my journal. Oh yes, I once won a short story award in the 6th grade. It was a Christmas story about Santa's elves going on strike and the scramble to get the toys delivered in time for Christmas. That was the extent of my literary recognition. Still, I often sat in cafes and scribbled out story scenarios but never followed through with a finished product.

***

It was now my third week in Paris and my money was going fast. I needed an immediate income. I debated calling Dad and asking for a bailout but if I did that I knew that he would want me to come home. The money would be contingent upon that. No, I would wait a while.

I started tracking the want ads in the *International Herald Tribune* again but they had become increasingly scarce because of the holiday season. Maybe I would have to sell the newspaper on the streets after all. Still, I vowed not to give up.

Also, I resurrected one of my schemes for traveling to Africa. I spent a couple days going around to various international agencies such as CARE to see if I could get on as an overseas field representative. The man at the Paris CARE office described what they were looking for. Someone footloose who could travel to the world's trouble spots, usually Africa, to make an assessment in terms what was needed for food and medical aid and report back. He seemed interested in me but added that I had to make formal application in person in New York City. Was it worth going back to New York on the chance that I might be hired? I had to think about that.

As mentioned before, I had heard from a couple of Peace Corps volunteers in Nigeria that it was possible to simply fly down there and get hired at the local secondary schools without a teaching certificate. All I needed was proof of a college degree. I did have my college transcript with me so I could prove that.

I also answered an ad for teaching on American military bases in Europe but the Defense Department wanted certified teachers with two years of teaching experience so I never heard back.

To earn some immediate spare change, I checked out the world of movie extras. Unfortunately, no movies were being shot in Paris at that moment but Seth had an idea.

"I know a guy, a film producer and he throws a party every Friday night for people on the film scene in Paris. He also has a pipeline for getting extras jobs. You might want to check it out." Seth scribbled down the address of the producer's place, somewhere in Montparnasse.

And so it was one Friday night that Gerard and I found ourselves at a chi-chi party in a coach house in a Montparnasse courtyard. It was all very elegantly designed with a loft, a spiral metal staircase and patio glass doors that looked out onto a lighted garden and a fountain. Free wine and appetizers. I was dressed in my New York business suit. Gerard was in a new Euro suit, looking very French.

The milling women looked like off-duty models in their little black dresses. The men — mostly model handsome except for a few scruffy, behind the scene types. The host, an Anglo/Frenchman his 40s, wore a silk dressing gown with a scarf, the epitome of the Hugh Hefner cool à la Europa. Snatches of overheard conversations in French and English:

> "Why yes, my agent has a line an upcoming movie to be shot in Paris. I might have a small speaking part. Just background stuff."

> "I'm leaving for Spain tomorrow. It's only a spaghetti western, but at this time of year you can't be choosy."

> "Bah, Godard is a patsy. He doesn't push far enough with this social commentary"

Off in the next room, a movie projector whined, running off some unedited footage of a documentary on the Paris slums.

The host stroked his Van Dyke beard as Gerard hit him up for a possible dubbing job, "If a dub version of the film is going to be released in America, you need some real American accents. That's where my friend here, Al and I come in. We offer not only American accents but pure California accents as well. However, we're flexible." Gerard then handed the host his card.

"I certainly will keep it in mind," said the host stuffing the card into the front pocket of this silk dressing gown. "But right now there's nothing on the horizon."

After this little pitch, Gerard and I tried to hustle some of the female models, but they ignored us; their obvious goal was making contact with the big man producer himself. These gals stuck me as vapid creatures, skeletally thin, the result of starvation diets. Only a fat English character actress surrounded by the gay looking male model types was having a good time, loud and cheery. I joined her crowd of admirers while she held forth.

She pulled me over and gave me a fat kiss on the forehead. "Now look here, you chaps. A pleasant looking, all-American boy in his button-down business suit. What can he be doing here in evil movieland...hmm?"

"Just checking the scene out," I said. "Maybe getting some extra work."

"Do tell, ducky," she clucked.

"Chaps, do we have extra work for our American boy."

Snickers emanating from her entourage.

"Ah, I have to be going," I said backing away. "Great meeting you all."

"Ta, ta, ducky."

I grabbed my overcoat and Gerard and I split into the stormy Parisian night as she called after us. "You boys take care tonight."

So that was movieland French style. Work was possible but I would have to hang around until spring to latch onto it. It was back to the want ads.

***

The only ads that I spotted in the *Herald Tribune* for immediate employment were for sales. Sales of cars to military personnel. Sales of mutual funds to both military and civilian. Fluency in either French or German required in addition to English.

And lastly, an ad for the American Library Society: *Sell encyclopedias primarily to American families stationed in Germany. German helpful but not required. No cold calls. Leads provided. Draw against commission.*

Hmm. I reviewed my options.

No way was I going to sell cars. I didn't know anything about cars and I could not see myself as a huckster in a plaid sports coat and white buck shoes pushing automotive merchandise.

I barely knew what mutual funds were. Something about pooling a bunch of stocks together into a fund of varying degrees of risk. I wasn't a financial guy. It seemed too complicated but there was the promise of big money if successful.

Encyclopedia salesman? Maybe. I knew a fair amount about the kinds of things you looked up in encyclopedias—history, art, literature, science. Or at least, I would know more than the typical G.I. about those subjects and could probably bullshit effectively in that area. Still, being a door-to-door salesman in Germany did not immediately appeal to me. However, the ad did say leads would be provided. No cold calls. And a draw against commissions. I would have money immediately.

After a day or two of pondering my options, I sent off a resume to the American Library Society headquartered in Vaduz, Liechtenstein, care of Chuck Roberts, President. Then I waited for a response.

***

During those days of waiting, I vaguely considered other possibilities ranging from the fanciful to the terrifying. As Seth had mentioned, he was going to go on an overland trek come spring to Nepal on his way to Vietnam. He was encouraging Gerard and me to come along. "Look, fellows, you only go around once in this life. Experience the overland route to Asia as the ancients once did before it's fucked over with Holiday Inns. It's dirt cheap, about five hundred dollars. Food is provided. We go in a Land Rover with some English outfit, camp out along the way."

"Sounds grungy," I said

"Grungy, yes, at times. But think of it," he said launching off into a travelogue. "We start off tame enough, traveling through Eastern Europe to Istanbul. See the standard sights, then overland to Persia. See Tehran and the ruins of Persepolis. Next on to Afghanistan. Camp with Afgan tribesmen. Later marvel at the gates of Lahore in Pakistan. Next, stay on a houseboat in the Kashmir. Then cross into Nepal. You can trek up to sixteen thousand feet and get a close-up view of Everest. Lots of great grass in Katmandu. Then we descend back into India. Check out the holy men in the Ganges and the burning funeral pyres. Maybe a widow burning. Strange body piercings. Sexy Indian women doing weird contortions. Do the Buddha thing. Gain enlightenment. Now we are fortified for Southeast Asia. Trek through Burma; see the ruins of Pagan, hang out in Mandalay. Down to Thailand. A little relaxation in Bangkok getting our pipes cleaned and then on to Saigon where opportunity awaits for anyone who can put two words together. What do you think?"

"Uh, it's mind boggling," said Gerard. "You really plan to do all of that?"

"Sure as shit," said Seth defiantly.

"Jeez, I'd love to too," said Gerard, "but I have to stay in Paris and get my Certificate of French Studies or my parents will kill me. About all I can manage is a quick trip to Majorca or maybe the Canaries to escape this winter gloom."

"What about you, Brown?"

"Ah, let me think about it, Seth," I said, my head spinning. "I'll get back to you."

And think about it I did. Thoughts ran through my head such as, "once in a lifetime...cheap...see a hidden part of the world."

I figured I could always skip Vietnam. End the trek in Bangkok. Maybe dip down to Australia, New Zealand and the Pacific Islands. I would need more dough, probably a couple of thousand. It was hard to believe that a few months ago, I had that much money but it was gone, mostly pissed away in New York. If I had come directly to Paris, I could have swung this overland trek. So what do I do now? Borrow it from Dad? Hardly. Save it up from selling books in Nürnberg? Not likely. Doesn't matter, just go. Look at Seth. He doesn't have a dime. He earns his way along, odd jobs at various embassies. Teaches English. Writes freelance. Maybe I could do the same. A glimmer of a life of adventure. I decided to decide later.

Then there was Charlie's way of dealing with the world. Passive Charlie, the one who stayed in his room gazing at pinups and supposedly writing an American abroad novel. The only time I ever saw him perk up with interest was when Jean-Paul asked him if he wanted to see Paris at its worst and find out what might happen to Americans who stayed too long. Jean-Paul said he knew about this place called "The Valley of Death," from the medical volunteer work he had done last year when he still took medicine seriously.

Curious myself, I followed along. Jean-Paul led the way through winding back alleys of the Latin Quarter. As we wandered along, the alleys became narrower and narrower and the overhanging buildings more rundown. I felt as if I had entered a time warp and we were walking through medieval Paris. I half expected to be sloshed with a bucket of shit. Eventually, we came to a dead-end alley. Strange though, here were head shops, cafes with the smell of incense and Indian raga music echoing in the alley. And scores of sleepy young men and a scattering of women, nodding off at the curb or wandering along the alley with thousand yard stares. Many were dressed in East Indian garb, others simply in T-shirts and jeans despite the cold and the ever-present drizzle. Their bare arms were pocked with bruises up and down their length. Off in one corner, I saw a guy with a rubber tube tied around his upper arm shoot up. This place was truly Gorky's Lower Depths. As Jean-Paul noted, this was where junkies came to die.

"Don't the cops ever bust them," I asked.

"No, what for?" said Jean-Paul. "The French cop's attitude is let them kill themselves, as long as it's confined to this maze of alleys."

"Makes sense," said Charlie. "In Chicago, the cops are always busting druggies, yet it does no good. They might as well legalize it. I myself need a hit of pot or coke now and then. It's a good thing. Clears the mind. I'm glad you showed me this Jean-Paul. I feel inspired now to get on with my novel. Maybe I'll have my hero fall prey to such a life. Make a nice bitter ending. Or maybe, if I want to sell to Hollywood, he'll be redeemed after a harrowing descent into hell."

I looked at these pathetic souls, most of them English or American. Dead-enders. Yet, I knew deep down that there really wasn't much distance between them and me. All it took was the right circumstances, the right set of attitudes and bingo before you knew it you were in the gutter. Selling encyclopedias in Germany was starting to look good.

***

However, the roulette wheel of life had spun and it appeared that my number had come up. Suddenly I faced the prospect of staying in France forever. Little Anne-Marie, who had been avoiding me for a couple of weeks, showed up out of the blue at our café hangout and announced she wanted to talk to me, somewhere private.

"Oh, oh," I thought. I suggested my hotel room as I led her out of the cafe.

"Yes," she said, "I will go with you but we must not go to bed again."

"Why not?"

"You will understand," she said defensively and then she shut up refusing to talk anymore as we made our way over to Île St. Louis. We stopped briefly at Notre Dame where she went into the nave, knelt at the altar and offered up a little prayer. I stayed in the rear of the church marveling at the gothic structure with its vaulted ceiling and eerie, stain glass windows.

When we arrived at my room, I offered her a coke that was chilled from sitting on the windowsill. She sipped it while we sat staring at the rooftops and the Seine. Then after a few minutes of silence, "Now what is it? Why have you been so elusive?" I asked.

"I have had to study," she replied. "I am not a fast studier. The students here are so smart. But now I have this problem."

"Ah, what problem is that," I said sensing what was to come.

"I have missed my period for two weeks. And it is always so regular."

"Gulp. So what do you mean?"

"I might be pregnant, Allan. And you are the only one I have been with," she said starting to cry. "And we made love right in the middle of my fertile period and you did not use protection."

She was right. In the heat of passion, my three-pack condoms sat in my toiletry bag all sealed up.

"There, there now," I said trying to comfort her.

"I am so stupid," she wailed. "I fell asleep when I should have used the bidet in the bathroom."

At this point, my mind was racing. Having been through this before, I calmly said, "Anne-Marie you must get a pregnancy test to make absolutely sure before you jump to conclusions. Periods are funny things. They are delayed for many reasons. If it turns out that you are pregnant, then we will consider the options then."

"Options! What do you mean? There are no options," she said her brown eyes blazing. "I am a good Catholic. If I'm pregnant, I will have the baby. I will drop out of school, go home to Montpellier and have the baby. Maybe put it up for adoption or maybe not. Depending."

"Take it easy. Let's wait for the test results. Come on, let's relax. I said moving over to the bed, and patting the space next to me.

She looked at me, hesitated and then came over, lying down. "Will you stay with me through this?" She said looking up at me with her big brown eyes.

I melted. She was a lovely little French girl. How bad could it be? We could live in the South of France with the baby. Maybe with her parents for a while. Her father was a doctor and probably well off. I could envision a dark-eyed son speaking French. I could maybe get a job teaching English or basic writing at the American Institute in Aix that I had attended a few years earlier. I knew they hired alums. Maybe I could get into import-export in Marseille. American companies were trying to crack the French market. Maybe I could become a representative for Berdau & Company in France.

Failing that, we could return to San Francisco where I would get a straight corporate job. IBM sales. I knew she would love San Francisco. It was the favorite American city of the French and she had asked my many questions about it. All was good.

"Yes of course, I will stay with you," I said, really meaning it.

Then, magically, our clothes were off and we were under the covers. Before we knew it was over and lay there panting, but she was restless.

"I must not make the same mistake twice. I will douche."

This struck me as not being very logical, considering her alleged condition but she was up, threw on my shirt which came down to her knees and scooted off to the bathroom in the hallway. I heard water running for a few minutes and then I heard a little squeal, almost a scream. She came rushing back into the room holding her dainty little left hand out. "Look, Allan. Look. Blood. It's all coming out. Our sex must have started my period."

"Whew. What a relief," I mumbled to myself.

We lay in the bed for a while longer thinking about what the might have been. I was almost sorry. I sensed she was too. Finally, I said, "Why don't we go to the Alsatian restaurant and celebrate your freedom."

"*Bonne idée*, but I do not want to return here. You are going away, I think. I do not want to hurt anymore."

She was right. The American Library Society had written back telling me that I appeared to be a good candidate and that they wanted to interview me in Nürnberg.

"I am going to Germany. I need to make some money," I said. "But I'll be back in the spring one way or the other to see you," I promised.

"*Peut-être*," she said.

We got up and dressed and went out to a nice dinner at the Brasserie, sipping only a small glass of white Alsatian wine. I walked her back to her student dorm near the Sorbonne and gave her a kiss on the lips. We said goodbye for the moment.

"You won't forget me will you," she said, her dark brown eyes searching.

"Never," I said.

20. NÜRNBERG

On the map, it didn't seem so far to Nürnberg from Paris, about 760-kilometers or 470-miles. An easy eight to nine hours by car. However, I was not traveling by car. I was on a local, stop-and-go train and it took over fifteen hours to travel to Nürnberg. A night and a morning. This involved traveling from Paris to Strasbourg on the French border; a change of trains and then a short stretch to Karlsruhe, Germany. From there it was on to Nürnberg, located in the middle of the Federal Republic of Germany or as the Germans officially called their country: *Bundesrepublik Deutschland.*

I managed to sleep some on the Paris to Strasbourg run but after that, I just sat in the grimy second-class compartment, feeling sticky and dirty in my slacks, cotton turtleneck and topcoat. The good news was a bright penetrating sun cracked through clear blue skies at dawn. A sun I hadn't seen during my time in Paris. When I stepped off the train briefly at Karlsruhe, a sharp chill penetrated my topcoat. I bought a bratwurst, some cheese and milk from a vendor and climbed back on the train, readying my mind and body for my adventure in Germany.

I had been to Germany once before during my junior-year-abroad, visiting a girl in Heidelberg over thanksgiving weekend. I had met Ursula a few months earlier at Cap d'Antibes on the French Riviera. Alas, as it turned out, Ursula had a boyfriend in Heidelberg who hovered about during my visit. Plus, the late fall weather in Heidelberg was miserable, foggy and wet.

I spent Thanksgiving at my hotel eating goose with a group of pissed off Air Force reservists who had been activated by President Kennedy during the Berlin Wall crisis of 1961. Still, I loved the town and loved the beer and vowed someday to come back and do Germany justice. In addition, I wanted to explore the mystery of how a nation that seemed so sensible and organized could go crazy and follow a nut like Hitler. I thought I might gain some insights in Nürnberg which had been the center of the Nazi empire.

***

The train rolled into the Nürnberg train station (*Hauptbahnhof*) around eleven. I grabbed my trusty Samsonite suitcase and disembarked. Looking around, I found myself disoriented in the cavernous neo-Baroque structure. All the signs were in German. Big surprise. I had never taken German but I could make out some of the signs such as *Ausgang,* (Exit), *Eingang* (Entrance). I desperately needed a Nürnberg city map to locate a Hotel Mercure where the American Library Society President, Chuck Roberts was staying.

I changed a hundred dollars' worth of traveler checks into Deutsche Marks, had another bratwurst and then picked up a cheap tourist map from a newsstand that showed the highlights of Nürnberg. But alas, there was no indication of Hotel Mercure. So I gave up and got into a cab in front of the station.

"Hotel Mercure," I said. The cabbie, a Turkish looking fellow, looked at me and shrugged. He then proceeded to drive two blocks and there it was. Hotel Mercure. I felt foolish. I paid him four marks ($1.00) and got out.

Hotel Mercure was a cozy looking place in the German Alpine style. At the reception desk, a well-coiffed woman in her forties spoke to me in English. "Oh yes, Herr Brown. We have been expecting you. You have room 203. A nice room looking out on the street. It will be forty marks a night. You are booked for a week."

Ten bucks a night! That was steep for me with only a $200.00 left. But at this point what choice did I have. I shrugged and lugged my suitcase up to my room. What a change after Paris! The room was sunny, bright and freshly painted. A big fluffy comforter covered the queen size bed and pictures of Bavarian scenes lined the wall. After all, Nürnberg was part of Bavaria (Middle Franconia) although the Alps were far to the south. This room would do nicely.

I grabbed a large fluffy towel and checked out the bathroom down the hall. There a clean, spotless white tile tub with bear claw legs waited for me. In a flash, I was out of my grungy travel clothes and soaking in the tub, wallowing in the height of luxury. Boy, unlike the French, these Germans knew how to do bathrooms.

After a thorough soaking, I returned to my room and fell asleep on top of my comforter for a couple of hours. When I awoke around three, I went downstairs to have the concierge ring Chuck Robert's room.

"Oh, I am sorry, Herr Brown. I cannot disturb Herr Roberts. He is resting. He left a message for you to meet him in the bar at 5 p.m."

I returned to my room to read and dress more appropriately for my impending job interview. I unpacked my suit, hung it in the closet, hoping the wrinkles would fall out.

At 5 p.m. sharp, I entered the bar all spiffed out in my New York finest, ready to begin my sales career. A slim, middle-aged man from one end of the bar looked up. Dressed in an impeccable custom-tailored German business suit, he stared at me through his steel-rimmed glasses. He smiled and motioned me over. "You must be Mr. Brown. Chuck Roberts," he said holding out his hand. I shook it with a firm but not too tight grip.

"Glad to meet you, Mr. Roberts."

"Chuck. Call me Chuck," he said in a flat Midwestern accent. Did you have a good trip from Paris?"

"Ah, not bad. Long."

"Yes, it is far. But what a city. It's been a while since I have been to Paris. So tied up here in Germany, you know." He smiled, flashing a gold eyetooth, apparently a sign of fashion and affluence.

"Would you care for some good, local beer?"

"Certainly."

After the beer was served in a big pewter mug, we went over to a table and Roberts began an informal interview starting with the standard question, "So, tell me about yourself."

I began by telling him I was from California, a Berkeley graduate who had been visiting friends in Paris and then decided to try working in Europe for a while, hopefully gaining some experience that would stand me in good stead when I returned to the States.

"Yes, yes," he nodded. "Sales is sales no matter where. If you develop sound sales skills here, you can sell anything from books to mainframe computers. It doesn't matter. I myself like the small-scale stuff like encyclopedias. I make a good living here in Germany. And you can too. You have a nice appearance and are well spoken but definitely American. That will go over well with our primary market, the American military. By the way, can you go out tonight on a training run?"

"Uh, yes, sure," I said, not sure. I hadn't expected to start right away.

"I know it might seem kind of sudden," he said, "but it's the best way to find out if you are right for the job and the job is right for you. You will only be observing."

"Sounds good."

He continued, "Another job applicant is due to arrive, a Negro fellow from New York but very cultured. He should do well. And of course, my main salesman, Mike. This guy is a wonder. He sometimes sells more than I do. And that is saying a lot."

We sipped on beer and munched on some pretzels and cheese appetizers while Chuck filled me in on his background.

"Yes. Life is funny. Here I was a kid, minding my own business in Kansas City trying to go to college when the Army drafted me at the tail end of World War II. They tested me, decided that I was good in languages. I did have a family background in German. The Army gave me a quickie course in advanced German and sent me over here for the occupation. I did my two years, mostly in civil affairs. I had a great time. The women here were hungry. Boy, what you could get for a pair of nylons! "

"I can imagine," I nodded.

"Yes, well, I decided I liked Germany. Kansas City was dull by comparison. So upon my discharge, I enrolled in the University of Nürnberg in economics, paid for by the G.I. bill. Of course, the cost of the university was zero and living was cheap. I lived like a king on the G.I. bill."

"However, after a couple of years, I became bored with student life, dropped out, went to work for the European Post Exchange as a buyer. This agency supplies all the PXs in Europe. I bought a nice little sports car and zoomed around Europe doing business for the Post Exchange Service."

"Eventually, I went out on my own selling cars, insurance, whatever to the G.I.s and I did rather well. Five years ago, I got the exclusive franchise on the World Knowledge Encyclopedia. I created the company I call the American Library Society. It's a take off on the American Library Association"

Clever I thought.

"Although, ALS is officially incorporated in Vaduz, Liechtenstein, the whole German market is mine, plus Greece and Italy. I have access to all the military bases. This has been a real gold mine. Education is king in the military. Anything that caters to education is a surefire seller like encyclopedias. Now, I'm trying to develop Greece. I plan to spend most of the winter there. Mike will be in charge up here in Nürnberg. You'll be working mostly with him. So that's about it."

About this time, Mike and the black fellow showed up. Mike was a stocky guy with a G.I. crew cut and a broken nose. Although he was wearing

German civvies, he still looked military.

"How you guys doing," said Mike with a crooked grin. Roberts introduced me to Mike who gave me a vigorous handshake. "Great to see you, Al. Christ knows we could use some help here pushing these sets. Christmas season and all. The pocketbooks are open. Except we can't guarantee delivery by Christmas. But we can bullshit around that."

"I'll do my best," I answered.

"Sure as shit you will do your best. Saw your resume. Impressive. College degree and all. Look good too. You'll be a hit with the officers' wives. They call the shots."

Meanwhile, the black fellow hovered in the background. Mike bought him forward.

"Al, I'd like to introduce you to Woodrow. He's a New York cat. Been around. Smooth. He'll do well too. Hit those nigger apartments. He'll have them eating out of his hand."

"Now, now Mike. Don't be so crude," chided Roberts. "Woodrow is a gentleman and could probably teach you a few things on how to conduct yourself in polite society."

"Ahem…" said Woodrow, clearing his throat. " No offense taken. Mike is a product of his environment. But I'm sure his salesman instincts are correct. I will probably do well with the black G.I.s. I may be an uptown Negro, but I can talk the talk with the best of them."

Woodrow had a polished, New England accent. He was a startlingly handsome guy, in an impeccable Brooks Brothers suit. As I was to learn, Woodrow had been a male model and sometime gigolo in Manhattan. Which sex he catered to was a mystery but after I got to know him, I decided it was probably both.

As Woodrow told us later, "God, you don't know how demanding my clients can be, especially those Fifth Avenue bitches. Perform all-night or you're off their list. Three hundred dollars a session. But my god, it's hard. I have to take vitamins and drink power drinks all day to keep it up."

Woodrow said he finally had to escape. He was burned out with the hustler scene and needed a vacation but like me blew most of his money in Paris having a high time and spotted the same *Herald Tribune* ad as I did. His main concern in Europe was eating healthily. As he said, "My, my. I can't do this German food. It's too heavy and greasy. I'll just haunt the farmer markets on the Hauptmarkt for my veggies."

Chuck drained his beer and carefully put it down. "OK, fellows let's go to work. Mike and I'll show you how to do it. I thought we would hit Fürth.

There's a little U.S. military apartment complex out there that I haven't milked for about six months. It should be fertile ground. If we are successful, I'll treat you all to dinner."

Outside, we piled into Chuck's big Mercedes and he took off, wheels squealing. Woodrow and I sunk back into the plush leather seating, as Chuck cut through city streets and barreled down the highway to Fürth ten kilometers away.

***

It was pitch black as we rolled into the Army apartment complex. No security, no gates. Wide open to the public at large. The three-story brick buildings were a sterile looking bunch with tiny windows and narrow stairwells. Chuck explained that these were the enlisted personnel apartments. We split into two groups. Mike and Woodrow went off to one building, Chuck and I to another. It was so dark and forbidding inside that I wondered if anyone would open their doors to two strangers on their stairwell. Chuck was unfazed, as if he was expecting a big welcome wherever he went.

"The first rule of door-to-door salesmanship is getting your foot in the door," instructed Chuck. "Once you get inside an apartment, the rest is easy. If someone slams a door in your face, just move on. It's all a numbers game. Hit enough doors and you will get in somewhere."

Knock. Knock. Knock. A door opened a crack. A sergeant looking type in fatigues and slippers peered out. I could hear screaming kids in the background. A likely prospect.

"What can I do for you guys," he said.

"Good evening Sir. My colleague and I are conducting a survey on the reading habits of American servicemen and their families serving overseas. Might we come in?" said Chuck in an authoritative voice.

The soldier, slightly befuddled and used to kowtowing to authority figures, paused and then said, "Yeah sure. Hon, we have two gentlemen here taking a reading survey."

We entered the small apartment cluttered with toys and two little boys drawing with crayons in the corner and a TV blaring. An overweight bleached blonde came in from the kitchen wiping her hands on an apron. "Reading survey, huh? That's easy. We don't read anything except fan and hunting magazines."

Chuck, seeing an opening, remarks, "What about your children. They must be learning to read in school?"

"Ah, I suppose," said the woman.

"May we sit down and ask you a few questions."

"Sure."

Both the sergeant and his wife dutifully sat down on the couch. Chuck and I sat across from them on dining room chairs. Chuck went down a checklist of questions asking what the couple read. Of course, the main purpose of this so-called "survey" was to determine if there was a set of encyclopedias in the house. Finding no evidence of an encyclopedia, Chuck launched into the second part of his spiel stressing how important it was for a child's education to have a good reference work in the house. Both parents nodded in agreement. He then segued into a special offer that the American Library Society was making to inspire kids to read—a free paperback mini-encyclopedia which he gave them. The parents thumbed through it. It was a brightly colored mini-reference work with a lot of pictures and not much text, designed for little kids. The parents seemed to like it.

"This is just one of a series we are offering free in conjunction with a full set of encyclopedias at a very reasonable price. Chuck handed the parents a composite encyclopedia book of World Knowledge that appeared to me to be a cheap knock-off of the *World Book Encyclopedia.* Both parents looked through it, nodding their heads in approval. Chuck closed in for the kill.

"So now just imagine how great and accessible this set would be in your home. Not only for your children but for yourself as well,"

"Yeah, it looks nice," said the sergeant. "Probably better than sitting around all day watching TV."

His wife nodded. "How much would something like this be?"

"I'm glad you asked that question," said Chuck pulling out his order book. "It's a small monthly outlay of seven dollars a month for twenty-four months with only a twenty-five dollar down payment now. We will take check or cash. If you order tonight I can get you the set at a discount and we may be able to have it delivered in time for Christmas."

The sergeant looked at his wife and then at Chuck. "We don't have the cash right now. How about a check?"

"Say, never mind the check. Why don't you give me whatever cash you have on hand now," said Chuck, all smiles.

"Well we do have is our grocery money, about fifteen dollars," the woman said pulling out her purse. "I can cash a check tomorrow."

"That will do just fine. My colleague, Allan here, will collect the rest tomorrow," said Chuck already writing out a receipt and filling out an order form before the couple could change their minds. He stuffed the cash into his pocket. Then got up and bid them goodnight. Total time elapsed for this sale: twenty minutes.

"Not bad for starters, but we have to keep moving," said Chuck as he headed up another flight of stairs.

Two hours later, Chuck had sold four sets of encyclopedias and had about a hundred dollars cash in his pocket plus a check.

I was amazed. Chuck was like a magician, conjuring up rabbits out of thin air or in this case, cash. His presentation was very smooth, almost hypnotic. He knew how to talk to enlisted men and their wives. A couple of wives were German, and Chuck charmed the socks off them with his flawless German in a Nürnberg dialect no less. In addition, he knew how to play on parental guilt. All parents no matter how poorly educated want their kids to have a good education. As Chuck presented it to them, a set of encyclopedias would give the kids a leg up on other kids in school, a jump-start on their education.

On the way back to his Mercedes, Chuck told me the cash collected was to be kept by whoever sold the books. This money was not sent in with the book orders. It was in effect, part of the salesman's 30-percent commission. It was, as he explained, "eating and sleeping money." The rest of the commission would be paid to the salesman at the end of the month. What Chuck did not say, as I was to later learn from Mike, was that Chuck also collected another 30-percent on each set sold by any salesman. So essentially, there was an over a 60-percent markup on each set sold.

When we met up with Mike and Woodrow, they too had made several sales. Overall, it was a profitable night and all done in a few hours. It was only 10 p.m.

We climbed back into Chuck's Mercedes and barreled back to Nürnberg and Hotel Mercure where we dined on wiener schnitzel and a liter of fine Bavarian beer. Day one in Nürnberg was over. I was feeling confident that I could hack this sales game.

***

I spent the next day in my room going over the promotional and sales materials that Chuck had given me on the *World Knowledge Encyclopedia*. The set was certainly not the *Encyclopedia Britannica,* nor the *World Book*. But it wasn't bad. In addition to an adequate text, the artwork was colorful and the photos many, something that was attractive to kids and their parents. I felt I could sell this in good conscience.

That evening we went out again to the same complex but this time we all split up. I was on my own. It might have been beginners luck, but that night I sold three sets of the encyclopedia and had seventy-five dollars cash in my pocket. It was easy. Like taking candy from a baby.

First of all, the soldiers' families were glad to see me. As one described it, it was like a visit from home. All they ever saw in Germany were military types and German civilians. An American civilian was a rarity. And all they wanted to talk about was the U.S. and what was going in sports and politics. I kept abreast of currents events and sports via the *Herald Tribune*.

We would sit in the living room and chitchat for a while sipping coffee or pop. I had decided to drop the phony reader survey bit and would begin talking directly about college and its importance. This hit a nerve. Most soldiers had enlisted in the Army right after high school or had been drafted. But after a few years in, they saw the importance of education. And to be fair, the Army stressed that too, offering college-level courses either in classroom settings or via the University of Maryland correspondence courses. So when it came to their kids, it was an easy sell. Add to that the spirit of the Christmas season. Christmas was only a week away. So the pocketbooks were open.

My sales spree went on for the next week, right up until the day before Christmas. I was making three and four sales a night. Mike and Chuck, five or six. Woodrow was doing at least three. It turned out he was selling to both white and black servicemen. We expanded our sales territories to include other military complexes such as Erlangen and Schwabach, nearby suburbs of Nürnberg. We had cash in our pockets.

Still, although I had "eating and sleeping" money, I was not getting ahead. It was all coming in and going right out. And it was a long wait for my commission check. The main problem was Hotel Mercure. It was too expensive. I started looking around for cheaper digs. Eventually, I found a decent place more in the center of town, Pension Avalon on the Königstrasse, for about half the price with maid service twice a week. Right across the street were several cheap eateries. I moved into my new room a few days before Christmas.

***

After I moved to Pension Avalon, I spent several days playing tourist and exploring the town. The days were bright and sunny but cold, somewhere in the high 20s. With a sweater and a topcoat, I managed to stay warm roaming around but I wrote my parents asking them to send my down ski parka because I knew it could become much colder in this region of Germany.

My first stop was the Christmas Market in the Hauptmarkt Square, a square dominated by the *Frauenkirche*, a 14th-century church with an impressive mechanical clock. This contraption had seven courtly figures rotating out of their enclave and sounding the chimes at various times of the day. The square itself was filled with booths and stalls selling every imaginable Christmas item from chocolates to toys, to candles, to ornaments.

The food stalls featured such local specialties as bratwurst, gingerbread, and mulled wine along with the freshest fruit around. I gorged myself on oranges and apples imported from somewhere in the Middle East. I ate delicious bratwurst while marveling at the intricacies of all the mechanical toy contraptions the Germans were famous for constructing. I spent many happy hours here at the Christmas Market especially after dark when it glittered under a light mantle of snow like a fantastic medieval wonderland.

For an overall look at the old city center, I hiked up the hill to the Kaiserburg, the local imperial castle, and wandered around its battlements. The earliest part of the castle dated back to the eleventh century and featured the Round Tower which from the top offered even more dramatic views of the city. This castle had hosted many imperial meetings throughout its history. At one time it was occupied by Frederick Barbarossa, the Holy Roman Emperor in the 12th-century.

Being at the center of four major trade routes during the middle ages, Nürnberg was chock full of such history much of it set off by the Pegnitz River which wandered through the old section of town, spanned here and there by charming covered bridges and lined with half-timbered houses. Everywhere, you turned were quaint rathskellers, restaurants, shops, and municipal buildings adorned with historical murals and sculptures depicting the glory days of Nürnberg.

A casual observer would never suspect that most of the old city had been destroyed in World War II. The city center had been lovingly restored since, although, around the edges, you could still see the rubble of bombed out buildings. Still, you could get a sense of the city's medieval past, even though it was primarily a reconstructed illusion. Of course, a dark shadow hovered over all of this—the shadow of Nazism. A shadow that still lingered in late 1964, almost twenty years after the end of World War II.

21. ARMY HOTEL

Soon it was Christmas Eve in Nürnberg and I was alone. Mike was with his family. Chuck had split to Munich to see a girlfriend. Woodrow was off somewhere. I wasn't sure how he would be celebrating Christmas and didn't want to find out. No, I would have to get through this alone. My choices were sitting in my room, reading or maybe sleeping. Or I could go out to dinner somewhere nice, but cheap. Also somewhere where I might run into other homesick Americans. There was one such place: The Army Hotel near the train station. Its official name was the Bavarian-American Hotel but everyone called it the Army Hotel.

This hotel catered to military and American civilians who were connected to the U.S. government. Theoretically, anyone could stay here but there were never any rooms available. The hotel set aside most of its rooms for long-term stays and for military transients. It was a big barn of the place, about six stories high, done up in a vaguely Bavarian style. But despite the Germanic décor, it was American through and through. Here, one could have a decent hamburger and milkshake. Here one could quaff American mixed drinks like Manhattans and Martinis. Here one could drink American beer without feeling guilty. One could also listen to the latest news from back home and the most popular American radio shows courtesy of the Armed Forces Network which broadcast from studios in the hotel basement. The hotel also had a spacious dining room that was currently featuring the classic American Christmas dinner—turkey with all the trimmings as well as baked ham.

I suited up and made my way over to the hotel around six. The dining room was jammed but the maitre d' said I could be seated immediately if I was willing to share a table. I glanced around. It was mostly military types out of uniform but with the tell-tail G.I. haircuts. I shrugged. Why not. I had been in the Army. I could relate. So I was seated at big round table with four single guys, all tough looking mutts. I introduced myself as Allan Brown and they nodded and introduced themselves by their first names only. Initially, they were polite but distant. One wanted to know if I was in the military. I told him no, that I was in Nürnberg selling encyclopedias to the military.

"Encyclopedias?" said one, thinking it was a joke.

"Yeah, a set of ten books."

"No shit. G.I.s buy encyclopedias?"

"Well," I responded, "as you probably know, many troops are here with their families and they want to lead a normal family life as far as possible, so they think an encyclopedia will be good for their kids."

One thick neck type, narrowed his eyes and said, "You have a clearance to get onto these bases?"

"Of course, although no one ever checks. Here," I said handing him an ID card that Chuck had given me introducing me as an employee of the American Library Society.

He looked at it and then handed it back. "I guess anything goes now."

Another guy, looked me over in my spiffy suit, "So, where you are from."

"California, Bay Area," I answered breezily.

"How did you wind up in Nürnberg?"

"I was visiting friends in Paris and ran out of money so I answered an ad to sell encyclopedias here."

"Just like that?"

"Yeah, just like that."

"You look like a college boy."

"That's right. I went to Berkeley."

"No, shit," said the suspicious one. "That commie school."

"Only a few of us are Commies," I joked. That went over like a lead balloon.

"Ever do time in the service?" asked another.

"Sure did. I'm in the Army Reserves. I was in the propaganda wing, broadcast specialist."

"Nice duty," said one raising his brow.

I went on to explain what I had done in the Army, including my time at the Presidio which they acknowledged was their favorite Army base on U.S. soil. After a few minutes of my recitation of my brief military experience, they decided I was OK. By this time our food had arrived, turkey again with all the trimmings. We dug into it along with several half liters of German beer. One of the brighter guys, now feeling no pain, began to wax on how great military life was, especially what he was doing.

"Lots of opportunity in the Army. It's not all grunt work. Like, take this unit. We go around the world and train police and armies of various countries in the arts of war. We show them how to contain the communist elements within their country."

"Like Vietnam?"

"Vietnam is nothing. We're up to eyeballs training troops how to deal with guerrilla warfare in South America, especially Columbia and Bolivia. Now we're heading down to Africa. A lot of the rulers want to make sure they have the military know-how to keep in power and rid their countries of the commie rebels. We live well in these joints. Great combat pay, usually great digs except when we are out in the field. Nice women. Real sex machines. It's a great life. Of course, we're all single. No time for wives or kids or anything like that. Maybe later."

"So you guys are part of the Green Berets?" I asked.

"Shit no. Those guys are pansies compared to what we do. Our unit takes the cream of the Green Berets and other elite units and trains them specifically for these special assignments. Officially, we don't exist," he laughed. "But then I shouldn't be telling you this. But what the fuck, it's Christmas Eve."

Secret Cold War warriors, I mused. A shadow Army. What would President Johnson think of next?

My dinner finished and tired of hearing about their macho gung-ho Army life, I excused myself and wandered into the bar and lounge for an after-dinner drink.

***

It was all very mellow in the half-filled bar. A pianist in the lounge tinkled out Christmas songs. A tree in the corner sparkled with ornaments and lights.

I was a sipping a cognac minding my own business when I noticed a blonde at the end of the bar by herself, swaying to the music, half-smiling. As I glanced over there, she smiled and nodded. I raised my drink and wished her a merry Christmas. She did the same. Emboldened I moved over to the stool next to her.

"Want company?" I asked.

"Sure, have a seat," she said in an American accent.

"Are you in the military?" I inquired, somewhat stupidly because it was obvious she wasn't.

"No just killing time between trains."

"Where are you headed?"

"Oh, I don't know exactly. I thought I would wander around Eastern Europe for a while and wind up in Greece to visit my father," she said swishing her long blonde hair back. It fell over her shoulders and down her black turtleneck sweater that showed off her full, ample figure. She was a bit hefty but in a pleasant Rubenesque way.

"Ah, are you Greek?"

"Not at all," she said ordering another Martini & Rossi. "I'm basically Scandinavian, originally from Minnesota but I've lived all over the world. My father is a diplomat, right now assigned to Athens. I'm on Christmas break from a Vassar program in London."

She introduced herself as Cybil and seemed a very self-possessed chick. After all, as I learned, she was traveling on her own. For some reason, she was late getting to Athens but she said her father and mother were divorced and he didn't care about Christmas. She would get there eventually.

I finished my cognac and bought another round. We moved over to a table and listened to the Christmas piano music. We talked about this and that.

She said she had spotted me immediately at the bar and knew that I wasn't a military type. She decided on the spot that she would be friendly. Just how friendly, I was soon to discover.

"Say, why don't you stay over in Nürnberg for a day or two?" I said. "I can show you around. It's an interesting little town."

"Well, I would love to see the Christmas Market?" she said with a sly smile and a tug on her long blonde hair. "Say, do you know a good but cheap hotel where I can stay tonight?"

"I have a good idea," I said.

***

We spent Christmas Eve, Christmas day and the next day mostly in bed at my pension. It was all one big carnal blur but I do recall we went out a couple of times for dinner and a quick look around the Christmas Market, the castle, a Rathskeller or two. Other times, we soaked in the bathtub down the hall to recuperate from our labors. I was amazed at her energy. She bordered on fat but still was nicely proportioned with silky, smooth skin. Very fair all over.

By the end of day three, Sunday, I was exhausted and sore. She was finally winding down too. I think she sensed that our libidinal binge was waning. So that evening after a dinner out, Cybil announced she had to get going. She wanted to make a 10 p.m. train to Prague, spend a day or two there and then head down to Athens through Yugoslavia. She asked if I would accompany her to the station.

"Sure, I said, "Let's drink to our chance encounter."

"Yeah, just a couple of ships in the night," she said lightly, but also a little sadly.

"Ships in the night," I repeated.

We clicked wine glasses. She wrote out her address in London and her home address in Minneapolis and made me promise to write her. She said she might stop in Nürnberg on the way back to London.

We went back to my room which had been destroyed by our rutting. No maid service over the long weekend. I helped Cybil pack up and we took the tram to the train station. There, I waited with her until her train arrived and then kissed her goodbye. Once aboard she turned and blew me another kiss as the train moved on out the station. So much for ships in the night.

Je baise. Je m'en vais.

22. NAZI GHOSTS

I awoke late Monday morning to a knock on my door. Shit! It was eleven. Still exhausted from my long weekend with Cybil, I slowly got up, threw on my topcoat which I used as a bathrobe and opened the door. It was Ulla, my maid. I let her in and plopped back down on my bed. She took one look at the room, shook her head, and said in her broken English, "Herr Brown, this room is kaput. You must leave while I clean it up."

She bent down and picked up a bobby pin off the floor, carefully laying it on the dresser. Then she picked a long blonde hair off my lipstick-stained pillow. She said nothing, just smiled. I got up, dressed and left Ulla to do her work.

Ulla was an interesting person. Rather pleasant looking with a nice spirit. She was about twenty-years-old and she told me that she was an American Citizen.

"An American citizen?" I asked puzzled. "How is it that you are an American citizen?"

"My father was an American soldier and he made a baby with my mother who was German."

"No kidding."

"*Ja*, here I show you my passport." She proudly pulled an American passport out of her satchel. "My father left when the war was over and my mother raised me. Sometimes, he sends money."

"So they never married?"

"No, it was not possible. She was, as you say, busy with other men."

"Oh," I said not wanting to go further. Still, Ulla always wanted to talk to me about America. In fact, she invited me to come to her house and meet her mother and her stepfather for a New Year's Day dinner. Curious and feeling sorry for her, I said I would.

In passing, she had mentioned that her stepfather was a cripple, wounded on the Eastern Front and that he had been a sergeant in the Waffen-Schutzstaffel, better known as the SS. That little bit of information was a further enticement for me to meet Ulla's parents.

***

Christmas in Germany was a weeklong affair. Everybody seemed to be on holiday. Chuck was still in Munich. Mike, Woodrow and I went out several times to nearby Army bases in Erlangen and Fürth, but made few sales. I sold only four sets of encyclopedias for the whole week. Those who were home were not in a buying mood. Most had blown their money prior to Christmas. As a result, I had time on my hands. So I spent the days wandering around Nürnberg and its outskirts soaking up its more recent history.

Like everyone, I had seen the old newsreels and documentaries of the Nazis on parade through the streets of Nürnberg with banners flying, crowds cheering, "*Sieg Heil*" filling the air. Hitler standing in his motorcar with a stiff, comical salute and a silly Charlie Chaplin mustache. The Nürnberg rallies had been an annual weeklong event for several years in the 1930s, elaborately staged and at one point, filmed by Leni Riefenstahl in *Triumph of the Will*.

So why was Nürnberg chosen for these events? After all, Hitler and his gang hung out in Munich during the twenties and when he came into power in 1933, he operated from Berlin. Historians say Hitler chose Nürnberg because it was thought to be the spiritual heart of the Fatherland. Also, the Nazis had the bedrock support of the people here, although the locals to this day still deny it. It was here that the Franconian Party Chief Julius Streicher published his anti-Semitic newspaper *Der Stürmer* and who later promoted the enactment of the Nürnberg Laws in 1935 depriving Jews of their rights as citizens. These laws later became the legal rationale in the campaign to exterminate the Jews.

It was precisely because Nürnberg was the symbol of Nazi power that the Allies chose it for the location of the Nürnberg Trials, trials that took place in the Palace of Justice on Fürther Strasse on the edge of town. It was here that the surviving head Nazis such as Von Ribbentrop, Keitel, Jodl and Speer were tried. It was here that Hermann Goring committed suicide in prison before he could be tried.

One day I took the tram out to the gingerbread Palace of Justice and wandered around its endless hallways. One would never have guessed that the infamous trials took place here. There might have historical plaques somewhere, but I didn't see them. Unbeknownst to me, Room 600 on the top floor was where the actual trial took place. As far as I could tell, the Palace of Justice on that cold wintery day was simply a busy, officious place housing the offices of the U.S. Military's European Exchange System and other administrative offices.

On another day, I wandered through the western section of the old city near the wall. This area still had stretches of rubble and was still undergoing reconstruction, although some of it had been purposely left as a reminder of war's destructive powers. Surveying the ruins, I felt as if the Allied bombing runs were yesterday. Here and there, single walls stood like sentinels, silhouetted against the blank, winter sky. Window openings looked out on nothing. Chimneys with no buildings. Entrances to rooms that had long vanished. It was a surreal, Salvador Dali landscape. All that was missing were the watches with broken hands or the melting timepieces warped by the heat of some unseen conflagration. Indeed, some sections were still off limits with signs that there was unexploded ordinance about.

Nearby was the newly opened Holocaust Museum of Nürnberg. This was a low-lying structure built almost like a bunker. Jewish groups had financed the deal, thinking a memorial to their people in the city where their persecution began would be a fitting tribute. The current city fathers of Nürnberg could hardly refuse. The museum featured mostly photomurals of starving Jews, SS guards with vicious looking dogs and short film clips of piles of dead bodies, piles of gold teeth, metal rim glasses and jewelry. Then there were the poignant artifacts—yellow Star of David patches and armbands, Jewish identity cards, ration cards, pieces of tattered clothing and shoes.

Most Germans at the end of the war claimed they had no knowledge of the extermination camps. The common refrain was: "We had no idea what Hitler and the SS were doing. We knew that our Jewish neighbors had disappeared, but we thought they were being deported out of the country or perhaps to work camps for their safety."

Of course, the city officials in various towns, including Nürnberg, had no qualms about taking over Jewish property once their neighbors had disappeared.

As the CBS wartime correspondent, Howard K. Smith described in his book, *Last Train from Berlin*, most Germans barely noticed these disappearances in 1940 and 1941. They were too busy living high on the booty and riches confiscated from the captured countries of Poland, Czechoslovakia, France, Holland and Austria. All was well until the German defeats on the Eastern Front. Then it was crunch time for the Nazi regime and the German people. The war had come home.

***

A few days later, I took the tram out to the Luitpoldhain, a municipal park in the southeastern part of the city. This was the location of the infamous Nazi Party Rally Grounds or as it was known locally Zeppelin Field. It was a dazzlingly bright but frigid day. Well-bundled children played on the crumbling concrete steps of the neo-classical stadium and old men sat in their overcoats blinking in the sun. This was where many of the most extravagant Nazi processions were held with Hitler perched high on the reviewing stand.

I climbed the steep stairs to the reviewing stand and stood where Hitler once stood gazing out over the parade grounds that went on forever. I could almost see and hear the Nazi multitudes goose-stepping their way to an illusory glory. At that time in the late 1930s, Germany believed itself invincible.

At one end of the parade ground were chunky, bunker type buildings that had apparently housed offices and living quarters for the participants in the rallies. I wandered through these concrete quarters, now dank, deserted and full of graffiti, trying to imagine what it had been like here during the war years. I envisioned Nazis bureaucrats scurrying back and forth, up and down the long concrete hallways, armed with documents and papers, trying to keep everything on schedule. The Nazis were very good record keepers which later provided a damning paper trail for Allied prosecutors. You could almost hear sounds of clacking typewriters and shouts of "Sieg Heil" echoing in the halls.

Before I left, I gazed at the uncompleted Kongressbau off in the distance. Designed by Hitler's favorite architect, Albert Speer, this was to be a civic hall patterned after the Roman coliseum. Speer's plans had called for a vast roof with no underpinning structure stretching over an interior court where fifty thousand people could assemble. This half-completed project, situated on the banks of a frozen lake, perhaps best summarized the delusional nature of the Nazi regime, a regime which predicted a thousand year reign but which in fact crumbled only after only twelve harrowing years of Nazi excesses.

***

New Year's Day, I showed up in my tweed jacket, tie and slacks at the apartment of Ulla's parents on the outskirts of Nürnberg. I was bearing a bottle of Rhine wine and some Belgian chocolates that had set me back forty marks ($10.00), money that I could ill afford to spend. Ulla was looking very pretty in a black and white lace dress. Her mother, now a faded beauty, was fixed up in a splotchy blonde way. The stepfather had made an effort, wearing a tie knotted around an ancient white dress shirt and a pair of dark pants but it was hard to tell because he was confined to a wheelchair. He had a dark complexion with stringy black hair and a twisted face with a jagged scar running down the right side. This guy looked like he had been through a lot. Ulla had told me he did not work but rather lived on disability payments from the German government.

Ulla introduced me. Mom nodded and smiled. Herr Müller, the stepfather, held his hand out to shake. We sat in the living room which had a view of the city off in the distance. Still, it was a rather modest high-rise apartment with only two bedrooms, a kitchen and one bathroom as far as I could tell. The dining room table had been set up in the living room. A large black and white TV was in the corner, showing a soccer game with the sound turned down.

The mother spoke some English. However, Herr Müller was nearly fluent, although rusty. As he explained, "I worked for the Americans in the Occupation. I learn much English there. They say they need us Nürnbergers to show them how to make Nürnberg run."

"How to make Nürnberg run?" I repeated, puzzled.

"Ja. When General George Patton's Third Army shows up in Nürnberg, we think it is all over. But no. Big surprise. Patton's officers want to use our Nazi know-how running Nürnberg and other Bavarian cities. Patton says now that the war with Germany is over, Russians are the real enemy. Of course, he gets into trouble for saying that and for the way he treats the Jews. And Eisenhower kicks him out. Later, Patton die in a car accident. Many Germans think he is killed by U.S. Army."

Herr Müller went on to say he had nothing but admiration for the Americans. "Thank God, the Americans got to Nürnberg first. If not, we are kaput like *Die Deutschen* across the border," he said waving one hand towards the picture window, facing east.

During the course of the afternoon, we sipped on aperitifs and then sat down at the dining room table and feasted on a delicious roast goose with all the trimmings—cabbage, dumplings, sauerkraut and various relishes and my Rhine wine. I complemented Frau Müller on her tasty meal. Ulla sat demurely by, saying very little but beaming now and then as her stepfather continued to praise the Americans.

"President Kennedy was a good man. It is not good he was assassinated. He knew what Russians were up to. He stood up to them over the Berlin Wall. But he was smart. He didn't make the mistake Hitler did by going to war with them."

Since he obviously wanted to talk about the war, I asked him how he was wounded.

"Bah, it was bad chance. Shrapnel but it did a lot of damage. It sliced my face and cut my body and hurt my back. After I was healed, it wasn't bad but later, years go by and my spine goes kaput and now I cannot walk."

Ulla began to talk now, feeling a little tipsy, explaining how Herr Müller had saved her and her mother from poverty, taking in a child who had another father.

"He is a good man," said Ulla. "He is very kind to us and very generous."

The mother nodded, tears in her eye. Then she said in broken English. "Ulla is an American. She go visit America someday, maybe to live."

"Oh, oh," I thought. Here it comes. They want me to take Ulla off their hands. She was attractive and sweet but a little rough around the edges. Not my type. Too uneducated for me, really too German despite her American citizenship. Nevertheless, after dinner, I invited her to a movie. She happily accepted.

We said goodbye to the parents and took the tram into the old city where we saw *Schick mir keine Blumen* (Send Me No Flowers) with Rock Hudson and Doris Day, all dubbed in German. Ulla loved it. Doris Day was big star in Germany. Ulla told me Doris Day was really German. Later, I learned she was right. Doris Day's original name was Doris von Kappelhoff, of German extraction, born in Cincinnati, Ohio.

After the movie, we wandered through the Christmas Market; then I kissed Ulla on her cheek and put her on the tram back to her apartment after thanking her for the wonderful New Year's dinner and silently grateful for allowing me an insight into the mind of one old German Nazi.

23. NEW YEAR '65

So here it was: *Neunzehnhundertfünfundsechzig*. What the hell is that? That's "1965" in German. And that's the problem with German. It takes too long to say anything. *Neunzehn-hundert-fünf-und-sechzig* is five words run together or twenty-nine letters long. "Nineteen-sixty-five" is only three separate words or seventeen letters long in English. So you see, German is a very clumsy language compared to English but as I discovered not without its charm. Since it appeared that I would be spending some time here in Nürnberg, I enrolled in a conversational German course at the University Extension. Among the twenty or so students were American G.I.s, American businessmen and an assortment of foreign students. The teacher was a German graduate student, a very sharp, no-nonsense fräulein who launched right into the language.

"Guten Tag"
"Guten Abend"
"Sprechen Sie Deutsch?"
"Wieviel kostet es?"
"Ein Bier, bitte."

And so on. Simple stuff, but it made it easier to get around and order beer or dinner.

But back to the point at hand. Here it was 1965, half-way through the decade of the 1960s and I was sitting in my pension in Nürnberg without a clue. Where had the time gone? It seemed like yesterday that I was splayed out on the family front lawn on New Year's Eve, a drunken frat boy, celebrating the dawn of the sixties decade. Eisenhower was still president. Crew cuts and pegger pants were still in fashion. The cars still had big fins and everybody was dancing the Twist with Chubby Checker. I had two more years of college ahead of me. Good times were rolling. Everything was cool.

Now five years later, I was almost twenty-five. Still undirected, still no career job. Just wandering around in life. In another five years, I would be thirty which was inconceivable to me. Thirty was nearly middle age. It was an age when you had a wife, kids and a career, maybe even a tract house in suburbia and a new car in the garage. Barf.

Yet, I wasn't doing much here in Nürnberg. Just dealing with the consequences of a spur of the moment trip to Europe and except for a dribble of cash and checks from selling encyclopedias, broke. Oh, well, soldier on. I was hopeful this sales gig would lead to something more solid in Europe. Take Woodrow for example. Woodrow had served notice that he was splitting for Geneva to sell mutual funds for the Investors Overseas Services run by the American, Bernie Cornfeld.

"The money is going to be unbelievable," he explained. "No more dicking around with a hundred here and there. We are talking thousands in a good sale. Mutual funds, that's the key. Commissions are forty percent."

"That all sounds great, Woodrow, but who exactly are you going to sell to? Most G.I.s are broke or nearly broke and can barely afford a set of encyclopedias," I countered.

"You are missing the point, Allan. We don't sell to enlisted G.I.s, only to the top brass. Or to other expatriate Americans such as businessmen, trust fund babies, rich Europeans, anyone with cash to invest."

"Sounds too good to be true. How do you get leads?" I asked.

"Well, according to Bernie, he provides the leads. No cold calls. No standing on doorsteps. Appointments, seminars, meetings. High-level stuff. I know I can do this. After all, I am a Manhattan Negro. And thanks to those Fifth Avenue bitches, I know my way around money."

"Good luck."

When I asked Mike about Bernie Cornfeld, he was dubious. "Look, man. I'm just an ex-G.I. grunt. I know zilch about mutual funds, but it looks like a shell game to me. Chuck is not perfect but he pays on time. I'll stick to what I know—talking dumb-shit G.I.s into buying encyclopedias."

Chuck, who had returned from Munich, nodded in agreement. "This has all the makings of a Ponzi scheme. The old pyramid trick. They are selling dreams. Stick to the tangible," he said holding his up composite encyclopedia book.

Time would prove Chuck and Mike right about Bernie Cornfeld's mutual fund scheme, but in January of 1965, it was manna from heaven.

Woodrow reported back that he was making more money than ever and urged us all to leave the encyclopedia business and sell mutual funds. I must admit that I did give it serious consideration. Our sales were pathetic. Nobody was buying. We were traveling farther and farther from Nürnberg, looking for fresh territory. We even hit the American base at Regensburg about seventy miles away, right on the Czechoslovakia border.

I continued to live hand-to-mouth and even resorted to a bit of black market trading. I would cash my checks at the Army Hotel and get ten or fifteen dollars worth of Kennedy half-dollars in change. This 50-cent piece was truly the coin of the realm. Ninety percent silver, they had just been issued and were already a collector's item. One side of the coin had a profile of JFK and the other side, the American eagle.

Coins bulging in my pocket, I would go over to the train station and hang around, looking like a conspicuous American tourist until some German would invariably come up and ask me if I had any Kennedy half-dollars. "Yeah, I have a few," I would reply nonchalantly.

"*Sehr gut*. I am willing to buy whatever you have for four marks a piece"

I would proceed to sell a few Kennedy half-dollars for four marks, doubling my money. Later on, I was getting eight marks for one Kennedy half-dollar. I vaguely wondered I could be arrested for this but I had to eat and pay my pension.

***

As the January winter closed in, temperatures plummeted. But thanks to the arrival of my winter down parka, I was warm and comfy on the streets, although still broke. Chuck had left for Italy and Greece to sell encyclopedias at various U.S. Naval bases. When I asked about going along, he said, it was really a one-man show and that there was a lot of territory left to milk around Nürnberg.

"Don't worry, Al. By the end of the month, the G.I.s wives will be going nuts with the kids and they will be willing to buy them anything to shut them up," said Chuck as he drove off.

As if to show his faith, Chuck had hired two more salespeople—a New Zealand woman and her boyfriend, an American Southerner. They had their own car, an old 1938 Mercedes staff car and went off to sell on their own. Liz was a character. She traveled around with an ironing board in the back of the Mercedes. She always hand washed her own laundry. She didn't trust the German laundries. A short, dumpy brunette with a head of curly hair, Liz had been on the road in Europe for a couple of years after fleeing New Zealand which she said was the most boring place on earth: "All there is to do is sit around and watch the sheep graze and fuck."

"I heard it's a beautiful country," I replied. "My father has always wanted to travel there to go trout fishing."

"Oh yes, 'tis a beautiful country," she continued. "Great fishing, but unless you're a tourist, New Zealand is boring. And the food is terrible. Bland, boiled mutton. After eating in Italy and France, I'm never going back."

Her boyfriend was Gerald, an older man in his fifties. He was a soft featured gentleman with a courtly air and fine southern manners. Originally, from South Carolina, he had lived for years in Europe on family money which apparently was running out. Hence, he had to go to work. His career of choice was sales. "I feel I can empathize with the military man. After all, most are from the South and they will respect a southern gentleman," he explained.

Mostly though, Gerald simply found excuses not to go out, spending days in bed with various ailments he said were brought on by the cold. "I say, I do need a warmer climate. I hear Morocco is nice this time of year."

"No way," Liz would reply. "Get your bottom moving. We have to make some sales."

Liz took care of Gerald like a child. They were staying in a large double room in the same pension as I and I constantly ran into them. They spent a lot of time in the bathroom, taking baths together. Weird couple.

Mike didn't like them at all and constantly made fun of Gerald and Liz. "I don't think poor Gerald can get it up anymore. She probably has to suck him off. Yuk."

"Now, now Mike. Don't be so harsh," I counseled. "As long as they sell books."

"Yeah, they do all right. I don't know how. I wouldn't let them in my house."

"Probably the southern gentleman bit," I speculated.

"Probably."

I grew to like Mike. At first, I thought he was just a dumb G.I. type. But as I discovered, he was a resourceful guy and a hell of a salesman. As he put it: "I have to make my nut every week. At least four sets of encyclopedias. One a night. About 200-bucks in commissions. I have to buy booties for my kids and feed my family."

Mike was married to a German woman whom he had met while in the

Army here in Nürnberg. As he explained it, he knocked her up and then did the right thing and married her.

He and his new wife returned to Mike's hometown in Ohio where he had a job waiting for him in plumbing. But his wife, Maria, hated small town Ohio, refused to learn English and begged Mike to return to Germany. The plumbing gig wasn't working out. Construction was slow. In addition, Mike was bored too with small town life in Ohio. So the family returned to Nürnberg where Maria had family. Mike bounced around at various jobs, working in the PX, selling cars to G.I.s until finally he hooked up with Roberts a few years ago, and has been making good money ever since selling encyclopedias.

I went over to their apartment twice for dinner. It was a nice set up, a clean modern apartment on the edge of town. Now with two cute kids, Mike was a good father, speaking to them in baby German and English. "*Sagst*," he would say. "*Sagst*." (Talk)

Later, he mused. "Life is strange Allan. I never in my wildest dreams imagined that I would be living my life in Germany. Me a small town boy who had never been anywhere until the Army. I love it here. I love my kids. I love my wife. I love the beer." That was Mike morphing into a German.

***

Mike may have been selling, but for some reason I was not. Already I was tired of the sales bit. I was feeling hemmed in. The pension was costing too much money. Luckily, I stumbled onto a little known loophole at the University Extension. Since I was enrolled as a foreign student, I was eligible to live at the student dorm for only forty dollars a month (160 DM). The problem was there were no rooms available. I checked in with the housing office daily and made friends with a well-groomed middle-aged woman who ran the place and seemed to like me.

"Nothing today, Mr. Brown. Check tomorrow. I think you may have luck."

After a week of checking in, something did open up. Room 211. A foreign student had dropped out of the University leaving a vacancy.

"Do you mind sharing with his roommate?" she asked. "A Norwegian student."

"Uh, not at all," I said wondering if this room was a dump or if my potential roommate would be a jerk.

"Uh, there is one thing," she said. "This room is not the nicest. It has a hole in the wall and can be noisy. Maintenance has not gotten around to fixing it."

"Well, I'll take a look at it and let you know."

I trudged over to the student dormitory which was connected to the student union and a student restaurant. As I walked into the entrance hall and up the stairs to the second floor, I noticed a hole in the wall of the stairwell, about eight inches in diameter. Could this be the hole mentioned by the housing lady? Yes, it was. Room 211 was adjacent to the stairwell with the hole. Oh well.

I knocked on the door. Nobody was in, so I used my key and entered the room. It was not a bad room, large for a student room. One side was neat and tidy with a narrow bed. Posters of Norwegian fiords lined one the wall. On the desk a few family photographs of my roommate-to-be and a small portable typewriter. The other side of the room appeared to be vacant. It had a bed, a small desk, an empty closet and oh yes, the gaping hole about six inches above the bed. I could hear the clomp, clomp, clomp of students going up and down the stairwell. I immediately saw that with some rearrangement, I could cover the hole with a dresser and I would still have just enough room for my bed. So I moved the furniture around, hoping my roommate to be would not object.

Next, I checked out the bathrooms down the hall. Nice. Big bear claw tubs, tiled shower stalls with unlimited hot water. Plenty of basins, a row of toilets all housed in private stalls with doors that locked. Once again, the Germans proved they knew how to do bathrooms.

I went back to the housing office told the lady the room would do fine. Next, I bid goodbye to Pension Avalon and lugged my suitcase and a box of ALS stuff over to the student dorm.

It was now around 5 p.m. and as I was getting settled, my roommate walked in, did a double-take and said, "I see you made the hole disappear. I was thinking to do the same," he laughed.

A tall, skinny guy with red hair and a red beard, he reminded me of an underfed Leif Erickson. He introduced himself as Eric from Oslo. In impeccable English, he said he was studying common market economics. The University of Nürnberg was a noted school for that.

"Maybe someday we can be as prosperous as the United States," said Eric.

"It's an illusion," I said. "Everyone lives on credit in the U.S. It will come crashing down someday."

"Perhaps. However, it is an illusion in which I would like to participate while I can. Shall we go to dinner?"

"Sure." I followed Eric to the student dining room which looked like a former beer cellar with a low beamed ceiling and sturdy wooden tables and benches. Unlike other student cafeterias in France, servers brought the food to your table and everyone ate boarding house style. The cuisine was heavily Germanic (big surprise!) Piles of potatoes, cabbage, pork rinds, bits of ham, maybe lamb all piled on top. Heavy soups and a plate of green leafy lettuce. For desert, an apple or an orange with a little bit of cheese. The saving grace to all of this was the half-liter bottles of beer that one could purchase at a bar in the dining room. A couple of bites of this pig food and a large swallow of beer made it palatable. Now to be fair, the food was healthy, and definitely more substantial than food served at the typical French student cafeteria.

"So now what brings you to Nürnberg?" asked Eric.

"Ah, well a job basically but I also want to learn some German so I enrolled in a beginning German class which qualified me for student housing."

"Yes, yes. The housing is important. Very cheap. You are lucky my other roommate had to go home to the Middle East. Some trouble back home."

"Yeah, as they say in America, 'shit happens'."

"Oh, that is good," said Eric laughing. "You must teach me your slang. I will help you with your German. I have been to America, you know, for a few weeks touring around. I was working on a freighter as a deck hand. Norwegians can do that on their own shipping lines. My father is in the shipping business. That's what I will do once I earn my degree."

We talked for a while and then I had to excuse myself to go sell some books. Mike was due to pick me up any moment. Eric struck me as a pleasant, easy-going fellow. Not uptight as many Germans tend to be. I was looking forward to sharing a room with him for only forty dollars a month.

***

After a few days of my new digs, life settled into a routine. I could almost believe I was a student again. My day went like this: Up at eight or nine, over to bakery across the street where I purchased a chunk of apple strudel, a piece of cheddar cheese and black breakfast coffee to go. Sometimes, I would venture farther to a bratwurst stand and have a bratwurst, often with a beer. A beer for breakfast! What was I doing? But man, it tasted good. And I noticed that it was a popular breakfast for many Germans. Sometimes, I just had beer and apple strudel. Forget the coffee.

Then with a mild buzz, I would retire to my room with my goodies and read or study German until I fell asleep. Around noon, I would rouse myself for lunch or supper, the main meal of the day. Following that, if I had not drunk too much beer, I would go out and wander about the city until three when I had my class. For two hours we would practice intensive beginning German. I enjoyed it. Unlike French in my college days, there was no grade pressure. And I found to my surprise that I was picking it up fast. I could even spit out a few phrases that Germans actually understood. Then it was back to the student cafeteria for a light dinner, usually leftovers from lunch. And finally, I would suit up or more frequently, sport suit up, wearing my ski parka, slacks and a sweater and go out selling encyclopedias with Mike until ten.

After that, I would usually go out with Eric and a few of his friends to a local beer cellar and drink and munch on appetizers until midnight or so. These were groovy little beer cellars tucked away here and there in the old city. The beer was always locally brewed, often right there on the premises. The half-liters were always served at precisely the right temperature as determined by the thermometers stuck in them. The beer was so good, so fresh, so chock full of nutrients that I believed I got most of my nutrition in Germany from beer. Perhaps, man could live by beer alone. Such was life in Nürnberg.

24. FRÄULEINS

As January wore on, my social life picked up as well. This was the Fasching period, the weeks before Lent. Every weekend there were parties, often costume parties here and there around the city and at the student union. The cutest women always wore the sexiest costumes. But when I tried to make time with anyone desirable, I struck out. After hearing my story, most decided I was a flake and lost interest.

I discovered German women were very practical about men. "You must have good prospects, be a gentleman, and speak some German." Unspoken was "You must spend a lot of money on me so I can have a good time." The Americans who did well with sharp German women were military officers, captains and above, and those employed in good jobs with the U.S. government or with international American businesses.

Andrea was one such German woman. I had met her in an upscale bar one night. I was suited up and on the prowl. She was sitting there with a girlfriend, very well groomed, ash blonde hair, sly, green cat eyes, and a charming dimpled smile. Also, while not very tall, she had nicely turned legs and a full chest rising and falling through her cashmere sweater. It was the lesser attractive girlfriend that broke the ice by asking in stilted English if I were in the American military. I said I wasn't but that I was a businessman doing business in Nürnberg.

"Oh, are you with the PX service?" Andrea chimed in. I discovered the PX service always attracted a German girl's attention because they knew that through a serviceman they could get cheap nylons, makeup and other American goodies.

"Not exactly. I deal in books."

"How interesting."

I guess I led them to believe I was some traveling executive supplying books to the PX.

I bought them both a round of drinks but when the girlfriend noticed I was more interested in Andrea than her, she excused herself to the ladies room and then joined some other friends at another table. I chatted on with Andrea. She said she had just graduated from the University of Nürnberg and was now working as a legal secretary but that someday she wanted to go to law school. Then she claimed her English was so bad she wanted to speak German. So I gave it a try. She smiled and switched back into English.

"You have much to learn, Allan. I do hope you stay with German because it is a beautiful language."

"I'm trying. Say, why don't we go see the new James Bond movie *Goldfinger*."

"I would like to, perhaps this weekend. Let us say Sunday night," she said, checking her little black book and marking the date.

I remarked that she was so well organized.

"Yes of course. Most Germans are that way," she replied. "They always know months in advance where they will be on a certain day. It is only logical."

"I'm impressed."

We talked about traveling around Europe which she had done but mostly she liked to vacation with her family in the Alps during the summer.

"It is so beautiful there and so much to do." She smiled dreamily.

I walked Andrea back to her apartment on the edge of the old city. Before I could move in for a kiss, she simply held out her hand and said, "I will see you here at six on Sunday, Allan and we will go to this *Goldfinger* movie."

***

Sunday at 6 p.m. sharp, I knocked on her door. This time I was dressed in my tweed sport coats and slacks and topcoat, looking rather collegiate, I thought. She came directly out, not inviting me in. But was very smiley and personable. "It's been so long since I have seen a movie. And I do like Sean Connery. He is so handsome."

As I discovered, going to a popular movie in Germany was a big deal. For a movie like *Goldfinger*, I had to make seat reservations a day in advance. It was a lavish theater with many upscale munchies. No popcorn or coke here. One could buy beer or have a coffee in a little cafe in the lobby.

Aside from Sean Connery, the movie starred the German actor Gert Fröbe as Auric Goldfinger. And of course, it was all dubbed in German with no English subtitles which made it difficult to understand, although I enjoyed the obvious visual thrills—the alpine car chase, the laser sequence, the Fort Knox heist, Pussy Galore and her flying dykes and of course, the ticking nuclear bomb. Andrea loved it, her cat eyes sparkling in the semi-dark.

After the movie, we retired to a little beer cellar and had a beer and bratwurst for a late night dinner. "That was enjoyable, Allan. I don't get out much with work and such."

"Well, we can solve that problem I said, holding up a beer mug in a toast."

"Yes, well you see. I have recently split with a longtime boyfriend and I have not felt like going out."

Andrea proceeded to tell me of her sad little story. How she had gone around with the guy for four years during the University. How he had to do his military service for one year and then they were going to be married. But he had changed. He had decided he wanted to travel overseas and not become tied down. So everything was put on hold. He then broke everything off by letter from somewhere in Asia.

"Oh," I said, trying to commiserate but I could think of nothing else to say, except to ask her out for another date next Friday. She accepted but I could tell she was not terribly enthusiastic about it. In fact, she mentioned that she had to go out of town for a few days.

When I arrived for our Friday date, I knocked at the door. No answer. I knocked again. Waited a minute. Still no answer. Then I noticed a note sticking out of her mailbox addressed to me: *Sorry you called in vain. I am in a bad state. I have too many troubles. My trip to Frankfurt was not too nice as the reason was not the best but take it easy. See you maybe Sunday night at 6.*

When I arrived Sunday night at the door of her apartment, I found another note. This one was a terse little kiss off: *I am sorry, Allan. I cannot not meet you again for reasons that I am not able to tell you. I have to stay in my room.*

What! This sounded bizarre. The first thing that flashed through my mind was she had been pregnant and went to Frankfurt to have an abortion. But I never found out because Andrea simply disappeared. When I returned to her apartment building a few days later, I discovered a for-rent sign for her apartment posted in the entranceway.

A couple of weeks later, I ran into the friend of Andrea at the bar where we had first met. When I asked about Andrea, the girlfriend told me that she had left town and gone to live with her parents in Bonn. I wasn't sure if this was all an elaborate kiss off or a real life situation. But, it was obvious I was out of the Andrea game. So much German women. Or so I thought until a week later.

***

"They are both very cute," announced Eric. "I will be with Ingrid. You can be with Zoë."

"Sounds interesting," I said while dawdling over dinner—another pile of potatoes and cabbage with a hairy pork rind on top. Eric and I were dining in the student union with our half-liters of beer. He had met a pair of German high school girls who had taken a shine to him. Although Eric was engaged to a girlfriend back in Norway, that didn't seem to slow him down as far as women were concerned.

"How old are they?" I pressed. "You said they were in a gymnasium?"

"*Ja*, an advanced secondary school. This one, private. Next year they go to the university."

"How old?" I asked.

"Ah, I don't know, Allan." Young. I would guess around seventeen."

"Whoa! That's jail-bait," I said.

"Jail-bait?"

"Yes, under the age of legal consent for sex."

"What! That's ridiculous. Not in Germany. However, I am not talking of sex," said Eric indignant. "I am talking about two nice girls to go out with to the Fasching parties. I, myself, am engaged, as you know. I would not think of such a thing."

"Sure, sure. OK. Let's set something up. Coffee maybe."

"All right," said Eric, then adding. "Oh, by the way, Zoë is the daughter of the Lord Mayor of Nürnberg."

"No kidding," I replied. "Well, I guess I will have to behave myself."

I was dubious about this whole set up. Too young. After all, I was almost twenty-five. If Zoë were only seventeen, I would be eight years older than she. But when the four of us met for coffee, I was pleasantly surprised. Zoë and Ingrid drove up in a brand new yellow Volkswagen Beetle with a sunroof. Ingrid was truly a Nordic blonde, tall, shapely. I could see why Eric was attracted to her. Zoë was shorter, with a buxom peasant build but still attractive with a pretty face and long dark hair. As it turned out, neither spoke English other than a few words. No problem for Eric who spoke fluent German but a challenge for me. A challenge that I was to profit by greatly because during my time with Zoë, my German improved a thousand percent. She did not speak in the local Nürnberg dialect, but in a clear, clean, pure German, probably the product of years of expensive schooling. After a few weeks of going around together, I fancied myself nearly fluent in conversational German. But I'm getting ahead of the story.

Our time with the two young but game German girls went like this: A couple of Fasching costume parties, several movies and dinners and one trip to Munich and the Bavarian Alps for skiing. It turned out these two high school girls were from well-off families and had cash to spare. They footed the bill for most everything except the movies and beer. Eric being cheap but not broke and I having no money, didn't protest. We felt like trophy boyfriends, as the girls showed us off to their friends who would remark, "Oh, so cute, so handsome, so *schön*, so sophisticated. Older, don't you know. Foreign too."

We were an adventure to them.

For instance, the first Fasching party was a costume party. I was planning to go as a cowboy, but Zoë, insisted that I come as I was, simply an American. So I dressed in a black turtleneck, black slacks and wore a black mask and that seemed to please her. She came as a German peasant which was a role she fit into perfectly. Note, one nice thing about German girlfriends was that they never introduced their boyfriends to the parents unless it was serious. I was relieved. I did not have to meet the dad, the Lord Mayor who probably wielded much influence with the local police and who if he didn't approve, could have me whisked away from Nürnberg in the dead of the night.

Father or not, Zoë was undeterred. She was determined to hang out with me. She would come over to my room and we would listen to records on Eric's little portable phonograph, maybe have a sip of schnapps, doodle around, practice some German grammar, and I would teach her a few words in English. She actually knew quite a bit but was self-conscious speaking it. Oh, yes and perhaps a little making out, nothing heavy. I was, in fact, a perfect gentleman with this seventeen-year-old.

***

Sometime in mid-February, Eric and girls were itching for a ski trip. Being Norwegian, Eric was a dedicated cross-country skier and accordingly, he had brought his gear down to Germany. Like me, Zoë and Ingrid had done downhill skiing but never cross-country skiing. After listening to Eric rave about it, we were eager to give it a try. The plan was to drive down to the foothills of the Bavarian Alps past Munich to a Nordic center that rented the gear and had some groomed trails.

Thus it was, early one Saturday morning, we four squeezed into Zoë's Beetle, and made our way down the autobahn towards Munich. I had been on the Nürnberg-Munich Autobahn only once before and that was with Chuck in his big-ass Mercedes, going at about 100 miles an hour in the fast lane. Still, even bigger Mercedes would come up behind us, blinking their lights for us to move over to the slower lanes. You see, there was no speed limit on the autobahn. A Beetle like ours, rolling along at about 70 mph, had to hug the right hand lane to keep out of way of the rocketships. As a result, it took us over three hours to get to our destination, about forty miles past Munich at a small ski area in the rolling foothills of the Alps.

Once we arrived, all four of us were soon on cross-country skis, sliding along the snowy trails in a peaceful landscape of rolling hills, lakes and meadows. In the background, loomed the jagged peaks of the Alps near Garmisch. Down here, there was no clank of chairlifts, no shouts or screams of over-hyped downhill skiers, no crowds. Just the chirp of an occasional bird, the whispering pines, and acres and acres of blinding white snowfields.

I found it easy to master the cross-country skis. Long, narrow, skis with a type of binding that allowed the heel of the soft boot to lift. This mobility made it easy to pole along, sliding first on one ski and then another, like skating. Zoë had no problem learning the basic stride nor did Ingrid. Of course, Eric was a pro at this and he would ski ahead in long graceful strides, with great rhythm and speed. Then he would stop and wait for us to catch up or ski back towards and ski circles around us.

"In Norway, I can do sixty or seventy kilometers in a day," bragged Eric. "We stay in huts along the way and ski for days on end. March is the best. It is warm and there is plenty of snow."

"OK, Mr. Eric," I say panting out of breath, "Just have mercy on us beginners."

"But of course," said Eric. "I will take a few extra tours while you three make your way back to the lodge."

Three hours of cross-country skiing was enough for me and the girls and we made our way back to the lodge. Twenty minutes later, Eric arrived out of breath. He had been sprinting about. We relaxed, drinking hot red wine and munching on sandwiches that the girls had made. Following a bite to eat, we lazed around in recliners outside the Nordic center, basking in the warm sun. Eric went for another quick run and returned pooped ready to stop for the day. We handed back our rental skis and then decided to drive back to Munich for a beer-hall dinner.

***

We had many beer halls in Munich from which to choose but in keeping with tradition, we went to the granddaddy of them all—the Hofbrauhaus. This was a cavernous beer hall that encouraged drinking and eating to excess at the massive, communal tables. All inspired by the cheery barmaids and the beat of the ohm-pa-pa music played by a band in full Bavarian dress.

It was hard to imagine that this cheery place was where Hitler delivered his first speeches to form the National Socialist Party and later where he staged the Beer Hall Putsch of 1923. However, we weren't paying much attention to history that night. We were too busy drinking delicious Bavarian beer and dining on bratwurst, sauerkraut and potato salad.

Eric was the champion beer drinker but even he after a couple of liters was bombed and I followed close behind. More worrisome was Zoë who barely had a liter. She complained that she was dizzy and could not possibly drive back to Nürnberg. Ingrid didn't drive at all. Also, it was snowing heavily, so we decided we would have to spend the night in a pension. I remembered vaguely where some were located based on my previous stay in Munich but it was Eric who knew exactly where to go.

An hour later, we found ourselves ensconced in two rooms in a cozy pension, a few blocks from the Hofbrauhaus. Zoë had phoned her father that she was stuck in Munich but that all was well. She and Ingrid would share one room, Eric and I another. Still, Zoë said her father was not happy about his daughter and her best friend being off with two male foreign students but there was not much he could do. I wondered if he would sic the Munich police on us but he apparently put his faith in his daughter's good sense.

I had vowed to behave myself but Eric with his beer buzz was unleashed and scooted off to Ingrid's room. Zoë feeling embarrassed as Eric and Ingrid misbehaved came over to my room where we listened to the radio for a little while and then found ourselves making out on one of the big fluffy beds with a billowy comforter.

One thing led to another, and before we knew it we both had our shirts off and were bare chest to bare chest. I was confronted with luscious, Germanic, peasant breasts, free at last. But when I pressed further, she pulled away and muttered something about not being able to go on.

"*Bitte*," she pleaded.

All of a sudden I wondered what the hell I was doing with this little German high school girl in a nowhere situation. For that matter, what was I doing in Germany? I began a serious reevaluation of my situation in Nürnberg.

25. BROKE

Essentially, the source of my problems was that I was forever broke. I had to scrape by on the money I collected from my customers who forked over the down payment on the encyclopedias. That meant ten dollars here, twenty dollars there. It was late February and I continued to live a hand-to-mouth existence. All because Chuck had not come through with the rest of my commissions, around four-hundred dollars. He was still off somewhere in Greece and Italy supposedly selling at the naval bases, but I suspected he was goofing off, playing *Zorba the Greek*, dancing, drinking ouzo and breaking plates in out-of-the-way Greek taverns.

So I resolved to try to find a real job in Germany, perhaps with the European Exchange Service. This was the purchasing service for all the military post exchanges in Europe. I knew from Chuck that they employed buyers to scour Europe and the U.S. for goods that the G. I. s would buy. That kind of job intrigued me. Best of all, the European Exchange Service (EES) was headquartered in Nürnberg at the Palace of Justice.

I had run into an American in a rathskeller who was a buyer for the service. Ralph said it was the best job he had ever had in retailing. He traveled around Europe, the Middle East and occasionally to Asia tending to the PXs. He also spent time in the U. S. on buying trips.

"It's a great gig. I have a hot Corvette that snows the European chicks. I have to beat them off with a stick."

"So how does one get hired there?" I inquired.

"Well, it was simple in my case. I had had a few years in retailing and was bored. My fiancée had bailed on me. I was looking for adventure, so I answered an ad in the *Stars and Stripes* that I had been subscribing to since my Army days. The EES wanted buyers in Europe. I applied and a few months later, after an interview in Washington, I was in. That was a couple of years ago and I've been based in Nürnberg ever since."

"Well, my retail background is minimal but I do have sales experience," I explained. "Do you think I'd have a shot?" I asked sipping a beer.

"Maybe. Buyers are always coming and going. If something opens up and you're on the scene, you just might get on," said Ralph. "Here I'll give you the name of the guy to see."

A few days later, I found myself at the Palace of Justice in the waiting room of the purchasing director of the EES. I had set up an appointment to see him, using Ralph's name as a reference. I was all spiffed out in my New York suit with a fresh haircut, shoes shined, topcoat. Updated resumes tucked into my slim leather valise. I was on deck.

After a ten minute wait, a rumpled, swarthy guy, with sweat rings on his dress shirt came out tugging at his tie.

"Jesus Christ, these Krauts keep the heat up in this joint. I'm sweating like a pig," he said holding out a wet hand for me to shake. "Ben Epstein, here. Glad to meet you, Allan. Come on in."

He motioned me to follow him into to his sauna bath office.

"What I would give to be back in L.A. instead of this winter sweatbox. But this is Europe. Culture capital of the world. It could be worse," he laughed. "I could be in bum-fuck nowhere."

I didn't know what to make of this guy. He certainly wasn't the polished marketing type that I had expected.

I sat down and he settled back in his leather chair which seemed out of place behind his Army surplus battleship gray desk. "So what can I do for you, Allan?

"I'm interested in working for EES as a buyer," I said in my most ass-kissing corporate manner. "I have a resume here that outlines my previous experience. I've been selling encyclopedias here for the past few months and I think I have a feel for the goods and services the American G.I. wants. Also, as noted in my resume, I do have some retail experience, mainly working for a vendor who supplied Christmas articles to Bay Area department stores. Plus, I've been on active duty in the Army Reserves and spent a lot of time shopping in various PXs."

I handed him my resume. Ben glanced it over and then leaning back in his leather chair, he said, "O. K., Allan. Here's the deal. You make a good impression. You probably aren't bad as a salesman. Door-to-door is great learning experience. Your actual retail experience is minimal but that can be picked up. The EES has its own quirky retail ways that often makes it hard for civilian retailers to adapt to. It's almost better to start from scratch. You're probably a quick study. In other words, I would give you serious consideration if a slot were open. Unfortunately, there's nothing right now here in Europe, but you might have better luck by applying at EES headquarters in Washington. They serve all the U. S. military bases around the world. Of course, this takes time. Many months and a fair amount of red tape. How long are you in Nürnberg for?"

"Indefinitely," I said. "I have no immediate plans to return to the U.S."

"Well, good. Hang in there. Something might open up in a month or two. That's when we start buying for fall and winter. Where can I get a hold of you?"

"Ah, student housing at the University." I handed him the address, shook his hand and left as he continued to bitch about the steam heat.

So there it was. A tantalizing possibility. I could almost taste it, see it. A cool apartment, a sports car, nice suits, and plenty of German women around seeing a good prospect. But still nothing certain, nothing immediate. No income. I can't hang waiting. Have to do something. Maybe it was time for plan "B."

***

Even though I had told Ben, I had no plans to return to the U. S., I was, in fact, thinking about it more and more. I didn't have time or money to wait around for a job to materialize in Germany. I was spinning my wheels. In a month, it would be spring. The surveying season would be underway in California. I would have the chance to make some real dough throughout the spring and summer and go graduate school in the fall. And to top it off, even though I was broke, I had a Lufthansa Airline ticket in my hot little hand that would take me back to the U.S.

How did I come by this ticket? Answer: In a low moment after my arrival in Germany, I had picked up a Peace Corps application from the American Consulate and filled it out. I was curious to see if they would re-accept me and also what kind of assignment they would offer me. I was still smarting from my dismissal from the Peace Corps a year-and-a-half ago. Still, they had encouraged me to apply again promoting my surveying skills. A couple of days before my interview with the EES guy, I found a Peace Corps packet in my mailbox. They had accepted me, offering me a slot working as a surveyor in Morocco. They were about to undergo a big road building program.

Hmm, Morocco. French speaking. Exotic. Intrigue. The Casbah. But near to Europe. Surveying roads. Doing some social good. Also skiing in the Atlas Mountains. Included in the packet was an airline ticket to the U.S. for training in Baton Rouge, Louisiana scheduled to begin in April. Why not?

However, after staring at the Peace Corps offer for a few days, I decided that I really didn't want to spend two years in the Peace Corps being bossed around by officious little pricks worried about the American image abroad. The Army had been bad enough. I would rather freelance it around the world. Still, that Peace Corps airline ticket was burning a hole in my pocket.

My conniving, little mind went to work. I noted the price tag on the ticket, some five hundred dollars. Shit, if I could it cash it in, I could fly home for half that price on Icelandic Airlines and have $250.00 dollars to live on for another month in Europe. I had cashed in other airline tickets now and then for some aborted trip and figured this would be no different.

I made my way over to the Hapag-Lloyd Office to cash this baby in. The travel agent lady at the counter took one look at the ticket and handed it back to me.

"Herr Brown. This is a U. S. government issued airline ticket. It cannot be cashed in. If you do not use it, you must notify them and return to the issuer."

I gulped. "Are you sure?"

"But of course, I am sure. I deal with the American military all the time using these government issued tickets."

"Do tell," I said, realizing this lady was no fool. She probably encountered a lot of hard-up G.I.s trying to cash their tickets in. I left the Hapag-Lloyd office looking at my useless ticket. Then a light bulb went off. Hey, no one ever matches the name on an airline ticket with the actual passenger. Not even when a passport was required to enter and leave a country. As long as you had a valid airline ticket in your hand, no one cared. I had known frat brothers who flew on tickets in the name of someone else. Maybe I could sell this ticket on the black market. Maybe I could find a German who wanted to fly to New York. He could bail out there and not continue on to New Orleans. Who would be the wiser?

However, after an hour or two at the train station, trying to pinpoint a likely customer, I was having second thoughts. This was too complicated. Too risky. Selling Kennedy half-dollars was one thing but selling an airline ticket was something else. I could get in real trouble. Also, I noted in the fine print of an insert to the ticket that if I didn't show up at the intended destination, or return the ticket, the Peace Corps would hold me responsible for the ticket at the regular coach price—five hundred big ones. Shit! I resigned myself to returning the ticket to the Peace Corps and telling them that I was not available for that particular tour of duty.

No, if I were going to return home without begging money from my parents, I would have to get what was owed me from Chuck. Even though he was in Greece, his main office was in Vaduz, Liechtenstein and that was where they cut the checks. Mike was desperate as well. He had had it with Chuck who owed him over a thousand dollars. He had been borrowing money from his father-in-law to feed the family. He was game to go down to Vaduz too.

As he put it, "I'm going to rip that office off, if that fucker off doesn't pay up."

So the next afternoon, Mike and I climbed into his beat-up Volkswagen Beetle and took off for Vaduz, Liechtenstein.

26. VADUZ

Liechtenstein is a screwy little country tucked away in a mountain valley between eastern Switzerland and western Austria. In 1965, this country of only 160-square kilometers was known for having almost as many banks as people, banks that guarded the secrecy of its depositors even more tightly than Swiss banks. It was thus known as an ideal place to launder money. As a result, the banks housed the ill-gotten gains of dictators, drug lords, mafia types, arms dealers, embezzlers, and any other criminal enterprise that one could think of.

Much of Liechtenstein's population of some twenty-five thousand residents consisted of foreign expatriates, many with criminal or shady backgrounds. Liechtenstein had no extradition treaties. If its criminal residents behaved themselves within its borders, all was well. The rest of the population indigenous to Liechtenstein were usually connected to some form of banking service, and often grew fat and sleek off the fees that they charged.

Liechtenstein was also headquarters for hundreds of international corporations escaping the tax obligations of their home country. Most were only a postbox at a local bank. In short, Liechtenstein was the perfect spot for Chuck Roberts to headquarter his American Library Service company. Mike explained bits and scraps of this as we made our way along the autobahns of Bavaria to the Liechtenstein border on a Sunday night.

We found a dumpy hostel filled with Turkish guest workers on the outskirts of Vaduz and crashed there for the night, occasionally choking on the acrid smoke from their cigarettes. The next morning went into town for a café-au-lait and rolls before we made our way to the ALS office.

Driving through town (a village really), I noted that Mike was right. The narrow main street was nothing but wall-to-wall banks, cozy looking places in faux-alpine style. After we parked the car, I poked my head into the entranceways of a few of these banks. Through the windows, I could see the rows of mailboxes and with discrete, anonymous numbers on them. The banks themselves were often nothing more than small offices.

We spent an hour in the cafe drinking café-au-lait, munching on croissants and pastry, and watching the banker-types going to work. Only a few dressed up in suits; most were casual in sweaters and slacks. Now and the, someone came by wearing ski pants as if they were going skiing on their lunch hour which in fact they could do since the local ski resort was only a few kilometers out of town.

"OK, here's the deal, Al," said Mike, screwing up his resolve. "We'll storm the ALS offices like we mean business and demand our dough on the spot. We'll accept no excuses, just cold hard cash."

"Sounds good but what if the money is not forthcoming?" I asked.

"Don't worry, his secretary Zelda knows how to get hold of Chuck. She probably talks to him every day. That fucker had better cough up. I'm tired of begging for money from my father-in-law."

"OK, OK, Mike. I hope you're right," I said with a knot in my stomach, sensing that this situation could turn ugly.

The town clock struck nine and probably little cuckoo men rotated out and around the bell tower somewhere but we didn't see them because Mike and I were driving up the hill behind town to the office of the American Library Society. The office turned out to be a two-story chalet with a spectacular view of the valley. Mike explained the house belonged to Chuck, although he spent little time there. Upstairs were the plush living quarters. Downstairs, a basement apartment and the office.

Mike buzzed the doorbell. A few seconds later, a big hulking guy let us in. His eyes widening a little as he encountered a red-faced Mike. "Herr Mike," he said, "What a surprise."

"Yeah, yeah, big surprise, Hermann" said Mike pushing past him. The hulk seemed soft to me and not tough at all.

"Where's Zelda?"

"Working in the office. Right this way," said Hermann in a stilted German accent.

We entered the living room and went downstairs to the office and there sat Zelda at a large IBM Selectric typewriter, typing away. She was a pleasant, thirtyish blonde of some vague European origin. Mike had told me she was one of Chuck's old girlfriends but instead of dumping her as he did with most old girlfriends, he made use of her office skills. Her fingers flew across the electric keyboard with the rotating type-ball spinning madly. She was obviously an efficient secretary.

"Oh, Mike," she said looking up but continuing to type. "How nice to see you. It's been a long time since you have visited us."

Mike, now in his Southern Ohio gentlemen's mode, said, "Zelda honey, I always enjoy seeing you and Hermann. I know my book orders are in good hands with you two. I know they will always reach my customers in a timely fashion."

"But of course. That's why we are here. Who's your friend?"

"Oh, this is Al. Al, Zelda. Al is a fellow salesman. He's rather new but he is doing well. Unfortunately, the fruits of his recent labor have not been rewarded lately. Now that I think of it, nor have mine."

"Yes, yes, of course," said Zelda briskly. "Hermann and I are in the same situation. We have not been paid either. Chuck is still in Greece. I talk to him most every day reminding him that the checks have to go out. I can't do a thing without his OK."

"OK, I understand except the situation with me is critical," said Mike. "Screw the checks, honey. Have Chucky-boy wire a cash transfer, today, immediately. Al and I have waited long enough. You know how to get a hold of him. He's probably still asleep at his Athens hotel. Give him a call now."

Zelda gulped, somewhat taken aback at Mike's insistence. "Yes, yes, Herr Mike, this I will do right now, but please leave the room so I can talk in private to him. He will be very grumpy at waking up so soon. Usually, we speak in the afternoon."

"Whatever. Come on Al, let's go look at the view from the sundeck."

We walked out on the sundeck and gazed at the snow-covered mountains off in the distance. So peaceful, so bucolic. One would never know that this place was ground zero for nefarious dirty deals. The thought passed my mind that once we secured our money, I might rent some skis and try out that local resort.

Fifteen minutes later, Zelda came out on the deck, shaking her head but smiling.

"Wow, what a grouch. Boy, did he swear at me out for waking him up. He had just gotten to bed after a wild night in the Plaka. But when he calmed down, I explained that you both had traveled all the way to Vaduz to collect your commissions. I guess that shamed him and I also reminded him that Hermann and I have not been paid either."

"So what's he going to do," asked Mike impatiently. "Do we get paid or not?"

"He said he would wire the money this afternoon. He promised that it would be here before the close of business today probably, around 4 p.m. How's that Mr. Mike and Al?"

"Sounds good to me," I said relieved.

Mike, though, wasn't so sure. "I'll believe it when I see the money in my hands. And it damn well better be before the end of the day. Chuck is such a flake."

We both left the house and climbed back into Mike's Beetle.

"Hey Mike, cheer up," I said. "We're going to be flush in a few short hours. Zelda promised. Let's enjoy ourselves. Let's go see the castle here and check out that ski resort. Maybe have a large wiener schnitzel lunch with a liter of beer. And when all that is done, our cash will be waiting. "

On that happy thought, we drove down the hill and into the valley for a bit of sightseeing.

***

Driving around Liechtenstein was a brief affair. As I said, only 160 square kilometers, a twelve-mile long valley with an autobahn running through it. I wondered why Liechtenstein was ever a country. Why hadn't been swallowed up by either Switzerland or Austria? Maybe it had served as a buffer zone. It was now ruled by a guy called Prince Franz Joseph II who apparently had quite a bit of power. He could dissolve parliament and veto any act before it became law. In other words, he was sort of a dictator. The good prince presided over his realm from a castle overlooking the town.

We chugged up a winding road for a closer look at the Prince's castle. For a medieval castle, it seemed to me a rather squat affair with no towers, high walls or moats but it did feature two round bastions dating from the middle-ages. Mike said he had heard that the Prince had a great collection of knights' armor and weapons inside along a bunch of rare paintings and other artworks which the public rarely saw.

Indeed, the whole set up here in Liechtenstein seemed like something out the movie *The Mouse that Roared*—a quirky, toy kingdom with a bark, but no bite. Liechtenstein had no military and relied on Switzerland for its defense, currency and foreign diplomacy.

After a brief look at the castle from the roadway, we drove on through the mountains until we came to the Malbun Ski Resort—a little ski resort tucked away in the southeast corner of Liechtenstein. It was a charming place nestled at the foot of a modest mountain with about a thousand vertical feet of well-groomed slopes. Obviously, a resort for beginners and families. However today, there were no children or families were in sight. The resort was filled with attractive young women. Mercedes sedans and sports cars filled the parking lot as the women strutted around in slim, clinging stretch pants, fluffy cashmere ski sweaters, fur-lined après-ski boots and glittering gold jewelry. Most carried the latest in ski equipment, usually Kastle or Head skis. These women appeared to be the trophy wives or mistresses of the rich and reclusive. All were in their late twenties or early thirties, all were very shapely, very well groomed. The best that money could buy. I wanted to rent some skis and join them on the slopes, take a few runs, maybe strike up a conversation. But to reiterate, we were down to our last few *pfennings* (German pennies.) All Mike and I could do was stand next to his shabby Beetle with our tongues hanging out.

"Nuf, of this shit," said Mike finally. "This is torture watching these babes. Let's get out of here. Let's go have a decent lunch, get our money and go home."

"I guess," I said, reluctantly getting back in the car.

We drove down the hill to town and dined at one of the older restaurants with the Alpine bric-a-brac, giant beer mugs and a wiener schnitzel that filled the plate. By the time we got out of there, it was nearly three o'clock. It was time to check out the progress of the money, so it was back to the ALS office.

***

"O. K. Zelda, dear," said Mike in his is soothing southern Ohio twang. "We are back and ready to be paid."

Zelda looked up from her typewriter, frowned and then trying to be charming. "Mike, I don't know what to say. Chuck swore that he would send it straight off but it has not yet arrived. I just checked with the bank down the way."

"That's O. K.," said Mike pleasantly. "We'll wait upstairs. I'm sure it will come through."

Mike and I trooped upstairs and read magazines for an hour and stared out the picture windows at the mountains beyond. Soon it was after four o'clock. The banks would close at five.

At that point, I asked Mike what we were going to do if the money didn't show up.

"Well, we'll see," said Mike thoughtfully. "Chuck has a lot of great furniture and appliances here. Maybe we should cart some of it off and sell it."

"That's a joke, isn't it?" I said.

"Yeah, right now it's a joke," Mike laughed. "Let's see how Zelda is doing."

We went back downstairs and confronted her. Now all the pleasantries were gone.

"I'm sorry to have to tell you fellows but it doesn't look like the money will be wired today," said Zelda, looking down at her paperwork. "I checked with the bank again. So far, they have received no notice that the money will be wired and they're getting ready to close up shop for the day."

"Well, shi--eet, Zelda," said Mike with fire in his eye. "I want my dough now. Go down to the bank and get it out of his account."

"I have no way to do that Mike. I can't access his account. Remember, Hermann and I have not been paid either."

"Not good enough," said Mike defiantly. "I have a wife and babies to feed. I guess I'll just have to take this brand new IBM Selectric and pawn it off. Mike pushed Zelda's papers off her desk and picked up the heavy Selectric with the cord dangling down.

Zelda, wide-eyed, scooted back in her swivel chair and called for Hermann. Hermann was nowhere to be seen. Then collecting her composure, she coolly said, "Mike, you better leave before I call the police."

"Yeah, sure," said Mike oblivious to her threat as he cradled the typewriter in his arms. "What did this cost? Probably around four hundred dollars. This baby should be worth a couple of hundred at least in a pawnshop. We saw a little pawnshop on the main drag, didn't we Al? I'll have to get over there before it closes.

At this point, Hermann stuck his head in the door and quickly withdrew it.

"Sorry, Zelda, it looks like your boyfriend is not going to help," Mike scoffed. "Come on Al, let's get out of here."

Finally overcoming my disbelief of what was happening, I said, "Stop this shit Mike. You can't steal their typewriter. She'll call the cops. Put it back and let's go."

Meanwhile, Zelda was frantically going through her desk drawers until she pulled out an envelope.

"Here, Mike. Take this. It's petty cash. Hermann and I have been living on it.

I think there's about a four-hundred Swiss Francs left."

"Shi-eet, that's nothing," Mike sneered, "A lousy one-hundred dollars."

I grabbed the envelope. "Come on, Mike lets go. I'll bet Hermann has already called the police."

Mike grunted and suddenly lifted the heavy typewriter over his head as if to throw it down. His arms shaking, the typewriter teetering up there, I had a flash image of the Selectric shattering on the concrete basement floor. But after a few seconds, Mike lowered the typewriter and gently put it back on Zelda's desk. He smiled a tight smile and grabbed the envelope from my hand saying, "See you around honey." Then we were gone.

We drove for several kilometers outside of Vaduz, and then pulled into a tavern, where we had a beer and calmed down.

"Are you fuckin' crazy Mike?" I reiterated once again. "Once Zelda tells Roberts what you did, you'll be lucky to have a job."

"Don't worry, Al. I've made these threats before," said Mike hunching over the bar on his stool. "I know the fucker will pay up. He always comes through. We've been together too long. And after all, I am his ace salesman in Germany. He won't fire me."

***

The most amazing part of this episode was that a few days after we returned to Nürnberg, Roberts did come through with the money. Mike was flush with twelve-hundred dollars and I felt almost as rich with my four-hundred dollars. I immediately made plans to leave for Paris and eventually home.

However, there were a few loose ends to tie up. Eric and I went out for one last beer blast at local rathskeller and exchanged addresses. He vowed to come and see me in the Bay Area. I also said goodbye to Zoë. She treated me to a nice meal of sauerbraten at a plush German restaurant. After a beer and a lingering kiss in our cozy booth, she said goodbye with tears in her eyes, her American adventure over.

Zoë wrote me a letter in German months later, saying she was attending the University of Nürnberg and very happy with new friends, but she said she still thought of me. I was touched.

I never did see Chuck Roberts again because by the time he returned to Nürnberg I was long gone. Also gone was my life as a door-to-door encyclopedia salesman. I was homeward bound, back to the orchards and hills of sunny California. But first a stop in Paris.

27. FLY ME

My resolve to return home immediately dissipated upon my arrival in Paris which was experiencing an early spring in March. People were going nuts, dizzy with the sunny, balmy weather in the seventies after months of cold, wet, dreary weather. Tops were down in convertibles buzzing around the city, women were in light sundresses, guys in shorts and sunglasses as if going to the beach even if the trees were still bare. The old hands said the spring-like weather would never last. The gloom and drizzle were bound to return. Whatever, it worked for me after the frigid temperatures of Germany. I spent hours sitting in outdoor cafes, meeting old friends—Gerard and Jean-Paul, Seth, Denise and Dede—and wondering where some had gone, including Anne-Marie.

"Strangest thing," said Gerard. "She just up and left a few days after you went to Nürnberg. She also said she might transfer down to the University of Montpellier. She was having a hard time with the Paris weather."

"Oh," I said, wondering but not wanting to pursue this any further.

Seth was up to his same old tricks, telling everybody he was about to set off in a month on the overland trek to Asia. Charlie still spent most of his time in his room but he had stashed the Playboys and was reportedly banging out a first draft of his novel. Gerard was still following his courses at the Foreign Institute but was getting antsy and ready to return to the Bay Area come summer. Jean-Paul was engrossed in his comparative lit courses, but he too was thinking about returning to Cal, because, as he put it, it would be easier to get a Ph.D. degree at Berkeley in comparative lit than at the Sorbonne. "Here, everyone in my major speaks and writes in several languages fluently. I'm just one among hundreds. Back in Berkeley, few do. I would be a standout. The professors would take notice, plus there's less red tape."

Denise was still hovering around the group. She had grown more sophisticated, and her French had improved dramatically. She had come a long way from being a Southern Bell. I had noticed her a few months ago during my first stay in Paris, but then I got caught up with Anne-Marie. But now, no Anne-Marie and Denise still seemed interested. So one Saturday night we did the Alsatian restaurant thing, and I told her of my time in Nürnberg.

"Wow, wild," she said. "I'm surprised you returned. Sounds like you could have made a life there."

"Oh, no. It's time to go home to the good old U.S. and earn some decent money."

"I know what you mean," she nodded. "I'm tiring of Europe too. After school ends, I'll be touring around for a month and then head back to Nashville. Good old red-neck Nashville, home of Hank Williams and Johnny Cash."

"Don't knock it. That's seminal American culture," I replied.

I didn't know whether it was our mutual homesickness or what, but by silent agreement, Denise came back to my hotel room and we explored our American roots.

***

Sure enough, after a week or so of warm spring weather, it turned ugly and I decided enough fooling around, I had to go home. Already I had spent a hundred of my four-hundred dollars. Before it was all gone, I hot-footed it over to the Icelandic Airline office and bought a one-way ticket for the advertised two-hundred dollars. This left me with a measly one hundred dollars to make my way from New York to the Bay Area. Not enough for airfare, maybe enough for a train or a bus. We would see.

When I announced my impending departure to the gang, Seth talked me into going over to Harry's New York Bar for a final farewell. "You can't just leave like that, Brown without hoisting a few."

"Ah, OK," I said dubiously, mentally counting my change. "Just a couple."

Once word got around there would be a farewell bash for Brown at Harry's, my Paris acquaintances came out of the woodwork. People I had not seen since November as well as the regulars, including Denise who gave me an open invitation to visit her in Nashville this summer.

"Come on over, ya all, I'll show you a real good time in fine southern style," she said in an exaggerated southern drawl.

"I'll definitely keep it in mind," I said, mentally reviewing our little tête-à-tête a few days ago.

In short order, our gang had taken over the rear of the bar and was ordering rounds of half-and-half. That's Bass Ale mixed with Guinness. It was indeed a merry time, as we reminisced about the good old days in Paris, back when writers were writers, and painters, painters. We felt the ghosts of Hemingway and Fitzgerald were smiling down upon us.

The downside to this frivolity was that I had to buy several rounds of drinks and that set me back thirty bucks. I now had only seventy dollars and some change to make my way from New York to Berkeley. I eventually made my escape, while the others were happily drinking now on their own dime. I spent my last night in Paris wandering around by myself saying goodbye to the city of light. The next day, I lugged my suitcase over to the American Express office where the airport bus to Luxembourg was waiting.

***

The bus arrived at the Luxembourg Airport two hours before my flight was to leave. I hung around the airport for a while, and then the hunger pangs hit. I had not eaten since breakfast and I figured I would not have the chance for a decent meal for a while, so I treated myself to a steak dinner at a nearby restaurant. A good chunk of pepper steak with a boatload of French fries, washed down with a fine Belgian beer. Cost, five dollars' worth of francs. Then I hiked back to the airport and waited in the lounge until my flight was called.

The passengers were an assorted bunch ranging from budget business travelers to a scattering of student types. One young lady in particular, caught my eye. She was a dark brunette, with cherry red lips and light make up, all bundled up in a heavy fur coat. Probably a money student, spending her daddy's dough in Europe. She boarded the plane several passengers before me, and when I made my way down the aisle, I discovered that I had a seat next to her. What were the odds of that happening? Usually, when I see a hot chick by herself on a plane, I never have a seat next to her. She was in the aisle seat, I had the window. As far as I could tell the center seat was empty. It was a light load that night.

"Pardon, me. It looks like I have the window seat."

"Oh, do tell. Lucky person. I had asked for the window seat, but they had none left," she said, removing her coat from the center seat and standing up so I could get by.

"Say, why don't you take it?" I said. "I'm happy sitting on the aisle. Saves you from getting up and down. I like to wander around the plane. I can't sit still for a ten-hour flight."

"Thanks. I do plan to sleep," she said moving her stuff to the window seat. "Say, since we are going to be seatmates, what's your name?"

"Allan."

"Hi, Allan. I'm Rachel."

"Hi, Rachel."

"Student?" I asked.

"Yes. I spent the fall semester in Vienna and traveled around a bit, but now I'm going home to meet my fate."

"Fate?"

"Yes, I'm going to be married," she said flashing a large diamond engagement ring.

"Congratulations."

"Thank you."

We continued to chat as the Icelandic Jetliner rolled down the runway for the take-off. I told her that I too was a student of sorts but had worked in Germany.

"Oh...that sound's interesting."

So I described my days as an encyclopedia salesman.

"I'd like to try something like that," she said. "I've never really worked. Oh, one summer as a camp counselor in New England." Rachel was from Connecticut and went to some women's college that I had never heard of. She continued "But, sigh, my fate is sealed, so to speak."

"Aren't you looking forward to getting married?" I asked.

"Sure, but I would still like to work. I don't want to have kids right away but maybe George does. He's a bit older than me, a bond trader on Wall Street. Ready to settle down."

"I see."

We chatted on while dining on the airplane meal which was surprisingly good with Icelandic cold cuts and beer. By and by, the lights dimmed as the plane droned on into the night. I reclined my seat and tried to sleep. Rachel had her big fur coat draped over her as she dozed in the window seat.

I don't know how long I had dozed, but Rachel had changed position and was now leaning against me. By and by, I felt her hand take mine and squeeze it. She opened one eye and winked.

"Your hand is so warm. You don't mind?"

"Ah, not at all," I said wondering what was up.

"I always feel so lonely and cold on these night flights," she said. "Just imagine the Atlantic down there. What would it feel like to crash land in that water? Freezing."

"I'm sure."

You don't mind if I snuggle down some more. You have a nice shoulder," she said squeezing my hand again. On an impulse, I gave her a little kiss and she didn't resist. Before we knew it, we were making out, her hand resting lightly on my crotch, under the covers of course.

I always wondered what it would be like to become a member of the "mile-high club." Now through sheer chance, and seating proximity, I was about to find out. By and by, she unzipped my fly. I slipped my hand under her blouse in the darkness and felt her breasts. I slipped my other hand under her dress, now hiked up to her knees under the blanket and went to work.

It was a heady experience, this mutual getting off in an airplane seat, in the dark with other passengers around, oblivious, hurtling through night skies at thirty-five thousand feet above the ocean. Still, I was eager for some real action. I debated trying to make it in the bathroom, but that seemed so gross and uncomfortable.

I checked my watch and noted that we were due to land soon at Reykjavik, Iceland for a two-hour layover. This was part of the deal flying Icelandic Airlines. You had to spend time in Reykjavik. Supposedly, the plane was refueling but actually, they wanted you to shop. I thought maybe we could get a motel room at the airport but didn't have the money to spare.

As the plane came in for a landing, we straightened up and went to the bathroom, looking almost presentable as we de-boarded the plane. Rachel and I dutifully browsed around the duty-free shop for a while, but our minds were not on merchandise.

We went outside into the freezing night air; she all bundled up in her fur coat and me in my ski parka. Over near the edge of the airfield, I noticed an abandoned guard shack. It looked like it was left over from the U.S. military when there was an Air Force base here. I suggested we go on a little walk to get the blood circulating. Rachel gamely agreed. All the time, squeezing my arm.

The shack was deserted but it had a bench and a table and the dirty windows provided some shelter from the wind. I figured the temperature was in the twenties. But it was somewhere in the hundreds between Rachel and me, as we grabbled and groped in the shack, barely lit by the runway lights a hundred yards off. Before I knew it, she had her panties off and was straddling my lap as I sat on the bench. Soon we were going at like a couple of rhesus monkeys. Hot and cold at the same time, sucking in the chill night air, yet burning inside each other. She was hot, hot, hot and hungry. As we rutted along, I couldn't believe that she was engaged to another. Soon, too, soon it was over, and we were panting. Afterwards, she shivered. "Gosh, I don't know what got into me. I guess it's the adventure of the unknown."

"What about George?"

"George? He'll never know the difference, she said tossing her hair back. "Right now is all that counts."

***

We returned to the plane and both fell immediately to sleep, her head on my shoulder, sleeping like a child. As the sun arose in the Arctic morning, the plane skirted Newfoundland, Nova Scotia, Maine and finally Kennedy Airport. Our encounter seemed like a dream.

Minutes before we landed, Rachel woke up, went to the bathroom and made herself up. She had told me her fiancé and her parents would meet her. I wondered how she could pull this off so coolly after being with me. As we disembarked from the Icelandic Jetliner, I said, "If you ever break up with George, here is my number." I handed her my home address in Martinez and telephone number.

"Allan, don't worry. I'll not forget you. But right now I have to go along with the plan."

She walked ahead of me into the terminal and into the waiting arms of George and her parents at the gate. I followed a few yards behind, smiling, wondering what George, a big serious looking Jewish guy, would do if he knew. I marveled at Rachel's coolness and duplicity and thought that this gal would go a long way in life.

28. HELLO AMERICA

A big, nasty, indifferent New York jerked me back to the reality at hand, reducing randy Rachel to a fading wet dream as the airport bus made its way to the Port Authority Terminal. Greyhound operated out of the same terminal.

After due consideration, I decided what the hell. I'll take the Greyhound to Oakland. Although it would be a three-day trip, it would cost only fifty dollars. Otherwise, I would have to beg for money from home to fly or take a cross-country train. Here was Greyhound right in front of me and ready to go. The next express left for Oakland at noon and points in between.

I settled down in the waiting room. It wasn't too bad, somewhat scruffy but at least it was relatively clean. The worn plastic seats were fairly comfortable. The people were a varied lot ranging from students to the elderly, to the immigrant types, to middle-class folks who could have afforded better but for some reason preferred the bus.

After sitting for a while, I began to smell myself. It was not good. What with all the activities on the plane and the constant travel, I felt cheesy. I had a clean change of clothes in my suitcase but I needed to wash up. Dare I make use of the Greyhound facilities? Yes, give it a try.

I went into the men's bathroom and lo, off in an alcove there was a row of lockers and shower stalls with doors that locked from the inside. Why not? I had done this at the bathhouse in Paris. How much worse could this be? So I rented a locker and a towel from a little man behind a counter. I locked up my clothes and stepped into the shower with a towel around my waist. The shower stream was not strong, but warm enough and I proceeded to lather up and cleanse my body and soul from the dirt of Europe. Twenty minutes later, I stepped out as a new man, a newborn babe in the land of a new America.

Following my shower, the time passed quickly and before I knew it, I was boarding the noon express bound initially for Chicago with a full load of passengers on this dreary March afternoon. I managed to find a window seat near the front but spent little time looking out the window and was soon fast asleep.

The first rest stop came in the middle of a heavily forested section of Pennsylvania. My stomach was growling. I hadn't had anything to eat for hours except a hot dog at the bus terminal. I went into the Howard Johnson Restaurant and Inn and had a bowl of soup with a sandwich, all the time wondering how I was going to make my meager funds of now only nine dollars last for three days. Somehow, I had to reduce my eating expenses. The only thing I could think of was to buy a large loaf of hardy bread and some cheese and cold cut slices. I could drink water for liquids. So following my soup dinner, I went over to the bakery and deli section of the Howard Johnson complex and bought a crusty loaf of German type bread with a chunk of cheese. That left me with only five bucks. It would have to do.

I climbed back on the bus with my goods, stashing them in the overhead bin, and then settled down to sleep some more. However, I now had a seatmate, a nice middle-aged woman going home to Chicago. She had gotten on the so-called express at the Howard Johnson. After twenty minutes of chitchat, I closed my eyes and zonked out lulled by the hum of the bus, the surprisingly comfortable seats, and the fact that I had not slept for 24-hours.

On and on, the bus went through the night along Interstate 80, through Pennsylvania, Ohio, and Indiana. Finally, in the wee hours of the morning, we rolled into Chicago. Seven hundred and ninety miles in eighteen hours. Not very speedy but at least I was getting somewhere. We had an hour layover in Chicago and then it was into the great heartland of Illinois and Iowa. I had thought this portion of the trip would go fast. Wide open spaces and all. But I soon discovered that Illinois and Iowa were hardly wide open. The Interstate was clogged with car traffic and eighteen-wheelers and when we approached the Quad Cities on the Mississippi, our express bus slowed to a crawl and suddenly degenerated into a local, making stops every few miles.

The Mississippi River, itself, wasn't very impressive. Simply a broad, slow moving, muddy river with grain and freight barges plugging along past dirty, industrialized shores. Hardly the romantic stretch of water that I had envisioned from reading *Life on the Mississippi* by Mark Twain. Where was Huck? Where was his sidekick, "nigger" Jim? Maybe a hundred miles south or so, near the town of Hannibal, Missouri.

We were now off Interstate 80 on a secondary road, crawling through the remnants of harvested cornfields under gunmetal skies which threatened to rain or possibly snow. The trees were all bare. No leaves in sight. Not even an evergreen. God, how drab the Midwest was in March.

Finally, we came to Iowa City and the University of Iowa and here the half-empty bus filled up with college students bound for Des Moines. From the chatter I overheard, they were eventually going south to Mississippi to register voters as part of a Civil Rights drive. I wondered where they got the idealism and energy. Didn't they know white people who try to sign up voters disappear and/or are murdered down there? Just last summer, the so-called "Freedom Summer," the bodies of three civil rights workers were found buried in an earthen dam. I suddenly felt old and out of touch with this generation of college kids, although I had graduated only two years earlier.

After a late dinner stop in Des Moines, a minor crisis developed. An elderly lady had taken too many blood pressure pills and felt sick. A half hour later, she passed out. People wondered if she was dead. Somebody felt her pulse. It was weak but there. The driver called ahead for an ambulance to meet us at the next town. As she was loaded into the ambulance, we thought we had seen the last of her.

Moving on, the bus began to make time, speeding towards the Iowa/Nebraska border. Once we hit Nebraska, the driver opened up and the miles clicked off as we traveled on through the night. The next morning, we were into the heart of Wyoming with a breakfast stop at Laramie, the home of the University of Wyoming. From what I could see, it was a charming little western town.

Back on the bus, I gagged on the smell of curry and urine. An East Indian in a filthy looking turban and long coat had boarded the bus at Laramie and now sat in the rear. He smelled as if he had not bathed in a year. He sat silently by himself and stared out the window. Other passengers were mumbling. I couldn't believe that the driver let this guy on. More riders got on and gagged. The bus was packed like a sardine can. We rolled out and people started to openly complain. Finally, a couple hours later, we stopped in Rawlins Wyoming. The East Indian left the bus for a stretch and when he tried to re-board, the driver stopped him.

"You better hit the showers here, fellow. I can't take you like that. Too many complaints. You can catch another bus in an hour," said the driver, apparently imbued with the authority to bounce people from the bus if he so desired.

The East Indian said nothing but bowed his head and retreated to the rest stop. The passengers cheered.

On and on we went. Now the Rockies were closing in. I could see them off in the distance. The pass that we were traveling through was the same one the covered wagons took over a century ago. It was formally known at the South Pass. Somewhere along this stretch, the immensity of the United States struck me. Europe seemed old and cramped compared to these vistas.

Somehow, this endless panorama of forests, plains, high desert and mountains made me feel proud that I was an American and that my fate was inextricably caught up with the continent. I suppose it was a frontier fever that I felt, riding this bus, the fever of endless possibilities if you just kept heading west.

Finally, we turned south to Salt Lake City. It was early evening with snow covering the Wasatch Range, reflecting the setting sun in a golden haze. No wonder the Mormons thought they had reached the Promised Land. We had a mysterious layover of nearly three hours in Salt Lake City before the run to Reno. So I used the time to walk around Temple Square. All lit up, the temple was an imposing hulk of a building with six spires, almost medieval looking. I didn't know what to think about Mormonism. Some said it was a crazy, faddish religion, a cult. Others said the Book of Mormon was simply the updated word of God. All of that was debatable, but when it came to farming and business, the Mormons were experts, essentially making this high desert country a land of riches.

I made the rounds of Temple Square with Max, an older bus mate who was retired and did nothing but ride the Greyhound for half the year. He said he always sat in the seat behind the driver. He bought into the Greyhound motto, "Leave the driving to us."

As he put it, "It's cheap and painless. I can stare out the window for hours. The best part is out west when you hit those national parks. Amazing what you can see from the window."

"Doesn't that get old, riding the dog?" I asked.

"Sure. About every fourth day I get off, find myself a motel room and clean up for a couple of days, but then I'm raring to go again. I don't drive. I wouldn't want to drive. Living in Brooklyn, I have no need for a car."

***

During our Salt Lake City layover, the lady with high blood pressure caught up with us. She had been on another Greyhound a few hours behind. "Yeah, I told those idiot doctors, I didn't need to stay in the hospital. I was all right. I just got up and walked out and caught the next bus along. I'll be going out on your bus with you all." She smiled.

Swell.

A new driver came on at Salt Lake City. He didn't have a clue about the blood pressure lady. And judging by his demeanor, he probably wouldn't have cared. Most new drivers greeted and kibitzed with the passengers. Not this guy. Immaculate in his freshly pressed uniform, hat just right, shining black driving gloves, you could tell he meant business.

We rolled out of Salt Lake City around 11 p.m. on the five-hundred mile run to Reno across the great Nevada desert. We could see nothing in the darkened desert but we could hear the wind noise whistling by. We could feel the motion of the Greyhound, although we had no definite notion of its speed. Up to this point in the trip, five hundred miles on the "dog" meant at least ten hours. But somehow, this driver was granted a dispensation. Woosh into the night. Seven hours later, we pulled into Reno. He had averaged nearly 75-miles an hour with only two rest stops. As soon as the bus was parked in the station, our driver got up and stepped down without a word, although one lone passenger in back clapped and said, "Well done." The driver nodded and then disappeared.

It was now 7 a.m. in Reno with the sun breaking over the desert and striking the Sierras looming to the west of the city. It was relatively warm, somewhere in the sixties. We had a one hour wait for the last leg of our trip.

To pass the time, I chatted with a woman with three little kids. I had babysat her kids on the bus for a few hours while she slept. She was a nice lady in her thirties who had just divorced and was trying to start a new life in Sacramento where she had a sister.

"Judy says she can set me up. I'm in the beauty parlor business. At least that's what I did before I got married to that no good son of a bitch."

"Well, I wish you all the luck. Lots of opportunity in California. The state is growing like a weed," I replied trying to be encouraging.

I excused myself, went outside the station, and gazed at the Truckee River running through a downtown park. Reno at this hour was serene with the babble of the river and the chirp of the birds. No one gets up early in Reno. It's a late night gambling town.

I bought a coffee with my last few dollars and a couple of muffins, having already devoured my loaf of German bread and hunk of cheese. As I soaked in the early morning sun, I thought it wasn't far now. These were my old stomping grounds. Five hours max to Oakland on a clear March day with hopefully dry, snow-cleared roads over Donner Pass.

The call came to board the bus. A half hour later, we were sailing over the Donner Pass on a new stretch of Interstate 80. All of a sudden, everything was green. Green pines, green grass. Clear blue sky setting off snow topped granite mountains. An hour later, we were plunging down I-80, through the forest, into the foothills, the grass now even more emerald green. A quick rest stop in Auburn. I got out and breathed in the sweet, clear air. This was a real California spring. None of that faux stuff as in Paris. No gunmetal landscape as in the Midwest. Down, down we went. I opened the bus window; it was warmer still, maybe in the 70s as we hit the Sacramento Valley. Woosh, over around and into downtown Sacramento. A half-hour at the Sacramento bus station and then we were on our way again.

On and on we went—Davis, Vacaville, a quick stop at Travis Air Force Base, then Vallejo, over the Carquinez Bridge, Hercules, San Pablo, Berkeley, traveling along I-80 which had morphed into the East Bay Freeway. Finally, we pulled into the Oakland Bus Terminal. I was high. I was energized. I was back in the Bay Area—Europe a cold, distant memory. I retrieved my suitcase and in a flash was on a Muni bus going up Broadway to Berkeley. Soon, I was at Bancroft and Telegraph and hustled over to the Cal Book Store where Bobbie now worked.

She was busy stocking books in the back of the store when I approached. I stood there quietly until she looked up, startled.

"Boo, I'm back," I said.

"Allan, what a surprise!"

"Surprise?"

"Yes, Tom and I didn't think you were ever coming back judging by your letters," she said as she gave me a little peck on the cheek. "The last we heard was that you had a job in Germany selling books."

"Ah, well, I'm back. Back for a good long while. I had a chance to sort out my priorities. But right now, I need a bath. I stink from riding a Greyhound for three days in a row."

"Yes, you do stink," she said wrinkling her nose. "Tom is on campus. Here's my house key. Go take a bath."

"I thank you from the bottom of my heart." I wanted to give her a real kiss. She was still so fresh and appealing. But I restrained myself and hustled over to her apartment with my suitcase.

A half-hour later, I was soaking in their bear claw bathtub with all the implements for a good scrub. It wasn't quite a German bathroom, but it would do. I slipped down in the warm water, almost to my nose and dozed off. I was home.

BOOK TWO
1965—1968

1. THE APARTMENT

There it was: my dream apartment in the Berkeley hills. True, it was only a sublet for the summer, but for me, it was nirvana. Up at the end of Virginia Street, nestled in a grove of redwoods, overlooking the whole Bay Area. It was the first story of a two-story redwood shake building with a flagstone fireplace, beamed ceilings, and a sunken living room. All furnished in an upscale 1960s décor with original oil paintings on the wall of Berkeley scenes and a big king-size bed in the one bedroom. A nice kitchen with all the appliances, even a dishwasher. The bathroom was small and off to the back. A minor consideration. Also, a back porch and a sundeck with view of Berkeley and the Bay Area.

The Jewish couple living there were graduate students, she an art major, he going for a Ph.D. in psychology. They were returning to New York for the summer.

"Please, please, take care of it," she pleaded. "I'm sure you will agree that it's a beautiful apartment."

"Don't worry, I will. I will. It's just me. I'll take care of your stuff," I assured her.

"You sure?"

"Yes, I'm sure. I won't be here much. I'm working in San Leandro."

"Well, if you're sure," she said somewhat reassured, "then that'll be the first and last month rent, please. Four hundred dollars."

Yes, it was not cheap but I was hooked. Also, I was making good money surveying so I had cash on hand. I moved in early June. But let's back up here. What was I doing living in Berkeley again?

***

After my return from Germany in late March, I had lolled around a couple of days at the apartment of Tom and Bobbie and then feeling guilty, useless and broke, I went home to Martinez to a mixed reception.

Mother: "Thank God, you're back."

Dad: "Have a nice trip, son? What are you going to do now?"

Mother: "Now don't badger Allan. Let him get his bearings."

Dad: "Surveying season is starting soon."

Mother: "Stop it Ray. Look at him. Doesn't he look great?"

Dad: "Yeah, a lot better than the first time when he came back from Europe sick as a dog."

And so it went. I was reminded by Dad that I was going to be twenty-five in a few weeks and that I had better get cracking with my real life instead of running around. I mentioned that I was thinking about going back to school, San Francisco State, maybe in Film and Television.

"Fine, fine, Allan," he said. "But you'll to have to do it on your own. I think we have done our bit in helping you and Don through college."

"No argument there," I replied. "I plan to survey for the season. That should give me a couple of thousand bucks."

"Well, get cracking. What about the Army Reserve? Don't you have to go meetings?"

"Yeah, don't worry, Dad, I'll take care of that. Right now, I'm in a control group. No meetings required."

"Humph," snorted Dad. "Well, the Army Reserve sent me this letter inquiring as to your whereabouts. I'll leave it to you to inform them that you are back. Just remember to do your duty."

"Sure Dad."

What I did was fill out the Army Reserve form using my Nürnberg address and then sent the form to my Norwegian friend Eric who was still in Nürnberg. He sent it on to the Army with the Nürnberg postmark and voilà, I was golden. Still in the control group with no obligation to go to meetings.

***

Two weeks at home was enough to convince me that it was time to move out. I was too old to live at home for an extended period. However, in order to get out, I had to first find a job.

To expedite my search, I reclaimed ownership of the old 1955 Chevy station wagon. Even though it was now ten years old, it still ran great with its big V-8 engine. I made good use of it tooling around the East Bay. Dad still had his 1964 Buick.

First, I went by Wilson and Company looking for surveying work, but they claimed they didn't have anything. I think they were still pissed that I quit in last fall. It was all right for these firms to lay you off, but heaven forbid if you quit. Luckily, through the union hall, I learned that an engineering firm in San Leandro was hiring crews to do preliminary surveys for the Bay Area Rapid Transit System or "BART" as it came to be known. The dream of a rapid transit system linking the Bay Area was indeed going to become a reality. I went down to San Leandro and was hired on the spot.

"You seem to have the experience we need, Mr. Brown," said Ron, the head surveyor. "Good chainmen are hard to find. Let's give it a try. You'll be on Len's crew."

Len was a jolly, heavyset guy with a southern twang. In the fifties and early sixties, he had worked around the Pacific on various government construction projects—Guam, Micronesia, the Marshalls Islands. Exotic, far away stuff. He even claimed he had surveyed the damage following the A-bombing and H-bombing of the Bikini atolls.

"I'll probably die from radiation poisoning," he said one day while sitting in the survey truck, "Although the counters weren't clicking much. The government boys said it was safe. Still, I would have liked to seen those bombs go off."

"Yeah, it must have been quite a sight," I replied.

"Boy, they sure fucked up those atolls," he continued. "Hardly anything left. A few just disappeared. The Marshallese are still wandering around dazed, wondering what the fuck happened. Some of them are having fucked up babies. Most are drunks now, the women whores. I did a stretch on Guam. That was more civilized than the rest of those islands, but I still had to get out of there and come home."

As I was to learn, Len knew his stuff. He had quite a brain in that fat head. And best of all, he was not a slave driver. As he put it: "When it's time to hump, we hump but this is a cost-plus government job. Accuracy is far more important than speed. We will do it right the first time."

What we were doing was surveying the BART right-away along some old Southern Pacific tracks. It consisted mainly of taking elevation profiles of the ground at fifty-foot intervals. It was boring work but good money, around $5.00 an hour with time-and-a-half on Saturdays. My duties consisted mainly of holding the elevation rod, pounding a few stakes, and now and then running the transit and calling off the elevation to Len who got tired of squinting through the instrument and held the rod himself. We were a two-man crew and we took long lunch breaks and I heard his life story over and over.

Len was a paradox. Born and raised in the South, yet he lived in a black section of Oakland and had a Guamanian wife. One time we drove to his house and he went in to visit his wife. I waited in the survey truck and munched on a sandwich. When he returned, I heard this: "The Micronesian women are great. They have a different attitude about sex. Any time, any place but they are still not whores. She'll be making dinner and I'll come up behind and grab some. She'll calmly turn off the oven and we'll go upstairs. She's a good mother too. That's why I married her. We have two cute little half-breeds."

"Sounds like a good life," I said finishing my sandwich, wondering if I could settle for so little down the road. Once again, I couldn't see staying in this surveying game long. It was great money for the moment but not a long-term prospect for me. I was more than ever determined to go to graduate school.

***

I settled in rapidly and began my daily routine. Up at six, a cold cereal breakfast. Down to my Chevy station wagon parked on a steep, narrow side street, wishing it were a sports car. Drive to San Leandro via the Mac Arthur Freeway. Seven thirty the workday began. Back in Berkeley by five. Making good wages, about a grand a month with overtime.

After work, I would chill on my back porch, barbecuing steak and sipping red wine, and watching the sunset over the Golden Gate. Living here was everything that I had hoped except for one small detail. No one was around from my old gang. Jean-Paul and Gerard were still in Europe, although both were expected back in a month. Brother Don was still in Australia although there were reports that Nancy wanted to come back to California.

Most importantly, there were no women around from the old days. I had to strike out anew. One day while I was drinking beer alone on my back porch, I chatted with a next-door neighbor lady watering her flowers in her garden below me. Joyce was a pleasant looking lady, probably in her early forties, married to a math professor. She was still trim and for some reason concerned that I, a bachelor, was, eating OK. I assured her that I was.

"Well, maybe I can interest you some home baked chocolate chip cookies."

"That sounds good," I replied, trying to be polite.

The next afternoon, Joyce knocked at my door. I had skipped work that day because of a cold. I was taking a snooze in my big double bed when I heard the knock. I answered the door and there she stood in a low-cut peasant blouse and shorts with nicely tanned legs. Joyce was holding a platter of cookies covered with cellophane. Hmm. It appeared that she was offering more than cookies. I was taken aback. This was a married woman with four kids. Of course, hubby was down on the campus. The kids were off at school. I invited her in.

"I saw your car here and wondered if you were sick or something," inquired Joyce.

"Slight cold," I answered. "But really just taking the day off. Have a seat," I said waving to the couch.

"Ah, I can't stay," she said nervously. "I have to get back. I have a lot to do before the kids come home. I just wanted to deliver these cookies."

"Oh come on Joyce, let's have a cookie or two. I have some cold milk, or maybe a beer," I offered.

"Ummm, I would love to but I really can't stay. Maybe I can come back another day when I have more time."

"Oh, OK. That sounds like a good idea," I replied, thinking she is having second thoughts. Also, I wasn't sure I wanted to get mixed up with a married woman. Maybe her mild-mannered husband wasn't so mild when pissed off. I didn't need the grief. Still, we would see. In any case, Joyce faded from my mind as other opportunities opened up in the female world in which my apartment played a critical role.

***

At one point, I thought I was living in Scandinavia because my apartment soon saw a procession of blondes that rivaled Stockholm. How that happened, I didn't know except by chance. It was amazing that it did happen because my preference was usually for brunettes. Nevertheless, I managed to cope.

There was Klara, a Swedish woman who worked at the Swedish Consulate. I met her at an open house there. The Swedes loved to throw parties for the San Franciscans, as did many other consulates. It was part of the diplomatic culture in the City. Brother Don had clued me in on that a couple of years ago when he palled around with an Aussie named Mike who

California Split

was a driver at the Australian Consulate.

"Good food. All free," Don used to say. "The women aren't bad either."

Since I was nostalgic for all things Euro, I made my way over to one such gig in mid-June and lo, I ran into Klara who worked for the consulate as a secretary. She was older than I, in her early 30s but at the time she seemed interested in me. I was all dressed up in my blue business suit, looking like a diplomat but with a deep tan. I guess that intrigued her. She had short blonde hair with startling blue eyes and a very womanly chest. She was new to the Bay Area and was curious about Berkeley. So I made a date to show her around.

The next Saturday, we wandered around campus, up and down Telegraph Avenue and wound up on the Northside which she liked the best. After a couple of beers at La Vals, we headed up to my apartment where we chilled and I barbecued a steak. After dinner, and a few glasses of wine and some raga music, things began to get cozy, but alas, when she sensed where it was headed, she announced that she had to go back to the City. Would, I drive her please?

"Of course, of course."

As I drove her back in my grungy station wagon, I sensed that she couldn't deal with an obvious blue collar, student type. She was after bigger game. Probably a lawyer, a doctor or at least a real diplomat.

***

However, I struck gold one night a week later while doing my laundry at a laundromat on Hearst Avenue. She was a stunning looking Nordic blonde in a long flowing dress that nevertheless, showed off her body. It appeared she wore no bra. Very smashing looking with her long, almost white hair. She smiled as I went about my business washing my jeans, shorts and T-shirts, filthy from surveying

"Boy you sure have a lot dirty clothes?"

"Yeah, when you work in the dirt all day, it gets that way?"

"What do you do?"

"Oh, surveying. We layout subdivisions, lots, roads, that sort of thing."

"Are you an engineer or something?"

"Something, like that. I just do this for money until I go back to grad school."

We chatted on as we washed our clothes. Her name was Lina and she was staying with some friends in the Berkeley for a few weeks. She had just graduated from Mt. Diablo High School in Concord and was scheduled to go to Diablo Valley College next fall but wanted to transfer to Berkeley.

We talked for a while as we watched our laundry going around and around in the dryer. She mentioned that she had just bought the *Freewheelin'* Bob Dylan album, and pointed to a shopping bag that she had been lugging around.

"Cool. I have a great stereo if you want to hear it right." (The Jewish couple's stereo.)

"Really," she said sounding pleased.

"Yeah, look we could listen to it at my place up the hill and then later I'll drive you wherever you are staying."

"Oh, I'm staying with some friends off Grizzly Peak Road. She smiled and agreed. "Also I have some pot."

"Sounds like a plan."

Well, back at my pad we listened to Dylan and smoked a joint. The music was great, the pot even better. Before we knew it, we were sprawled on my king-size bed. I began to undress her. She offered no resistance, only giggled.

She was absolutely stunning, fine boned, fine blonde hair everywhere, perfect skin, full breasted, tapered waist, long, shapely firm legs. Un-fucking-believable. Lina also had a nice smile. As we made it, I vaguely wondered if she was eighteen yet.

As it turned out, she was certainly enthusiastic but not too experienced. Really, Lina was too beautiful to fuck. It was better just to look at her. However, her personality, while sunny, was bland. Afterwards, she slept in my arms like a child. I felt like I had taken candy from a baby.

The next morning, I proposed that she could hang out at my place if she wanted for a few days. She considered my offer but said she her friends were counting on her staying there. I was perturbed but it was probably for the best. I would be like a parent taking care of a kid. Therefore, I drove her up to her friends' pad, a large A-frame shack on a back road off Grizzly Peak. I made a date to see her in a few days.

But on the appointed day, Lina was distant and didn't want to do anything so we listened to "Blowin in the Wind" and sipped on white wine. I think she had come to realize that I was too old for her. Her friends were young, just out of high school. All had long hair, smoked pot and listened to Bob Dylan. Lina told me she wanted to do some sort of hallucinogenic drug that was fast becoming popular, called LSD.

"It's supposed to blow your mind. Put you into another world," she enthused.

"Really," I replied. "Why would you want to blow your pretty little mind?"

I don't think that last remark went over well with her. Anyway, the last time I saw Lina was at a party I threw. She came with a couple of cute girlfriends and impressed the hell out of my old fraternity brothers whom I had invited. But Lina remained aloof and distant. I think by that time she had another boyfriend.

***

Next, I went back to my roots in Martinez. I had run into Kate, a girl that I had known in high school. While very nice and pretty, she was considered a freak since she was six-foot-three. The kids called her "Amazon." No one, including me, ever went out with her in high school although I was friendly and felt sorry for her. Now, when I spotted her at the Martinez Safeway one weekend, she came off as an elegant blonde giant, possibly a model. She had recently graduated from nursing school and worked at UC Medical Center in San Francisco. She told me she had an apartment in San Francisco and invited me over, giving me her phone number. I knew that she had had a crush on me for years. In fact, I had gone to a nursing school dance with her a few years ago. Still, it made me feel odd.

Anyway, I yielded. I phoned her up and suggested we to go a movie in Berkeley. She said, "I'll drive over to your place and we can go from there."

"Great."

On the appointed night, she drove up in an Austin Healey, looking very chic and with it. We went down to Telegraph, had a bite to eat at a Middle Eastern Restaurant and then saw a flick at the Cinema-Guild. I think it was Fellini's *Eight and a Half*. Afterwards, it was back to the apartment for a good night. I was ready to end the evening right there, but Kate, said she wouldn't mind sharing a joint. So I put on an old Georges Brassens record and we shared a joint. By now, it was obvious, she wanted something more. She had let it be known that I intrigued her. She called me "Tom Jones", especially when she saw me in the black turtleneck sweater that I was wearing on that cold Berkeley night.

Well, one thing led to another and soon I was in bed with a giant. It felt odd being with someone my size. On the other hand, it was exciting. There was so much of her and she was strong. We were like two gladiators on the field of battle. By morning, I was worn and bruised and begging for mercy. I stumbled out of bed and fixed some coffee.

Kate nonchalantly got up, took a shower, fixed her hair while humming a little tune and kissed me goodbye. She had an afternoon shift at the hospital.

"I hope to hear from you soon, my Tom Jones," she said as she headed out the door.

Yes, I knew I was living irresponsibly. But I didn't care. Thanks to the apartment, the good times were rolling. And they were about to roll even faster.

2. HOSTEL

Early July, Jean-Paul and Gerard returned from France. Jean-Paul had apparently given up on the Sorbonne and would now be pursuing a PhD in Comparative Lit at Berkeley. Gerard also planned to continue in graduate school for a master's degree in Comparative Literature.

I saw Jean-Paul only briefly as he was headed down to San Mateo to stay with his mother for the summer. Gerard was staying with his parents for a few weeks as well. The family had just moved from Martinez to Berkeley. Gerard's father, a former French high school teacher, was now a professor of education teaching graduate students at Cal how to teach French.

Gerard and Jean-Paul had brought along four little French girls. They had driven cross-country from New York in a banged up station wagon, stopping in Nashville as guests of Denise, the girl I had "known" briefly in Paris. All were enthused by the country-and-western scene, so much so that the girls bought themselves cowboy hats, Levis, and cowboy boots.

"*C'était formidable!*" exclaimed Viola

"*J'aime bien Nashville,*" confessed Jeanette

"*J'aime Johnny Cash,*" cooed Lilly

"*C'est vraiment américain,*" assessed Nicole.

As soon as Gerard saw my pad, his eyes lit up and suggested that maybe his little flock of French girls could stay here since I appeared to have plenty of space. His new Berkeley abode was in total disarray from the recent move by his parents.

"Ah, well. I don't know," I hesitated. "This is a sublet. I have to be careful of stuff."

"Come on Al, do your part for Franco-American relations."

"Yes, Al" chimed in Nicole, the cutest of the French girls, a shapely little blonde who came from a wealthy Parisian family and who was an English major. In a precise English accent, she announced, "We will cook and clean for you, take care of everything. This apartment would be very nice for us."

Well, what could I do? I relented. Of course, it meant giving up my bedroom with my big king size bed. All four could sleep in the same bed since they were so tiny. Nicole, the tallest, was about five-four. I would have to sleep on the daybed in the living room.

The girls took over. First, they gave the place a thorough cleaning, top to bottom, especially the bathroom and kitchen. They did all the laundry including mine and ironed it. For a while, I thought I was living in a Chinese laundry. They cooked all the meals, breakfast, lunch and dinner, making delicious omelets, fish and beef dishes etc. I had to give them rides to the Berkeley Coop for their natural foods. I also took them out to Martinez for a swim at the Forest Hills pool. They were interested in small town California, so I showed them around Martinez in my grungy station wagon. My parents held a backyard barbecue for them. My father was dazzled and my mother amused. She described the girls as little birds.

At one point, we had a party at the apartment which featured me barbecuing a slab of chuck roast and they, fixing elaborate side dishes, washed down medieval style with red Pisano wine which the French girls diplomatically pronounced as decent table wine. Besides the girls, Gerard, and some old frat brothers were there. Even my upstairs neighbor, the Contessa, put in a brief appearance at the party, sniffed at the goings on and then left. (More about her later.)

After everybody went home, all four girls collapsed on the bed, half-drunk with hard rock pounding in our ears. On an impulse, I plopped down beside them on the bed. At first, they were startled, then one started to giggle, another gave me a kiss on my cheek. I leaned over to Nicole and gave her a little peck. Then more laughter and rolling around and light making out and I'm thinking, "Hey this could turn into something." But just at the point that things were getting promising, Nicole got up and like a mother hen ordered me out. "This has gone far enough, Allan. I think you should go to the other room."

"Uh, OK," I replied groggily.

The other three girls just giggled.

Then, softer, Nicole added, "Do not think we do not appreciate your hospitality but I think we are all tired tonight."

"Uh, fine," I said dragging my ass out and collapsing on the daybed in the living room and falling sound asleep.

I don't know how long I slept, but I felt a soft, nude female form slipping into my daybed. I didn't know if I were dreaming or what. But I woke up and found the Contessa beside me, saying, "Hush. I need you now."

A half hour later, she slipped out of my daybed and climbed back into her jeans, and left saying, "I guess that'll show those little French snots."

Female jealousy. What a trip!

***

My housing situation became even more complicated when André, Gerard's German friend from Paris arrived fully expecting to bunk at my place. André was a cool guy with a beautiful fiancée who was to join him later in San Francisco. She was a Lufthansa stewardess. However, based on what I saw of André in Paris and here in Berkeley, it was an open arrangement. Gerard had promised him a place to stay at my apartment but I was not in the mood for any more guests. It just so happened that I saw my neighbor Joyce a day before Andrés' arrival watering her plants in her garden. She remarked on my little French guests.

"My, how exciting, playing host to all those French girls."

"Well, yes, it has its moments but we are packed to the gills. It's hard to turn around here."

"Well, if you are short of space, I'd be glad to take a couple off your hands,"

"Really?"

"Well, yes. Michael is gone for a week on some boring conference. I would be glad to play hostesses."

"Uh, I can handle the French girls, but I have a German friend coming, André who needs a place to stay. He's the son of the mayor of Bonn."

"Really?" her eyes widened.

"Yeah, he's a cool cat. A gentleman."

"I'm sure. I would certainly love to have him as a house guest too," she purred.

"I think you have yourself a deal."

When André arrived, I told him of the arrangements. He was cool with that. In fact, when Joyce came over to introduce herself in her low-cut peasant blouse and shorts, André got that gleam in his eye, turned to me and winked.

So there we were, all snug as bugs in a rug for a couple of weeks. Again, eating and feasting well, partying and staying up half the night. I managed to get through days of boring surveying, half-asleep, but Len didn't seem to notice.

Towards the end of their stay, André and the girls begged me to take them up to Lake Tahoe for the weekend. They wanted to swim in the lake and gamble at the casinos along the South Shore. I recruited Gerard and his old Hudson to share the load and we drove up to Lake Tahoe early Saturday morning in two cars. We arrived around noon, found some rooms in a motel by the beach. The girls thought Lake Tahoe was spectacular and indeed it was looking good that day with the mountains in the background, clear blue skies, warm in the 80s, the lake sparkling, the water crystal clear. André and the girls tried water skiing with mixed success. Gerard and I gave it a pass, content to lie on the beach, soaking up the rays and drinking beer. By and by, the afternoon waned. We went back to the motel, took showers and Andre, Gerard and I put on Hawaiian shirts and white khakis for our outing to the casinos.

Our first stop was the buffet dinner at Harrah's Casino. A sumptuous feast with prime rib, shrimp and crab all laid out buffet style for only $4.95 per person. The girls could not believe their eyes.

"*Mon Dieu*, so much food."

"I'm going to become a cow with all this *boeuf*."

"This will make me fat," said Nicole, "But that's OK because I will starve back in Paris."

We all loaded up our plates and went at it, washing the buffet down with beer and wine.

Following dinner, it was time to hit the casino. I wasn't too enthusiastic about throwing my money away but André was especially eager. He wanted to play every game in the room—blackjack, roulette, craps, etc. I informed three of the girls that since only Nicole and André were over twenty-one, they would simply have to watch at the gaming tables. Gerard, Nicole and I played the slots for a time while André studied the blackjack table but he then decided it was too complicated to learn on the spot. He wanted simple fast action. Meanwhile, Gerard and I moved over to the roulette table and started playing. André came over and watched. I managed to lose twenty bucks but Gerard made about twenty-five. André was intrigued.

"It looks so simple. You bet on whether that little ball lands on a red or black. That's a fifty-fifty chance."

"Yeah, but see that green zero and green double zero on the wheel," I said. "That means you have less than a fifty-fifty chance of hitting on either black or red. It's the same idea for the even and odd numbers."

"Bah, it so simple, so easy a baby could play." And André proceeded to spend the next couple of hours at the roulette table. He was up big and then down big, then up big, all the while mesmerized by that spinning wheel. We tried to convince him to give up and walk away while he was ahead.

"Leave me alone. I know what I am doing," he protested.

Finally, on a downswing, he bet it all, convinced his luck would change. It didn't. He lost over five hundred dollars, essentially all his spending money for his one month stay in America. He smiled weakly, saying, "Well, that was a thrill. Now I know how Dostoevsky's gambler felt. I'm sure I can get more money from my father. "

As it turned out, back at the motel on a long-distance call to Germany, the good Mayor was royally pissed. Not only did he refuse to send money, he ordered Andre home immediately on the return portion of his round-trip ticket.

"But what about, Karen," he pleaded. "She is to meet me in a few days. We were going to travel throughout California."

According to André, his father simply said something to the effect of, "Too bad. She can go on by herself or come home with you."

Two days later, André bid us goodbye and headed over to San Francisco International Airport for the flight home.

A few days after that, the four French girls kissed me on my cheek and said goodbye. They were off on a cross-country Greyhound bus trip via Yellowstone, the Black Hills of the South Dakota, Chicago and thence to New York and Paris.

My role as an international host was over and I was relieved.

3. THE CONTESSA

Let's back up here and introduce you properly to Sigrid Von Plante or as we referred to her, "The Contessa." She lived in the upstairs apartment. I met her a few days after I moved in. She had come down to "borrow a cup of sugar." Actually, she was just curious about the young man (me) who had taken the sublet. She was tall and thin, with light honey brown hair and chiseled aristocratic features. Not exactly beautiful, more handsome but still very attractive in a haughty sort of way. She formally shook my hand and introduced herself in a British accent with a hint of a Scandinavian lilt. I figured she was in her late twenties but I later learned she was my age, twenty-five. She also claimed she was descended from a long line of Danish nobility.

I told her I had no sugar but she was welcome to a beer. She accepted and we sat down in the living room and drank a couple of Heinekens.

"You know, I have never been inside this apartment," she said looking around. "I always kept my distance from those New York Jews. But it is rather interesting with those paintings. That one for instance reminds me of a woman's genitalia," she said pointing to a pink flowering thing.

"Really? I always thought it was some flower, kind of like a Georgia O'Keeffe painting," I replied.

"Perhaps, but the main reason I came down here was to ask a favor of you. I have graduate classes at the University in Art History and I have to come and go at various times, especially in the evening. And I have two small children. One is only eleven months old. I was wondering if you could keep an eye on them when I step out, if you're around."

I didn't have a clue she was a mother. I had never heard a peep out of any kids upstairs. Heavy. I explained that I worked during the week and sometimes on Saturday.

"I understand, but if you are here sometime and I have to go out briefly, I wish you would be a good neighbor and watch my kids. It is so hard being a single mother," she sighed. "I do have a regular housekeeper/babysitter but she sometimes does not show up and is never here on the weekends."

Jeeze, she didn't mince words. She was bold and demanding, very straight forward. She explained that she was recently divorced from another Dane in Santa Barbara and that she moved up to Berkeley to go to graduate school and to get away from him.

"Uh-huh," I nodded, not quite taking this all in. Then, "Well, if you're in a jam and I'm here. Sure, I'll watch over your kids."

She invited me to her apartment to meet her babies. When I saw the apartment, it was more like a house with three bedrooms, two baths and an expansive living room with a stunning view of the Bay. It made my apartment look like a hovel.

It also had a glassed-in sun porch with a wide-angle view of the Bay. Sitting in it, you felt as if were hanging in the air hovering over the pines and Berkeley below.

Oh yes, the kids. The little boy was three and busy buzzing around. Very cute, very bright, playing with his Montessori type blocks. The girl was indeed a baby. All pretty and pink in her little dress, sitting strapped in a rocker. I briefly wondered how Sigrid could leave these kids alone even for a minute to come down and see me.

I played with the little boy, building a tower and then later held the girl as I fed her a bottle. This was heavy. This was serious. This was real life. A single mother burdened with two children. Did I want to get involved in this? I immediately felt the burden.

Well, to make a long story short, I did become involved. I found myself playing weekend babysitter a couple of times while the Contessa flitted off on various chores. It wasn't too hard. I already knew quite a bit from helping raise my brother Kenny, eleven years younger than me. I knew how to fix a bottle. I knew how to change shitty diapers and I knew how to play with a three-year-old or how to read him a story. Still, it made me nervous. Motherhood was such a heavy trip.

Sometimes, I helped out while the Contessa was there as she went about cleaning up her place. When she was gone in the evening, I would crash on the bed in the glassed-in porch and fall asleep amidst the star spangled night and glittering Bay Area lights. Other times we went on various shopping expeditions to the grocery store, the hardware store, etc.

It was on these expeditions that I noticed the Contessa was an expert shoplifter. Not that she was subtle about it. She would simply stuff whatever she wanted—clothing, food, small appliances—inside the pockets of her trench coat that she invariably wore, rain or shine when she went shopping. I once saw her take a hair dryer and slip it into an inside pocket, right in front of a sales lady, and walk out of the store. The sales lady didn't do a thing. She most likely could not believe her eyes. That was part of the Contessa's *modus operandi*.

"Shock, baby, shock," she smirked. "Most people don't believe what they see at first. By the time they figure it out, it's too late. I'm out of there."

"Yeah, but they are going to nab you someday," I predicted. "You have money. Why do you shoplift?"

"Yes, I have some money. I get alimony from my ex-husband and I have money of my own but why should I waste it on overpriced merchandise. Those Jews mark up the stuff sixty percent. That's not a fair profit."

"How do you know they're Jews?"

"Aren't all merchants Jews? Just look at them. You can tell."

"Whatever."

I stopped going on shopping trips with her. It was too dangerous. I just stayed back at her apartment and babysat the kids. Of course, I had my little rewards with her on the sleeping porch. We used to get it on high on pot to the beat of Jamaican reggae with exotic incense filling the air, and those star-spangled views.

As far as the Contessa was concerned, this was strictly a servicing procedure for her. No offense intended. She said she dug my body. She told me she had to get with me a couple of times a week to keep her head clear for her really important work, namely finding a rich husband.

The Contessa led a rather active social life in this regard. She went out with a network of single professional men who worked in San Francisco. Lawyers, doctors, well-off stockbrokers. Even some old money. When she was dressed to go out to the city, she was stunning in expensive evening gowns and reeked of regal class with her natural hauteur and chiseled good looks. She was so obvious in her pursuit that I was amazed her dates fell for it. But fall for her they did. I knew because I would be in bed on the sleeping porch as she bade them goodnight at her doorstep, not even inviting them in for a nightcap.

One of her dates was one of my old fraternity brothers, Bob, who was doing well as a lawyer in the city. He had met her at one of my parties and was stunned. He badgered me for information about her and how best to approach her. I suggested that he stand in line and ask her out for a date which he eventually did. He too got the doorstep kiss off. And after some banal conversation and an appointment for another date which I overheard from my bed, he shuffled off into the night. Two minutes later, she was in my bed. I vaguely wondered if I should someday in the far future tell Bob what had been going on.

***

The Contessa had a fraternal twin brother who lived across the street in an alpine-like redwood cottage. Lars was even stranger than his sister. He too had that tall Scandinavian look, with dirty blonde hair. He too had gone to the University of California at Santa Barbara. The surfer school as he called it.

"Surfing gets boring, man. Most of the guys are dolts. I need some intellectual stimulation. That's why I came up with Sigrid to hang out at Berkeley."

"Are you a student or something?"

"Or something. Not a formal student. I audit courses that interest me."

"Do tell."

"Yeah, but to be honest, I'm also in the car import business. I import them from Europe."

"What do you import?"

"Come here I'll show you." Lars led me downstairs to a two-car garage that he rented. Inside were two mint condition 1930s Rolls Royces, one a convertible. He backed out the convertible.

"Want to go for a ride? We'll do some mobile advertising."

"Sure."

Lars explained that he would go to Europe and scour the countryside in Germany, France and England looking for the old luxury cars, Rolls, Mercedes, etc. and ship them back to the states. Then he would have them fixed up at a local shop in Oakland. Not a complete restoration, just cosmetics so they looked good and then sell them to whomever. Apparently, there was a market. Old professors, antique car buffs, even a rich student or two, sometimes car dealerships or high-end auto repair shops that wanted an antique car in their showroom.

"I can make a hundred percent profit. I buy them for two or three grand and then sell them for maybe four or six thousand. It's enough to keep me in beer."

Soon Lars and his cars became a fixture around my apartment. He liked the parties and the procession of young women parading through. One, in particular, inspired him.

"Jesus H. Christ," he said one day. "I was up in my sister's apartment minding my own business on the sundeck, drinking beer when I happened to glance down to your sundeck. There was this chick stark naked stretched out on her back on a recliner. Built like a brick shit house. You banging that, Brown? If you are, I won't tell my sister."

"Uh, no way. That's Annie, the cousin of one of my Martinez friends. She's going to summer school here. She wanted some place to sunbathe so I said sure."

"Hey, if you are not interested, do you mind?" insisted Lars.

"Not at all."

So Lars introduced himself, took her over to his apartment and the rest was carnal history.

Anyway, our gang would go out tooling around Berkeley and San Francisco in Lars's vintage Rolls Royces, like early 20th century plutocrats. All that was missing were the top hats, the monocles and the diamond-studded walking sticks. Although, it must be noted that Lars did dress the part now and then, even coaxing his sister into a frilly Great Gatsby gown. We would park in the no parking zone in front of various outdoor cafes and watch the pedestrians ogle the cars. Even the cops were impressed and never gave us a ticket. This show of ostentatiousness eventually paid off with a couple of well-heeled stockbrokers buying the cars right off the street. No matter, Lars had a few more cars down at the Oakland docks ready for pick up.

***

So all was going well with the Contessa and her brother Lars and the general scene that had started out so meager but was now so rich. I dearly wished it could have gone on forever but alas, that was not to be. I think it started to fall apart when Gerard and the Contessa got into a big fight at La Vals. We were all down there having a pizza and beer and were planning on a movie right after. Gerard casually asked who was taking care of the kids. The Contessa gave him a blank stare.

"Why no one right now. They're in bed asleep. I'll check up on them in a little while."

"No one?" said Gerard, eyebrows raised.

I too thought it was scary. I knew it was a habit of hers to leave the little ones alone now and then for an hour or so. But she explained she was the mother and knew what was best for her kids.

Anyway, the Contessa took offense and said something to the effect of mind your own business to Gerard. Then Gerard, an only child who always wished for a sibling, muttered something that sounded like *merde* (shit) into his beer.

The Contessa went off on him. "Just like a fuckin' male. No idea of the pressures a single mom is under. Your kind makes me sick. At least Allan here helps me out."

I should probably point out that there was a history here of mutual antagonism between Gerard and the Contessa. Essentially Gerard didn't approve of her and thought she was a phony and could not understand why I wasted my time with her. The Contessa for her part thought Gerard was a weakling who probably couldn't get it up.

"I hate that type. Weak blond, deceitful. He reminds me of my ex-husband," she once told me.

Well, after the uttered *merde,* the Contessa simply got up with her mug of beer and walked around the table and poured it on his head. Gerard startled, pushed her off and then she came at him with her claws, scratching his arms and the side of his face.

I pulled her off, as Gerard sputtered, "Get that crazy bitch out of here before I coldcock her."

The Contessa merely sneered and walked off. I caught up with her and we returned to her apartment. The children were sleeping peacefully in the land of dreams. But I was now having serious second thoughts about the Contessa. I thought she had a screw loose. What would she do if she really got pissed? Later, she told me she had stabbed her husband in the shoulder with a steak knife because he was such a prick.

After that revelation, I started to pull a slow fade of not being available on the weekends. For her part, she found a part-time job at an art gallery in San Francisco and brought in the babysitter to live in the apartment full-time. We kept on good terms however, even though we were no longer shacking-up. (I think she found a likely husband prospect and was screwing him.)

When my lease was up and I was in the processing of moving to San Francisco, she promised she would come and see me. She did once with her kids. We went to the Fleishhacker Zoo and had a picnic. That was the last that I saw her. I always wondered if she ever did land a rich husband.

4. ZEITGEIST '65

Let's pause here and take stock of the times in the mid-summer of 1965. Examine the *Zeitgeist*, if you will. Even though I was primarily in my own little world of work and hedonistic pursuits, I was not unaware that "the times, they are a-changin'," to quote Bob Dylan.

The Vietnam War was revving up. The first contingent of U.S. Marines had landed at DaNang in March 1965 supposedly to defend the U.S. airfield. There were now over 75,000 U.S. troops in Vietnam, heading for a goal 125,000. Also, a bombing program called Rolling Thunder was underway over North Vietnam.

On the homefront, the selective service was gearing up, drafting ever more young men. President Johnson had increased the monthly draft call from 17,000 to 35,000. Still, hardly any of the draftees were college students. Educational deferments were easy to obtain. As already noted, I was in a reserve control unit and the likelihood of me being called up was remote at that point. No, the ones who were being sent were the high school dropouts, the poor and the minorities, especially the blacks. By the way, President Johnson had rescinded Kennedy's deferment for married men. So those poor suckers who had married to avoid the draft were now being plucked off the streets of America.

In one of the rare instances of TV news sticking its neck out on the Vietnam War, CBS News aired a piece in August by correspondent Morley Safer showing American troops setting fire to thatched huts with Zippo lighters. When Johnson saw that he fumed that Safer must be a communist. Informed that Safer was not a communist but rather a Canadian, Johnson was quoted as saying, "Well, I knew, he wasn't an American."

Along with this was the growing anti-war protest in the Bay Area and elsewhere. There had already been a Vietnam Committee teach-in in May in Berkeley with thousands in attendance, with another one planned for the fall. In another demonstration, protesters sat on the Santa Fe tracks down by the Berkeley waterfront in an effort to stop the troop trains. The demonstrators had also tried to march on the Oakland Induction Center but were blocked at Oakland/Berkeley border by the Oakland cops. A mêlée ensued with the cops cracking heads. Still, a majority of the American people backed the war. "Ballad of the Green Beret" topped the pop charts.

In addition to the anti-war movement, the student Free Speech Movement was still alive and well at Berkeley. Hundreds had sat in Sproul Hall in December of 1964. Although I was in Paris when it went down, I had caught the headlines of the sit-in in the French newspapers. I remember many French students sitting around the left bank cafes debating whether to stage their own protest over what they considered the dictatorial policies of the University of Paris.

Eventually, Cal University officials backed down. The Free Speech firebrand, Mario Savio, was the hero of the day. The new chancellor, Martin Meyerson, announced new guidelines in keeping with the FSM demands. Students were working to reform student government and organizing a teaching assistant union. All seemed well but there were rumblings on the far right about the spoiled brat students at UC Berkeley, and their communist inspired protests. Some of these utterings came from none other than B-movie actor Ronald Reagan who was now a declared Republican and thinking about running for governor against Pat Brown in the 1966 election.

In August, the Watts riots broke out in Los Angeles and before it was over, thirty-four people were dead, mostly blacks, and a thousand were injured. Some six hundred buildings were damaged or burned, mostly businesses. Damage was estimated at 35-million dollars. The National Guard patrolled the streets of Watts for weeks afterwards.

I had a personal interest in this because my Uncle Jack was a captain in the L.A. Fire Department at the time and he worked out of a firehouse in the middle of Watts. He got through unscathed but quite of few of his fellow fighters were injured, one died. He never said much about it except that the Watts residents were crazy.

"I mean, how stupid can you get," he said amazed. "Destroy your own neighborhood. And for what? Just because some spook is stopped by a highway patrolman."

Uncle Jack added that he was looking for a transfer which he later got to the L.A. Waterfront Fire District.

***

Essentially, all of these events were so much background noise to me. I was focused on a different pursuit—the life of the mind or more precisely the life of my mind. I had jotted down various scribblings in my journal that reflected that state of mind.

1. The "why" is adolescent speculation. Only the" how" matters.

2. The line is all, the content nothing. The posture or stance defines. Baudelaire creates new poetic forms purely for form's sake.

3. Pop Art explores the surface aspects of the material artifacts of our society. It seeks to elevate the common. A beer can achieve a transcendence of sorts. Andy Warhol has made a career out of this.

4. The conscious man sees the futility of his actions and proceeds to rationalize his inactivity. As Camus says, twentieth-century man will be remembered for nothing more than reading the newspapers and fornicating.

5. We have programmed ourselves into the realm of the marginal. Man is superfluous in a world of his own making.

6. Perhaps Bobbie is right. Family and a sense of purpose are important but most people around here are too weak to appreciate it or even do anything about it.

I should probably expand on this last point. Bobbie had become my minder of sorts. She and Tom had moved from their Southside apartment to a nearby apartment on the Northside. "So much nicer than the Southside," she had said.

I was puzzled because the apartment I had found them on the Southside apartment was big, the size of a house with two bedrooms and a large living room. Their Northside apartment was a tiny one bedroom and a cramped little kitchen.

"It's not so bad Allan," she rationalized. "We can see each other all the time and eat pizza together at La Vals."

Hmm. I wasn't too excited at having them so close at hand. As noted, I was having a rather active social life and didn't need Bobbie's surveillance. She and Tom had come to one of my parties and Bobbie was shocked at the goings on.

"All those loose women," as she put it, half-kidding. Later, when I saw her alone, she chided me for leading such a dissolute, undirected life. Why didn't I settle down with a nice a girl?

I was merely annoyed and wondered why she even cared. She had made her choice. In fact, at one point I said, "Well, all of this could have been prevented if we had gone into the Peace Corps together."

"Oh don't be silly, Allan. That was impossible. We were too different," she replied wistfully.

I thought to myself, "Well then stay out of my life. I have other fish to fry."

Anyway, by the fall, Bobbie and Tom had moved back to the Midwest. Tom had been awarded his master's degree but somehow was out of the running for a Ph.D. at Berkeley. However, he had been accepted at the University of Michigan to finish his doctorate. I did not see them again for years.

***

Well, all this philosophical speculation, existential angst and wandering in the wilderness of willing young women had gotten me exactly nowhere. I had to decide which direction I should pursue in my upcoming graduate studies.

Initially, I was set on television and radio, something I had seen close up in the Army and actually had a modicum of experience with. San Francisco State had a well-known television and radio department. And word was, one could actually get a job in the broadcasting industry if you had gone to SF State. That was something practical to think about. Although, as noted, I thought that television in particular and broadcasting in general while exciting, were essentially banal. I wanted a higher art form.

In the summer of '65, I was attracted to the so-called "New Journalism." A type of reportage that dealt with the inner feelings and thoughts of the real-life principals and done in a narrative manner with scene and dialog. Some of the foremost practitioners of this art at the time were Norman

Mailer, Tom Wolfe and Gay Talese. Even Darrah was part of the trend. I saw an article in the Daily Cal profiling her as one who had made it in journalism. She had taken a job with the *Boston Globe* as a "lifestyle editor." Her mission was to write about the youth of the 60s and the emerging counter-culture movements, including of course the anti-war movement.

My favorite "New Journalism" writer was Tom Wolfe and his pop art style in *Esquire Magazine*. He caught my attention with an article about Junior Johnson and the North Carolina stock car racing scene. A wild, over the top article full of "wows" and "bams," sort of comic book cartoon writing. Or his collection of sixties essays entitled "The Kandy-Kolored Tangerine-Flake Streamline Baby" in which Wolfe explored the world of the Beatles, bouffant hairdos and car customizers. Then there was Wolfe's *Electric Kool-Aid Acid Test*, a book just out about Ken Kesey and his Merry Pranksters riding around in a psychedelic colored bus throughout the Bay Area. As Wolfe put it:

> *I make out a school bus....glowing orange, green, magenta, lavender-chlorine blue....vibrating off each other as if somebody had given Hieronymous Bosch fifty buckets of Day-Glo paint.*
>
> (My thanks to Tom Wolfe)

I wanted to write like that. Journalistically accurate, yet free and easy. Going after the poetic truth, as well as the literal truth. Concocting a detailed account of a city council meeting or rewriting a corporate news release did not interest me. Not even getting the so-called big scoop of a current news event. I was looking for something else. Of course, if I wanted to enter the lists of journalism, I would have to pay my dues and start at the bottom of the rung, probably writing obituaries for the *Oakland Tribune*. Although I did note that a couple of underground newspapers had started up, namely the *Berkeley Barb* here in Berkeley. They would publish anything of a counter-culture nature by anybody. But I found the writing shoddy and ill-informed. I guess I was still too much of a traditionalist.

At the same time, I was being tugged in another direction—film. Why film? I had this unreal feeling all the time of seeing everything in life as if it were a film. My eye as the constantly moving camera—turn head, pan right. Background music swells. It was really very simple. Shoot reality as it is. Andy Warhol did it. His camera held steady on one New York building for forty minutes. Another held steady on the face of queer getting a blowjob. It was easy. Or take the movie *Georgy Girl*. Run around London and up the stairs into the flats. Iron fence posts flashing by as the camera trucks along. Why not?

So I enrolled in a film history course at SF State in July. It was a three-hour class, one night a week. We watched all the early classics—*Great Train Robbery, Intolerance, Birth of a Nation, Dr. Caligari's Cabinet, Greed,* and *Citizen Kane*. The instructor took it all very seriously but most of the students were there for a lark filling an easy course requirement. But I sensed there was something there for me. The final was a joke, a simple multiple-choice test based on the lectures and the films that we had seen. An easy "A."

I had plenty of time to ponder all of this because by mid-August our work on BART had come to an end. I was unemployed. No matter. I had saved money. I needed a rest. So I would sit for hours at a desk in my cozy alcove overlooking the street and write in my journal or write little bits trying to imitate Tom Wolfe or simply gather wool. Ultimately, I would fall asleep on my daybed couch in my cozy apartment in the Berkeley hills in the dreamy, warm sunlight of forever afternoons.

5. THE DOLE

Wake up! Wake up! There was work to be done. Plans to be made. Action to take. My time in the apartment was coming to an end in a few short weeks. I had to start thinking about where I would live next, but I didn't have a clue other than a vague notion that I would be moving to San Francisco. I was content to ride out the string.

A few days after being laid off, Len called me up and urged me to apply for unemployment.

"Unemployment?"

"Yeah, unemployment insurance, dummy. The government pays you money when you are laid off from work. I'll be getting about sixty bucks a week."

"No kidding."

"Yeah, not great but better than nothing until I can find another gig. Go down to the unemployment office and apply. Before you know it, you'll be collecting."

"It's that simple?"

"No, there are a few details, like proving you are looking for work but since we are in the Operating Engineers Union and they have a hiring hall, all you have to do is tell them you are available."

"Uh, OK."

This was all new to me. I had heard about unemployment insurance but never thought that I would be able to collect it. But as I learned, since I worked six months in surveying the prior year, I had enough quarters to qualify. Hmm, I thought. That sixty bucks a week would come in handy. Maybe I could go to school and still collect unemployment. When I went down to the

Berkeley unemployment office, a nice lady explained all about it.

"Yes, Mr. Brown. That is possible, as long as your classes don't prevent you from being available to work. That usually means taking night classes."

This was encouraging since according to the latest San Francisco State course catalog, there were now many evening classes to choose from in Film and Television, although there was one day class that I had to take, basically a film production class for their master's program.

So I signed up for unemployment and was ready to collect my checks and loaf until the beginning of school, a month away.

***

A few days later, ring, ring. I picked up. It was the union rep from the Operating Engineers.

"Al, I see here that you have been laid off from Ray Engineering in San Leandro and you have indicated that you are available for work."

"Uh, yes, I guess I am."

"Well, we have something for you. It's short-term job, probably about two months with Parsons & Company in Martinez. As you may know, they're expanding Shell Oil Refinery and they're hiring survey crews. They put in a request for a head chainman."

"Really?"

"Yes, are you interested?"

"Uh, hold on a sec." I paused, not really interested. I was looking forward to coasting on unemployment until school started. But if I said no and word got back to the unemployment office, they could cut me off. If I said yes, I would have a job I didn't want. But it was only for two months, about a month of that during school. I could probably swing that if I stuck with night classes. Do the day class later. Also, I could use more money in the bank. So I said yes and agreed to show up at Parsons & Company the next day.

Normally, I was optimistic when I started a new job. Usually, I met new characters and worked in new areas. While we often had to work hard, there was usually a fun, hang-loose element to it. Based on my experience, most land surveyors were individualists, iconoclasts. They loved to roam over the countryside, digging for corner markers, measuring the land off. They loved the outdoor work. No closed in cubicles for them. However, I had a bad feeling about this Parsons gig. It was plant surveying usually considered the dregs of land surveying. All you did was locate where buildings and tanks were to go, maybe survey an elementary access roadway. Nothing very challenging, but I decided to make the best out of it. After all, it was only for a couple of months.

So the next day I drove over to the Shell Oil Refinery at Martinez which was weird in itself since I had grown up with Shell Oil and knew people who worked there. But this was an entirely new wing on the edge of the existing plant and construction was in full swing.

I checked into the contractor's office and some skinny bureaucratic type in a white, short-sleeve shirt and clip tie made me fill out a ton of paperwork, all about hazards and safety procedures and sign releases to the effect if I was poisoned, gassed or blown up, I would not hold Parsons & Company responsible. Then I met the party chief, George, an older guy who looked like he had been around for a while. George was cool, laid-back. He didn't believe in breaking his ass. As he put it, "It all pays the same." I was on a crew of three, George, a rear chainman and me, the head chainman. After the first day's work, George told me he appreciated a chainman who knew his stuff. Like I said, it was simple layout stuff. I worked with George for a week and it was an easy gig. We got off early, around four p.m. so I would go to the Martinez Forest Hills pool for a swim and then go home to eat dinner with my parents before returning to Berkeley.

"Why don't you stay here until school starts?" asked my mother. "Save some money."

"Uh, thanks for the offer, Mom, but I'm paid up until the end of August on this sublet and I have all my things there."

Really, I just wanted to keep living my bachelor life unimpeded and far from overseeing eyes.

Then at the end of August, I was transferred to another surveying crew. This time the party chief was another little red-haired prick, feisty, noisy, but dressed in neatly ironed buttoned-down shirts and khakis. Randy was his name and I had noticed him in the office before complaining about his chainman. He eventually fired the sucker and I apparently was his replacement.

Randy hung around the office after hours, schmoozing with the higher ups, the engineers. He somehow thought he was a big-time player, forever talking about his golf game and challenging the engineers to a round after work. Word was he was gunning for a construction supervisor spot.

Right away, Randy got on my nerves. "College boy, huh, Al? What are you doing surveying? Flunk out of engineering?" (Later I learned that he himself had flunked out of engineering at San Jose State.)

"Uh, no Randy. I do this to make some money," I explained. "I'll be going back to school."

"Where did you say you went?"

"Berkeley."

"Oh, yeah... You're not a commie are you?"

"Don't think so."

"Well, doesn't matter. Just so long as you do your job. I keep up a fast pace here."

"I'll do my best."

Actually, Randy was slow as shit. I don't think he knew his craft very well. He took forever to turn an angle or make a simple calculation. But he expected you to move, to knock in those stakes and measure with pinpoint precision to the hundredth of a foot. This was a waste of time since anything within a half-tenth for a roadway or a building or tank location was plenty adequate for refinery work.

Randy was always bugging me to make sure I had enough stakes and equipment on hand. He had declared that I was to be in charge of all supplies and woe to me if we ran short in the field, even though it was a five-minute drive back to the supply shed. I dutifully made sure that we had the proper gear available.

Then one day, after acting buddy-buddy for a few days, he asked me if I could get some tickets to a Cal Football game for him and his golfing buddies. He needed five tickets. Since I was an alum, he thought that I could get them cheap. I told him the price was the same for me as anyone else. The only break you got was if you bought season tickets. When I hesitated, he insisted, "You live over there, Al. Drop by the ticket office and buy them. That'll save me a trip. I'll pay you back."

Hmm. This did not please me. I had better things to do than hang around the Cal Ticket Office on a Saturday morning and buy football tickets. And use my own money to boot. This was bullshit. But what could I do? Randy could make things unpleasant here. So I wasted half a Saturday and spent sixty dollars on tickets. Not quite end-zone seats but close enough. That was all that was available. Needless to say, Randy was not happy but he coughed up the sixty bucks and went to the game with his buddies and later bragged about what good time he had and how they got drunk on a flask of whiskey and ogled the cheerleaders, even though the Cal Bears lost. He didn't even say thanks.

By this time I had decided I had to get out of Parsons. School was to begin in a week and I didn't want to both work and go to night classes. The commute from Martinez to San Francisco in traffic would have been a killer.

But I couldn't quit outright because the penalty would be to wait at least six weeks before collecting unemployment. So I let myself be fired. It wasn't hard with a little prick like Randy. I conveniently neglected to stock up a goodly supply of marker stakes for three days in row. This necessitated a fifteen-minute break while I went back to the supply warehouse and retrieved some more stakes.

The first time, Randy was just pissed. The second time he was rip-shit.

"How can you be such a fuck up, Brown? Here I thought you were a professional. I'm very disappointed."

The third time he just did a slow burn and then disappeared an hour before quitting time, telling us to cool our heels in the truck. He came back waving a check, saying, "You're out of here Brown. I am not going to have you screw up the production of my crew. You're making me look bad."

I grabbed the check and said, "See you around, Randy." As I walked off, I added under my breath, "Sucker."

The next day I re-applied for unemployment in Berkeley, explaining to the lady that I had been unjustly fired. Parsons & Company in the person of Randy protested me receiving unemployment checks saying I was not qualified for the job. The good lady replied that I had a long record of satisfactory employment as a chainman at many engineering firms in the area and put my firing down to a personality conflict.

"Mr. Brown, you will receive your unemployment checks but we will have to impose a three-week wait. In the meantime, notify your union hall that you are available for work."

By this time, I was attending classes at San Francisco State, including that day class in film production. The union hall never did call because the bulk of the surveying season was over and no one was hiring. Three weeks later, I began receiving the first of six months of unemployment checks. I was golden until spring.

When my father learned of my financing arrangement for my graduate education, he disapproved. I pointed out that I had earned the right to receive unemployment checks because I had worked for it. It was an insurance that an employer buys into and counts as an employee expense. Still, my father was not happy but he could do nothing other than appeal to my conscience.

"That's nothing but welfare, Allan. You could get another surveying job tomorrow if you wanted. Let it go to some other poor guy who can't find work and has a family to feed."

"Sorry Dad," I replied, thinking that if he was so concerned, he could pay for my graduate education.

6. BY-THE-SEA

What with my hassle at Parsons, general malaise and reluctance to move out of my apartment, I stayed over into September. The Jewish couple had written me that they would be back around September 15th but to be sure that I had vacated the apartment by September 1st.

I thought, "What the screw. They're not here. They won't know when I move out. I can stay over a few days."

Well, the very day that I finally packed up and lugged my suitcases up to the Contessa's place for temporary safekeeping, the Jewish couple drove up in their little car. I was upstairs at the Contessa's that evening when it happened. I looked down at the street in disbelief. They had arrived on the 10th, not the 15th. Even though I had cleared my possessions out, the apartment was a mess. I heard them banging around downstairs and I heard the wail of the wife about what a pigsty the place was.

The Contessa just laughed saying, "Sounds like she is going to castrate you, Allan, if she catches you."

I laid low until about midnight and then after bidding the Contessa goodbye, I snuck out her entrance to my station wagon parked down the block. At first, I thought about driving home to Martinez but that would be admitting defeat as an independent soul. Instead, I drove over to Jean-Paul's place, a studio apartment on Dwight, and knocked on his door. He answered, pissed.

"I need a place to stay for a couple of nights, Jean-Paul. Can you help me out?"

"Well, yes but as you can see, Al, this place is small," he said groggily. "You'll have to sleep on the floor."

(The only bed was a sofa bed that Jean-Paul slept on.)

So I spread my sleeping bag out on the hard kitchen floor and tried to sleep. I spent the next few days there but it was obvious that I couldn't stay long. Jean-Paul was basically annoyed at my presence. However, we did have some good times.

One night we went upstairs to a party given by a gal who had just returned from Paris from a year abroad. She had been chasing Jean-Paul ever since.

"Alice is not pretty, but very lively and interesting," opined Jean-Paul. "I could never get involved with her but I like her as a friend. And she does speak French rather well for an American."

When I met Alice, I too noted her plainness. But she was indeed lively and bubbly. She didn't pay much attention to me but rather continued to focus on Jean-Paul, jabbering in excellent French. She explained that her goal was to finish up at Berkeley and then go back to Paris for training as a chef.

As it turned out, years later, Alice would succeed beyond her wildest dreams.

***

I thought I had made a clean escape from the clutches of the Jewish couple until a few days later. I was minding my own business, eating a breakfast on the Terrace when I heard, "So, here you are."

I looked up and there hovering over me was the Jewish couple.

"We have been looking all over for you," said the wife. "Sigrid said she had no idea where you were staying."

"So?"

The Missus sat down at my table across from me, while her nerdy husband, embarrassed, looked off in the distance.

"So, we figure you owe us two weeks rent plus another fifty dollars for cleaning up your mess."

"Whoa, wait a minute," I protested. "The place might have been messy, but I damaged nothing and preserved your treasures. I think you got a good deal, or at least peace of mind while you were in New York."

"OK. Forget about the clean-up fee," she relented. "How about the rent? We know that you stayed there for nearly two weeks this month. Sigrid told us that."

"She did, did she?" I'm thinking what a double-crossing bitch. But they did have a point. I was caught.

"OK," I agreed. "I'll send you a check for two weeks of rent, now leave me alone."

"Are you sure?"

"Yeah, I'm sure. You'll get it in a few days. Here, I'll give you my Martinez phone number. If you want to follow up."

"Thank you," she said relieved. "Let's go, Ned, we still have more cleaning up to do.

***

After a few nights of sleeping on Jean-Paul's floor, I was desperate to get out and move to San Francisco. But where? I hadn't done any scouting around and I knew San Francisco rents were high.

As if on cue, I ran into Chris in the San Francisco State student cafeteria. A big, heavyset guy, Chris was a graduate student, studying industrial arts. He wanted to be a high school shop teacher. He was also the older brother of a girl that I had met in the Squaw Valley bar two winters ago. His sister Rebecca was a dark, raven-haired beauty that I went out with once back then but never bedded.

Then in the midst of my Nordic exploration this summer, I went out with Rebecca again to break up the blonde monotony. When I phoned her up for a second date, Chris answered the phone and told me Rebecca had died in a car crash. The beautiful Rebecca had wrapped her little red MG around a cable on the San Francisco-Oakland Bay Bridge and had died as a result. She had been driving back from a wedding and probably had had too much to drink.

I was stunned. Here one minute, so lively, so beautiful, gone the next. I even went to the funeral in Hayward where they lived and joined the mourners. There she was in the casket. Her face was made up but swollen, plastic looking. I guess the undertaker did the best he could. It was painful to see. Later, Chris thanked me for coming.

So I guess when Chris saw me sitting in the cafeteria reading the *San Francisco Chronicle* and marking apartments for rent, he felt a bond. He offered to let me stay at his two-bedroom apartment in Pacifica, south of San Francisco. We would share rent.

"It'll be great, Al. I have all the furniture, even an extra bed in the second bedroom. It's right on the beach. There's still some good weather left. We'll have some great parties. "Louie-Louie, rock-on," he said doing a bump and a grind.

Big Chris was still a frat boy at heart from his days at San Jose State. I wasn't too far removed from that scene myself. So I thought he might be a congenial roommate and I was curious about living on the ocean. And the price was right. My share was only a hundred a month.

I packed up my station wagon, bid Jean-Paul adieu, and drove down to Pacifica, a little dump of a town about ten miles south of Daly City, right on the ocean. It was sort of a white-trash community by the sea. Most of the year it was dank and foggy, but in the fall the skies were blue and the sea calm. Almost Mediterranean. It was even possible to go swimming off the beach but you had to be careful of riptides. Chris's apartment was on the second story of a two-story building right next to the beach. It had a sun deck and picture windows with a stunning view of the Pacific. Chris said he rented it because it was cheap and relatively close to SF State. Also, he said he had always dreamed of living on a beach.

Well, it worked for me too. I quickly ensconced myself with my meager belongings in the extra bedroom. I bought my own food and was ready to rock. No sooner had I moved in than Chris decided we needed an inaugural party. So we bought a bunch of wine and a keg of beer. Chris had a great stereo and the latest hits excluding the Beatles. He hated the Beatles. But the Rolling Stones were OK. We also listened and danced to the Beach Boys, Chubby Checker and of course, Chris's favorites, "Louie Louie" and "Wooly Bully."

Chris had invited a bunch of his buddies over with their girlfriends. His own girlfriend, Erica, fixed the food and set things up. She was a sweet, charming girl and it was obvious she was serious about Chris. Erica worked as an executive secretary in the San Francisco financial district. I was with nobody having left my Berkeley base but I didn't care. It was good being a frat boy again and I schmoozed it up with one of Erica's working girlfriends, a down to earth bunch and nice looking to boot.

The party was a great success. We drank and danced until exhausted and then hit the beach in our shorts dodging the waves until somebody said, "Fuck it" and plunged into the surf. Then we all plunged in and kicked around in the small waves, finally coming out and warming ourselves up by a roaring bonfire. Frat life was good. Beach life was good. The Pacific sparkled in the moonlight, the waves lapped gently. I could almost imagine I was on Malibu or Redondo Beach.

Soon I was feeling right at home in Pacifica and ready to do battle at San Francisco State. A student again! Whee!

7. MOVIES

San Francisco State hadn't changed much in the year since I had dropped out. Was it a year ago? Yes. Fall of 1964. It seemed like a century ago. As noted before, the college still reminded me of an overgrown high school with its boxy, mass produced buildings, softened here and there by landscaping. Students poured off the 19th Avenue Muni Street car for the many evening classes it offered. The students looked about the same with button-down types at night; beat looking types during the day in beards and sandals totting book-bags, looking either very serious or very spaced out. Then there were the live-wire creative types—drama students, music students, and yes, film students, flitting around, chattering, laughing, high on their art. That was the group that I was about to join, I hoped.

Once again, enrolling as a graduate student was a cinch. Any Berkeley graduate was an automatic admit, no matter the grade point. All it took was a Cal transcript and a one hundred dollar registration fee.

I signed up for four courses, twelve units in all—*Documentary History, The Films of Alfred Hitchcock, Business of Broadcasting* and *Film Production 1-A*.

Why these four? Well, let's take them one by one.

I thought the documentary film history course by Dr. Goldner would make a good compliment to the history of film course that I had taken in summer school. And documentary filmmaking interested me the most at that point. We watched documentary classics such as Robert Flaherty's *Nanook of the North* and *Moana*; the Russian Kino-Pravda (Newsreels); Leni Riefenstahl's *Olympia* and *Triumph of the Will*; Pare Lorentz's *The Plow That Broke The Plains* and *The River*; a couple of Frank Capra's *Why We Fight Series* and for a taste of the modern, *The Making of the President 1960* by Mel Stuart.

The question that we often asked ourselves about these films was did they depict objective truth or were they propaganda? In the case of *Olympia* and *Triumph of the Will*, the answer was obvious: brilliant Nazi propaganda. Even the Lorentz Depression films were designed to persuade. We concluded that there was always bias, no matter how objective the documentary filmmaker tried to be. The mere pointing of the camera at a particular object and not another, implied choice. Then there was the shot selection during the editing sequence. Some shots were used, others not for a variety of reasons. Again a distortion of reality. And finally, there was often active staging of an event, such as Robert Flaherty's insistence that his Eskimos use harpoons to kill seals rather than their preferred method of shooting them with a rifle.

The Hitchcock course interested me on another level. I had always been intrigued by the master intriguer. The course was given by a Dr. Fell, a straight looking film professor who unlike the others wore a business suit with white shirt and tie. We watched many of the Hitchcock classics including his early English films such as *Blackmail, 39 Steps, The Man Who Knew Too Much* and *The Lady Vanishes*. We then had to write a paper on a particular theme relevant to his filmmaking technique. I chose as my theme his "cinema of appearances" and wrote the following:

> We find in Hitchcock's works a cynical manipulation of appearances, causality and continuity. He plays with audience expectations in an almost ruthless way: a body the audience believes dead gets up and walks away (Sabotage). A little boy carrying package with a time bomb is not saved at the last minute but is blown up along with his dog (Sabotage). Cops become crooks and a murderess preserves the legal system (Paradine Case). Later when asked if he would do any of these sequences differently, Hitchcock said upon second thought, he would have spared the dog.

***

I took the *Business of Broadcasting* course because it fulfilled a master's degree requirement that we explore the commercial side of the media. I thought it would be dry and uninteresting, but it was an eye-opener. It was taught by a former spot salesman at one of the local TV stations. He briefly reviewed the history of commercial broadcasting, the creation of the FCC, the role of advertising on radio and television and the nitty-gritty of ratings and the buying of spots. He also gave us tips on job hunting in radio and

California Split

television, pointing out that we should all subscribe to the *Broadcasting Magazine*, the bible of the industry. The back of the magazine listed nearly all the broadcasting jobs available nationwide. This was later to prove an invaluable resource.

The film production class was a nuts and bolts primer on filmmaking. First, there was a brief introduction to the craft of film dealing with camera composition and editing aesthetics. Then it was on to the mechanics of camera operation, film stock, lighting, sound etc. We fooled around with the Arriflex and the Eclair, two 16mm cameras with sync sound capabilities. We ran the Nagra sound recorder and spent hours editing silent film footage film that we had shot on little 16mm Bell & Howell cameras. It was a hands-on experience that involved checking out equipment, lugging it around, lining up people and shots. It was in short, the grunt work of shooting a film but it was exhilarating and I learned a lot.

***

I was also exposed to the experimental style of filmmaking predominate at San Francisco State. At a student film festival, I saw several good films including Gerald Varney's *Watts Towers*, an eight-millimeter extravaganza on the towers built in Los Angeles by an illiterate Italian workman. The 93-foot towers were a construction of steel pipes, rods, wire mesh coated with mortar and embedded with porcelain, tile and glass and other found objects creating a colorful, mind-boggling display.

Even more impressive was Scott Bartlett's *Metanomen*, a dazzling experimental film that used flashing positive and negative images of an urban landscape of bridges, freight yards, trains, and a fleeing woman, all to a pounding surreal beat. Some said watching it was like getting high on acid. Others said it was the filmic equivalent of a pop art movie. Whatever, I found it mesmerizing, almost hypnotic.

At one point, I met Jerry Slick, an older, slightly seedy graduate student who had been at the school forever making films, including one I think he called *The Landscape Is Part of the Trip*. Essentially, it was a road trip with a camera stuck out the window a car, rolling on the passing countryside with a jazzy soundtrack. Jerry mentioned that his wife Grace Slick was the lead singer in the local rock band, The Great Society. He said it like I should be impressed but at that point, I had never heard of her.

All in all, I was inspired. It seemed it was all happening right here at San Francisco State. I decided I had to start making my own documentary film.

***

The subject matter wasn't hard to figure out. It was going down right before my eyes—the anti-war protest, now in the form of mass rallies of the Vietnam Day Committee. The next scheduled rally was on Friday afternoon, October 15th at Berkeley. It was to feature Ken Kesey, the writer and the Merry-Prankster-in-chief. I decided the best way to film this was to keep equipment at a minimum. I would only use the 16mm Bell & Howell silent film camera and worry about adding sound later, maybe some voice-over narration or newsreel sound clips of the rally.

On the appointed day, I drove over to Berkeley and wandered around the student union and Sproul Plaza where the rally was to take place. Already a mob was there, several thousand I estimated. The Merry Prankster bus was parked in the plaza in all its day-glow psychedelic glory, topped by a sign called "Further." I began filming it, even stepping inside the open door and checking out the interior, a crazy mess of couches and old bus seats with various pranksters sitting around smoking weed.

"Far out, man," said one.

"Film away," said another.

"Yeah, get the message out."

There was no sign of Kesey himself.

The Pranksters were no stranger to film. They had gone on a cross-country road trip filming hundreds of hours of their trip. The Prankster bus had been driven by none other than Neal Cassady, a Beat elder, immortalized in Jack Kerouac's *On the Road*. The Pranksters' goal had been to meet Timothy Leary at his home in Massachusetts and learn about LSD. I had seen some of their film at SF State. It was tedious, self-conscious, "look-at-me, ma" stuff.

Soon the official rally was underway with a series of speakers, all condemning U.S. policy towards Vietnam and the deployment of American troops there. Most ridiculed the concept of the domino theory and said the war was merely an extension of dominant colonial powers subjugating the colored races.

Kesey, a husky guy wearing a World War One helmet, finally came up to the podium to speak but instead of taking the expected anti-war stance, he began playing "Home on the Range," on his harmonica. Between blasts on his instrument, he uttered things like, "Holding rallies and marches, you're playing their game," or "Just look at the war and turn your back on it and say 'fuck it.'"

I had mixed feelings about Kesey. I had read his *One Flew over the Cuckoo's Nest* and thought it brilliant. He had based it on his experiences working in a mental hospital while attending Stanford University. Next, he wrote *Sometimes a Great Notion*, about a family logging business in Oregon, a less impressive work, I thought. Nonetheless, Kesey had made a pile of dough from his writing and appeared to be spending most of it on these Merry Prankster characters running around the nation on his bus or partying at his La Honda pad west of Palo Alto. I wondered if he was still a serious writer or if his mind had become addled by taking too much LSD. Nevertheless, I filmed away.

Needless to say, Kesey's light-hearted approach upset the rally's MC but he tried to paper it over by urging everyone to join a march to Oakland. Their goal was to shut down the Oakland Army Terminal where most of the troops boarded ships and sailed off to Vietnam. (In 1965, they took troop ships over to Vietnam. Flying troops to Vietnam came later.)

***

Following the rally, hundreds of protesters gathered on Telegraph Avenue for the march to Oakland carrying banners that read "International Days of Protest." Already rumors were rife that the Oakland Cops were waiting to knock heads at the Oakland border about a mile away.

I filmed the beginning of the march and then jumped into my car and drove down to the Oakland/Berkeley border on a side street. There, I spotted some TV camera crews on top of a building. I found the stairwell leading up to the roof and joined them for a birds-eye view of the proceedings. Below was a phalanx of Oakland Cops blocking the street. They were a hard-bitten bunch, wearing their white riot helmets, standing grimly at attention, their billy clubs at the ready. I had heard about the Oakland Cops, commonly referred to as "fascist pigs" by the Berkeleyites. I had heard that many had been recruited from the South specifically to keep the Oakland blacks in line. It was also apparent that they hated the anti-war protesters and loved to beat them up. Well, we would see.

Presently, the marchers arrived at the border, pausing about a half-block away. After a tentative probe by a few lead marchers which was met with threatening truncheons, the protesters wisely decided not to push it any further. Instead, they taunted the Oakland Cops from a half block away, calling them pigs. To their credit, the cops stood their ground and made no a move this time. Having made their point, the marchers soon melted away.

It had all been recorded by the local TV news stations and was sure to be on the 11 o'clock news. The images of the peaceful but boisterous marchers juxtaposed against the images of tough unyielding cops would be seen throughout the Bay Area and perhaps across the nation. I too had captured those images on a special fast film with a high ASA rating in the now dark evening. I carefully removed my film from the camera and put it in my camera bag, along with some other rolls that I shot.

Another march was scheduled the next day but I couldn't make it which was too bad because there was actually some action between the cops and a group of hecklers.

The following week, I had my film developed and it came out spectacular. The black and white images were crisp and clear even in the dark. Goldner, who taught the film production class as well, took one look at it and declared it fantastic. He advised me to have a work print developed from it so I could edit the piece without damaging the original. I agreed, putting the film in my locker and locking it up (or so I thought) for the night.

A few days later when I went to fetch it from my locker to send it off for a work print, I discovered the film was gone. Gone, gone, gone. Somebody had apparently broken into my locker and lifted it. It was nowhere to be found. I looked high and low in the locker and equipment room. I collared my fellow film students and quizzed them. Some were insulted, others indifferent, a few concerned but none knew anything about such a film. I even offered a reward for the return of the film, no questions asked. But no film turned up.

Goldner was sure the footage would be returned. It never was, although years later I did see footage suspiciously like my own in various documentaries on the anti-war movement. A lot of similar footage was being shot in those days. It was probably just a coincidence. Still, my first attempt at documentary filmmaking was shot down by a thief. No matter. I felt I would have other documentary opportunities. Also at the time, I was becoming involved another major student film production, *Mike Angels*, a comedic, 1940s detective mystery, with the goal of a theatrical release.

Dr. Goldner announced the project in his class one day and asked if anyone was interested. As bait, he said, "If you put in the time and document your efforts on it, I could get you a couple of units of graduate credit."

My ears pricked up. I could use a couple of more units of graduate credit.

After all, I was starting from scratch at SF State. Every easy unit counted towards my master's degree. Also, I was interested in working on a theatrical film. The word was the student writer/producer, John Newton, had a bunch of money and was willing to spend it on production. So I volunteered.

***

Pant, pant. It took three months of shooting mainly on weekends to get the job done. We shot in mansions, on the seashore, in Golden Gate Park, and staged chase scenes in vintage cars and even in an airplane. We had a femme fatal that motivated the story plus many local character actors, one of whom played the noir detective, *Mike Angels*. When it was over, I had built a breakaway set for a car crash scene, ran the camera occasionally as an assistant cameraman and did sound. In general, I was an all-around grip, often hauling film equipment around in my old station wagon.

I learned a lot but it was exhausting. Some Mondays, I could barely make it to class. However, there were compensations other than learning how to make a relatively big budget student movie. There was the camaraderie of the film crew. We would often party together at the director's place on Carl Street in the Haight Ashbury. The director, Tom Bullock, would also have beer busts and pizza out on the locations where we shot.

Some of the women involved were cute and available. I was particularly attracted to Lucy, a slightly spacey, yet attractive young lady who served as a script girl and continuity director. It was she that took the Polaroid photos for continuity, making sure the actors wore the same clothes as in the prior scenes and that the props were identical. One night after, a day of shooting around Petaluma, we snuggled down in the back of my station wagon and it was like old times again in my high school days.

After the shooting was over, much work remained to be done on the movie, namely the editing and laying in of the soundtrack and music. My role was effectively over. I duly wrote up a paper on the making of Mike Angels and received an "A" by Goldner and two units of graduate credit.

However, Newton and Bullock were never able to achieve wide distribution for the film. It was only 45-minutes long, too short for commercial release and when I saw its debut showing at the Surf Theater, while well shot, it had some obvious problems with continuity and storyline. After a week at the Surf Theater and screenings at various student film festivals, it went into the vaults never to be seen publicly again.

Still, it was this experience that got me to thinking that perhaps I should look into a more traditional film school like UCLA to continue my studies. I was fascinated how the scriptwriter John Newton had concocted his script. How he dreamed up the idea and realized it scene by scene with dialogue and shot description. I also recalled Joel and Bruce pounding away all night on a typewriter back in my Army days, writing a script called *The Sergeant*. I remembered my input into that and what a rush it was coming up with a finished product.

In fact, I was working on my own movie script about a free-spirited chick with a crazy gay boyfriend who builds incomprehensible structures in his studio. Gloria is also a top model in San Francisco and we see her often walking down a San Francisco hill in freeze-frame shots. I also had some good scenes involving an ad guy living in plush suburban Orinda with wife and kids, part of the country club set. Yet he is fatally attracted to Gloria. This script didn't make much sense yet but I was confident it would jell. In any case, it had all the appearance of a real script with dialogue and shot descriptions and camera direction.

All of this taken together, made me resolve to head down to UCLA for a long fall weekend to attend a student film festival and to see what was going on in Hollywoodland.

8. HOLLYWOOD

A week or so later, I caught an afternoon flight to Los Angeles on Pacific Southwest Airline (PSA) to attend the UCLA student film festival. When I phoned ahead to make reservations, the PSA lady said, "Come on down. We're like the Greyhound bus. You show up and you're on. We have flights every half hour. You buy the ticket on board."

Wow! I thought. What a contrast to the uptight major carriers which wanted your reservations and re-confirmation in blood. And the cost was cheap, around fifteen dollars one-way.

When I got to SF International and made my way out to the PSA gate, I thought I had stumbled onto a rock concert. A band was rocking away and a line of "go-go" girls in short, miniskirts were kicking it up. A temporary PSA bar had been set up selling frozen daiquiris for a buck a piece. Thirsty, disheveled businessmen with silly grins on their face bellied up to the bar. Me too. Let the party begin.

Once on board, the little 727 jet took off like a rocket and before we knew it, we were leaving the coastal range mountains and flying out over the Pacific now glittering in the afternoon sun. Almost as an afterthought, a steward came through collecting the fare for the tickets. Right after him came the munchie cart and then the frozen daiquiri cart, still for a buck. Meanwhile, the sound system was pumping out rock. It was all going on with the stewardess in orange miniskirts buzzing up and down the aisles, smiling and flirting with the business types and making sure everybody was having a good time. A mere ninety minutes later, we were approaching LAX, half-bombed and happy. PSA sure knew how to run an airline.

***

Corrine, an old girlfriend of Jean-Paul, was there to meet me at the airport. She was working at UCLA and she also had a new boyfriend, Brett. I had phoned her up and told her I was coming down. She invited me to stay with them. She looked worn out when she picked me up. She seemed to have aged, no longer looking very fresh but still very cute with a pixie cut, or as I liked to imagine it, her Jean Seberg cut.

I wondered if I should tell her that Jean-Paul was back at Berkeley pursuing a Ph.D. in Comparative Literature. But it turned out she already knew that from some mutual friends.

"So, how is Jean-Paul?" she asked.

"Back."

"Yes, I know," she sighed. "Remember, I told you that he would come back. He's been too Americanized. Over there, he's just a little Frenchman. Here, he can be a character and an intellectual."

"Whatever. As far as I know, he just wants to get his Ph.D. at Cal and then maybe return to France, "I replied.

"Does he have a girlfriend?"

"No, not that I know of. At least nobody serious."

Back at her apartment in Westwood, near the University, I met Brett. He was already in his thirties with graying hair in a ponytail and a lined face. He looked as if he had been around a while, the perennial graduate student. Actually, he had spent ten years in Army, seen service in Korea and Europe. He got out before Vietnam heated up and was pursuing a Ph.D. in Psychology. Still, he struck me as a burnout, maybe shell-shocked and he smoked pot all the time. So did Corrine. No wonder she looked tired. Brett was especially proud of his home brewed beer. He brewed it in his bathtub. I wondered where they bathed. He gave me a bottle to drink. It tasted god-awful, but I managed to get it down.

"Not bad, eh?" He smiled sadistically.

"Gasp, uh, interesting. I've never had beer like that before."

"Yeah, well it grows on you. Has a good kick, like the German beer. Here, have some weed. Makes it taste better."

"Uh, thanks. I took a deep drag. As the weed went to my head, it felt a damn sight better than the grotty beer.

After some more pot and listening to Brett's exploits on the Korean DMZ and his time in Germany, we listened to the latest LA rock band, the Byrds, doing Dylan's *Mr. Tambourine Man*. Then we crashed for the night. I slept like the dead on their couch in their tiny, cluttered one-bedroom apartment.

***

The next morning, I caught a ride over to UCLA with Corrine, ready to explore what the school had to offer in its film department. With time to kill, before meeting with one of the film school deans, I wandered around campus. Most of the major buildings dated from the late 1920s, reddish-tan brick structures done in a Romanesque revival style featuring square towers with intricate filigree design. Of course, all of this was set off by lush Southern California landscaping with the ubiquitous palm trees and fountains. Another, more modern section of campus built in the 1950s was a collection of modern slab buildings with a lot of windows and outdoor arcade walkways. These too were softened by the lush vegetation. Functional I suppose, but not too interesting.

The students who were up and about seemed more laid-back, more serene, less harried than those at Berkeley or for that matter SF State. Most were still dressed in khakis and neatly pressed shirts, in the late fifties style, a style that I still wore myself, although I was starting to branch out into jeans and flowery shirts. A few students here and there, dressed in the surfer mode sporting sun-streaked hair, surfer shorts, Hawaiian shirts and deep beach tans. Others emulated the beat style with beards, sandals, tattered jeans and book bags.

I found the film school tucked away in the basement of one of the newer Arts buildings. Film students were rushing up and down the hall, chattering excitedly about this project or that project as they made their way to class. I waited patiently in the reception area for an assistant dean to interview me. I had brought along my Cal transcript and my San Francisco State class schedule and enrollment documents. I was all dressed up in a blazer and slacks with a tie. Still, I was nervous and wondering if they would even let me into this place. After all, I had been a mediocre student at Berkeley and had yet to prove myself at SF State.

By and by, a tweedy Mr. Leon came out, introduced himself and beckoned me into his office, an office lined with photographs of famous directors including Billy Wilder and movie stars on one wall. On another, photos of UCLA film graduates who were making it big in Hollywood.

"Well now, Mr. Brown. So you want to come to our little film school," Leon said leaning back in his plush leather chair.

"Well, at least I want to take a look at it. I've heard good things."

"Of course. We do do good things in the industry. Take a look at the photos of some of our more successful graduates." He said with a sweep of his hand. "Now, based on your letter, you said you were enrolled in the San Francisco State film school. A fine school, I might add. Very good at what they do, documentary and experimental. Why do you want to switch?"

"As I indicated in my letter, I would like to gain experience in the more commercial end of filmmaking, theatrical films. I feel my talents lie there, especially in the realm of script writing."

"Oh, have you written a script?" he asked, raising one eyebrow.

"Ah, yes. I can send it to you. It's not complete but you'll get the idea."

"Ah, no matter for the moment."

"But I do have my transcripts from Berkeley and course description from SF State," I said pulling them out of my satchel and handing them over. Leon glanced through the documents.

"Well, yes, a Berkeley graduate," he nodded, looking over my transcript. "That would bode well for gaining admission here even though you were not, shall we say, a stellar student. Of course, that is buttressed by your current attendance at SF State. And I note a year abroad in France. Plus your age. Twenty-five. You have had time to look around a bit and decide what you really want to do. I don't think you would have a problem gaining admission here at the UCLA film school.

"I wouldn't?"

"No, we love stealing SF State film students," he smiled. "They often bring a jolt of needed creativity here. Sometimes the students here are too focused on emulating the industry. Not that that's not important. We do have very close ties with the industry. Several well-known directors teach here on a casual basis. Billy Wilder shows up often."

Billy Wilder? My mind was racing. Of course. *Sunset Boulevard* and *Double Indemnity.* Masterpieces of film noir. Also his *Some Like It Hot*, a hysterical gangster picture with Marilyn Monroe.

"And we do have the latest in equipment and production facilities, much of it donated by the major studios," Leon continued. "I'm sure you would like to see all of that. I'll have one of our graduate students take you around. Oh, by the way, don't forget to take in our Fall Student Film festival tonight. There you will get a feel for what we do here."

"Yes, of course. I do plan to attend. Thank you for seeing me," I said as I shook his hand.

***

Meryl, the graduate student, was a skinny Jewish looking guy with a scraggly beard. He told me, he too thought of himself as a scriptwriter. "I don't like all of that running around a director has to do. I prefer to offer the blueprint of the film, the road map so to speak that drives the whole endeavor. Everything begins with the writing. That's what Billy says.

"Billy Wilder, right?"

"Right, Billy Wilder," said Meryl as he continued, "Of course, screenwriters get no respect. The smart ones become producers so their stuff gets on the screen with some semblance of what they intended. Nonetheless, we have to be knowledgeable about the hardware of filmmaking."

Meryl let me into the equipment and repair room and there before my eyes was a staggering array of cameras, lights, and sound equipment, editing Movieolas and other film paraphernalia that put SF State to shame. They had the usual 16mm Eclairs, Arriflexs and Nagra sound recorders but instead of one or two of each, they had a dozen. Also, they had several 35mm cameras.

"Wow! Big time Hollywood!" I exclaimed.

"Yeah, the 35mm is reserved for major film projects around here, usually by graduate students with access to some funding," Meryl explained. "They shoot in 35mm to impress their contacts in the industry. In effect, it's a film resume with particular attention paid to the mechanics of filmmaking, camera composition, lighting, editing, and so on."

After the equipment room, Meryl led me into a classroom where a class in graduate film production was about to get underway. A bunch of students was sitting around talking about this project or that. I kept hearing the name "Francis" pop up.

It was "Francis" this and "Francis" that. Or, "Francis has a new project with Roger."

Who was Francis? Who was Roger? Whoever they were, they were referred to in very reverential tones. Later, I asked Meryl who Francis was.

"Oh, that's Francis Coppola. He's technically enrolled here in the master's program but we hardly ever see him. He works for Roger Corman on Corman's schlock films."

"Corman?"

"Yeah, Roger Corman. He produces films you may have never heard of such as *Swamp Women*, *Bucket of Blood* and a bunch of movies based on the stories of Edgar Allen Poe. Corman sometimes hires UCLA students, mainly because they work cheap."

"Still," I countered. "At some level, it must be a good experience."

"Ah, yes, if you want to do direction and production. But he doesn't have much to offer would-be scriptwriters except formula crap."

***

By now, it was noon, so I joined Meryl and other film students for lunch at the student union. They were a lively bunch, so eager, so ready to kiss ass to get some lower-rung job in the Industry. They loved to name drop and tell about their experiences as unpaid interns on films shot around L.A.

"Hey, it's a foot in the door," said one.

"Fuckin' eh. I'd suck cock to get in with some of the directors," said one fat guy, half in jest.

"You'd have better luck bending over with the fag directors," said another.

"Hey, cool it guys," said Merle. "It's talent and creativity that is going to get you there in the long run."

I soon tired of hearing this stuff. Except for Meryl, I felt like most of these students would wind up as hacks. As I was about to excuse myself, Meryl mentioned there was a party after the film festival in nearby Westwood. He wrote down the address. I thanked him for showing me around and bid them all good-bye.

I spent the rest of the day at the UCLA recreation center, lying by the pool. The day was very warm, even though it was mid-October. I had brought my bathing suit. How can you come to L.A. and not have a bathing suit handy? I was able to get a guest pass as a fellow student. I would have preferred going to the beach but the pool did have its attractions such as scores of bikini-clad co-eds prancing around in firm, tan bodies. Some making a display of reading books, other lazing in the sun, applying suntan lotion. Quite a contrast to the Berkeley and San Francisco State women. Perhaps another reason to come down here to go to school.

Following an afternoon at the pool, I met Corrine and we went out for a Chinese dinner at a nearby restaurant. She said that Brett had a night class, so she was relieved of her cooking duties. I remarked she acted like a little old married lady.

"Never. I'll never get married. I don't trust you guys. You hurt too much."

I was worried about Corrine. She seemed on a path of self-destruction.

California Split

***

At seven p.m. sharp, I showed up at the auditorium where the student film festival was being held. The place was jammed with film students, regular students and a number of older industry types with notepads. Hey, I realized. This was for real. You could be noticed here as a budding young filmmaker.

Alas, the films didn't amount to much. Mostly dutiful, straightforward, functional vignettes about student life and student crises. A guy losing and then regaining a girlfriend. Someone having his car stolen. Endless shots of LA Freeways and driving around side streets. A few sequences of life on the beach, a traveling shot down the Venice Beach boardwalk. A surfing sequence or two. Nothing major or extended. By these standards, *Mike Angels* was a creative, far-out, clever film. There was nothing approaching the experimental creativity of a *Metanomen* or a *Watts Towers*. One of the more banal films was *Induction* by a Ray Manzarek, a tale of lovers lost and found. Interestingly, I would read about Manzarek a few months later as being the musical brains behind a new underground rock band called the Doors.

In summary, I thought, if this is the best film work that UCLA had to offer, it wasn't much. But, the school did have the pipeline into the industry. Exactly how the pipeline worked I was to find out at the party that Meryl had clued me into.

***

For a film party that was supposed to attract industry types, the setting was pretty prosaic. No mansions in the Hollywood hills for this party. It was being held in a modest bungalow in Westwood, the home of a film professor. It was a two bedroom, one bath job. A small front yard and a smaller patio out back. Of course, no pool. On the other hand, it was crammed with people and the rum punch in a large bowl was strong. Women were scarce probably because those enrolled in the film school were mostly males. However, everyone was friendly. You could tell who the industry types were because each one had a cluster of wanna-be filmmakers surrounding them. I hung back for a while, and then spotted Meryl coming through the door. He said hello and helped himself to the punch.

"Look around, Al," he said. "It's disgusting. Most of these industry guys are third or fourth directors acting like big shots when all they do is fetch coffee for the main director."

"Still, I'd like to meet one of them," I said.

"Sure. I know George over there." Meryl pointed to a heavyset guy with balding hair and a paunch. We went over and Merle introduced us.

"Al here is thinking about going to UCLA in theatrical film. Maybe directing."

George looked me over and said, "It's a long haul kid. I've been in the business about ten years now. I'm still only a third director."

"What does a third director do?" I asked.

"Well, it's a step up from being the fourth director who is essentially a gofer. At least I don't have to fetch coffee anymore. You're in charge of logistics, making sure everything and everybody is ready on time for the shoot. I also track down the stars, making sure they know their lines. Taking care of crises that pop up. A lot of non-technical rat shit. But critically important to shooting a film."

"So, when do you think you will be able to direct?"

"Hard to say," said George looking into his punch drink. "On average, the typical Hollywood film director doesn't get a shot at being full-scale until his late thirties or early forties. I'm about due. But first, I have to spend a couple of years as a second unit director. Then I'll get into the real nitty-gritty of filmmaking. Running around with a second unit cameraman doing pick-up shots on location. It's a lot of fun."

"Late thirties, huh?"

"Yeah, that's the average age unless you're born into the industry or are some hotshot kid that gets in on a fluke."

After George, Meryl introduced me to a cool looking dude leaning up against the wall. No one was hanging around him. His name was Sterling and he told me he was a script reader and a screenwriter. It was obvious Sterling was Meryl's hero.

"Yeah, I give Meryl advice about how to break into screenwriting."

"So how do you break in?" I asked

"Become a script reader," he replied. "It's a logical entrée. You spend all day reading scripts coming in over the transom or scripts from bona fide writers or their agents. Depending. The studios give you a list of categories they're interested in, and within those categories critical elements, they are looking for. In the industry, we refer to them as 'beats' or 'hits' that make the script commercial and make it move. You read mostly garbage, but now and then you find a jewel and promote it to the studio heads, writing little summaries."

"So how does that translate into becoming a scriptwriter?" I asked fascinated.

"It's simple man," Sterling replied. "You see what the market is, you see what sells. Reading those scripts is a real education on what to do and what not to do to sell a script. I have a couple of my own scripts in the works right now. But it all takes a while. I've been script reading for about three years now. If I'm lucky, I'll get a movie made out of one in a few more years."

***

So there it was. If I wanted to go the Hollywood route, go up through the system, I would have to spend years doing it. Doing essentially dumb-shit work, maybe some script writing on the side. But ultimately, not making movies on any terms. All of a sudden, San Francisco State didn't seem so bad. At least you had the creative freedom to explore without worrying about hooking into the industry. One could develop one's real talent to the fullest. Or so I thought at the time. I sensed that UCLA film school would be too constricting for me. I wanted to move fast, free, wide and open. But I would hold off for a while before making a final decision.

After the party, I walked over to Corrine's apartment and crashed for the night. The next morning Corrine took me to the airport. I kissed her goodbye on the cheek, still worried if she would survive life with Brett. And then I winged my way on PSA back to San Francisco.

9. SASHA

It was one of those rare, blazing hot nights in San Francisco in late October when the valley winds were blowing out of the east and the fog was miles offshore. I was on my way to the San Francisco Film Festival. This would be my second night at the festival which so far had failed to inspire me, except for *Crazy Quilt*, a film by local filmmaker John Korty.

As I stepped off the cable car at the Masonic Auditorium on Nob Hill, I spotted an attractive, yet exotic looking woman outside the auditorium, smoking a cigarette. At first, I thought, she was going to board the cable car, but no, she let it pass, preoccupied. For some reason, I stopped and asked her if she was lost.

"No, not at all," she smiled, grinding the cigarette out under the spike heel of her high heel shoes. "I am merely enjoying the warm night. Usually, I am freezing in this city."

She spoke with an odd Spanish accent as if mixed with an East European language. As I got a better look at her, she struck me as a dead ringer for the Greek movie star, Melina Mercouri, younger of course and maybe not as tall. She had ash-blonde hair, wide Egyptian type eyes and a charming, slightly ironic smile. Shapely legs and a narrow waist, dressed in European fashion. This was not your average American girl.

She noticed me checking her out. "You must think I am a woman of the streets. I am merely passing time here until the festival begins."

Hmm, I thought. "Say, have you bought your ticket yet?"

"Why no. Why do you ask?"

"Uh, I have some free passes to the festival courtesy of the San Francisco State Film Department. Would you like one?"

Without answering my question. "You are a film student?"

"Well, yes. It's an assignment to come here and check out the festival. Also, I know the guy who runs it, Albert Johnson."

"That's nice. I will accept your offer," she said with a smile. "Perhaps we could sit together. As you can see I am alone here."

"Wow," I thought. "That's one of the easiest pickups ever."

"How do you know the festival organizer?" she asked. I thought that a curious question as if she was fishing to see if I knew somebody important.

"Oh, Albert Johnson has been on the Bay Area film scene for years. He's also a Berkeley English professor. I knew him from my fraternity days when he used to rent us 'Red Cross' movies for fraternity gatherings."

"You were a fraternity boy?"

"Well, yes in my former life."

"That is a social club, isn't it?"

"Sort of."

"What are 'Red Cross' movies?"

"Movies that show a lot of skin and maybe more," I explained.

"Oh, dirty movies."

"I guess you could say that."

"Something to get the fraternity boys excited, no?"

Huh? I didn't respond. But I was beginning to realize that here was a woman on the make. Actually, it was more complicated than that. After watching a few banal shorts, during the intermission, Sasha told me a little of her history over a Martini Rossi in the lobby bar.

She said she was from Mexico City but was not Mexican. Her family was Jewish Polish immigrants who, failing to get into the U.S. in the late 1930s went to Mexico instead when Sasha was a baby. Her father, a tailor by trade, set up a clothing store on the Zocalo and prospered.

"Are there many Jewish Poles in Mexico?" I asked, surprised at this conjunction of cultures.

"Oh, yes, over a hundred thousand, I believe," she replied. "It is a very cohesive community. Well integrated into Mexican society as professionals and business people, but still considered apart from the Spanish and Mestizos."

Sasha went on to explain that she grew up in Mexico City and that during her secondary education at a Jewish school, she became attracted to the theater. Her teachers recognized her talent and recommended her to a drama academy. She spent several years there, acting in little theater and then met an American painter, Peter. Peter had come to Mexico to live cheap and paint. Sasha fell madly in love with him and they were married but while Peter was from a wealthy New England family, he had little money. Eventually, they decided to return to America. First, they lived in New York, where Sasha tried to get bit parts in Off-Broadway but to no avail.

"It was probably my accent. I did not speak English very well then. The best I could do was a walk-on as a Spanish maid."

As she later related, New York was a hard, cold demanding city. Peter wanted a sunnier lifestyle and was always fascinated by San Francisco which he had visited on several occasions. He thought he could paint here as well as hold down a full-time job. So they moved to San Francisco. Peter found a job as a driver on the Muni Street car. Sasha found work as a part-time social worker helping poor Mexican immigrants. She also managed to get small roles in various little theater productions in San Francisco. Then, just months after moving here, something happened to the marriage and Sasha moved out.

"I am waiting for my divorce," she told me. "Peter is a dear, but I cannot live with a painter. All he does is paint when he does not work. I need more attention. More fire and drama. Peter is boring. Also, he wants children. I cannot have children now. I want to be an actress. However, Peter and I are still friends."

I sensed this woman could be trouble. I calculated she was at least two years older than me. A grown, married woman, yet she was fascinating. A Polish Jew from Mexico who looked like Melina Mercouri, the star of *Never on Sunday*. How often do you run into that? I must have seemed like a callow youth to her, yet she was obviously interested.

After the film festival, we had an ice cream cone and walked around Nob Hill, past the Mark Hopkins and the glittering Fairmont Hotel in the still warm night. Then we boarded the California Street cable car and at her stop on Polk Street, she invited me to her nearby apartment for a shot of Tequila.

"OK," I said, "but please, no worms in the bottom of the glass."

"Don't worry. If you get down to the worm, you won't care," she answered saucily.

This is where we fade to black except to say, a married woman without a husband has her needs too.

***

Well, before we knew it, we were seeing each other two or three times a week. I would come over to Sasha's apartment after classes and she would fix some Mexican/Polish food or we would go out and eat or see a movie.

Sometimes, we would go out with her roommate Flora, a warm-hearted, thirty-something blonde and her boyfriend, Dan, a bit actor around town. Dan, a balding, comic looking figure, made a living as a character actor in commercials and comic bits.

I even met the soon to be ex-husband, Peter. At first, I was afraid he would slug me, but Sasha assured me he was harmless. Indeed, he didn't seem jealous at all. He seemed relieved that Sasha was interested in somebody else.

He was a tall and Nordic looking with a light goatee beard and short hair. A definite Vincent Van Gogh type. And he was an excellent painter. Sasha had several of his paintings hanging on the wall in her apartment including one depicting the backyards of a Mexican village up against a mountain. It reminded me of a Cézanne with its solid, cubist renderings of the buildings, the fences and the mountain beyond.

Peter and Sasha went off to the kitchen to transact some financial business. He was making good dough as a conductor on one of the trolley lines. His visit was brief. He was gone in an instant, and all was cool.

Wow, I thought. I just met the husband of a married woman. I briefly wondered what I was doing messing around with this serious life stuff. Yet in some ways, precisely because it was serious, I felt like I was participating in how life really was. Maybe I was growing beyond being a perennial college kid.

***

When Sasha wasn't working or seeing me, she was busy with her theater group, taking drama classes from the San Francisco Actors Workshop and/or auditioning for plays around town. In 1965, San Francisco had a thriving theater scene with many repertory theater groups, some of them equity which meant the actors were paid at union rates. Groups like the Playwright's Theater, Stage Door Theater and The Actor's Workshop Theater. When the actors were asked why they didn't practice their craft in Los Angeles or New York, the answer was usually something like this: "San Francisco is a theater friendly town. You can get a start here and learn your craft. Everyone here is supportive. You find none of the cutthroat competition here that you find in L.A. or New York."

I would sometimes accompany Sasha to rehearsals or classes and found it fascinating. The actors were so dedicated, so into their art and so into the philosophy of "my body is my instrument." It was Stanislavski-lite. Not only did they draw on their emotional memories, they drew on their visceral bodily memories, memories of movement, smell, taste and touch. It was a primordial regression to infancy, childhood and puberty.

There was a lot of talk of the proscenium, the "fourth wall" that separated the audience from the actors, of how it should be torn down, namely by addressing the audience directly or by staging the play in the round. Even going through the aisles, interacting with the audience. And why have a physical theater at all? Just do it in the street.

This was part of the philosophy of the San Francisco Mime Troupe. Street theater. The Mime Troupe, dressed more or less in Italian Renaissance costume and modeled after the Commedia dell'Arte, sought to shock, to involve, and to politically agitate. The Mime Troupe was frequently cited for being obscene. I had seen the group a couple of times in Golden Gate Park. One of the members of the troop was John Broderick, a grad student at San Francisco State. I thought them amusing, but not to be taken as serious theater.

And why have a script? Make it up. Improv. It was being done already and successfully by the Committee, the improv comedy group, somewhat modeled after Chicago's Second City. They lampooned the local and national politicians, and corporate life in San Francisco, as well as the trials and tribulations of young singles in the city. In addition to this was a flood of stand-up comedians with sharp social commentary who came through town, Mort Saul and Lenny Bruce, among the many.

Occasionally someone would ask me why I didn't try acting. As one very gay actor put it. "Say, you're a good-looking guy. You remind me of Rock Hudson, tall and dark." (This is before I knew that Rock Hudson was gay.)

While it was flattering, I didn't have the acting bug in me. I thought being an actor required more than looks. It required ego or paradoxically, it required no ego, only a desire to escape the reality of oneself. Also, I thought of actors as puppets, bossed around by directors. To me, the real creative brains of theater and film were the writers and the directors. I didn't want to be a puppet. Also, I felt self-conscious on stage. I had briefly audited an acting class at SF State, but after a few classes of trying to emote or even move correctly on stage, I gave up.

Sasha had no such inhibitions. She was ready to do drama anytime, anywhere. Not only straight drama but also comedy. She was an excellent comic. She could change moods on a dime, going from being goofy to being tragic in an instant. She claimed she was only truly alive on stage.

"I have much to give, Allan. I am always going around feeling like I am going to burst. I need this outlet. I am miserable without a dramatic outlet.

Of course, I am often miserable with my gift as well, miserable that I cannot do more because of this stupid accent, and afraid that I may never become recognized. Some days I feel more like Anna Kedrova than Melina."

As you may recall, Anna Kedrova played the dying whore in *Zorba the Greek*.

***

Since my film on the Vietnam Day Committee had vanished, I still had a film to do for my film production class. So I thought I would do my own experimental short, playing with time through editing. Sasha happily agreed to be my little star. It was a simple thing to shoot. Basically, her walking down the street in front of City Hall, getting a newspaper out of newsstand and then continuing to walk. I shot the action on the 16mm Bell and Howell from a variety of angles—long-shots, closes-ups of Sasha, the newspaper stand, the newspaper. Then back in the editing room, I fooled around with it, jumbling the time sequence and continuity of the walk, the procuring of the newspaper, and the walking on.

When I finished editing it and showed it to Sasha, she frowned, "What is this, Allan?" she said puzzled. "This makes no sense. It jumps all over the place."

Sasha was very literal.

"As I told you, it's an experiment with continuity and time," I said defensively.

"Hmm, well at least I look good in close up," she said, preening before a mirror "I've never been on film before. Maybe someday, we can do a real film piece together."

"Sure."

Well, at least Dr. Goldner like it. He thought the idea was interesting, even if it left something to be desired technically. He gave me an "A" on the film and on the paper I submitted explaining what I was trying to do.

***

On her days off, sometimes in the mid-week, Sasha would take a bus down to Pacifica in the afternoon and we would hang around the apartment or go walk along the beach. By now, it was often foggy and rainy, making the ramshackle town even more depressing than usual. But we managed to amuse ourselves, eating at a local cafe or having drinks at a local bar. The local men always did a double-take at Sasha. She was so different from the women they knew, the beat-out country and western gals.

Chris didn't know what to make of Sasha. She was unlike any girl he ever knew. Sometimes, he became downright hostile.

"Boy is she different," Chris would exclaim. "A Mexican Jew. I didn't they know they even existed. What's a matter, Brown? Can't find an American woman?"

"Get lost Chris," I would reply, annoyed. "I'm not interested in any of the Sally types you and your friends hang around with."

Chris was offended. And it was true, there was a real culture gap going on here. Chris was all-American even if he was second generation Rumanian and even if his girlfriend Erica was of Hungarian extraction.

"Sasha looks older than you," Chris teased.

"Yeah, she is."

"Divorcee too. Bet she's horny"

"Shut up Chris or I'll throw something at you."

Actually, I thought it was Chris who was horny. While Erica often slept over, I don't think they ever made it. She was a traditional girl waiting for the ring.

To tell the truth, I was tired of living with Chris, reliving frat days and commuting down to foggy Pacifica. He did have a sweet set up with nice furniture and he ran a well-ordered household. I was materially very comfortable, right down to using his thick, plush towels after showering and drinking his beer. Chris was very generous, although I did make an effort to pay him back. But I could no longer relate to his scene, especially now going around with Sasha. Plus, my station wagon had broken down in December and I didn't have the money to fix it. I was reduced to bus transportation to the City which made it a hassle to commute to Pacifica.

The breaking point came when Sasha took the Greyhound Bus out to see me one day and I wasn't there. In order to get down to the apartment, she had to hike three-quarters of a mile in the high heels over a rocky, barely paved road. By the time she arrived at the apartment, her feet were killing her. Only Chris was there and apparently, she did not feel very welcomed. He never even offered a class of water. She left in a huff, her feet still hurting her, and hiked back to the Greyhound bus stop.

I got an ear full from Sasha later. "That fat slob. How can you live with such a person? And why weren't you there?"

"Uh, I thought we were going to meet in the City. I went to your apartment," I said.

"No, I have it right here. Right in my appointment book." She waved her little appointment book at me. "You are so disorganized. My life is too busy to be wasting time going down there."

She looked at me and then softened. "Oh, I don't know. I feel so lost sometimes. That day in Pacifica, I felt like a real stranger in this country. I felt like I was back in Israel with my sore feet and all."

"Israel?"

"Yes, did I not tell you about Israel?"

"Not in any detail, except to say you went there to visit," I answered.

"It was more than that. Growing up in the Jewish community, all we heard about were the glories of Israel. Young people were encouraged to go there and work on a kibbutz, maybe even emigrate there. They made it sound very tempting. All expenses were paid, airfare, hotels and transportation to the kibbutz. So I went when I graduated from my secondary school. I was eighteen. I loved Tel Aviv with its cafes and seashore. It was a very vibrant city. But that only lasted a couple of days. We took a rickety old bus to a kibbutz in the middle of nowhere. It was dusty, dirty and hot. And you had to go to the bathroom in a shack outside and take a cold shower outside."

"No, shit."

"And the work was hard. I worked in the fields in the middle of the day in the sun. That was crazy, nobody works in the middle of the heat in Mexico. One day I became sunstroke and after that, they let me work inside, mostly in the kitchen. I had to wash pots and pans. That was not me. I like to keep my fingernails pretty. And I hated wearing those boots."

"I can imagine," I replied.

"Also the Jews there were so different. Many had come directly from Eastern Europe. They were like peasants. For them this place was paradise. The women ran around half-naked all the time. The men had all of these crazy women they wanted. I was innocent and shocked."

"Finally, I couldn't stand it anymore. So I ran away. I simply left, walking out of the place in my high heels, down a long dusty road. My feet hurt so but I was not going to give up high heels, nylons and makeup to live in Israel. Soon a bus came along and took me to Tel Aviv. My father wired me money and I spent a few days in Tel Aviv having a good time, but I was homesick so I flew home."

Turning to me, she said, "Now I feel the same way. An outsider. A foreigner here in this town. I cannot go down to Pacifica anymore."

"OK, OK."

10. TENDERLOIN

January I gave my notice to Chris and moved to a shitty, little furnished studio apartment on Eddy Street in the heart of the Tenderloin. This was essentially a skid row section of town where you kicked empty wine bottles down the street and where hookers of dubious sexuality hung out on street corners, not to mention druggies nodding off in alleys. But it suited my purposes because it was cheap and I was running out of money. Also, it was near Sasha's apartment on Polk and the theater scene where she hung out.

However, after a week of living there and staring at water stained walls in my three-story walkup, I wondered if I had made a mistake. Luckily, the Chinese landlord had not insisted on a lease so I could bail anytime.

"You pay month to month, Mr. Brown. In advance. That good enough."

"Whatever you say Mr. Lee."

I tried to alleviate my depression by sprucing up my apartment. I painted the mottled the walls green. This only made me more depressed. But the real cause of my depression was Sasha. She took one look at my place and refused to stay the night.

In addition, she had landed a part in "The Man Who Came to Dinner," and she was busy rehearsing day and night. Essentially, she had no time for me. The theater came first. As she described it, "It's like a family, Allan. We are so close, so tight knit. It has to be that way. I am sorry, I cannot see you often."

I also thought she was becoming interested in one of the handsome lead male actors, somewhere in his mid-thirties. Now I knew how Peter felt. Eventually, I felt relieved. Sasha was a handful. Her intensity had worn me out. I needed to concentrate more on my studies and eventually find another surveying job because my unemployment checks would run out in March.

After Sasha split, I rationalized that living in the Tenderloin wasn't so bad. It was centrally located. Public transportation was good getting out to San Francisco State. Further, I had a great bar nearby, the Edinburgh Castle. This Scottish pub was a friendly, comfortable place of dark wood and great beer. It was a favored hangout for Brits, Canadians, New Zealanders and Aussies, most of them in the military. The routine was to order fish and chips from a deep-fry joint around the corner, wrap it in a newspaper and carry it over to the pub to be consumed with a pint of bitter. Following that, a game of darts and social mingling with the Anglo Empire.

"Bloody great town, this San Francisco."

"Best in the U.S."

"Great, easy women."

Yes, some single women did hang out here. The sporting girls. The ones into tennis, skiing, biking and generally keeping fit. Most were a little too butch or plain for me.

But the Anglos didn't seem to mind. I was still attracted to Jewish girls like Sasha and Darrah. Even though they could be a real pain in the ass, they had soul.

***

I was down at the Muni Station one Friday morning, waiting for a bus to Berkeley. Gerard had a new apartment that I wanted to see. He had described it as "real groovy." I was lost in these thoughts when a young lady asked me if I knew where the California School of Deaf was located in Berkeley. I looked her over, young, attractive and sweet. Innocent. Jewish.

"Sure, I know where it is. I'm going to Berkeley to a friend's house a few blocks away. If you want, I'll take you over there."

"Oh, that would be so great. I'm so lost up here." She smiled gratefully.

We boarded the bus and sat together as it pulled out and wheeled its way across the Bay Bridge. Her name was Silvia and she had just graduated from a UCLA teachers program that taught how to teach deaf kids. She was going for a job interview.

"That's interesting. How is it you want to teach deaf kids?" I asked.

"Oh, my younger older sister was born deaf and I grew up knowing sign language. Since I was interested in teaching, I thought I would put those skills to good use."

"Let's see."

Silvia proceeded to talk to me in sign language with fluid graceful movements of her hands. Of course, I didn't have a clue what she was talking about even though years ago, I knew some basic words because we used to fool around with sign language in Boy Scouts.

"So what did you say?"

"I said 'Thank you for being my guide in finding this school.'"

Like I said, a charming, sweet girl.

We changed buses at Dwight Way and took another bus up to Piedmont Avenue, just south of campus, beyond fraternity row. It was here the school was located. I bid Silvia goodbye, but before I did, I casually mentioned that Gerard's apartment was nearby and that if she wanted to come over and hang out after her interview, she was welcome.

"We'll go out for dinner and I'll give you a little tour of Berkeley."

Much to my surprise, she jumped at the chance. "I'd be delighted. I don't know anyone here. I've always wanted to see Berkeley."

I gave her the address and a couple of hours later, she did show up on Gerard's doorstep.

***

We sat around, sipping wine, listening to the Rolling Stones and grooving on Gerard's new digs. It was the second story of an old craftsman house with a sundeck, plenty of woodwork and alcoves with a redwood tree out back.

Gerard was eyeing Silvia. Damn, she was attractive. Around five-seven, slender, very dark hair, nice skin, good teeth, dressed in a little black silk suit that must have cost mucho bucks. Her family lived in Brentwood, a plush section of L.A. Her father was a lawyer. Gerard thought her young. I guessed she was about twenty-one.

After listening to some records, we went out to eat at Larry Blake's and then wandered up and down Telegraph, checking out the cafe scene and the bookstores. Then noting that it was getting late, she said she had to get back to the YWCA where she was staying in San Francisco. They closed their doors at midnight. Not wanting her to ride the Muni at this hour alone and traipsing through the Tenderloin where the Y was located, I decided to return to the City with her, thus giving up my weekend in Berkeley.

She thanked me profusely for accompanying her. "Boy, it sure is nice to have a protector and an escort. Your friend Gerard seems very nice. I'm looking forward to working at the School for the Deaf."

It was nearly midnight by the time we got to her Y. At the elevator, I told her at that I would be willing to show her around San Francisco the next day.

"Oh, that would be great." Then she held her head as if she was expecting a little kiss. I duly complied. She was so young, so fresh. Then I turned to go. She paused and said, "Wait. Why don't we go to your place? I have a couple of little bottles of wine they handed out on the airplane."

"Uh," you sure?"

"Yes, I don't want to go up to that cold, anonymous room right now. You said you lived nearby."

"That I do. Come on then."

Well back at my apartment, the inevitable happened.

Afterward, she told me that she was engaged to be married in a few months. "My fiancé will be working in San Francisco. He's just graduated from law school."

"Well, then what was this?" I asked puzzled, seeing no engagement ring on her hand.

"Oh, I suppose it was my last chance for a fling before I become a beaten down teacher and a drab housewife."

I felt like replying, "Well glad to be of service," but said nothing. Indeed, I recalled Rachel on the Icelandic Airline flight and concluded last minute flings were apparently a Jewish tradition.

The next day, we wandered around the city and out to Golden Gate Park, visiting some friends in the Haight-Ashbury, and then back downtown where I put Silvia on an airport bus to the San Francisco Airport.

A week later, I received a postcard in the mail, thanking me for the great time we had in San Francisco. That was sweet, but Silvia was a fast fading memory. I didn't have much time to reminisce because I was in the process of packing up and moving out. I was done with Tenderloin. Hello Haight-Ashbury.

11. THE HAIGHT

The Haight. The intersection of Haight Street and Ashbury Street near Golden Gate Park. I wondered what all the fuss was about in early 1966. Initially, all the Haight meant to me was that it was a cheap place to live for San Francisco State students. Tom Bullock had told me about an apartment in his building on Carl Street that had just opened up. It was a large one-bedroom and that if I wanted it, I should act quickly because the area was hot and good apartments at reasonable prices went fast. I took one look at the furnished apartment and grabbed it.

It was a typical San Francisco Victorian apartment with a long hallway leading to a spacious living room with large picture windows that had a good view of St. Ignatius Church across the way. The living room was furnished with a rattan couch, a daybed, a rickety coffee table, an old but comfortable easy chair and a couple of floor lamps. Along one wall were bookshelves and a mantle over what had once been a fireplace but was now sealed off. The bedroom was large with a lot of natural light, and a queen-size bed that looked dubious with a sagging mattress but was surprisingly comfortable.

The kitchen off the living room was a dark hole with old appliances and a beat-up kitchen table. A lone window looked out on a stairwell between the two wings of the apartment building.

The bathrooms were interesting. I use the word in the plural because there were two bathrooms. One was merely a toilet but it had a little vanity and basin. It was referred to as a "water closet." The other was a full-scale bathroom featuring a bear-claw tub with a shower arrangement and a basin but no toilet. The Victorians were fastidious. They didn't bathe and shit in the same place. I thought this arrangement quite sensible.

Overall, I found this apartment at 150 Carl Street quite pleasant and roomy. All it needed was some color on the blank white walls to brighten it up. It was not as interesting architecturally as the Virginia Street apartment, but it was all mine for as long as I wanted it. And for only a hundred dollars a month.

***

Once settled in with my meager belongings, I went on a tour of the neighborhood. Right outside my door, the N Judah Line ran out to the beach in the Sunset District and in the opposite direction, downtown to Market Street via a tunnel through Buena Vista Heights.

A block away was a corner grocery store with produce and meat run by a fat little Italian. That would be my food source. On the corner of Carl and Cole was a drugstore for my toiletries and pharmaceuticals. Across the street was the Free Store run by the Diggers. I thought that might come in handy if I ran out of money for food but I heard they handed out mostly macrobiotic rice and weird vegetables.

Walking north on Cole, I eventually found myself down on Haight Street, the main commercial strip of the district. By early 1966, Haight Street had made a rapid transition from staid traditional businesses such as hardware stores, clothing stores, five-and-dimes to the counter-culture hippy establishments such as the Psychedelic Shop.

Walking into this shop, you were overwhelmed with the smell of incense and mind-boggling array of pot paraphernalia—roach clips, rolling paper, clips, beads, bells, Buddhist medallions, psychedelic posters, books on drugs and oriental philosophy. I didn't know there could be so much to smoking a joint. At the time, pot was cheap at eight dollars a lid and available on every street corner in the Haight. The cops were nowhere in sight.

Other nearby hippy stores included: Xanadu, a leather store and the place to go if you wanted a custom-made pair of sandals; In-Gear, which featured mod clothing from Carnaby Street in London and the Print-Mint with the largest collection of wild, mind-bending posters around.

In addition to the shops were several hangout cafes such as the Blue Unicorn and The Drogstore Cafe where one could sip organic coffee from remote corners of the world and peruse the latest underground newspapers like the *Berkeley Barb* and the *Oracle*. Nearby was the Straight Theater which hosted concerts, lectures, and poetry readings but rarely put on a regular play.

Heading west on Haight towards Golden Gate Park were a variety of restaurants including my favorite take-out place, The Foghorn, which specialized in authentic British style fish and chips wrapped in a newspaper.

On the corner of Stanyan and Haight was an ordinary Safeway store in contrast to the health food stores nearby. On the other corner was McDonald's where I must confess I occasionally dined.

Across from Stanyan Street was Golden Gate Park or more specifically Hippy Hill which was not much of a hill at all but merely a rise. When the weather was sunny and temperatures reached into the 60s or 70s, the hippies turned out in full regalia, gathering there. Young men lounged about in antique military jackets, leather vests and old top hats with psychedelic headbands. A few donned Indian robes with a feather headdress and danced in circles waving totem sticks. Others chanted mantras, sitting on the ground yoga style in East Indian outfits. Many women with paint on their faces and flowers in their hair wore sweeping calico granny dresses and sported tiny colored glasses. Others pranced about in leather mini-skirts with high heel boots and crazed embroidered vests. A few would dance topless to beat of conga drums, tambourines and flutes or sway to the strains of Indian raga. The smell of incense, pot and hashish permeated the air. It was indeed a mellow bacchanalia.

In short, the Haight-Ashbury was a happening place. Still, I was living in my own little world oblivious to much that was going on since I was busy with school. Eventually, though, I decided I had to upgrade my image from that of an aging graduate student dressed in khakis and button-down shirts. I found the British Mod style attractive and bought a couple of flowery, billowy silk shirts with tight black pants and shiny half-boots with high heels. This along with a pullover sweater with a rawhide drawstring and a Navy pea coat. For more casual dress, I bought a few wild tie-dye T-shirts to wear with my Levis and a pair of custom made sandals. I let my hair grow long, well below my ears but couldn't bring myself to grow a beard or even a mustache. Even so, after my wardrobe upgrade, I felt more suitable hip.

Still, I was not a hippy. I found the word itself annoying. "Hippy." Obviously, it derived from "hipster" a common term used by the jazz musicians of the 40s and 50s and adopted by the Beats. It was really a term of derision used by the present-day Beats seeing these young wannabes coming onto the scene.

Most of the hippies I saw were in their late teens or early twenties. They came primarily from the middle-class suburbs of the Bay Area and Los Angeles. A few had made it out from the Midwest and the East Coast. Many had dropped out of college to follow the advice of their LSD guru Timothy Leary, namely to "tune in, turn on and drop out." Some claimed to be seeking a higher reality but most I suspected were just looking for a good time and the freedom to do what they wanted such as getting high, doing acid and getting laid.

There were a lot of one and two-year-olds running around naked with names like Sunshine and Destiny. No one was quite sure who the fathers were and no one apparently cared. Many of the women were stunningly attractive, reminding me of Lina, my hippy acquaintance from the laundromat, but elusive, reserving themselves and their young bodies to their own little communal group of hippy guys through which they would rotate. Other, less attractive women often wound up doing the cooking, cleaning, and other grunt chores of the living arrangement while the men would lounge around on their batik pillows and plot out their next move in getting "bread" for an upcoming concert.

The more creative and energetic hippies were engaged in various activities such as making music, designing posters, fabricating jewelry, leather goods and baking bread. Some wrote, others did little sketchy films on eight-millimeter film that featured hours of boring street scenes. A few landed real jobs, the favorite being a postal carrier delivering mail in the Haight. The hippies liked this job because they were on their own on the streets and could deliver the mail according to their own whims. The recipients rarely complained to the post office about late or undelivered mail. The hippy mail carriers were the ones with the money and benefits who shared it all with their commune.

Then there were the business hippies who were really businessmen in hippy disguise. Profit was their game in selling the hippy paraphernalia but they took great care in concealing their profit margins since profit was considered uncool. A few were successful but most little businesses came and went in a matter of months. However, the vast majority of hippies did little or nothing. They were too busy "being."

My peek into this world came through Mimi, a friend of Lucy's. (Lucy, the *Mike Angels* girl that I hooked up with.) Mimi was cute as hell with dark hair and big wide eyes, but spaced-out. She was a sometime student in theater at SF State but had no ambition whatsoever other than being a visual prop for film and television students. In one short film, she was depicted staring at a Kachina doll for about five minutes, then picking up an ice pick and stabbing it mercilessly until it fell to pieces and throwing it at the camera.

However, at the moment, she was taking a break from the rigors of acting and was drifting around from crash pad to crash pad in the Haight, going to concerts, and in general hanging out. Even Lucy was concerned.

"Your mother is not going to like this," Lucy would chastise her.

"Leave me alone. I'm meeting interesting people," Mimi would protest. "Plus I don't have any bread. My parents cut me off when I dropped out this semester."

Mimi took Lucy and me on a tour of her latest domicile. It was a notorious crash pad on Oak Street in an old rundown Victorian house with five or six bedrooms and two bathrooms only one of which was operational but so disgusting that the both the guys and the girls used the weed-choked backyard for pissing. In each bedroom, several mattresses were scattered on the floor where hippies of both sexes would "crash." The living room was a collection of oversized beanbag loungers, a couple of old moldy couches. In the center, a glass-top coffee table in surprisingly good condition on which people kept their pot paraphernalia and other drug material. In an effort to beautify the place, the latest psychedelic posters were plastered on walls.

The kitchen was covered with gooey, congealed, substances of various origins. Dirty pots and pans filled the sink. The garbage overflowing in the garbage bins was being picked over by a stray cat and perhaps a few unseen rats. The stove was encrusted with more grease and burned food. It was doubtful if the burners even worked. All in all, a disgusting mess.

Nobody paid rent to stay here. Nobody knew who owned the place. It just was. Manna from the hippie god. So said the inhabitants of the Oak Street crash pad that we saw that particular day. All young, all aimlessly sitting around or stretched out on the mattresses, sleeping off a long night or a bad trip. Despite their colorful costumes and youth, many seemed weary, worn out. Dark circles under the eyes, gaunt features, underweight, pale, and listless. Faint body odors. Tired. Beaten down by life in the crash pad.

"It's not too bad," Mimi insisted. "And the people are nice."

After surveying the squalor, Lucy announced. "I don't care. You're getting out of here. Come stay with me. My roommate is never there. She's always off with her boyfriend."

"Well, maybe," Mimi sighed. "But I've learned a lot staying here. About sharing, about loving, about just "being," but a clean place would be nice. "

"Don't worry about rent for right now. I'm sure your parents will be happy to see you in some place decent," said Lucy. "Come on Allan, let's get her stuff out of here."

Of course, decent was a relative term. Lucy's pad, a little house in the Sunset, was no jewel, but at least it was cleaner than the crash pad.

***

So that was the hippy life that I encountered in the Haight. The other action going on in the Haight was the rock scene. Really, a rock renaissance. San Francisco was producing its unique brand of rock music. Some called it "acid rock." The main practitioners of this new rock were the *Jefferson Airplane, Grateful Dead, Big Brother & The Holding Company, Quicksilver Messenger, Country Joe & The Fish* and *The Family Dog,* all local bands.

Their music featured long, repetitive, hypnotic takes with hints of Indian raga and blues. Melodies would appear in unexpected places, mostly improvised. Other times, the music was simply rock-and-roll with a pounding beat and highlighted by amplified, electric guitars. The bands wrote most of their own music, music that some said was best appreciated while high on pot or acid. No short three-minute cuts for radio play for these bands. Although, there were two radio stations in town devoted to long cuts, namely KMPX and KSAN, the main venue for their music was various auditoriums around town, including the Longshoreman's Hall, the Avalon and the Fillmore Auditorium.

My first introduction to the San Francisco rock scene came at the Longshoreman's Hall in the fall of 1965. The concert featured the *Family Dog,* the newly formed *Jefferson Airplane* and the *Great Society* with Grace Slick as the lead singer. All the bands were inspiring but Grace Slick was truly hot. Jerry Slick, her estranged husband, had understated his case to me when he referred to her as a sometime singer. She looked great up onstage in a white leather fringe costume, long-legged, tall, model-like, long dark hair, a supple low voice, belting out the songs like "Somebody to Love." This was no little sweet lady chanteuse. She was a rock siren.

Adding to the atmosphere were the light shows of liquid plasma displays, and projected psychedelic designs, although not on the scale that was to be seen later. I had gone to the concert with a few of the *Mike Angels* crew, leaving Sasha at her apartment. She was not interested in what she called vulgar American rock music. No matter, I had a good time dancing the night away with Lucy who, as a semi-hippy chick, fit right in. The next day the *Chronicle* music critic Ralph Gleason gave the concert rave reviews. The San Francisco rock Renaissance had officially begun.

The next major rock event I attended was a concert at the Fillmore Auditorium in December that featured the *Jefferson Airplane, The Great Society* and the *Warlocks*, now renamed, *The Grateful Dead*. By this time, the light shows had become full-fledged theatrical productions put on by some students from San Francisco State. They featured oil and water floating blobs on screens, bits of crazed movies, swirling psychedelic light patterns, flashing strobe lights—all creating a disorienting maelstrom of color and sound again best confronted high on acid, pot or liquor.

I skipped the Ken Kesey's Trips Festival that was being advertised as a three-day event at the Longshoreman's Hall in January of 1966. The Trips Festivals was based on the earlier gatherings that Kesey had hosted at his place in La Honda where attendees paid a one-dollar cover charge and were treated to a cup of "electric" Kool-Aid and to the music of the Grateful Dead. Now Kesey was going public with his Trips, encouraging everybody to take acid and get their groove on. LSD was still legal although there were moves afoot to make it illegal.

To make sure order was maintained at the Trips Festival, the Kesey people enlisted the Hells Angels who stood around dumbfounded at the goings on but intrigued by the music and the free and loose hippy women. Actually, it was the Hells Angels that made sure mayhem ensued along with an occasional gang-bang of an overdosed hippy chick.

Kesey apparently thought he could tame the goons with a dollop of acid. It never happened. They became more unruly than ever. However, today the Hells Angles are still around and Kesey and his Merry Pranksters are long gone. The Trips Festivals came to a crashing end when the cops busted Kesey for possession of marijuana for the second time and he fled to Mexico.

***

So with all this LSD around why did I not partake? Good question. A fellow named Owsley was making it by the tub full in a secret lab in Berkeley and the Haight was flooded with it. Still, it would have taken an effort to go and find a tab and then worry how pure it was. Also, I kept hearing stories about "bad trips." Of people going into paranoid, hallucinatory states and never coming out of them, even when the acid had worn off. Then there was the potential brain damage associated with long-term use, assuming one got hooked on it. Finally, I noted that those high on acid were dull, just wandering around with silly smiles, not making much sense when they talked. "Oh, ahhh, groovy, far out." This could go on for hours. You could see them up and down Haight Street, licking on ice cream cones, a favorite treat when high on acid. The local ice cream parlor in the Haight was always busy, making a mint from the stoned hippies.

Once driving down to Half Moon Bay for the day with Lucy and Mimi, another couple in the back seat had dropped some acid for what they called the real trip. They proceeded to get off on the passing scenery for a few hours talking gibberish and then fell asleep. Boring. No, I knew acid was not my thing. I liked being in control too much. I figured I could groove enough on my own without the help of acid.

Just listening to the music around with an occasional joint could get you high enough. Songs like the Stones' "Satisfaction, I Can't Get No" filled the streets of the Haight. At San Francisco State, the song was incorporated into many short student films as a soundtrack. No worries about paying royalties for its use, because, hey, we were students.

The live music scene further picked up in June. I kept hearing about a great blues singer with *Big Brother & The Holding Company*, so a group of us went down to the Avalon and listened to a Texas chick named Janis Joplin. Although, rather plain and dumpy with a rough looking face and stringy hair, Joplin had a voice like a foghorn and really belted out her bluesy tunes. Still in early twenties, she nevertheless had the look, the swagger and the singing style of a lady blues singer in her forties or fifties. I wondered how long she would last. Still, at the time listening to her was a heady, soul wrenching experience.

Later that fall at another *Jefferson Airplane* concert, I heard Grace Slick again. She was now with the *Airplane*. This was the first time I heard her sing "White Rabbit," the hallucinogenic song set to a rising crescendo that comes to an abrupt end. "White Rabbit" perfectly summed up the spirit of San Francisco acid scene: *"One pill makes you larger, one pill makes you small."*

***

Despite the hippy scene going on around me, I was into my own thing hanging with Lucy, Mimi in their little house in the Sunset. After, Sasha split, Lucy and I started seeing each other now and then, nothing heavy, just an occasional joint at her place and a screw in her shower. She liked running water going over her while she did it. Lucy with honey blonde hair had a peasant, mother-earth build.

But she was spacey, at times almost going into a trance, staring into space for hours, while gently petting her cat in the living room of her little house. Sometimes she was remorseful, about a former boyfriend whom she nevertheless saw now and then. Martin was an astronomer at Stanford, engaged in a project that involved listening to radio signals from far-off solar systems, possibly an indication of life on other planets.

"Christ, he had a dick, like a baseball bat," she said nonchalantly. "He can hardly get it into me. Not like yours."

"Mine?"

"Yeah, we fit just fine," she smiled

"Glad to hear it."

Now that Mimi was living with her, our encounters grew more complicated. Mimi was currently without a boyfriend. So sometimes she wound up in the same bed as we, apparently hoping to participate. I was all for the idea, but Lucy, still with her bourgeois hang-ups, would resist.

"Hmm, if you want to make it with Mimi. Go ahead, but I'm going to go sleep on the couch."

I took that as a signal to cease and desist. However, one night after quite a bit of pot, wine and steak and a lot making out with both Mimi and Lucy, both high and horny, we did fall into bed for a threesome. I won't go into the gory details, except to say the combinations and permutations of three far exceeded that of two. Such was my scene in the spring of 1966. On the fringes of the rock and hippy revolution.

12. KEMP

In the midst of my fun and games in the Haight, my unemployment checks ran out and so had my savings. I could no longer be a full-time student at SF State. So that spring I duly enrolled in two night classes (film directing and film theory). I also began looking for another surveying gig which in March of 1966 was not that easy. My basic problem was I wanted to stay in my apartment in San Francisco. Most of the surveying jobs were in the East Bay and in Contra Costa County. I didn't want to commute across the Bay Bridge everyday by Muni since I was still without a car. When I notified the union hall that I was available, I stipulated that I wanted an engineering firm in the city.

"Uh, that's going to be hard, my friend," said the husky voice at the Operating Engineer's Union. "Nothing going on there. How about the Peninsula? Lots of construction down there."

"Not if I can help it," I replied.

"Well, I'll see what I can do but don't hold your breath. More than likely you'll wind up in the East Bay."

"Uh, OK," I said, half resigned to the inevitable.

I decided not to wait on the union. I resolved to do some job hunting myself in the city. I checked the yellow pages and noted there was an engineering firm out on Judah St. in the Sunset District, Nicarao Engineering. Why not give it a try?

Nicarao's office was located in a squat, one-story stucco building that shared with a dentist and a beauty parlor. An unlikely place for an engineering firm. However, one glance around inside the office with its rows of drafting tables and maps on the wall, told me that this was indeed the place. A draftsman looked up from his work and asked if he could help me.

"Uh, is Mr. Nicarao around? I'm looking for a chainman job."

"Why yes, go to the back and knock on his office door."

I made my way through the drafting tables and knocked on the door.

A voice with a Hispanic accent said, "Come in."

I entered and encountered a tall, sleek looking Hispanic, looking more like a used car salesman than an engineer. He had thick black sweptback hair, a mustache and flashing white teeth.

I introduced myself, saying I was looking for work as a head chainman.

He nodded, saying, "Very good. What is your experience?"

I outlined it briefly and handed him a resume of my experience. He looked it over and nodded again. "You appear to have some good experience. You may be in luck, Mr. Brown. It does so happen that we will be putting a crew out in the field in a couple of weeks. I have two big jobs coming up. But first, I would like you to meet Kemp, my party chief. He is out doing lot surveys right now. Can you come back around five today or tomorrow?"

"Sure. How about tomorrow? I have class tonight."

"Oh, you are student?"

"Part-time at SF State."

"Oh, yes. Perhaps you are studying civil engineering."

"Ah, film."

"Really," he nodded, preening a little. "How interesting."

What a strange dude. What a strange set up. As I later learned, Mr. Nicarao was the brother of the Nicaraguan Consulate to San Francisco. He sported diplomatic plates on his Cadillac. He apparently had good connections with rich Nicaraguan families who were investing in real estate developments in the Bay Area. Nicarao's job was to make their developments become a reality. While not a licensed civil engineer himself, he nevertheless had founded this firm, hiring all the expertise he needed. He had two licensed civil engineers on staff. George the fellow I met at the drafting board and Kemp whom I was yet to meet.

***

Kemp turned out to be a cranky, thin, wiry guy in his fifties with a faraway look in his ice-blue eyes. He said his distant gaze came from his forbears on the Arctic frontier, crazed, isolated Finns trying to farm and look out for Russians at the same time. Of course, that distant penetrating gaze at his natural surroundings helped him immensely as a land surveyor. As

Kemp often reminded me, he was a full-fledged, licensed civil engineer, a graduate from Cal, who chose to work in the field not at some drafting table designing subdivisions. As he said, "Gosh, I go batty indoors, all that sitting, all that cigarette smoke. It's unhealthy. I have to move around."

"I know what you mean. I like outdoor surveying too. Even pounding stakes," I said sucking up to him as we rode out to our first job, a simple lot survey.

"Yeah, sure. You'll soon get plenty of that. No, what gets me most about working indoors are the politics. I had enough of that working as a construction inspector for the City of San Francisco."

"Inspector?"

"*Ja*. My job was to keep an eye on those contractor sons-of-bitches. Always trying to cut corners. Use the cheapest materials. Do slipshod work. Get it done, pocket the bonus for an early finish. They were all crooked. Yet when I called them on it, they would go over my head. If they were connected politically to city hall, the chief Engineer would get a call from higher up saying that I was being a prick, a stickler. No flexibility."

"No flexibility? What do you mean?"

"I mean I was accused of making unreasonable demands that didn't amount to a hill of beans. So I would be told to back off. Eventually, I got sick of it and quit. Half the shit they built just a few years ago is already falling apart. Roads buckling, sewer lines coming apart. Curbs and gutters crumbling. You name it. Shitty work. Well enough of that, let's see what you know, young man."

The lot survey was easy. Kemp located the street monument which served as our reference point. We turned angles and distance off that to locate the corner of the property line of a small bungalow house in the Sunset. A few more angles turned, distance measured, a new stake or two in the ground to adjust the old property lines and we were done in three hours. On the way back to the office, Kemp told me, I would do as a chainman but warned me that we had a lot of hard work ahead.

"This is nothing. We have two major subdivisions to layout in record time. I told Nicarao he was crazy, but he wouldn't listen. You are going to have to hump young man."

***

Kemp wasn't kidding. He ran my ass ragged. He was another one of those *Energizer Bunny* surveyors. Running up hills with the transit over his shoulder, calculating on the fly with his Curta Calculator and scratch pad for figuring angles and distances. He more or less followed the layout on the blueprints of the subdivisions we worked on but as Kemp would say, "These plans are shit, unrealistic. I have to re-engineer most of it in the field. Morons in the office. It's that Nicarao. He insists that George puts out this crap. Crazy inclines, oddball lot sizes, grades steep enough for mountain goats."

Our first major project was laying out a subdivision on the outskirts of Napa. This was about an hour and a half drive across the Golden Gate Bridge, up 101, and then cutting across the mud flats of San Pablo Bay and up to Napa. We tried to avoid the traffic, taking back roads but were not always successful.

Since we were paid portal to portal, I was not too concerned about the commute which left us with only a five-hour workday. But Nicarao was. He was constantly nagging Kemp to work faster and to do most of his calculations back in the office early in the morning before he went out. The implication was he was to do this on his own time.

Kemp, resolving to give Nicarao his money's worth, would try to work double time in the field. He was relentless, having me set stake after stake as he hustled around with his transit, laying out the streets, the sewer and the lot lines throughout the subdivision. The blessing was it was a flat, pleasant place in the middle of an old orchard. On our brief breaks, we would lounge under a walnut tree, and listen to the plop of the walnuts as they hit the ground. We could smell the fermenting fruit from a nearby peach tree rife with yellow jackets feasting on the rotting peaches. Just about the time, I was nodding off, Kemp would leap up and shout, "Come on Allan. We have hundreds of feet of line to establish before we can go home."

So it was rush, rush, rush in the blazing hot sun. But at the end of the day, on the drive back, we would relax, often cracking open a can of beer. Sometimes were would stop and buy a huge slice of cold watermelon from a roadside stand and gorge on it while sitting on the tailgate of the survey wagon. All the while, Kemp would be going on about his passion, betting on the ponies. He claimed he had a system. "It's nearly foolproof."

"So you win all the time?" I asked.

"I didn't say that," he smiled with a dreamy faraway look in his eyes. "Actually, I break even but it's the thrill, the rush. And it gives me the excuse to travel. I've hit every major racetrack between here and New York. During the winter months when there's no surveying work, I hit Florida for a few weeks. I lounge around the pools and bet the ponies, sometimes the dog races. It's great life."

"No shit," I remarked, trying to sound appreciative but all the while thinking of the money he was wasting.

***

In contrast to the Napa job, there was the subdivision in Sausalito, a vast acreage destined to become single-family homes and duplexes set on a steep, hillside. This was indeed a job for mountain goats. Kemp wondered aloud why anyone would try to build here. One look around and the answer was obvious. It had stunning views of the Bay, Angel Island and the town itself.

In fact, most of the town was on a steep hillside except for the commercial strip down at the waterfront. Sausalito, a former fishing village, was now an elegant hangout for rich bohemians and the yachting set living in hillside villas. In my undergraduate days at Berkeley, I had spent many a day at Sam's Dock in Sausalito, munching on cheeseburgers and sipping beer after a hard days sail over from Berkeley with the Cal Yacht Club.

Sausalito was also an enclave of houseboat owners, some plush others grungy, gently rocking next to the docks on the muddy bay. Will Marchetti, one of the stars of *Mike Angels*, had a houseboat here with his girlfriend. It was an artsy, nautical abode with lots of throw cushions and an observation deck. I wiled away several afternoons here with the *Mike Angels* gang after a day of hard shooting. So steep hills or not, I was looking forward to working in Sausalito. It was short commute to San Francisco and it had great lunch offerings for our midday break, pizza by the slice, great burgers, even Thai food.

Initially, the mountain goat subdivision wasn't too difficult, except for the constant hiking up and down the slopes. A bulldozer had cleared most of the brush from the hill and last fall, Kemp had conducted an elevation profile of the contours of the hill and submitted the data to the engineer to layout the subdivision. So now, with the freshly minted plans in hand, the job was to finalize the main baseline and establish reference points for the layout of the streets, lots and sewer lines.

It was here that we ran immediately into trouble. Our main base line failed to close properly. It was off by several feet. This was the line from which all other layout points would be derived—the streets, the sewers and the lots. It was critical to adjust it so it would close at least within a few inches instead of feet. We spent a full day going over the line repeatedly. Kemp kept checking the figures. By day's end, he concluded that the error was in the subdivision plans not on the ground. So he sent the plans back for revision which the George, the engineer sheepishly did, adjusting sewers, streets and lot lines in the process.

Nicarao was pissed. "I lose days and plenty of money because of a small error that nobody would notice. Kemp, you should have fixed it in the field. I pay you *mucho dinero* to do that."

Kemp calmly replied, "Some things you can fix in the field, other things not. This is just one of those cases."

"*Ay, caramba!*"

Later, Kemp advised me to cash my paycheck fast because Nicarao had a habit of writing bad checks when he was angry.

Once the baseline was adjusted, the staking out of streets, sewer and lots went fast. Although it was a lot of up and down and stake pounding with a heavy sledge hammer, I was getting into even better shape. And with my tan, unusual in foggy San Francisco during the summer, I attracted attention in the Haight.

"Man, you from Florida our something?"

"Sure dude. Just up to see what's going down in the Haight."

"Far out."

So now that I was making good money with the prospect of employment through November, I began to wonder again if I should abandoned graduate school, and survey for a living. I could count on two or three months off a year in the winter during which time I could ski, travel, write or even finance a small film. Heck, I even had enough money to buy a six-year-old Mercury station wagon and maintain it. If I got ambitious, I could take a surveying course at SF State, to upgrade my skills and become an instrument man or even a party chief.

When I looked around at what most people my age were doing, I realized it was not for me. Either they were junior executives for mega corporations like IBM, or in advertising or teaching in a classroom—all at much lower wages. Even among the film majors, the most any could look forward to was a stint as flunky film editor inserting commercials into feature films at a local TV station. Hardly the big time. Still, I continued to be fascinated by film, not only the production aspects but also the theory behind it. So I plugged on with my studies.

13. FILMIC

The film theory course taught by Dr. Fell met one night a week for three hours. First, we read a work by the Russian film director, Sergei Eisenstein— *Film Form* and *Film Sense*. Eisenstein focused on the art of montage which was the juxtaposition of images to create a new film reality. His most famous example of montage was the massacre of citizens on the steps of Odessa in *Battleship Potemkin*. A sequence which featured a runaway baby carriage with a baby on board lurching down the stairs inter-cut with horrified bystanders and a quick shot of an old woman looking on with shattered eyeglasses.

Eisenstein also was a master at dramatic composition within the camera frame but he felt it was secondary to the dynamics of montage. Here is where the class turned to André Bazin, the founder of the French film journal, *Cahiers du Cinéma*. A prominent film critic and theoretician, Bazin believed that what went on in the frame in terms of composition and action defined the true artistry of film. He considered "montage" a form of deception. As far as he was concerned, film editing should serve only to link long sequences in a logical order. He championed the use of depth of field, movement within the frame and slow camera movements. He cited Orson Welles' *Citizen Kane* as a supreme example of the artistic use of depth of field with interior action, all expertly photographed by cameraman Gregg Toland.

Bazin was also instrumental in promoting the French New Wave films by Truffaut, Godard and others which sought to achieve a sense of documentary realism even though they were fictional films. Godard's *Breathless* was a prime example with the nervous handheld camera following Jean-Paul Belmondo and Jean Seberg as they raced through the streets of Paris.

Part of the course also dealt with the early German films as social statements. Dr. Fell claimed that an understanding of German film in the 1920s and 30s was vital since these so-called "street films" had a huge impact on Hollywood in the 1940s and 50s, especially in the production of "film noir." Fell screened such films as *Joyless Street*, *Last Laugh* and *Blue Angel* featuring a young Marlene Dietrich as "Lulu."

With all of this in mind, we were urged to see the applications of these theories in the major art films of the day: Fellini's *La Dolce Vita*, Antonioni's *L'Avventura*, *La Notte*, *Eclipse* and *Red Desert*, Truffaut's *400 Blows* and of course, Godard's *Breathless*. I had already seen these films but I didn't need much urging to look at them again. They played constantly in Berkeley and in San Francisco at various art houses.

There was a short essay final in the course which Fell gave because he had to. But as he put it: "Your grade will be based primarily on your paper. It should be twenty pages at least on some aspect of film theory. Don't simply regurgitate what you have learned in class. Launch out, go into some depth, blaze new paths in this ever fertile ground."

I took him at his word. My twenty-two page paper was entitled: "Tickle Me Again: Audience Involvement in the Film Medium." In it, I explored the visceral and psychological reactions of an audience while watching a movie. The essence of my argument was perhaps best summed up in Siegfried Kracauer's book, *Theory of Film*:

> *What drives me to the movies is a hunger for sensation, a tickling of the nerves by unusual sensations, fights, love scenes, crowd scenes, unknown worlds. The film as a whole may be bad, but given in the right mood, I am on the whole satisfied.*

Admittedly, I ignored the more intellectual approach to film theory, and instead concentrated on the vicarious thrills of movie watching which engaged all the senses except smell and touch. Dr. Fell was intrigued by my paper and gave me an "A," with a note saying I might have a future in Hollywood or at the very least a future in making skin flicks. I took that as a compliment.

***

So that was film theory. My other class was film directing. Or rather "pretend" film directing since we were not actually required to direct a film

California Split

or even a portion of the film. I guess you could compare it to Army recruits practicing marksmanship with wooden rifles instead of real weapons. Still, there was plenty to do for the course, mostly in the way of preparing to shoot a movie.

The professor, Ms. Reich, a stout middle-aged woman who reminded me of my old Geometry teacher, stressed to us that preparation was the key to success to making a film. As she put it, "Do not fall into the trap of thinking you can improvise scenes while filming. Only a few, very lucky directors have that ability and freedom. Most must plan ahead. Plan, plan, plan. If no other reason than budgetary considerations."

So my task was to plan ahead. We were supposed to write a theatrical film script of ten or fifteen minutes or so and break it down into a full-fledged shooting script with a storyboard of each scene followed by detailed camera directions, acting directions. Further, we were supposed to scout locations, map out logistics and set up a shooting schedule and concoct a budget. At the end of the semester, we were to present our project in both a written and lecture format.

To inspire us in our quest, Ms. Reich, used most of the class time showing us various film clips illustrating different directorial styles, as well as the "meat of potatoes" of directing a scene with the standard cover shots, cutaways and close-ups.

We covered such procedures as to how a shoot a classic chase scene, how to shoot a back and forth conversation between two actors and how to shoot a traveling shot while the actors are on a horse or in a car. I had already observed a lot of this while filming *Mike Angels*.

Since Ms. Reich had a family connection to Hollywood, she was able to obtain the original rushes of a film or two so we could see how the final product was assembled from an editing point of view. It was amazing seeing fifteen or twenty takes of the same scene which varied only minutely. I admired the actors for putting up with that, for repeating their lines and moving perfectly take after take. It was like repetitive factory work.

Duly inspired, I hauled out my old script about the married San Francisco Ad man and his mistress, Gloria. I figured it would run about ten minutes if ever filmed. First, I polished up the dialogue and then broke the script down into it various scenes—exterior shots of Gloria walking down San Francisco hills, the interior of the apartment of her platonic, crazy gay boyfriend who builds incomprehensible structures in his living room, scenes of the Ad guy, George's plush suburban home in Orinda and his country club.

Next, I went out and scouted locations. This was relatively easy. On one weekend with my little Kodak camera, I shot a couple of steep San Francisco hills, used my own apartment interior for the gay artist's abode. In Orinda, I shot a row of houses in an upscale subdivision. Then I went inside a furnished model home and shot interiors. Finally, I took some snaps of exteriors of the Orinda Country Club. My script was not fully documented but I felt it was good enough. Ms. Reich would get the idea.

Next, I attempted to storyboard the scenes and individual shots. This was what Hitchcock did. He drew an elaborate sketch of each and every individual shot, much like a comic book artist and then he followed it to the letter during shooting. Alas, my artistic sketch skills were such that I merely drew stick figures in simplified backgrounds and not for every shot. Again, good enough I thought. Next, I broke my script down into a detailed shooting script, indicating each camera placement, each shot, the actor's movements and dialogue.

Finally, at the last minute, I set up a hypothetical shooting schedule and concocted a budget of about five thousand dollars indicating the percentages allowed for materials, rental equipment, film stock, actor's salaries, etc. I typed all this up and assembled it in a package which included the shooting script, storyboard and production details. I was ready for my presentation.

However, my presentation was my undoing. Ms. Reich had been very emphatic about that. "You will have ten minutes to make your presentation at a very precisely scheduled time. Do not miss your slot."

My time was 8 p.m. in the 7 p.m. class.

The day of my presentation, I got back to my apartment from surveying about 5:30. I went over to Lucy's for dinner. We got distracted and before I knew it, it was 7:40. Lucy lived about twenty minutes from campus, so I drove like mad but hit some construction traffic and arrived ten minutes late. I had blown my presentation slot.

Ms. Reich was not pleased. During a break she informed me, "Mr. Brown, you have missed your opportunity to unveil your directorial plans for your project. Had you done this in the industry as a novice director, you would have been through. If we have time at the end of the class, you may offer your presentation but you will be marked down."

I finally did get my chance, but my presentation was rushed and off-handed. I had not practiced it at home. In addition, half the class had left to catch the late Muni. I handed my production package over to Ms. Reich. She nodded, took it and said nothing. I got a "C" in the course. My only "C" so far at San Francisco State. It felt like an "F."

***

Sometimes I did arrive at San Francisco State early for my night classes. On a couple of occasions, I used the time to inspect the new TV facilities in a wing that had just been completed that spring and was now being used for TV production classes. The studios were impressive indeed with state-of-the-art black-and-white cameras, advanced lighting, and audio systems. (Color did not arrive at SF State until a few years later.) The space age control room had banks of monitors to view the action and the latest in video switchers that allowed the director to cut, fade or dissolve from one camera to another. The switcher also had special effect keys for wipes of various geometric designs and one for the chroma key effect. The rest of the control room was actually a small amphitheater, allowing the students to observe the TV production up close. The physical studios consisted of one large studio to be used for major productions, usually a live television theatrical production and two smaller studios for interview formats or a news show.

Prior to this, those who emphasized "television" in their Film and Television major had to put up with scarce and outdated equipment with a control room little bigger than a closet. Now everybody, both film majors and broadcast majors were clamoring to use the new facilities. I could immediately see the attraction. New toys to play with and unlike film, any production you put on was immediately accomplished. No tedious, long involved shoots, no messing with film editing. And it was free. The only hassle was getting studio time to put on the production. The productions were recorded on two-inch videotape for later viewing but were actually produced live and that added an exciting element.

This all took me back to my days at the Presidio when we cobbled together Army public service shows for airing on KGO-TV. I remembered standing in the control room and marveling how the director could switch between three studio cameras, while interspersing film, slide and videotape sources and come up with a coherent, smoothing flowing show.

The student efforts I saw were of a different order. They usually featured a dance or a dramatic sequence involving effects which gave the images an eerie, ghost-like appearance. Most of these efforts were over-indulgent, incoherent affairs but one who did manage to put something interesting together was John Broderick, the SF State student who was a member of the San Francisco Mime Troupe. He would persuade a few of his fellow Mime Troupe actors to participate in a medieval romp before the television cameras and add special effects to produce an interesting, yet comic television version of a mini Mime Troupe production.

All of this started me to thinking. Film seemed like such a hassle. Except for a few little shorts, I had not filmed anything of major consequence. A fact that I was constantly reminded of by some members of the *Mike Angels* crew who themselves were now filming their own little theatrical shorts.

At one party, I had to hear this from Tom Bullock: "Shit, Brown, here you spend weeks working on Mike Angels, being a grunt but still getting all that good experience and you have nothing planned for your own film."

"Ah, nothing yet," I stammered. "Maybe down the road."

"Well, if you want to work in the film industry, you're going to have to have something major in the can," he declared. "Nobody in the industry will look at you unless you have something in the can. It's your resume, your calling card."

"Yeah, I know, but right now I'm just trying to get through my courses at SF State and work for a living," I replied.

"Yeah, its' tough," Bullock nodded. "I have to do the same thing, freelance editing. But, you still need to take the plunge."

"I'll take it under consideration."

I did briefly consider trying to shoot my Ad man script based on the work I had done in Ms. Reich's class. But I would need a few thousand dollars to do it, and lots of time. Time and money that I did not have between working full-time and going to night classes. But the essential reality was, I was tired and overwhelmed with all that filmmaking entailed—the planning, the logistics, dealing with a crew, and dealing with actors who mainly wanted to see how they looked on film, rather than work for the good of the production.

Then I thought back to my visit with UCLA film students, how pedestrian their film efforts were, how pathetic their ass kissing was—all to get a job in the Hollywood film industry as a fourth assistant director whose main duty was to fetch coffee. Or the job of a script reader wading through thousands of nothing scripts for years before getting a shot at having your own screenplay accepted. That further dampened my enthusiasm.

But lo! As I gazed at these new television facilities, I felt a new surge of energy, a reawakening of my creative impulse. I realized I could do minor theatrical productions quick, easy and for free without any of the hassle of film. I could get valuable experience that could transfer to film down the road. It had been done before. Many of the major live television directors such as John Frankenheimer, Sydney Pollack and Ralph Nelson had made the successful transition to film. It was this very point that Professor Herbert Zettl, the local pied piper of television's artistic potential, made time and time again.

"Ladies and Gentlemen," he would declare in his soft German accent. "We have only begun to scratch the surface of television's potential. Ignore the banalities that you see today on commercial television. Harken back to the golden age of live television drama and build from there."

I took his message to heart and resolved to take a television production course in the fall. In the meantime, I had a summer of surveying to get through in order to pile up some money for my next semester at SF State as a full-time student.

14. SASHA II

As soon as my spring night classes were over, I settled down to a more relaxed routine and began to enjoy some leisure. I would go out with Kemp to our various surveying projects, put in a hard day's work and come back pleasantly exhausted. But instead of rushing out to SF State, I could lounge about the apartment, maybe cook myself a little meal, maybe go out to one of the growing number of restaurants in the Haight or cage a meal at the Daltons who lived around the corner on Frederick Street. Lucy had returned to Menlo Park for the summer so there were no free meals and get-togethers at her house.

John Dalton was an old high school buddy who had gone to UC Davis for a while, then dropped out and later attended Berkeley. The last few years he had been living in San Francisco trying to make it in acting. At 6' 3", tall, thin with a jutting jaw, he certainly had the dramatic looks but so far, he had not been too successful. He scrapped by with small parts, commercials, doing kid shows on local TV and working part-time as a mover. He was now newly married to Marge, a set designer and they had a baby daughter. He and Marge had a cozy apartment and were warm and welcoming. I had many happy meals there during my time in the Haight. John and his friend Herman, another actor were currently all excited about the prospect of the American Conservatory Theater coming to San Francisco under the direction of William Ball.

"This exactly what San Francisco needs," said Herman. "A first-class professional repertory theater. No more amateur hour productions. Just think of it John, *Tartuffe*, *Under the Milkwood Tree*. First-class productions."

"Yeah, I hear they pay well," John replied while working on a gigantic hamburger that Marge had prepared. "I'd be happy just to be a spear carrier on one of their Shakespeare productions."

"Stop dreaming guys," cautioned Marge. "Get something going now. It will be a year at least before they are up and running."

This is how it went at John's place. It was a gathering spot for struggling actors and actresses, a place where they could chill while lounging on the spacious couches that Marge had built from scratch.

Marge was indeed amazing. Pleasantly stocky with long black hair, she was as strong as any man and more creative than most. She was a skilled carpenter, seamstress, and pottery maker. She kept the whole thing together.

Early July, Sasha began showing up at their apartment on a regular basis. She was now living a few blocks away on Clayton Street with one of her acting girlfriends. I had introduced her to the Daltons when we had been going together last fall and like everybody else, she had been taken by Marge. But when we broke up, she drifted off to another set of friends. I had not seen her since January. She looked frazzled, thin and pale.

As she explained it, she either had to give up her job or acting. "It's no good. Trying to do both. Something has to go or I will go crazy."

Our initial meeting was awkward. It rather annoyed me that she was hanging out at Daltons. I didn't know what to say but I was polite. But she put on the charm show, as if nothing had ever happened. After a couple of encounters there, one late night, as a courtesy, I walked her back to her apartment.

"You seem well, Allan. Very tan, healthy."

"Well, I work outdoors over where the sun always shines. Not like foggy San Francisco."

"Surveying? That seems like that would require a lot of skill?"

"I was born into it," I explained. "It comes in handy when I need some money."

"Oh, money. I hate money," she pouted. "It's the money that keeps me working at this crazy job dealing with hysterical Hispanics. It makes me ashamed of my countrymen. I would dearly love to quit and pursue theater full-time."

"Dream on," I said. "I'd like to do the same so that I could be a full-time student at San Francisco State."

When we got back to her place, she told me she would like to see me again and in fact had four free tickets to a new play opening in town. "We'll go with John and Marge."

Somewhat against my better judgment, I accepted the invitation. We saw an overwrought version of *The Iceman Cometh*. It was tedious and long. I thought Eugene O'Neill needed some serious editing. Still, the outing was a success and afterwards we had beer and sandwiches at Tommy's Joynt on Van Ness Avenue. However, I noted the old spark between Sasha and myself wasn't there, even though she gave me a kiss on the cheek as I bid her goodnight on her doorstep.

***

A week later, I was fixing myself a hamburger dinner in my shitty little kitchen when my apartment buzzer rang. I went out to the outer door to see who it was and there was Sasha with a suitcase.

"Allan, you have to help me out. I lost my apartment. I have nowhere to sleep."

"What! What happened?"

"It's a long story. Let me come in and I'll tell you all about it."

"Sure, come in."

Once settled on my couch, she continued. "My roommate decided to move in with her boyfriend. I could barely afford the rent on my own, but I was making it. Then my agency laid me off. Something about a lack of federal funding, but really, I think they wanted to get rid of me. Oh, it was probably my fault, I kept missing days of work because of theater and I think they wanted someone who looked more 'Mexican' to deal with their clientele."

"Wow."

"Yes, it was a financial blow. So now, I couldn't pay the rent. I had to leave. I've been staying with John and Marge, sleeping on their couch for a week. They've been very kind but I can't stay there forever. I thought of you and your apartment. Maybe I could sleep on your daybed." (Sasha had apparently heard about my daybed from the Daltons.)

"Uh, yeah sure. Make yourself at home," I replied, not quite realizing what I was in for. "This joint is not much."

She looked around at the spacious living room, and the big bedroom and two bathrooms. "It looks like luxury to me after that cramped apartment. I promise I'll only stay a few nights. I won't be any bother at all."

"Uh, sure."

***

Well, soon it was a month and counting. Sasha was no longer sleeping on the daybed. She had apparently decided that I wasn't such a flake after all. In fact, she was impressed that I had such a well-paying job and was behaving so responsibly. For her part, she made herself useful, cooking delicious Mexican meals, chicken mole being her specialty, scrubbing the place down, doing the shopping. And oh, yes, running off to one audition or another.

"Allan, this is my dream. Being with you and being free to pursue my acting career with no stupid job to worry about."

Sasha was not entirely broke. She still received some alimony from Peter, about two hundred dollars a month that she chipped in for expenses.

So I guess we were happy. I had to pinch myself that I was living with a woman, a former married woman at that who knew how to run a household. It was nice, it was so normal, so bourgeois. It was like a preview of marriage. So we floated along living in the domestic moment for the summer. I would go off in the morning surveying and she would be home at night getting my dinner ready. Then we would go out to John and Marge's or go to a movie or maybe a theatrical event. Sasha was taking more acting lessons but had not yet landed a part in any current production. But she was doing radio commercials for a Spanish language station. She had an excellent speaking voice and was very good at the zany, comic spots. That brought in some income.

Still, I was not saving much money. I was spending it on domestic upgrades, such as new, although used furniture, a better outfitted kitchen and a wall-to-wall paint job. I had undertaken to repaint the entire apartment. The landlord had gladly given me permission as long as it was white. So we traipsed off to Sears and bought a few gallons of paint, paint brushes, rollers, etc. and spent a couple of mad weekends slapping on paint. The long hallway alone took one entire weekend. I was bone tired from standing on the ladder and spreading paint, while Sasha did the trim. Several weekends later, we had the entire apartment repainted. It fairly glistened. But our prize was the kitchen. I had ignored the white paint mandate and painted the whole thing burnt orange with a bright yellow trim. It brightened up the gloomy pit.

Also, my food bill was climbing. We had started entertaining, paying back John and Marge, Herman and his girlfriend. Gerard and his current girlfriend from Berkeley and other assorted friends would show up now and then. In addition, my car needed a few hundred dollars in repairs. I was beginning to think my 1960 Mercury station wagon was a lemon. All in all, it was amazing how fast my paycheck could disappear, even with overtime.

Around mid-August, with school a few short weeks away, I realized that I would have to be a part-time student again. Even with unemployment insurance, I wouldn't have enough to go full-time. There was also the technicality of being laid off. Kemp and I were in the middle of laying out the Sausalito subdivision. If I bugged out, he would be screwed, as he often said. "You know the program here, Al. You're a big help."

"I'm just a humble chainman, Kemp, your loyal servant."

"Yeah, but I can trust you. You run the instrument pretty good and your measurements are accurate. You are a vital part of the team."

I didn't have the heart to bug out. And the way it looked, we had work through November. If I kept going, maybe I could save enough to finish off my master's degree at S.F. State and never have to go back to surveying again. But the financial drain, continued, drip, drip, drip. At one point I wound up paying for a month of Sasha's acting lessons when Peter failed to come through with the alimony.

Peter dropped by occasionally. He was a conductor on the N Judah line right out my front door. I was still amazed that he exhibited no jealousy at all. He just wanted to see that Sasha was being taken care of. He appeared happy to have her off his hands. I later learned that he had been on the verge of taking her back after she lost her apartment. But instead, I unknowingly stepped up in the nick of time.

So when school started, I once again enrolled in only two night classes, TV Production and TV Aesthetics course. Meanwhile, Sasha and I perked along like an old married couple but still without any hint of a long-term commitment. I certainly didn't want to get married and she was still consumed by her career as an actress. "One must sacrifice a personal life to be successful in theater," she constantly said.

And so it was, we were cruising along until late October when Sasha received a fatal telephone call from her father in Mexico City. Her mother who had been suffering from cancer was expected to live only a few days longer and she was longing to see her only daughter again. The two had been estranged for years. Sasha used to say one of the main reasons she married Peter was to get away from her mother, far away. Her mother used to drive her nuts, bugging her to forget about acting and get married at eighteen.

"At nineteen, you are an old maid in Mexico city," Sasha explained. "Mama had adopted the Mexican attitudes towards marriage. Also, she was old. She had me late in her thirties. She wanted to be a grandmother. She used to say she would die long before seeing any grandchildren."

Nevertheless, Sasha was out of my apartment in a shot. She packed half of her clothes and left on the next plane to Mexico City. In all happened in a space of a few hours. One minute, we were having a leisurely Sunday breakfast, reading the newspapers and the next minute she was gone, the empty metal coat hangers in her closet still banging together. She had taken a cab to the airport since my car was still undergoing repairs. It was a hurried kiss and goodbye.

The original idea was that she would go for only a week or two, enough to help her father settle her mother's affairs and come back to San Francisco, but two weeks stretched into three, then four. In the meantime, I was getting telephone calls from her explaining the situation that she couldn't leave just yet.

"There are so many things to attend to, Allan. And my poor father, he is so lost without her. He can't even fix a meal."

"Uh, I thought you had a cook and a maid."

"Yes, yes a maid but no cook now. Mom got rid of her a while ago, saying they couldn't afford it what with her medical bills and such."

"OK, I'll see you whenever."

"Don't worry, Allan. I'll be back on in your cozy apartment before you know it."

But she didn't come back. Not in a month, not in two months. I missed her at first, but then I thanked my lucky stars. I was free again. I decided playing house was too much like marriage. I set forth with a new burst of energy, energy I needed what with my night classes, and my surveying job.

15. TV LAND

"Let me repeat. Television has its own aesthetic rules and unique attributes. It is not film, although it does borrow many of its compositional and editing principles from film. Most obviously unique to television is the transmission of live images and the use of multiple cameras to follow live action but there are many other distinctive factors to consider as well, all of which we will go into in this course." Thus spake Dr. Herbert Zettl, at the first meeting of his Moving Image class.

Zettl stood before a portable blackboard in the control room of the main studio, a tall, slim, curly headed guy with the profile of an American Indian. But Herb Zettl was not an Indian. He was German as was obvious from his accent. He didn't talk much about his background except to say his early schooling was in Germany and that he was a student of the visual arts. At some point, he came to this country, attended Stanford University and received a master's degree and later a Ph.D. in education from Berkeley.

Somehow, he wound up in television working as a producer-director at a variety of stations including the CBS affiliate KPIX-TV in San Francisco. His specialty was live television, producing and directing scores of live concerts, operas, variety and public service shows. He even directed Edward R. Murrow's *Person to Person* when Murrow came to town. Zettl was also the author of a well-known television production handbook that many Radio-TV schools around the nation used, including San Francisco State. In sum, he was the local, and indeed the national guru on television production as an art form.

I had long looked forward to taking his Moving Image course. His classes were always full, even with film-oriented students because of the inspiring way he presented his material. He was open, creative, clever and always willing to listen to any hair-brained idea on pushing the limits of television. I was immediately swept up in the creative fervor that he sparked. He inspired his students to try something different and to do it now, live and instantaneous on TV. No time-consuming logistics or expense of film. See your realization immediately or minutes afterwards on videotape. That further inspired me.

Zettl initially lectured about the more general aspects of visual aesthetics. He gave us a quick overview of the history of perspective in painting from the middle ages through the Renaissance. He cited the use of chiaroscuro to indicate depth through lighting, the use of over-lapping of planes and foreground objects and size variation to indicate depth.

Zettl then traced the use of these techniques in the set design of theatrical productions, especially those of the great German director Max Reinhardt. Further, he explained how forced perspective found its way into television set design. As he said, "The frame of the television camera is so limited that much of the action has to take place in depth; that is movement to and from the camera." Zettl would then show us clips from the early German movies and some kinescope shots of the live TV dramas from the 1950s to illustrate his point.

Next, Zettl considered the use of multiple cameras in television production. "In film, usually all action is shot from a single camera, albeit, a camera that moves or is constantly repositioned. In television a two or three camera view of the action gives a more of a theater-in-the-round perspective of simultaneous live action. Note that even in the case of the lowly reaction shot, the live televised reaction of one actor to the words uttered by the another actor is much more convincing than the standard film practice of shooting reaction shots later, long after the speech is delivered."

In a couple of lectures, Zettl focused on the special effects possible in black and white television, primarily through the electronic manipulation of the image. He demonstrated a series of patterned wipes and fades such as diamond dissolves, star dissolves, vertical and horizontal wipes. Zettl was especially enthusiastic about the use of the chroma key in musical and dramatic presentations.

The chroma key was, in effect, an electronic matting device that could insert one picture into another, instead of superimposing it. It was developed for inserting printed words over a video image as in the case of identification in news program or in a commercial. But television experimentalists quickly found other uses for the chroma key such as juxtaposing matted images to create a kind of electronic video collage. Some played with the key effect to reverse polarity or to produce a grainy textured image that harkened back to the days of surreal photography in the 1920s.

"And of course you will note that all of these techniques are at your immediate fingertips in a live medium that only requires your quick reflexes and not months of tedious editing."

That was what inspired me. You could do it all on the fly. Like a live concert or a ballet. Rehearsal yes, but when it was show time, the show had to go on.

To further illustrate his points, Zettl showed us a the kinescope of the Playhouse Ninety production of *Requiem For a Heavyweight,* a live television drama aired in 1956 written by Rod Serling and directed by Ralph Nelson. The teleplay was chock full of the live TV techniques that Zettl had been lecturing about. Indeed, as a dramatic piece of television theater, it was stunning.

Afterwards, the author, Rod Serling, in person elaborated on the differences in writing for television and film. Serling was guest lecturing at various colleges following his successful TV series *Twilight Zone.* At first, I was taken aback by the guy. He seemed so Hollywood with his slicked back hair, dark, poolside tan and skinny Italian suit. But he knew his stuff when it came to writing for film and television. He said, in essence, live television drama was all about unity— unity of time, place and action. Film, he said, allowed the writer to travel to far horizons over vast temporal stretches, limited only by the film budget but film could also lose dramatic density in the process.

***

Duly inspired by the possibilities of live television, I paid serious attention to my television production course. This was taught by a Dr. Miller, a nuts and bolts TV instructor. Miller shunned theory. He emphasized "doing" in the real world of television. He had spent years in local TV doing everything from being a gofer to an on-air director of news, talk and sports.

Under his guidance, I went about mastering the television camera, moving it fluidly about dollying, panning, tilting, and changing lenses when required on various student productions. I also mucked about with studio lighting and dressed television sets. I operated the sound boom and inside the control room ran the audio board. I also played with the switcher on student news shows, switching from studio cameras to videotape sources or camera cards according to the director's cues. I did everything including directing a live news show at the end of the semester.

"Sports and news are the only 'live' you guys are going to run into these days in local television," Miller would remind us. "Until you get to the big time, forget about 'live' which is really 'live-on-tape.' Networks hate airing mistakes."

Thus, our semester end assignment was to write, produce and direct a live news show. However, our resources were limited. We did not have access to news videotape or news film inserts. All we had was a canned videotape opening and closing to the show with a pompous news theme. The live studio portion of the show all had to be done in a two-camera set-up.

So I set about writing a news script, mostly a rehash of a day's news from the *Chronicle*. Since we had no news film or tape inserts, I cut out appropriate pictures from *Time, Life* and other magazines that illustrated my news stories and pasted them on camera cards.

Next, I recruited Megan, an aspiring drama student with wholesome Midwestern looks in contrast to the hippy grunge look predominant on campus. She was happy to play anchor. In fact, she told me, "If I don't make it as an actress, I might try television as a hostess or a news reader."

"Far out. Then this should be good experience," I replied.

Once I had assembled all my elements, I sat down and marked my news scripts with cues, indicating which camera would be on Megan and which camera would be on the camera cards. Also, I had to indicate the cues for the opening tape of the show and the audiotape theme.

Other members of the production class functioned as the crew — cameramen, audioman, floorman and switcher. All of us would be wearing headsets through which we could communicate.

I adjusted my headset, set my stopwatch and gave the cue to roll the videotape opening with the audio cart. And the show was on. The red light flashed on the camera and Megan began to read the script, looking up now and then to maintain eye contact with the camera. (This was before the days of a teleprompter).

During her first story on the Middle East, I gave the cue to "take camera 2," which was on a camera card photo of an Israeli tank firing. After a few seconds, we switched back to Megan on camera 1 finishing the Mideast story and moving on to the next. This went on for about five minutes with Megan reading through seven or eight stories, all illustrated with the photos on camera cards. Then she arrived at the final sign off, with a brief weather forecast in the Bay Area. I rolled the closing video tape with the sign off audio and we were done.

Whee, no glitches. Smooth. My shirt was drenched with sweat. I felt like I had been through a ringer. I thanked the crew and collapsed in my chair at the console.

"Well, done Mr. Brown," said Miller right after. "You seem to have a feel for it. And your choice of talent was exceptional. That young lady might indeed have a future in television."

I got an "A" on that project, but more importantly, I felt that I had done something that was incredibly exciting. Maybe there was a future for me in television.

The next week, I was asked to be an anchor for another student's news show. I sat there in the small studio in my blazer and tie and pretended I was the new ABC anchorman, Peter Jennings. I looked into the glass eye of the camera with appropriate anchorman solemnity and read my script in carefully measured phrases. Later, several people came up to me and said in effect, "Jeeze, Brown, you looked and read like a real anchorman." I filed that observation away for future reference.

In summary, with these two television courses, I felt that my own personal course was set. My immediate field of emphasis was to be in television, not film and I planned accordingly for the next semester, a semester when I would again be a full-time student.

Meanwhile, my job with Nicarao ended mid-November. Nicarao claimed he had run out of work. That was debatable. I think it was more likely he had run out of money because the Sausalito project was still not complete.

"Next spring, young man, next spring, I will bring you and Kemp back. And we will finish up the job," he said.

"Don't hold your breath," I thought. "Unemployment, here I come."

16. BERKELEY REDUX

School may have been going great, but on a more personal level I was tired of the San Francisco scene after Sasha left. I was tired of the Haight with its increasing overflow of hippies, bums and even tourists. It lacked the intellectual caché of Berkeley. Plus my old friends Gerard and Jean-Paul were well set up in Berkeley and had an interesting scene going on there. Thus it was I began spending my weekends in Berkeley again.

Gerard was now a second-year graduate student in Comparative Literature at Berkeley. As noted, he had a rather nice second-story apartment on Benvenue in a large craftsman type house. It had a sundeck out back with a view of the Berkeley hills. He also had a daybed upon which I could sleep or listen to his many new LP's on his state-of-the-art stereo. Plus, he was now into fine California wine and choice grass. Furthermore, he had a charming girlfriend, Marie, whom he was seeing fairly constantly. She was still an undergraduate in Sociology and wanted to become a social worker. They had been going together for about a year and I assumed it was serious. After all, Gerard was pushing twenty-eight, two years older than I.

Still, as I was to learn, Gerard was not ready to settle down. When Marie was not around, he had a bevy of young lovelies trooping through his apartment. His natural charm and European savoir-faire learned in France proved irresistible. One coed who hung about was Lauren who lived downstairs. She was from Bismarck, North Dakota and was part Sioux Indian and a stunner. She had come to Berkeley as a junior because she wanted to flee the harsh winters of North Dakota and its boring Midwestern lifestyle. Another was a Jean Seberg type, little, lithe and sexy whose name was, in fact, Jean, from Southern California. She was married to a physicist but it was apparently an open marriage and she paid regular visits to Gerard.

Across the hall from Gerard's was an apartment occupied by a tall black dude from Boston, Dirk. Dirk was a graduate biochemist who had a job as a lab tech with the University. But Dirk also had a side-job of mixing various mind-bending chemicals, including LSD and selling it on the side. Dirk claimed he rarely dropped acid because he knew how bad the side effects could be.

"Hey, if you want to take the chance. Go ahead. But I know the downside of this stuff even when it's pure like mine. It will really fuck with your mind."

Gerard and I never bothered.

Dirk also had access to the finest grass around and was the main supplier to Gerard. Frequently, we would go over and hang out at Dirk's and listen to his stereo which made Gerard's sound like a tinny transistor radio. Dirk had decorated his apartment like the desert tent of a Pasha prince with billowy canvas overhead, large batik pillows and cushions on which to lounge and listen to the latest Stones' album.

Jean-Paul lived nearby on College Avenue with a brainy New York Jewess whose father owned a string of drugstores. Sometimes we would go over there to visit, but Jean-Paul was often testy, saying he had to study. Actually, he was into a new set of friends that interested him more than his old fraternity buddies.

His girlfriend, Judith, was rather remote and aloof. She was so different from Jean-Paul's old girlfriend Corrine. No passion or fire, just brainpower. And Jean-Paul had changed. No longer was he the old Jean-Paul of a booming voice, raucous humor and broken tooth. (He had fixed his tooth). He was now a serious intellectual as were some of his new friends. Further, he was into computers and was doing a complicated content analysis on various works of literature. This involved setting up punch cards, going over to the UC computer center in the middle of the night when time was available, and running data streams through on the giant IBM computers. Jean-Paul said he despised computers but he needed them to give a solid research basis for his on-going content analysis which would have been impossible to do by hand.

When I wasn't with Gerard or Jean-Paul, I would simply hang out at the Mediterannum Cafe before going to a movie. And there I would run into old acquaintances from my undergraduate days including Rory a friend of Darrah. Rory was studying for a Ph.D. in mathematics and philosophy. A brain. A bearded, heavyset fellow with black curly, hair, Rory also had a lively social scene going on around him.

The night I met him at the cafe he was with a stunning young blonde of East European extraction. Her name was Tara and she gazed at Rory with goo-goo eyes. Yet, Rory later told me she was merely a friend and that I could take her out if I wanted. I wanted. Rory invited me to one of his weekend dinner parties. It was an assorted bunch—professors, grad students, and a few unattached women one of whom was Tara. I sat next to her and chatted her up. She seemed pleasant but reserved. Still, very cute with her Czech accent. She explained that she had been in the U.S. for a few years living in Berkeley with her mother, an academic. She had graduated from Berkeley High. I asked her out on a date and she agreed.

A few days later, I drove over to Berkeley and we saw a movie at the Paramount Theater in Oakland and later went out for pizza. We seemed to get along but I could tell she was distant and reserved as if she was going through the motions of the date to please somebody else. When I moved in for a kiss outside her mother's Berkeley bungalow, Tara drew back and gave me one on the forehead instead. End of date. Oh, well. Struck out. Probably a virgin. Too young for me.

A week later, I went to a party at Rory's which was quite a bash. Cheap wine flowed and the music blasted. Tara was there too but barely acknowledged my existence. She was hanging around some older Italian guy who looked as if he had escaped from the Las Vegas Rat Pack.

Rory later told me the Italian was a photographer for *Playboy Magazine* and he had photographed Tara in the buff for a spread in the magazine.

"Tara!? In Playboy?"

"Yeah, Playboy is doing something on Berkeley Coeds and the Sexual Freedom League," he explained.

"The Sexual Freedom League?" I said puzzled. "Tara's not a member of that, is she?"

"Shit no," he said. "She's practically a virgin. I think they just want a pretty face to represent it, 'cause most of those chicks active in those orgies are dogs. They're just using her as a front."

"Practically a virgin?"

"Well," he smiled. "Let's not go into that."

It was then that I knew Rory had been doing the deed with my innocent Czech girl. Still, I was troubled.

The Sexual Freedom League had been getting plenty of publicity lately in the underground press with articles describing the goings on. Rooms full of writhing bodies. Girls and guys, girls and girls and even guys on guys.

The image made me cringe. I couldn't imagine Tara involved in that. Of course, a milder version of the SFL had been going on for years at Berkeley. Wife swapping parties, girlfriend swapping parties. But according to Rory who had attended some of these parties, most of the women were pretty aggressive, preying on guys. It was like playing caveman in reverse. Not for me. I would stick to my private little encounters.

***

They may have been private little encounters but they were coming thick and fast. Lucy had started coming over again since Sasha had left and I was also seeing my old platonic girlfriend, Clarissa. Cool, blonde, ethereal Clarissa. It had been two years since I had last seen her. She had finally gone off to be a flight attendant for Pan American Airlines but now she was back living in Berkeley and going to library school at UC.

"Ah, what happened to Pan Am," I asked later as we met at Larry Blakes over a beer one Saturday afternoon.

"Oh, it was great for a while," she said sipping her beer. "Seeing the world through sleep deprived eyes. But it got old and I got tired of being hit on by fifty-year-old copilots. I'm glad I did it but now it's time to get serious. That's why I'm going to library school."

"Why library school?"

"I love libraries and there's a real demand for good academic librarians. I can probably get a job at the Berkeley Library. It's only a year course."

"What about history? I thought you wanted to get a Ph.D. in that once."

"Oh, I did but I don't want to spend years and years in school," she explained. "I want to make some money and now they pay librarians pretty good here."

It was obvious Clarissa had changed, matured, as it were. However, we were still in the platonic mode, but I could sense she was wishing for something more. She said things like, "You know, Al. It's maybe too bad that we didn't get more involved back then. I was such a drip. So idealistic and naive."

"So you were."

"But that was then and this was now," she remarked lightheartedly. "Why don't you come over for dinner next Saturday? I can cook a good steak now. I have some great wine. And I can show you my new apartment. A real apartment. Not some dive."

"Sure."

So it was on one particular Saturday evening, all fresh from Lucy in the morning that I made my way over to Clarissa's apartment. Her apartment was indeed nice. She had furnished it well with earnings from her Pan Am days. It was the upstairs of a spacious bungalow on the South Side with its own separate entrance. She was wearing, one of those clinging Asian silk dresses, slit up the side. With her white-blonde hair up, she looked fetching indeed. I had a feeling that there was going to be more than dinner served. And I was right. Dinner by candlelight. Steak and wine excellent. Soft music in the background. Soon on the couch with a joint. Incense burning. Then the inevitable.

As she led me to her bedroom, she remarked. "You know Al, we have never made it. I always wanted to but you weren't around for that phase of my life."

"Well, let's make up for lost time."

While our encounter was pleasant, it lacked spark. Almost like a thank you for putting up with her past. I think she sensed it too. After a decent interval with a cup of instant coffee at her kitchen table, I made my excuses to leave, explaining I couldn't stay the night because I had a major paper to write for Monday. I told her that I would call her. She nodded and bid me good night. As I walked to my car, I wondered what was wrong with me. Clarissa was a gorgeous, smart girl but whatever sexual attraction I had once had with her was gone. She would remain just a friend.

***

That part about going home was a lie. I spent the night at Gerard's. The next day after a leisurely breakfast full of goodies fixed by Marie, and a reading of the Sunday papers, I bid them goodbye and went down to Telegraph to browse in Moe's Bookstore. There I ran into Joyce from my senior year. Dark, sexy Joyce. She looked about the same, except she was much better groomed. In many ways, she reminded me of Tami.

She told me that she was getting her secondary teaching credential in French. We chatted for a while, had a cup of espresso at the Med across the street and then she invited me over to her apartment that she shared with a roommate who was gone for the weekend. Along the way, I filled her in on my life and she did the same, letting me know that she was still unattached despite several offers of marriage.

"How come?" I asked.

"How come!" she exclaimed. "I don't want to settle down yet. When I get my masters in teaching this spring, I want to teach in France at the American high schools on the military bases. I still haven't been to France. Yet I can speak it pretty well from hanging out with the French around Berkeley and I know the grammar cold."

We sat at her kitchen table eating sandwiches that she had made. "How about you?"

"Uh, free as a bird right now." I said, looking her over again. God, she was sexy. Full breasted, yet trim ass, an Italian countenance with full pouting lips. I thought back to our encounters in my senior year when she would purr, *"Jolie Garçon."* I wondered.

Yet in the now fading afternoon light, I didn't have to wonder long. Joyce had gone and showered and came out in a short bathrobe, the belt loosely tied, revealing her full cleavage. In a matter of seconds, we were on the shag rug in her living room, entwined in each other.

Fireworks until dark. As we lay there afterward, I put it all together. Sparks were necessary. Intellect alone did not do it. Still, I was proud of my weekend triple play, sensing that probably would be a rare occurrence. Indeed, it was.

As the author Paul Bowles put it: "We often think of life as an inexhaustible well. Yet, everything happens only a certain number of times, and a very small number, really."

After that, I lost track of Joyce. I think she split for France.

***

A week later or so, I got a phone call from another voice out of my Berkeley past, Darrah. She said she got my number from Gerard and was surprised to learn I was living in the Haight. She was now a reporter for the *Boston Globe*. She was in Berkeley to interview Clark Kerr, the UC President under fire for allowing such student unrest. The new California governor-elect, Ronald Reagan, pandering to the conservative base that elected him, accused Kerr of being too soft on student protesters and was gunning for his removal.

"So what are you doing? Gerard said you were surveying?"

"Yeah. I have been but I'm done for the season. I'm at San Francisco State working for a masters in film and television."

"Great. I've always been interested in film. I think we talked about that a couple of years ago."

"Yeah," I said wondering what she wanted.

She finally got to the point. "Well, of course, I would like to see you but I'm also doing an article on the Haight. I understand that you live right in the middle of it. Maybe you could show me around?"

"Ah, maybe. But you have to realize, I'm not into the scene that much."

"Sure, I suspected as much but you must know something about what's going on?"

"Yeah, I know the basics, where things are and such."

"You know where the crash pads are? I would love to see a crash pad."

"Yeah, I know where one or two are."

"Good enough. How about tomorrow? I've already done Clark Kerr."

"Sure but make it around noon."

"OK."

She hung up. Darrah. The opportunist. Kill two birds with one stone.

***

She arrived at my apartment around noon, looking sharp, professional. A black silk skirt and an expensive white silk blouse, hardly the garb for slumming around in the Haight. She was taller than I remembered and now slimmer. Her dark hair, normally curly was now straight, well cut, and glossy. Quite a contrast to the bedraggled Columbia journalism student I had last seen in New York.

After a quick hug and peck on the cheek, she looked around my apartment remarking, "My, what a nice place. Good light,"

"It's OK," I replied. "It works for me."

"It's more than OK. You have space and light. An apartment like this would cost a fortune in Boston. And the weather, my god. Here it's November and I'm running around in a blouse and a skirt."

"Well, come on back to California,"

"I can't right now, maybe in a few years," she said thoughtfully. "Still, I'm tired of the cold, dank winters of back east. I guess I'm still a Southern California girl at heart."

"Well, should we get going?" I said. "I've got a crash pad lined up. A new one on Frederick Street. Fresh hippy arrivals."

"Sounds good. Let's go."

I led her over to Frederick Street and sure enough, we hit it just right. A group of bedraggled hippies was moving in with their meager belongings. It was a vacant basement in a commercial building that the Diggers supposedly owned or at least rented. Inside, it was dark and smelly, lit by dirty beams of sunlight coming through the basement windows and a dim naked bulb hanging down. Old mattresses were strewn around on the floor. Large beanbag loungers served as chairs, orange crates as bookcases and storage containers. Some of the hippy girls were working on decorations of one sort or another, lighting candles to get more light. The odor of incense, pot and bodies permeated the whole room. A young girl who could not have been more than fourteen was nursing a baby.

When they first saw us, they thought we were the "man" or maybe social welfare workers. Darrah quickly assured them that she was just a reporter trying to do a story from their point of view on the Haight scene. She interviewed three or four of the hippies while I sat down in a beanbag and read hippy comics.

Afterwards, as we walked up and down Haight Street, Darrah was amazed how young the hippies were and how impoverished and spaced out. "My god, they're just babies. Lost babes in the woods."

"Yeah, and sometimes they meet tragic ends," I replied. "The younger chicks are often gang-raped by their male peers. It's called "sharing." Many others have died of drug overdoses. A few from exposure trying to sleep in Golden Gate Park. Sometimes it isn't pretty."

"Well, it's a lifestyle that my paper is interested in because it sells," said Darrah defensively.

We had a sandwich at some health food store and then walked around some more checking out the sights, the Drogstore, the Psychedelic Shop, Hippy hill, etc.

As soon as we got back to the apartment, Darrah started scribbling out an article in a loose-leaf binder based on the notes that she had taken during our jaunt. I was impressed. Instant writing. It only took her about twenty minutes or so and then she telephoned her newspaper and talked to an editor, pumping up what we saw, making it seem more dramatic than it was. From I what I could determine, the editor was eating it up. I was amazed.

"Pretty dramatic recounting," I remarked.

"You have to sell the story, Allan," she smiled as she hung up. "If you don't have something compelling to report on these lifestyle stories, they don't make it into the paper."

So this was big time lifestyle journalism. But it figured because most of the major news media were lurking about in the Haight filing their exaggerated reports but essentially not having a clue as to what was really going on.

Meanwhile, Darrah had moved to the couch and was yawning. Her long sleek legs curled up under her. "Oh, pardon me, I guess I'm still on eastern time," she said arching back, her white silk blouse now tight across her chest. "Come over here and tell me about your life," she said patting a spot next to her. Against my better judgment, I did go over and sit next to her but we didn't discuss my life until much later.

That evening, we dined by candlelight on steak and a baked potato at my makeshift dining room table, listening to the theme music from *Jules and Jim,* Darrah's favorite movie. We talked about the old times at Berkeley. About my ill-fated time in the Peace Corps and the Army. She filled me in on her life in Boston, noting that she had been living with a psychiatrist but had broken up. She said she was getting restless living back East.

"God, how I want to return to California!" she repeated.

"Well, why don't you?"

"I can't just yet. I need to establish my reputation. I can only do that back east. But I want to come home someday and write from California. Eventually, I want to write a book or two, maybe about Berkeley."

"Sounds like a plan."

"Yeah, I want to live in a groovy little house in the redwoods in Marin County and write. Maybe you'll be around. I'll write and you'll survey," she said half in jest.

"Ah, I don't know about the surveying part. I'm on to other goals," I said knowing that this was all a pipe dream on her part.

As she left that evening, Darrah had a hint of sadness in her eyes. She said she would write to see how I was doing. And surprisingly, a week or so later she did write, a long letter describing how miserable she was in Boston and how she was trying to get a transfer to New York City and still work for the Globe. I never bothered to write back.

17. MEXICO

As the weeks slipped by towards Christmas, I was still feeling at loose ends and indeed even lonely in my Carl Street apartment despite my forays into Berkeley and the demands of my classes. I wondered off and on what Sasha was up to down in Mexico City. Her phone calls had become less frequent. I also wondered what I was going to do over Christmas break. Aside from spending Christmas day with my parents in Martinez, I had no definite plans. Perhaps I would go skiing for a few days. I hadn't been skiing for a couple of years and was afraid that I was losing my skills. My old Head skis sat gathering dust in the garage in Martinez. While I was mulling all of this over, I got an unexpected call from Sasha.

"Allan, you must come to Mexico City to see me."

"I must?"

"Yes, I want you to come here for the holidays and see how I live. See what my life and friends are like. I want you to understand."

"Understand what?"

"Understand why I don't think I am returning to San Francisco."

"Ah, really?" I replied, thinking that was no big surprise.

"Yes, yes. I know you are probably going on with your life. But even though, I think I want to stay here, I want to see you and want you to understand my life here. We will have a great time. I can show you all the sights in Mexico City and maybe we can even go together to Acapulco."

"Sasha, I have to think about this. I'll get back to you in a day or so." I said goodbye and hung up, with very mixed feelings.

One on hand I did want to see Sasha again. She was unique. She was exotic and she was also very sexy. On the other hand, she was a handful and sometimes trouble. Might it not be better to leave things as they were? It was a perfect set up for a split. But there was also the siren call of Mexico.

I had always wanted to see Mexico City and those Mayan ruins on the Yucatan Peninsula. Perhaps even make it out to the Caribbean coast of Mexico where I had heard about the crystal clear tropical waters where visibility was a hundred yards.

What else was I doing over Christmas? Just the same old stuff. I felt the need for adventure, something different. It had been almost two years since I had returned from Europe. I had been stuck in the Bay Area ever since. On an impulse, I called Sasha back and told her I would be coming down. Then I made airline reservations on Mexicana Airlines for a flight the next day, Saturday, December 17. The next three weeks were a blur.

***

The Mexicana flight was longer than I expected, five hours, some 1,900 miles with a stopover in Los Angeles. Luckily, the movies were free and the tequila and Carta Blanca beer flowed liberally along with some crazy south of the border music.

The Mexico City International Airport was a mad house. It was, after all, rush hour. As I de-boarded the plane, there was Sasha, looking tanned and fit. She had lost a few pounds, her hair had been frosted and she was wearing a fashionable outfit. An upscale Señorita. She was with a well-dressed gentleman that I assumed was her father.

"You came. You came," she exclaimed, hugging me.

"Well, of course. What did you expect?" I replied grinning.

"I didn't know. But welcome to my country."

I greeted the father who spoke only a few words of English but smiled a lot as he looked over my attire. A haberdasher, you remember. I had dressed for the occasion, wearing a Madras blazer, white shirt and tie with black slacks and my mod boots but it probably wasn't up to the standards of this elegantly dressed gentleman in a perfectly tailored continental suit.

I retrieved my suitcase off the carousel and we made our way to the parking lot to Sasha's little Volkswagen Beetle.

Soon we were on the freeway heading towards the center of town where my hotel was situated. Oh, yes. My hotel. I was informed by Sasha (out of earshot of her father) that I could not to stay at their house on the outskirts of Mexico City because that was not proper for a man to stay with an unmarried or formerly married woman. As Sasha later told me, "My father is afraid the neighbors and yes, even the servants would talk. He very much believes in appearances and I do not want to hurt my father."

I was annoyed at how easily this so-called liberated Mexican-Jew who once lived with me had become a society conscious Mexican. To say nothing about the extra cost I would incur by staying at hotels throughout my stay. I immediately began to think about shortening my stay.

The hotel turned out to be a big barn of a place on the square. It was supposedly a three-star hotel but it struck me as a soulless dump. I didn't mind dumps as long as they had some charm. This could have been anywhere USA; more specifically, it reminded me of the dumps I had stayed in in New York City.

To celebrate my arrival, Sasha and her dad took me to a nearby restaurant that passed for upscale and had decent food. I had a delicious chicken mole but was careful to point out to Sasha that her chicken mole was superior. After a few Sangrias, and a hearty meal, Sasha's dad loosened up and with Sasha translating, told me the story of how a family of Polish Jews came to Mexico City.

"It is good to know history, my friend," said Mr. Zielinski, lighting up a long, thin cigar. "As a young man, I knew my Polish history. It was a history of occupation and partition by many powers and a history of Jewish persecution. So when Hitler came to power in Germany in 1933, I along with many other Polish Jews understood it would only be a matter of time before he tried to reclaim the Danzig Corridor the region in which we lived."

"I'm afraid, I'm a little fuzzy on my history there," I remarked. "What exactly was the Danzig Corridor?"

Sasha explained that it was a corridor of land between Germany and East Prussia which allowed Poland access to the Baltic Sea. The Germans had been upset at losing control over it following World War One. The Poles wanted to keep it because it was their only access to a sea.

"Oh. Yes, I vaguely recall that in a history class I took," I said, not really recalling it. "Please continue."

Mr. Zielinski continued: "Well, I tried many times to immigrate to the United States during those years, but it seemed only wealthy Jews or those who had family ties in the United States were accepted. So now it was early 1939, and Hitler had recently annexed Sudetenland and Austria. I became desperate and decided to flee to Mexico with my wife and baby Sasha. I had some distant cousins who had immigrated in the 1920s and they wrote me that life was good there. "

"At the time Mexico was still open to Jewish immigrants, although, a few months later they would restrict such immigration. So we left just in time. In September, Poland was invaded by the Nazis. But we were now safe and snug in Mexico City and settled in the growing Jewish community. I set up my tailoring business and eventually opened a fine men's store which is quite popular with many important people, including politicians. It is useful to know politicians around here..."

I began blanking out, as he droned on. I had heard most of this from Sasha before. I was sleepy and wanted to return to the hotel. Mr. Zielinski paid the bill and twenty minutes later, I was back at my hotel. Sasha told me she would pick me up around ten the next day for lunch and dinner at her house. ZZZZ.

I slept fitfully that night and woke up early. Unable to sleep anymore, I went out and walked around the Zocalo. Nothing was open, but I was determined to find another hotel. I checked my Frommer guide to Mexico and noted a Hotel Cortez that looked promising. It was about a mile away from the Zocalo so I hiked over to Avenue Hildago and located it. Frommer described it as cheap but charming with rooms lined with colorful Mexican tile and an enclosed courtyard full of songbirds, tropical foliage and a splashing fountain. The sleepy desk clerk showed me a room which was even smaller than the one I had but was clean, had a bathroom and a balcony that looked out on the courtyard. Furthermore, it was cheap, about twelve dollars a night. I immediately felt I was indeed in Mexico. I went back, checked out of my hotel, and took a cab over to the Cortez. Then I phoned Sasha to inform her of my new quarters. Finally, I crashed for some more shuteye, being lulled to sleep by the cooing of the birds, and the gurgle of the fountain.

***

Sasha picked me up at eleven sharp in her Beetle and we drove out to her house near the Hippodrome. As we passed by the racetrack, Sasha mentioned that she loved to bet on the ponies.

"I sometimes win. My father is an aficionado too. He taught me some of the tricks."

I replied, "A guy I worked has played the ponies for a for a lifetime, spent tens of thousands of dollars, and claims so far he has only broke even."

"I know," she nodded. "But my bets are small, a hundred pesos or so."

We drove through an upscale hilly residential section to her house, a low-slung, one story rambling affair, around a small inner courtyard with a fountain.

"My father had this house built ten years ago. I love it but I have not spent much time here. As I told you, I left home when I was eighteen and when I came back, I married Peter and we moved to the United States. But now I feel so much at home."

What Sasha didn't say was her mother was no longer around to bug her. She was now the mistress of the household and as she pointed out, she was taking care of her father.

Inside, the house was very comfortable, modern with touches of old Mexico. Some faded pictures of the family in Poland and snapshots of Sasha and her younger brother Alberto sat on a mantel. There was even a photo of Sasha on a kibbutz, looking very much out of sorts in a smock she wore as she worked in a kitchen garden. I kept remembering her high heel story.

I greeted the father and he offered me a Carta Blanca and we talked while waiting for Alberto and his wife to arrive. In halting English, the father wanted to know my future plans. I told him I was interested in film and television and I was working for a masters in that. He nodded with approval. Meanwhile, Sasha was in the kitchen preparing some traditional Mexican dish that had to do with shredded beef. It turned out to be enchiladas with green sauce.

By and by, Alberto arrived with his very attractive wife, Delores. Alberto was tall and elegant looking, dressed in the latest casual Euro fashion. His English was fluent. I had met him once briefly in San Francisco when he had come to visit Sasha. He was also on an architectural tour of the U.S. since that was his profession. From San Francisco, he had flown to Chicago to check out its unique architecture by Louis Sullivan and Frank Lloyd Wright and then by car traveled to Wright's Falling Waters house in Pennsylvania. From New York, he flew back to Mexico City. Albert said in addition to his architectural duties, he was also involved in film with the University of Mexico, especially film on architecture.

"If, as some say, architecture is music frozen in stone, then film is architecture in motion. I find the two art forms very compatible," he noted.

We sat at a huge oaken dining room table with a view of the courtyard and dined on the enchiladas and salad washing it down with lots of Sangria. After lunch, Sasha and I walked around the neighborhood and over to a park in the warm afternoon sun. It was now almost eighty degrees. Eighty degrees in December! In addition, I could feel the high altitude taking its toll on me since Mexico City was at an elevation of 7500 feet. Even Sasha said it had taken her weeks to get used to it.

The heat and the enchiladas had made us all very sleepy and one by one, we drifted off to various couches and bedrooms and crashed for a siesta. Sasha escorted me to the guest room, kissed me on the forehead and apologized for not being able to join me but again it was a question of appearances, although I didn't think anybody was really fooled.

A couple of hours later, as it was growing dark, everybody was up and about. Alberto invited Sasha and me over to his house for a late evening supper. Sasha was eager to go since she wanted to show off her brother's brand new house in an even more upscale section of Mexico City. We said goodbye to Sasha's dad and followed Alberto to his new home about five miles away. In the twilight, I could still see that it was indeed a plush neighborhood with large villas dotting a hillside. I also noted a tin shack across the street from Alberto's house and asked Sasha what they were doing there.

"Oh, they are squatters," she replied. "Our zoning is crazy here. The squatters can stay until someone wants to build a big house and then they have to move. But they are useful. Alberto pays this group to watch his house. There are gangs of burglars around here that do nothing but break into the homes of the rich."

As I discovered, Alberto did indeed have a lot to protect. His house was, in fact, a mansion with an interior waterfall. I wondered how he could afford this on a young architect's salary. Then I remembered that Sasha had mentioned that he had married well. His wife Delores came from a very wealthy family and her father was seeing to it that his daughter lived in luxury and that Alberto had plenty of homes to design for his friends. It all made sense. Alberto was a made man.

And it turned out that Sasha was not doing too bad either. She had been doing some voice-over work for commercials and was getting involved in little theater.

"I feel appreciated here, Allan. They understand me. I don't think I will be relegated to roles as a Hispanic maid anymore."

"Good for you," I replied, happy that her talent was being properly appreciated.

After a light supper at Alberto's and a viewing of a short film that he had made on the architecture of the University of Mexico, we said goodbye and Sasha drove me back to my hotel. She declined to come in because as she put it, her father would be worrying about her. End of day one in Mexico.

Allan Brown

18. TOURISTA

I had the next few days mostly to myself since Sasha was busy helping her dad in his store during the Christmas rush. No matter, I knew how to amuse myself. I would have a leisurely breakfast with a delicious cheese and chorizo omelet in the courtyard restaurant while I decided what to see. The first day, I settled on an outing to the Anthropological Museum. I had been told that this museum would give me an overview of the whole Mesoamerican Indian scene.

On the way, I stopped off at Sanborns, a local drugstore chain. This particular Sanborns was housed in a tiled building that featured murals by Jose Orozco, a well-known Mexican artist. This was a way-station for tourists to gather their wits, buy anti-diarrheal medicine, send letters and postcards and eat cheap food that didn't make them sick.

Sanborns also had an excellent bookstore and I was looking for something to read during my stay in Mexico. I spotted an English paperback copy of Malcolm Lowry's *Under the Volcano* which I thought that might be appropriate. Jean-Paul had raved about the novel which he said was ostensibly about a day in the life an alcoholic diplomat who lived in Quauhnahauc (Cuernavaca) but really was a hallucinatory journey through 1930s fascist Mexico. Perfect since I was planning to visit Cuernavaca at some point.

But enough delay. The day was bright and clear and warming up fast. I was starting to love this climate. I hopped on a bus that took me down the Paseo de La Reforma and deposited me at the door of the Anthropological Museum which was situated on the edge of Chapultepec Park.

I knew something about the Mayans and the Aztecs but really nothing about the earlier Indian civilizations such as the Tolecs, the Olmecs and the Zapotecs. I began wandering around this never-ending museum, staring at the artifacts and steles of the ancient Mesoamerican past. The museum even included exhibits on the North American Indians such as the Anasazi and the Midwest mound builders.

All in all, the exhibits reminded me that the Americas were indeed a busy, populated place with thriving trade routes that spanned the continent long before the Europeans arrived. Some of their technological achievements were amazing as well, including the Mayan calendar more accurate than our own, pyramids that rivaled Egypt's, stone roadways more solidly built than our own superhighways and a form of brain surgery that seemed to work. Of course, by the time the Conquistadors arrived in Mexico most of these ancient civilizations had passed their prime. And a few decades later, these Indian civilizations were all but decimated by European viruses.

I lingered in the exhibit hall devoted to the Mayans, gazing at the large photomurals and artifacts of Chichen Itza, Uxmal and Palenque, thinking that I might actually visit these sites on the Yucatan Peninsula. Palenque of was particular interest to me because it was freshly excavated, much of it still swallowed up by the jungle.

Before I knew it, I had spent four hours in the museum and still had not exhausted its offerings. But I had to get out of its darkened halls and into the bright sunshine. I was overloaded with Mesoamerican culture. I checked my watch. Two-thirty. I grabbed a bite to eat at the museum cafeteria and then boarded a bus to return to the city center where I was to meet Sasha and her friends.

As I rode along the Paseo de la Reforma, I noted that it resembled a grand Parisian-like boulevard. As I later learned, it had, in fact, been patterned after such boulevards during the brief Mexican reign of the Austrian Emperor Maximilian. Scattered along the Reforma were imposing monuments, foreign embassies, cafes and restaurants and giant movie palaces. My journey along the Reforma ended as I changed to a bus which took me to the Zocalo and the haberdashery of Sasha's dad.

***

The clothing store was a modest little place but it was jammed full of the latest European styles. No synthetics here. Just the finest fabrics of worsted wool, cotton and linen. Double vented continental suits, double-breasted pinstripes and suits with narrow, Beatle-like labels. Plenty of accessories—

belts, sox, shirts, ties, even a modest corner for elegant, handcrafted shoes.

Mr. Zielinski was buzzing around a couple of customers trying to talk them into buying two suits for the price of one. With a tape measure over his shoulder, he was obsequious, yet dignified and of course impeccably dressed. Sasha sat at the counter behind the cash register, looking bored, reading a book, but now and then coming alive when a sale was finally transacted.

She looked up when I entered, smiled and stuffed her book in her purse, saying, "Let's go."

"Ah, why don't you show me around," I said. "This is interesting."

"Oh, sure," she smiled. "But remember I grew up with this. Dad, I love him, but it's so boring."

Sasha took me through the cramped aisles pointing out the finer suits her father had imported from Europe. And in her best salesperson mode, fingering the suit, she said, "Look here at this material, Allan. This is very superior material. You want I have my father make you a fine suit? Only one hundred American dollars. Much better than you can buy in San Francisco at that price."

"You're kidding, aren't you?" I said taken aback. "I'd have to go home tomorrow. I'll just have make do with my blazer and slacks."

"Well, at least let dad take your measurements so he can make a suit up for you when you become rich," she said half joking.

"I'll think about," I replied. "Let's go."

We walked over a few blocks to Sasha's favorite cafe in an upscale district of restaurants and cafes. She ordered mixed chocolate and coffee iced drinks for both of us. A few minutes later, we were joined by three of her girlfriends, all Jewish, blonde and green eyed, all chattering like birds in Spanish, even though all spoke some English. I sat there like a department store dummy, as they looked me over. Later, Sasha told me her girlfriends thought me cute but so young looking.

Soon their boyfriends arrived. Two dressed in stylish business suits, a third in a casual corduroy jacket and jeans. Geraldo was the artist/writer in the group. He spoke excellent English, explaining that he had studied at Columbia in New York.

"My god is Carlos Fuentes," he declared. "He can write in both English and Spanish and he is very stylish in both languages."

"Not a bad goal," I concurred.

Finally, tiring of the scene, I signaled to Sasha that it was time to go eat.

The others begged off, saying it was too early to dine and made fun of

Sasha for her American habit of dining early.

We decided to eat at my hotel which had the courtyard restaurant and modestly priced food. Following dinner, Sasha came up to my room for a tequila nightcap. When I suggested that she stay a little while, she replied, "I must go home. My father will be wondering where his meal is."

"God, what are you, his housekeeper? Can't he fix his own meal?"

"I suppose, but I am trying to be a good daughter. After all, I have been away so long. He is so happy that I am back."

I then broached the subject of going away for a few days together, to Acapulco.

"Allan, I know I mentioned that on the phone when you were deciding to come down, but I cannot," she labored to explain. "We are very busy at the store over the holidays. My father makes most of his income during these times. Maybe in a week or so after the rush."

I thought about that for a second and wondered again why I had bothered to come down here. I was barely seeing her, let alone bedding her. Then out the blue, she suggested that I should travel for a week or so on my own and see Mexico. "Go to Acapulco, maybe Puerto Vallarta. There are many beautiful places to see."

"Uh, that idea had crossed my mind but I'm more interested in the Yucatan," I replied. "The museum today inspired me. I want to climb those pyramids, maybe even go out to the Caribbean coast."

"Yes, yes," she said eagerly. "That is a good idea. It is very lovely there. I remember as a little girl we visited Isla Mujeres. I remember sticking my head in the water with goggles and seeing all those little fishes and beautiful coral. You didn't even have to swim. You could just stand on the bottom and look."

"That sounds good. Of course, it would be nicer with you," I said. "How about just a day trip to Cuernavaca. Can you get a day off?"

"No, Allan. As I told you, I must stay here."

"OK, I'll phone you when I get back in a week or so."

I walked her to her car, kissed her on her lips. She squeezed my hand. "When you get back, I will make sure we spend some time together."

As I watched her drive off, I was both pissed off and relieved. I felt I had been suckered into coming down here, but at the same time, I was eager to see Mexico. I went back to my room and started reading *Under the Volcano* while listening to the songbirds and the splash of the fountains. Just as Jean-Paul had said, the book was hypnotic, almost hallucinatory; an alcoholic haze permeated the pages. But slowly my eyes closed and before I knew I fell asleep.

Three hours later I awoke with jolt and checked my watch. Eleven-thirty. Still in my street clothes, I washed my face, combed my hair and went out again, seeing what was what in Mexican nightlife. I walked by an upscale nightclub with a long line of eager señors and señoritas waiting to get in. The guys were sharply dressed, mostly in black with tight pants and high heel boots, young Valentinos. The door checker seeing me looking on, and probably figuring I was a tourist, beckoned me forward and allowed me inside. The club had a colorful strobe light set up with hot Salsa music, blasting my ears. Most couples were simply writhing around, but some tried to keep to the traditional dance steps. I went over to the bar and ordered a large Margarita which kept me busy for a half hour as I watched the dancers on the floor. One señorita was giving me the eye as she sat alone at the bar but after my margarita, I felt sleepy again and in no mood for dancing. So I left, went back to the Hotel Cortes, half drunk and crashed.

***

I woke up the next morning wondering what to do. Sasha was out of the picture for now but I wasn't in the mood to leave right away for the Yucatan. I still had stuff to see around Mexico City. I decided to take a cab out to the Teotihuacán ruins and maybe after that I would check out the Our Lady of Guadalupe Basilica.

I had always thought Teotihuacán was an Aztec city but as I learned in the Anthropological Museum, it preceded the Aztec civilization by hundreds of years. The best estimates were the Teotihuacán Empire flourished from about 600 BC to 800 AD. At first view, the restored site of Teotihuacán was indeed impressive, covering hundreds of sunbaked acres. Its biggest pyramid, the Pyramid of the Sun, soared over two hundred feet high. So naturally, I had to climb it. Huffing and puffing, I made it to the top in the now blazing sun with not a drop of shade around. Still, from on high, I was able to get a view of the layout of Teotihuacán with its other pyramid, the Pyramid of the Moon, and its palaces, temples and plazas. The whole layout was bisected by a mile-and-a-half esplanade called the Street of the Dead. Back down at ground level, I hiked over to the Palace of the Quetzal-Butterfly and examined elaborately carved pillars and frescoes of ancient elites living in splendor. Of course, all of this elaborate construction was no doubt done on the backs of slaves but still it was impressive.

Even though I had barely scratched the surface at Teotihuacán, a couple of hours in the blazing sun were enough. How could the sun be so hot in

December!? Where was the nice, cool green jungle? Not here, not today. The jungled ruins would have to wait until I hit the Mayan trail. I had a coke and a sandwich at the museum cafeteria and then took a cab back to the city to visit Our Lady of Guadalupe.

Even though I had been warned December was peak time for pilgrimages to the basilica, I wasn't prepared for the mob scene that ensued. When I arrived, the expansive plaza in front of the 18th-century basilica was overflowing with pilgrims, most on their knees, crawling towards the entrance. It was a surreal, almost scary sight. Many were obviously peasants, others more middle class. A few were wearing basketball knee pads for the grueling crawl, other just rags wrapped around their knees, some on their bare and often bloody knees but all had a determined yet blissful look on their faces with an occasional grimace as they hit a ridge or a bump in the stone plaza.

Of course, the object of their devotion was the Lady of Guadalupe herself, a.k.a, the Virgin Mary. I managed to bypass the knee crawling crowd and got in line to view the image of the Virgin in the Basilica. What I saw after a half hour of waiting in the line was unremarkable. Encased in glass and hanging on a wall, was the washed out image of the lady emblazoned on an old cloak. She was portrayed as olive skinned rather than Caucasian, supposedly to appeal to the new nation of Mexico. Her origins were rather mysterious.

According to the legend, Juan Diego, an Aztec nobleman who converted to Christianity, claimed to have had a vision of the Virgin in 1531. This vision was somehow imprinted on his cloak to prove to the local bishop that the vision was indeed real. The legend has served its purpose. The Lady of Guadalupe has proved to be an enduring inspiration throughout five hundred years and the foremost symbol of a Catholic Mexico.

Of more interest to me were the many statues of a crucified Christ and various other saints, many crowned with thorns, others pierced with arrows, all bleeding profusely from their wounds, all appearing in agony. Blood was big in Mexican worship. One had to bleed to prove their devotion. Maybe it was a hold-over from the notorious human sacrifices of the Aztecs. Or perhaps a symbolic reminder of the bloody conquest of the Spanish Conquistadors. Or could it be just a simple and dramatic way to appeal to an illiterate peasantry?

***

The following day, I took a bus to Cuernavaca thirty miles away and found myself wandering around the main square looking for the volcano described so vividly by Malcolm Lowry in *Under the Volcano*. No obvious volcano in sight today. Maybe it was the haze. Technically, Cuernavaca, at an elevation of five thousand feet, was built on the lower slopes of Chichinautzin, a dormant volcano only twelve miles west of town. Although, Lowry explicitly states the volcano is Popocatepetl, the most dramatic and active volcano in the area, a distant 40 miles east of town. Methinks Lowry was taking poetic license with his geography so he could concoct a fiery backdrop to his novel, a novel which has been compared to a modern voyage through Dante's Inferno.

After the hustle and bustle of Mexico City, Cuernavaca was peaceful. I checked out the main sights around the plaza such as the Palace of Cortez once occupied by Cortez himself. Now the palace featured Diego Rivera murals depicting the atrocities committed by Cortez and his thugs. Next, I peeked into the Cathedral of Asuncion with an ominous looking skull and crossbones over the main entrance. Then I lounged in a garden next to the cathedral, the Jardin Borda. But mostly, I just walked around, up and down the hilly side streets, stopping now and then for a coffee or a beer and finally for lunch on an outdoor patio with a view of the plaza.

All of this was interspersed with reading snatches of *Under the Volcano*. I half-imagined myself to be another whacked out writer re-tracing the steps the Consul as he conducted his odyssey on the Day of the Dead. I even found a bar that claimed that Lowry had hung out here. (Probably there were many such bars.) After a strong margarita and some directions from an English bartender, I walked to the edge of town and onto a bridge over a deep ravine, the *barranca*, which traversed the countryside for miles around. In the book, it is into this ravine that the Consul's body is tossed after being shot by Mexican fascists. As the Lowry put it in his brutal final sentence, "Somebody threw a dead dog after him down the ravine."

***

Tiring of Cuernavaca, I climbed aboard a third class bus heading to a little village outside of town. Unlike the city buses, this was a rattletrap affair crammed with kids, baskets, Indians, suitcases piled precariously on the top and a few live chickens. The bus traveled along a secondary road which eventually turned into a dirt road. A few kilometers along, I got off at my un-named village and walked down a dirt path past fields being worked by the peasants. I ended up at a church, a simple but perfectly proportioned adobe affair. It had no real ornamentation or stained glass windows, only a scarred wooden altar with a cross, a small statue of Jesus and of course, a small statue of the Virgin Mary.

It was now four in the afternoon and the shadows were creeping across the fields, the heat softening. I sat for while on a hard bench pew soaking up the meager spirit of the place. Then I strolled around the grounds and fields. The Mexican workers smiled and nodded, probably wondering what this Gringo was doing so far off the beaten track. I finally hiked over to the main highway about a half mile away and flagged down one of the intercity buses heading back to Mexico City. An hour later, I was back at my hotel, feeling I had been touched by Mexico.

19. YUCATAN

The next morning, I set out on my voyage to the Yucatan. I phoned Sasha to tell her of my plans. That was cool with her. She simply wished me *"Vaya con dios,"* which of course made me wonder again why I bothered to come down here. Still, I was excited at the prospect of seeing those Maya ruins.

After throwing a few clothes and toiletries into a small knapsack that I had bought, I made my way over to the Eastern Bus Terminal for a bus to Veracruz, my first planned stop on my journey to the Yucatan. I bought a first class ticket and climbed aboard a sleek, new, air-conditioned bus with plush seats and large picture windows. This baby put Greyhound to shame. The passengers were an assorted bunch—businessmen in suits, students, one or two mothers with babies, but all middle class. No peasants here. I settled back for the 260-mile journey which would take me through the heart of eastern Mexico.

It was six hours of riding through high plateau countryside with stunning views of the volcanoes Popocatepetl and Ixtaccihuatl, through agricultural lands, scrub deserts and then a descent through the coastal range mountains towards Veracruz.

After the clear air and the bright light of the elevated towns of central Mexico, the town of Veracruz was another world. Low, humid, overcast skies hovered over rickety wooden buildings. It struck me as the bowels of the tropics. I made my way from the bus terminal down the main drag looking for a hotel.

I eventually found a dumpy place listed by Frommer near the local Zocalo. It was clean but depressing and stuffy despite a slow moving fan overhead that gave the room a faint hint of air circulation. A mosquito net hung over the bed. Malaria here? I didn't know but was too tired to worry about it. I dumped my knapsack on the sagging bed and hit the street, hiking around until I found a little seafood restaurant. At first, I was worried it would be indigestible, but as I discovered, seafood was Veracruz's specialty. I had a grilled red snapper that was delicious and cheap even if its dead eye stared at me as I devoured it.

To further amuse myself, I hopped on one of the many rickety streetcars that served the downtown area and rode around for an hour or so to get a lay of the town. Finally, I repaired to an outdoor bar and had a couple of strong Margaritas. Then I returned to the hotel and crashed in the humid night with the sounds of the Marimba and the screech of traffic echoing through the streets.

***

Slime. That's what I felt like the next morning after a hot, humid night under the mosquito net which by the way I discovered had a hole in it but luckily no bites. I was soaked with greasy sweat. My head ached from the humidity or was it the Margaritas I had the night before? Or maybe it was from the all night crowing of roosters even though dawn was nowhere in sight.

I got up and washed off at the basin with lukewarm water. What I would have given for an ice-cold shower. However, I made do. I dressed in a pair of shorts that I had brought along and a T-shirt and went out for breakfast. Although it was only 7:30, the town was already buzzing. Probably to get a jump on the heat.

For breakfast, I devoured another omelet chock full of chorizo, peppers and cheese and sipped an excellent coffee. Afterwards, I strolled along the waterfront, stopping now and then at various statues commemorating Mexican heroes.

Looking out, the port didn't appear too busy. Only a few cargo ships were in dock being loaded or unloaded by giant cranes. Despite its modernity, it wasn't hard to imagine the role the port played in Mexico's early history. It was here that Cortez and his gang of Spanish Conquistadors came ashore in 1519. These waters were also the gateway to other conquerors: the French in 1838, the Americans in 1847 during the Mexican-American war. And then the French again in 1863 to establish Maximilian as Emperor of Mexico. Finally, the Americans in 1914 to protect their interests following the Mexican Revolution.

Next, I explored the Castillo de San Juan de Ulua. This fort was an imposing, though crumbling monolith of stone towers and ramparts set on a small peninsula jutting out into the bay. It was a perfect location to protect the harbor yet this 16th-century fort actually failed Veracruz during its many invasions. The invaders would simply land farther up the coast and cut the fort off by land.

I spent an hour or so climbing around the battlements admiring the views of the bay. Then I descended into the dank corridors and checked out the small cells where political prisoners were held under the rule of Porfirio Diaz in the early 20th century.

By now it was time for a break so I sat down in a cafe on the waterfront and had a sandwich and a beer. The humidity was climbing so I decided what I needed was a swim. I returned to the hotel, grabbed my bathing suit and hopped a trolley to the beach, Villa Del Mar, just south of downtown. I wasn't expecting a pristine white sand beach with gin clear waters, but this beach was pretty dismal. Packed, grey-brown sand, lapped by even grayer, brown water. I noted the locals didn't seem to mind. The kids were whooping it up while the elders swam offshore in long graceful strokes. So I decided to give it a try.

I waded out a ways and swam around, at first being careful not to get my head wet and then saying the hell with it and dunking under. However, back on the beach, I immediately took a shower at an outdoor stall. As I settled back in a recliner, I belatedly noticed off in the distance a big-ass pipe spewing some dirty looking water directly into the bay. Was a fatal skin disease in the offing? That was it for the Villa Del Mar.

I took the trolley back downtown, getting off at the waterfront. Now powerfully thirsty, I ducked into a local dive for a tall cool one. I immediately noticed there was no place to sit. It was a stand-up bar filled with working stiffs and town drunks. Red bleary eyes and sly smiles greeted me as they looked the Gringo over. But nobody said anything. *"Una cerveza, por favor"* I uttered in my best high school Spanish. The bartender smiled and shoved me a bottle of Carta Blanca.

I was standing in the front of the bar where I had a view of the street and the waterfront activity, as well a hint of a breeze coming off the bay. But now and then, I smelled something very acrid coming from the interior of the bar. I peered through the gloom to the very back and noticed something odd. Several men were lined up at a tile wall with their backs to me. And I heard the faint hiss of water and gurgling sounds coming from a trough in the floor. No, it can't be! I went back to investigate. Yes, it was. It was an open pissoir right in the bar. Disgusting!

Yet when you thought about it, from the Mexican point of view, it was efficient and probably boosted sales. I had heard about this before, stories of men at the bar, a beer in one hand and their dick in the other pissing into a trough right under the bar. But I had thought that was just slander or at least confined to barrios. But here it was, right in the middle of a major city. I wondered if they had health department inspectors in this town.

In any case, I lost my thirst and walked out, leaving my half-finished beer on the counter. A few blocks away, I found a nice outdoor cafe with a real fountain and garden and had another beer, this time in a proper environment. Ah, Mexico.

I finished off my day with a nap at my hotel room under the slow moving fan and then had another delicious red snapper dinner with a Margarita on the Zocalo. Finally, to bed, feeling I had done Veracruz. Tomorrow: Villahermosa, the jumping off point into the heart of the Yucatan.

***

The next morning, it was another long bus ride to Villahermosa about three hundred miles away, around the bend of the Gulf Mexico and into the interior of the Yucatan Peninsula. I arrived mid-afternoon at the non-descript town and immediately took a cab to La Venta Park on the outskirts to gaze at the mysterious Olmec heads. Set in a jungle garden, these were massive, basalt heads, some seven or eight feet tall. I closely examined their features— thick lips, flat noses, closed eyes as if in meditation. Mute testimony to a long ago civilization.

Archeologists say the Olmecs flourished from about 1200 BC to 400 BC, long before the rise of the Mayan civilizations. Very little is known about the Olmecs except that they obviously knew how to sculpt heads along with other artistic skills. Some archeologists also credit them with a system of writing, the concept of zero and a calendar that may have influenced the later Mayans.

There is a lot of speculation about the Olmecs' origins. One school of thought is that they somehow migrated from Africa. This view is based on the Negroid features of the heads, totally unlike the features of the later Mesoamerican Indians. The more traditional view is that the Olmecs were indigenous to the region but of a slightly different racial type and just faded out before the rise of the more recent Mesoamerican tribes.

***

After a night in Villahermosa in yet another hot, sweaty dump, I continued my trek to one of the more mysterious Mayan ruins, Palenque. Of course, in the process of getting there, I had to endure a ten-hour wait for a train on Christmas day in Teapa, a god-forsaken village in the middle of the jungle. I wandered around town, ate at the local restaurant and took a short hike on a trail up to a jungled waterfall. The lowlight of my day was watching a pig give birth on the train station platform and then dealing with a bout of diarrhea.

When the night train did come, it was an antique, rattletrap affair, all second-class. The seats hard and unforgiving. I tried to sleep on the way but kept waking up as the train stopped every ten miles or so at every little settlement. As we penetrated ever further into the inky black jungle, I was beginning to feel like Conrad's steamboat captain going into the "heart of darkness." At one point while half-asleep, I thought I was hallucinating as figures wrapped in ghostly white robes drifted on and off the train. When I awakened with a start, I realized these visions were real. Deep jungle Lacandon Indians, probably descended from ancient Mayans, moved silently up and down the aisles. One sat across from me with a sheet wrapped around his head, staring at me. All I could see were the bright whites of his eyes and shiny teeth beaming out in a smile. Now and then I could hear them muttering among themselves in a language far removed from Spanish. I guess it was the ancient Mayan tongue.

Finally, around three a.m., the train rolled into Palenque Station, in the still pitch-black night. I got off with my knapsack wondering what to do next as the train chugged on. A little kid came up and pointed to a nearby barrack-like building, saying, "*Hotel, Señor?*"

I shrugged why not. I didn't want to hang around the train station for another three hours. The hotel couldn't be too expensive. So the little kid led me over. The place turned out to be a workers hotel or more accurately, a hostel. And it wasn't cheap. About twenty bucks. That must have been the gringo rate.

The clerk led me to a dormitory type room with six or seven bunks. I had three other bunkmates, happily snoring the night away. I figured I could stand it for a few hours. I lay down on top of the bunk fully clothed, my knapsack at my side and eventually fell asleep wondering if this was all a dream or a nightmare. Wondering if seeing these ruins was really worth it.

Four hours later, I was up and trudging along a dirt road that led to the ruins of Palenque. I had been told the ruins were only a few kilometers away, well within walking distance. There was no bus service and taxi service was spotty and expensive. Palenque was still not on the tourist radar.

What the hell, I thought. I could use the exercise. Trudge, trudge, trudge. Still, the day was heating up fast. My knapsack grew heavier and heavier and I was sweating like pig in my shorts and T-shirt as I hiked along through the scrub countryside. No jungle here. I decided to take a breather and sat down on a sun-baked rock. A few minutes later, I spotted a Land Rover coming down the road in a cloud of dust. On an impulse, I stuck out my thumb and to my surprise, the Land Rover stopped.

"Are you going to the ruins?" asked a female voice in perfect American English.

"Yes, I am."

"Good, get in."

I got in the backseat and was greeted by a little boy with big brown eyes. In the front seat were the dad and the mom. She was an American and he a Mexican doctor from Jalapa. The Señor made it a point of telling me that he was trained in New York.

"Small world," I remarked.

The couple was very friendly and concerned about my wandering around alone.

"It's easy to get lost in this country," she said.

"Really?"

"Yes, it happens all the time. Some die of thirst. Say, since you are by yourself, after touring the ruins, why don't you ride back with us to Villahermosa?" said the Señor. "It will save you a lot of hassle with trains and buses."

I hesitated. "Sounds like a good idea but I don't want to intrude upon your hospitality."

"Nonsense," the woman said. "We will meet you in the parking lot around two."

"Will do."

My transportation assured, I could now focus on these mysterious ruins.

***

Yes, the ruins. One was not allowed to roam them at will since it was a working archeological site. There were only a few tourists this particular morning but most were American so the tour was in English. Even the

Mexican family that had given me a ride joined in. The tour was given by a serious graduate student in archeology, a blond American with a goatee. He introduced himself as Tim. He first gave an overview of the Palenque site, explaining how Palenque was believed to be part of a network of Mayan cities. The zenith of Palenque was estimated to be from about 300 AD to 900 AD after which it went into decline with the rest of the Mayan empire hundreds of years before the Spanish arrived.

"Compared to Tikal and Chichen Itza, Palenque is rather small and as you can see only partially investigated. But the treasures it has yielded are abundant," said Tim pointing to the breathtaking Temple of Inscriptions, the classic Mayan temple with the steep stairs, situated up against a jungled hillside.

We proceeded to climb the stairs which were diabolically steep and required a high step to ascend. Thighs burning, I wondered how the Mayan priests could do this all day long. But as the guide reminded us, the temple was probably used only for ceremonial purposes, not everyday events. Indeed, its archeological importance was that it housed a lengthy Mayan text that appeared to record significant events in Palenque's history. It was a pictographic text that the archeologists were beginning to crack.

The other major attraction of the Temple of Inscriptions, other than offering a spectacular view of the surrounding countryside, was the tomb of the Mayan king, Pakal. Once we climbed to the top of the temple, we descended into a narrow, claustrophobic passageway to Pakal's tomb. There in a small room was his stone sarcophagus, the lid of which was carved with various images including one of Pakal as the Maize God. Corn was big in these parts.

Next, we hiked over to the main palace, a complex of terraces, buildings and a tower. Inside, the palace housed an array of sculptures and bas-relief carvings, lit up by floodlights. We watched as an archeologist/artist type seated at a drafting table carefully copied the images by hand.

All of this made me think about the reality of archaeology. It was much more than just ripping off artifacts and finding priceless treasures. There was the tedious grunt work. First digging up the ruins as was evidenced by the excavations going on here and then the measuring, the recording, the drawing and the photography.

Most of the archeologists around here appeared to be graduate student types both Americans and Mexicans with a few graybeards wandering around, nodding and approving as their student underlings showed off their findings.

After the palace, we hiked around some more with Tim pointing out what appeared to be various mounds and hillocks covered with jungle vegetation, saying these no doubt were other buildings waiting to be excavated along with a suspected ball court.

"We've only scratched the surface here," said Tim. "There are years and years of excavations ahead. You could spend a lifetime here and never unearth it all."

We ended the tour in a work area under a tent where archeology students were studying a stone fragment of a Mayan Calendar, a calendar based on precise astronomical observation said to be more accurate than our own. Interestingly, their calendars only went up to our year of 2012 which they apparently felt, would be the end of time. Even today, there are many nut cases who believed that 2012 would indeed be the end of time for us. Shit, in 2012, I would be seventy-two. Probably dead or almost dead anyway.

So here we were surrounded by all the signs of an advanced civilization and yet there was one surprising gap. The Mayans made no use of the wheel. Tim explained they had no use for the wheel because it was slave labor that supplied the muscle for transportation and the construction of their cities. It was possibly slave revolts along with human sacrifices and bitter wars over scarce resources such as water and land that led to their demise but who really knew.

Following my sojourn at Palenque, I rode back to Villahermosa in style with the Mexican doctor and his wife in their Land Rover. Then the next day because time and money were short, I decided to forgo the rest of the Yucatan and instead took a bus across the Isthmus of Tehuantepec to the Pacific coast where I planned to chill for a few days.

20. PACIFICO

The parrotfish is an interesting fish. In addition to being beautiful to look at with its rainbow of colors, it performs a remarkable task. It nibbles on coral to get at the embedded algae and then shits out the debris as sand. It's a beach building fish. The tiny damselfish are interesting little guys as well. Also, multi-colored with reds, grays yellows and black stripes, they dart in and out of the coral nooks and crannies and if you approach too close, they will attack you, their tiny little bites like a tickle on your arms or legs. All of this I witnessed as I snorkeled around in the coves of "El Pacifico," the ocean that fairly glistened and rippled in the sunlight and that stretched on forever. The ocean that Balboa viewed from a hilltop on a calm day in 1513 when the Pacific appeared as infinity.

I had arrived at this Edenic spot after a twenty-mile cab ride over a bumpy dirt road to a beach west of Salina Cruz. There I found a cheap hostel filled with hippies and beach bums lounging around in hammocks. The hostel consisted of a row of thatched hutches and a covered dining and bar area where, as I would discover, a local cook concocted fantastic seafood dishes. My favorite was a seafood salad with chunks of conch, lobster, snapper and grouper, all mixed with tomatoes, garlic, onion, and soaked with lime.

It was a mellow crew indeed that stayed here—snorkelers, scuba divers and surfers when the surf was up. These guys and gals were very unlike the stoned hippies that I had run into in the Haight-Ashbury. They weren't above smoking pot or dropping acid now and then, but they were into the outdoor thing. Tanned, muscled, healthy looking with long, sun-bleached hair. I felt right at home here.

I rented some snorkeling gear and spent three long days swimming, snorkeling, tanning, drinking beer, and listening to Mexican and acid rock. Several American hotties ran around in their string bikinis while sloe-eyed Indian beauties hovered about smiling, apparently available for a small price. In short, all the trappings of a little tropical paradise.

As Brad, one of the beach boys put it, "Why hassle with the states and all its hang-ups. I've been to the Haight. It's depressing and cold and cost a lot of bread. Down here I can live on a fraction of the cost and do my ocean thing. I'm never returning. The closest I ever want to get to civilization is a run up to Oaxaca for weed."

"Right on, man, I'm with you," I said as I sipped on a beer and lounged in my hammock, now and then gazing out over the tranquil, stunningly blue Pacific. Slowly, slowly, I was slipping into this mellow never-never land, my meager academic ambitions evaporating. Why return? I too asked myself. "Never return" was the immediate answer from this lotus land. Never return. I fell asleep in my hammock as the gentle trade winds caressed my bare skin.

Towards evening, I stood on the beach watching an Indian maiden outlined by a surreal sun setting into the ocean. She beckoned.

***

By day four, paradise was wearing off. I was sunburned so bad I was blistering. Also, I had been stung several times by little jellyfish lurking offshore and the stings seemed to be festering. Finally, I had eaten some bad fish or something, and my runs were returning and my crotch itched. To say nothing of the no-see-ums, little bugs that you can't see but leave a nasty bite that itches like hell. So I decided it was time to move on but I vowed to return someday soon to this hideaway paradise.

Early the next day I hitched a ride to Salina Cruz, a dumpy industrial town on the coast and then caught a bus to Tehuantepec up the road about thirteen miles. Here I had a layover before continuing on to Oaxaca. The Tehuantepec Zocalo was jammed with scores of little markets run by women in colorful full-length skirts. These were tall, often beautiful women, many carrying large baskets of produce and other goods on their head, a sure-fire formula for perfect posture. Others rode Vespas or bikes, skirts hiked up over the knees with the market goods on the bike rack, zooming up and down the narrow streets of Tehuantepec. I spotted a few men in the bars and the back streets, but mostly they stayed out of sight. There was no doubt that the women of Tehuantepec called most of the shots.

Soon I was back on the bus heading up to the highlands of Oaxaca on a narrow twisting road. It was a long, laborious drive of 150 miles with the bus pulling off the road every few miles to give trucks and buses coming down the mountain the right-away. Nonetheless, the many white crosses that dotted the roadside testified to scores of deaths on this highway, along with the visible wrecks scattered at the bottom of ravines.

We finally pulled into Oaxaca around four in the afternoon. The passengers filed off the bus as if in a trance. Exhausted from the crazed ride, I headed for a fountain and splashed water on my face. Then I scoped out the Oaxaca town square. It was by far the prettiest that I had seen in Mexico, lined as it was with scores of inviting cafes and restaurants and shaded by Indian Laurel trees. I immediately repaired to the nearest outdoor cafe and ordered a Carta Blanca while I got my bearings. My guidebook was rather useless at this point with only scant hotel listings for Oaxaca. Still, I was sure I would find some cheap accommodations near the Zocalo. I settled back, ordered a sandwich and sipped on my beer, soon becoming light-headed since I was now back up at the five-thousand-foot elevation.

I noted that the cafe was filling up with *Norteamericanos*, many appearing to be students or just young drifters. I spotted Brad. He nodded and beckoned me to come over. He was with a couple of American college girls.

"Yo, bro. Small world. Tired of the beach?"

"Yes, Brad. I'm not in my forever beach mode like you," I replied. "I actually have to return to the U.S."

"Too bad, but what the hell. I'm only up here on a supply run but already I can't wait to get back. Say hello to Jerri and Lois. Two lost souls who want to know about paradise down below."

I said hello, noting that both Jerri and Lois were rather cute, although both looked a little worn out from traveling. Lois said she and her friend were on Christmas break from UCLA. I mentioned that I had visited UCLA's film school once when I was thinking about enrolling.

"Oh yeah, film. That's quite popular at my school," Lois replied.

"Actually, I'm more interested in television," I explained. "I like the immediacy."

"Ugh, television is so mundane. Although, I suppose there's a lot of opportunity that," said Jerri. "Maybe I could be a weather bunny if this acting thing doesn't work out." Laugh. (Jerri was a drama major.)

"Maybe."

Changing the subject, we talked about Oaxaca, what there was to see, how much time was needed to do the city justice.

"Well, the big thing is Mt. Alban, the Zapotec ruins," said Jerri. "We saw them yesterday. Very impressive."

"Better than the Mayan?" I asked.

"Well, I don't know," she answered. "I have never seen the Mayan ruins."

I proceeded to fill them in on Palenque. The girls seemed interested. But when I told them what it took to get there, their interest waned.

"The best thing to do in Oaxaca is nothing," offered Brad. "Just lounge around the plaza, maybe take a little stroll up and down the side streets, maybe score some grass."

That was advice I was willing to listen to. So in line with the do-nothing policy, we all sat around getting bombed drinking margaritas. After all, it was New Year's Eve. 1967 was rearing its ugly head on the morrow and who knew what it held. But hey, eat drink and be merry.

Somewhere along the line, we had dinner. I believe it was enchiladas and something, something. Now things were beginning to get hazy. We walked around, stumbling upon a New Year's fiesta. Everybody was dancing, clapping, the trumpets blaring—shades of Prez Prado. Mariachi madness. Little kids jumping up and down. More margaritas, more beer. Fuck it, straight tequila. Then a nightclub in a cave lit by torches. Dance, dance, dance. The stroke of midnight. Kiss, kiss. Then stumbling back to the girls' hotel right off the Zocalo. I was with Lois. Brad was definitely with Jerri. Up to Lois' room. A narrow bed with an overhead fan that didn't work, bathroom down the hall, street noises right outside. Drunken making out. Am I staying the night?

"I can't Allan," said Lois finally. "I have some sort of intestinal bug. It's a real mess. Maybe I'll see you tomorrow."

"Sure," I said too bombed to care. Plus I had my own problem with the trots.

I went down to the reception desk to get my own room. It was now well past 3 a.m., yet the noise went on. Still, I crashed and was out like a light.

I woke up around noon the next day, hung over big time. My head felt as if it has been split in two. I popped several aspirins and after a quick wash up, I stumbled down the stairs in the shorts and T-shirts that I had been wearing for several days now and which were beginning reek. It was definitely time to return to Mexico City and to my suitcase with its change of clothes.

I sat in the cafe, sipping on coffee and munching on a roll trying to decide on my course of action for the day. I finally decided to forego Mt. Alban and take the bus back to Mexico City.

Around five o'clock I trekked over to the bus terminal and bought a first-class ticket to Mexico City. According to the timetable, the bus left at 7 p.m. for the three hundred mile ride in the middle of the night.

Actually, it was a good thing the ride was at night, a pitch-black night lit only by the headlights of our bus. That way I saw only fleeting glimpses of the numerous white crosses along the roadside and saw nothing of the sheer cliffs and ravines that bordered the narrow road. Of course, there was a lot of horn honking by the bus driver as he careened around the blind corners on his downhill run. Good thing that I didn't see that. I only felt the swaying of the bus which lulled me to sleep along with the other jaded passengers who made this run routinely. Eventually, the road straightened out and widened and then the driver really kicked into high gear, streaking through the night towards Mexico City.

We rolled into the Central Southern Terminal around two in the morning. I immediately caught a cab back to Hotel Cortez where the desk clerk rented me another room. I fetched my suitcase that had been sitting in a storage room and hustled up to my quarters. As I crashed on the bed, I felt as if I had been in a dream, an unreal journey into the heart of Mexico.

***

Ring, ring. I groggily reached for the phone in my room and muttered "Ola."

"Where have you been?" said a very annoyed and almost hysterical Sasha.

"I'm here. I just got back."

"I was worried about you. I thought maybe you had gotten lost in the jungle or maybe eaten by a jaguar."

"No such luck. I just spent a little time on the beach. That's all. What's up with you?"

"I have to see you, Allan. Today. I'm not working at my father's store anymore. He doesn't need me."

"Ah, OK."

"Yes. I will pick you up at eleven and we will spend the day at my house. The housekeeper is off."

"Ah, OK."

"Doesn't that sound nice?"

"Sure."

"You don't sound too enthusiastic. I know I have not spent much time with you. But I will make it up."

"Ah, OK. Sasha, see you soon."

So that's how it went. In the shower, I had mixed feelings. Other than seeing Mexico, this trip had been a bust. I probably should have stayed home. In any case, I was ready to go back to San Francisco. In fact, I was leaving the next day. Even so, I felt obligated to say goodbye to Sasha, although I didn't want to reignite anything. I had already concluded that Sasha was never returning to San Francisco.

***

As promised, we did hang out at her house, munching on goodies, listening to music and despite my vow not to reignite anything, we did spend quite a bit of time in bed. She was in fine form, this actress who thought of life as one big dramatic production. But through it all, was a strain of sadness because we both knew that it was over even though she made vague promises that she would return to San Francisco in a few months.

By late afternoon, we were both depressed and decided that we needed to go eat a nice dinner out. She took me to one of her favorite little restaurants off the Paseo De La Reforma. Then we went to see a movie in one of the huge movie theaters on the Reforma. We saw the *Blue Max* dubbed in Spanish which I managed to follow. After all, how much language did you need to understand what May Britt and George Peppard were up to? And World War I dogfights needed no explanation.

Sasha dropped me off at my hotel, saying she would drive me to the airport the next day which she did. As my flight was called, I didn't know whether to shake her hand or give her a kiss. I gave her a light kiss on the lips and then boarded the plane. As I did, I saw tears in her eyes, even as she tried to remain cheerful. I wondered if I would ever see her again.

21. BEING

My body may have been back in San Francisco for the next couple of weeks but my brain and spirit were still hanging out on that beach in Mexico. I was seriously disoriented and unable to focus on my classes. Luckily, I had no final exams this semester, just a couple of short papers to write. One for Zettl on television aesthetics and the other a production journal summarizing my projects and production activities for the TV production class. Worse, my resolve to dive head first into television-land had dissipated. It seemed so stupid, so futile.

Looking around at the current programming, it was mostly junk except for the *Huntley-Brinkley Report* and a few documentaries. As far as live television drama was concerned, there wasn't any. Just a Playhouse Ninety production now and then that had been recorded and edited on videotape leaving it slick and clean. All sense of spontaneity had been erased. No more flubbed lines or microphone booms in the picture. Yes, at this point, I had an old black and white television set with rabbit years and fuzzy reception to view the current offerings, not that I spent much time doing so. Still, I went about my routine of attending the few classes left in the semester but I was also drawn back into the exploding Haight scene.

***

On Saturday, January 14, Golden Gate Park was the scene of the largest hippy gathering to date in the Haight-Ashbury. On a clear, bright but crisp day, tens of thousands of hippies along with straights and Berkeley politicos gathered at the Polo Grounds in Golden Gate Park for the first Be-In. Traffic was backed up for miles around the park. Police were towing cars left and right and buses could not get through. You had to hike a mile or so to get to the center of the action. I had seen the posters for the gathering, mostly psychedelic screeds proclaiming the gathering of the century which was to feature the beat poet Allan Ginsburg and acid guru, Timothy Leary among others.

By the time I arrived at the Polo Grounds, the Be-In was in full swing. I had missed the opening incantation by Ginsberg but there was plenty more to come. First the crowd. Yes, there was the expected hippy contingent with its far-out but now familiar costumes.

The guys: Indian robes with feather headdresses, Nehru jackets with psychedelic headbands, antique military jackets, decorated vests, stovepipe hats, square colored glasses. Others simply in tie-dye T-shirts and jeans with long flowing hair.

The women: Calico dresses, tiny granny glasses, leather mini-skirts, boots, beads and long dangly earrings. The bolder ones danced topless, covered with body paint or feathers. Others simply lay seductively on blankets caressing their hippy lovers, oblivious of the world around them.

However, a sizable contingent at the Be-In were student types in jeans, khakis, pea coats and Army fatigue jackets. Many were political activists from Berkeley and other area universities, including Jerry Rubin. One of the goals of the Be-In was to unite the acid-heads with the politicos and to move forward together to end the war and achieve a higher consciousness. As the Berkeley Barb put it:

In unity, we shall shower the country with waves of ecstasy and purification. Fear will be washed away. Ignorance will be exposed to sunlight; profits and empire will lie dying on deserted beaches; violence will be submerged and transmuted into rhythm and dancing.

Everywhere the smell of incense, pot and hashish. Soap bubbles and balloons floating around. Bouquets of flowers thrown about along with the ever-present placards with peace symbols and banners demanding the legalization of pot and withdrawal from Vietnam. Cops on horseback hovered in the background doing nothing. Groups of Hells Angles stood around supposedly protecting the stage but they spent most of their time getting high and ogling the topless women. The ever-practical Diggers handed out free turkey sandwiches.

Somehow penetrating the acid rock were sounds of the Hari Krishna chanting on the edge of the crowd in their Saffron robes. Elsewhere the tintinnabulation of cymbals, tambourines, and ankle bells filled the air. Throughout the crowd were jugglers, pied pipers on flutes and hippy magicians and one lone fire-eater.

On stage, short performances by the Mime Troupe, speeches that nobody paid any attention to and intermittent performances by a succession of rock bands—*Jefferson Airplane, Grateful Dead, Moby Grape, Big Brother and the Holding Company* among others. Some too stoned to perform. At one point, the sound system went out. A lull in the music. Timothy Leary, beads around his neck, a flower behind his ear and long gray hair flowing under his headband, ascended to the stage and bellowed out his famous mantra "Turn on, tune in, drop out."

It was a mad, merry circus, getting higher and higher as the afternoon wore on. Word was agents of Owsley were handing out free acid tablets. People kept looking skyward believing a rumor published by the *Oracle* that a flying saucer would land at any moment. Eventually, someone did parachute out of passing Cessna and into a nearby meadow and disappeared. Many people believed that they had seen God.

It all came to a crashing end around 5 p.m. when someone blew on a conch shell and Ginsberg led a closing chant. The crowds drifted off through the now darkened pathways of the Golden Gate Park and out into the Haight where they blocked the main streets. Fifty people were arrested for obstructing traffic. Others followed Ginsberg to Ocean Beach where they watched the last remnants of the sunset, lit bonfires and continued their chants. That night *The Doors* and the *Grateful Dead* played at the Fillmore. The day of the Be-In was over.

22. YVONNE

As exciting as the Be-In was, my mind was elsewhere. I had had an amazing encounter the prior evening which jolted me out of my lethargy. It was like a bolt from the blue. Actually, it was a bolt of orange to be exact. A big, wide brimmed orange hat, a burnt orange coat, open in the front revealing a shapely burnt orange mini-dress, and long, long legs in black high heels. Five-ten at least. Under the hat, flowing dark hair, sparkling blue eyes and a wide, wide smile. She came down her apartment hallway like a runway model, turning at the end, and looking back half askance at Marie, apparently confused over who her blind date was. Me or this pudgy little French professor who was with us in the hallway.

"Yvonne, this is Louis. Louis, Yvonne," said Marie immediately to clear up any confusion.

"How do you do," she said, holding out her gloved hand for a little shake.

"Enchantée," said Louis in his most debonair manner, kissing her on the gloved hand.

Yvonne smiled graciously and then glanced over to me. Marie caught the drift and introduced me to her. "Oh, this is Al."

"So pleased to meet you," she said in a faint European accent, holding out her hand again.

"Come on, let's get going," said Marie impatiently heading down the hallway.

I followed after Yvonne and the professor, wondering where did this babe come from? All I knew was that she was Dutch and a co-worker with Marie at Capwells Department Store. And that she was going on a blind date with Louis. Marie had apparently set the whole thing up. It seemed Louis was an advisor to Gerard in his graduate program. We were all on our way to a birthday party for Dede, a Lebanese friend from Paris who was now studying at Berkeley for a Ph.D. in Electrical Engineering.

We piled into Gerard's old Hudson out front. Yvonne got into the backseat in the center next to Louis. I sat next to her on the other side. Gerard was driving. Marie and her friend Peggy were crammed in the front seat. As we drove over to Dede's place, I managed to get a good look at this Yvonne person. She was making polite conversation with Louis, but now and then glanced over to me.

I studied her features—wide almond shaped eyes, slightly curved but delicate nose. Indian or Jewish? And generous lips with pearly white teeth, and silk smooth cheeks, with a faint Latin cast. Where had this gorgeous, exotic looking creature been?

Where indeed? Even though Marie had known Yvonne for months, she had never once mentioned her although Marie constantly blabbed about everyone else she knew—her former Jewish roommates, her old boyfriends. Indeed, she used to go and on about me and Sasha and telling everyone how we might be serious. After Sasha returned to Mexico, I disabused Marie of that notion. I guess as a consolation prize she had fixed me up with her friend Peggy, a buxom, little L.A. Jew, who was engaged to a Boalt law school student.

I had seen Peggy a couple of times, once at her apartment when she had me over for dinner. And just as we were about to get cozy, her fiancé, Ron, showed up. Ron, also Jewish, seemed nonplussed. He had come over for a book. And left immediately after. As Peggy later explained it, even though they were engaged, the marriage date was uncertain and, they decided to date other people in an open relationship.

As Marie further explained, Ron was going out banging everything in sight and little Peggy was thinking about doing the same. I was to be her first venture. But after that night, I excused myself from the triangle and hadn't seen her since until the night of Dede's party to which she had also been invited.

But back to Yvonne. Sitting there in the car, breathing in her perfume and dwelling on her remarkable good looks, I vowed that I would ask her out at the earliest opportunity. I would, of course, play the perfect gentleman at the party and not bird-dog her from Louis who was obviously in over his head. Further, I sensed Yvonne had absolutely no interest in Louis. Indeed, weeks later, she told me she was shocked that Marie had fixed her up with the likes of Louis. "Not my type at all and also I felt used."

Apparently, I was her type because she later told me when she first set eyes on me in the hallway, she had said to herself, "Hmm, I got to meet this."

I suppose I didn't look too bad in her eyes. I was tall, 6' 3", 200 lbs. with longish dark hair, in good shape from surveying and decked out in my madras sports jacket with a black turtleneck and black slacks.

***

The party was in full swing when we arrived. The little house was jammed with foreign grad students, many French as well as the Euro-American crowd, (i.e. those Americans who thought themselves more European than Yankee.) The music was French folk-pop and American acid rock. The punch strong. Dede was running around playing the ever-active host at his own birthday party and showing off his fiancée, a cute French blonde who was a hairdresser in Marin County.

The chatter was in French and English with Louis showing off his perfect academic French. Yvonne appeared unimpressed. Soon the conversation focused on the latest trends in films. This was home ground for me and I held forth on the New Wave and Ingmar Bergman as well as film noir. Yvonne even joined in, taking an art historian point of view. (She had been an Art History major at Berkeley.)

Meanwhile, Peggy who had been at my side wandered off, probably sensing I had other interests that evening. Then Louis eventually excused himself. I took the opportunity to ask Yvonne to dance. We danced a few fast ones to the Stones and then a slow dance. She melted easily into my arms. Hmm. Louis returned but seeing us dancing entranced, he got the point and started making polite conversation with Peggy.

Yvonne and I stuck together throughout the evening until we got tired of the noise and the heat and went outside to cool off in the crisp January night. It suddenly occurred to me that it was Friday 13. I noted the irony. Far from being bad luck, Friday 13 just might be the jackpot for me.

We walked up and down the block and then, while staring up at the stars through the bare branches of tree, I kissed her gently. Yvonne responded with an electrifying kiss, almost knocking me off my feet. A few minutes later, after the heat of the moment cooled off, I said, "Say, I'm tired of this party. What about you?"

"Me too," she said breathlessly. " Plus, it's late. I have to work tomorrow. Why don't you escort me home?"

I wondered if this was an invitation. We walked back to her apartment on Dwight Avenue. We hesitated at her door, kissing again.

"Shall I come in?" I inquired.

She paused, then smiled. "No, not tonight. But I do want to see you again, Allan. Give me a call."

"Will do. I'll talk to you in a few days."

She unlocked her apartment door and let herself in. I walked down the hallway, my head spinning wondering what had happened.

A few days later, I reached for the phone to call Yvonne for a date but she got to me first with her own phone call.

"Ah, Allan, this is Yvonne. I'm throwing a party this Saturday. A birthday party for one of my girlfriends. Gerard and Marie will be there. Are you interested in coming? You can bring someone."

"Are you kidding? I'll bring you."

"OK. Sure. But, I'll be busy being hostess."

"That's all right. I'll help out."

"See you then."

***

Yvonne had gone all out, decorating her apartment like it was the Fillmore Auditorium with rock posters on the wall, helium-filled balloons floating around, strobe lights flashing, a color wheel casting a kaleidoscope of colors on the walls, a lethal looking, bubbling rum punch, and of course, ear-splitting acid rock. Yvonne was stunning in a silk rainbow dress and her hair done up Asian style with a spike comb through a bun. But she was harried trying to get the party off the ground.

A varied crowd was there including the birthday girl, Vail, another tall leggy one that Yvonne knew from an art history class. Also on hand was her best friend, Kathy, a cute, little Japanese girl who had majored in interior design but was now a go-go girl in San Francisco. Little Kathy danced in a cage in a North Beach bar. She was, in fact, decked out in her go-go costume for the party, also tearing around making sure everybody's cup was full. Gerard and Marie arrived late and left early. I suspected they were just making an appearance to be polite. Gerard had told me earlier that Marie was still honked that Yvonne had ditched her blind date at Dede's party. Other grad school types shuffled in and out, mostly architecture and art students.

All in all, it was a good party but I hardly had any time to hang out with Yvonne. We danced a few times and at one point, I cornered her in the kitchen, making out a little but her mind wasn't on it. She was still distracted playing hostess. Finally, I made a date to see her the following Saturday. We would wander around San Francisco and do whatever, but most importantly, get to know each other.

***

On the appointed day, I met her at the San Francisco Muni terminal. She looked classy in a tailored, tan wool coat with matching hat, doeskin gloves and a stylish silk scarf casually looped around her neck. Again that big beaming smile and sparkling blue eyes, fresh, rosy-cheeked complexion. I felt like a grunge in my now well-worn Madras jacket, black stovepipe slacks, mod boots, but I was wearing a tie and a fresh white shirt. After all, downtown San Francisco was still a dress up city and I wanted to be presentable for Yvonne. But I realized that I needed to upgrade my wardrobe if I was going to keep seeing this lady.

After a kiss on the cheek and a hug, we made our way up Market Street to Powell where we hopped on a cable car for a scenic ride up Nob Hill and Russian Hill. Then it was down one of the steepest streets in San Francisco, Hyde Street where the view of the Bay Area on this clear day was spectacular. So clear, you could reach out and touch Alcatraz or even Angel Island across the Bay. I loved these San Francisco winter days. Brisk in the morning but often warming up to the 60s in the afternoon, and the fog banks well off the coast.

The cable car was so crowded we had to stand and hang from the straps to keep our balance. Yvonne didn't say much. She just smiled, beaming, looking around, as if this was her first ride on a cable car. I knew it probably wasn't but it was exhilarating plus the racket of the cable car, the grinding of the cables and brakes and the dinging of the bell, made it difficult to communicate. The pressure of her body against mine as we made the descent and rounded the turns was enough communication for me.

Down we went on Hyde Street, hanging on tight to the straps because of the incline until we came to the roundabout, the end of the line on Beach Street at Aquatic Park. We jumped off and walked around the waterfront park. A lone seal sunned on the breakwater while two humans swam off the little beach in the frigid waters. Brrrr.

Next, we checked out the nearby Maritime Museum, an Art Deco, nautical looking building that housed artifacts and ship models of the rich maritime history of San Francisco. Inside we examined the clipper ship regalia—wheels, ropes, capstans, charts, compasses, nude lady mastheads, and old photos. These were the clipper ships that had rounded the cape or circled the globe from Europe, Latin America, Asia and Australia bringing fortune seekers to California. On a more mundane level, there were photos, models and other bric-a-brac from the schooners that used to ply the west coast hauling redwood lumber for the construction of San Francisco.

"A city founded on dreams and quick buck artists," I observed.

"Oh, I know," replied Yvonne. "I used to hear about the glories of San Francisco as a little girl in Holland. It was the California dream that eventually brought my family to California."

"Holland to California? That's quite a leap."

"Not really, my dad's side of the family is originally from South America, Surinam to be exact."

"Where's Surinam?"

"Well, it's better known as Dutch Guiana."

"Oh yeah," I nodded. "I once did a 6th-grade project on the Guianas. Dutch Guiana, French Guiana and British Guiana, all crammed together into the far northeast corner of South America. Tell me more."

"Well, it's a long, confused story," she sighed. "I'll tell you but not now. Later when we have some time. Right now I just want to enjoy the museum."

Needless to say, I was burning about to know more about Yvonne's origins. She sure didn't look typically Dutch. I had known Dutch girls during my junior-year-aboard in France. And while not all were blonde, even the brunettes had that Nordic, pale skin look. Not Yvonne. She could pass for a high-grade Latin girl. I wanted to learn more right then but I contained myself.

After the museum, we wandered around Ghirardelli Square across the street. This was an old chocolate factory that had been gutted, remolded and filled with little shops all aimed at bilking the tourists. Next, we hiked over a few blocks to Fisherman's Warf and watched the live crabs boil to death in their respective pots. Yvonne cringed as the creatures emitted what sounded like a hissing scream in the boiling water. But after a few minutes of walking around Pier 39, we got fed up with the intense tourist scene and walked back to the Buena Vista Cafe for lunch.

I had rarely been to this cafe/restaurant during the daylight hours. My visits had usually been in the wee hours of the morning after a pub-crawl in the city during my fraternity days. It was at the Buena Vista Cafe where we party boys ingested cup after cup of the house specialty, Irish coffee, supposedly to wake us up but which got us even more plowed than ever.

Still, even in the daylight, it was a popular place, with the bar full of tourists and locals downing the Irish coffee. We lucked out and were seated on the restaurant side of the establishment where we had a view of the waterfront. We both had an Irish coffee to start things off and then we ordered the local hamburger specialty of the house.

As we waited, I probed Yvonne for the rest of her family story, "You mentioned Surinam. How did your family get from Surinam to Holland to the U.S.?"

She took a deep breath, as if not certain how to begin. Finally, after another sip of Irish coffee, she launched into her tale:

"The Schuster family has been in Surinam since the Dutch took it over in the 17th-century."

"Really?"

"Yes. It all started with the Dutch swapping Manhattan Island with the British for territory in South America that came to be known as Surinam. This swap was part of a settlement following the Second Dutch-Anglo War in 1667."

"Wow, you sure know your history," I said amazed. "I didn't know that the Dutch had fought the British."

"They beat it into you in the Dutch schools," she smiled. "Glory of Holland and all of that. Anyway, at the time, the Dutch were convinced there was more money in slave sugar plantations than in commerce in Manhattan so they were happy with the swap. Only later did they realize the British had gotten the best of the bargain."

"Those crafty Brits," I smirked. "Please continue."

"Yes, as I said, the Schusters were among the first colonial administrators and plantation owners in Surinam in the 17th century. There's a family bible that documents all of that. The family has been a fixture down there ever since and was quite wealthy for a while."

"For a while?"

"Yes, my great-grandfather invested heavily in the Trans-Siberian Railway in Russia. That was in the 1910s. You know what happened in 1917."

"Yes, the Bolshevik Revolution."

"Of course. Well, the railroad was taken over by the Bolsheviks with no compensation to the shareholders. That bankrupted great-grandfather. And then there was the banana rot in the twenties. All our plantations went broke and the United Fruit Company took over. Still, the Schusters remained quite prominent in Surinam. My dad's brother was once the Economic Minister of

Surinam. Now he's a diplomat in Holland representing Surinam's interest."

"OK. So how did the Schusters get from Surinam to Holland?"

"It was simple enough. The Surinamese can come and go to Holland as they please. Many emigrate there for work. Papa was a ship's engineer. He sailed the world in the 1930s, finally winding up in Holland just before the war. It was there he met my mother, a beautiful blue-eyed blonde. Blondes are rare in Surinam. That might have been the basis for the attraction."

"Makes sense. Opposites do attract."

In fact, I might as well tell you, my father is of mixed blood. His father, Gustav Schuster was white. His mother was a black woman with Amerindian blood. In Holland, Papa was considered a mulatto but the Dutch are very tolerant, unlike the South in the U.S. where we once lived."

"You lived in the South?"

"Yes, in the late fifties just before all the civil rights turmoil. We lived in Baton Rouge."

"So how come your family came to the U.S.?"

"Well, after the war Papa had his own engineering business in nearby Belgium doing insulation for oil refineries. He worked with the Americans. But something happened and the company went broke, so Papa decided to immigrate to America in hopes of finding work in the oil industry where he had contacts."

"That must have been quite a change for you."

"Oh, yes. America was a cultural shock after tidy little Holland. We had a nice home in Rotterdam and lived very well. I was only thirteen, my sister Jeanette nine and baby Ingrid eleven months when we flew to New York."

"Where did you live when you first arrived?"

"Well, we were lucky. Our family had been sponsored by the Dutch Reformed Church in Bronxville, a wealthy New York suburb. We lived with an old established family there, the Clifford's in their big mansion. I went to school with all the rich kids. They even had their own school psychiatrist. These kids had everything. I felt out of place. I was considered exotic, although I did better than most of them in language. I could spell better in English than they could, plus I knew German and some French. Still, our stay in Bronxville didn't last long. Papa found the job in Baton Rouge with Kellogg, an engineering firm that specialized in refinery construction and we moved down there."

"That must have been a different world after New York."

"Oh, yes. It was the Old South. It was beautiful, very tropical. The blacks worked in the cotton fields singing their old songs. My dad loved it because it reminded him of Surinam. Then there was New Orleans. We thought it was fascinating."

"Still, it was tough on my mother living in the south with all the heat and the bugs. Then she got a bad case of poison ivy. All of this on top of caring for little Ingrid. But Jeanette and I loved it. We used to dress up in southern belle dresses and spend weekends at an old plantation mansion, learning how to be a gracious southern ladies."

"You must have been an eye-stopping southern belle."

"Well, maybe. However, after a year, the refinery job came to an end and Kellogg didn't have any more work for Papa in Baton Rouge and he was transferred back to New York where we again lived with the Cliffords. Meanwhile, my mother was homesick. She decided to return to Holland with Ingrid, Jeanette and me for while. So we sailed back to Holland. Papa was crying at the dock as he waved us goodbye."

"So your family was separated?"

"Yes, for a year. I re-enrolled in school in Rotterdam but I found myself way behind because American schools were so easy. I especially had trouble with Algebra and Geometry.

Finally, my mother got fed up with Holland and missed Papa, so she decided to return to America. He met us at the boat. Boy, was he happy to see us. But he had bad news. He had just been laid off from Kellogg. But being a very upbeat person, he decided to strike out for California. We crammed into an old station wagon he had bought and drove across the United States to Los Angeles where he had been told there were plenty of jobs in his field."

"That must have been exciting, seeing America like that."

"It was. We took our time and saw the sights along the way. All the red rock country in New Mexico and Arizona. The Indians in Gallup. The Grand Canyon, Phoenix, Las Vegas, Death Valley and finally L.A."

"What did you think of L.A.?"

"I didn't know what to think. I was confused. There didn't seem to be any center to it. It was all freeways and suburban towns with shopping malls. I know my mother hated it. She didn't drive. She was stuck in the little town where we lived, Ontario. Jeanette and I went to the local schools and made friends, although there were a lot of Mexicans and the Mexican girls used to get into vicious fights."

"Did your father find work?"

"Yes and no. He would work for a few weeks here and there and then be laid off. It was all very haphazard. Because he looked different and had a funny accent, he had a hard time keeping a job. I guess they thought he was black. There was a lot of racism in L.A. So we were broke much of the time. Luckily, Papa was a member of the Moravian Church and he had a network of support there. The church rented us a little house dirt-cheap and would deliver free groceries. Papa could have gone on welfare but he was too proud. About all he would do is collect unemployment."

"How did your mother feel about all of this?"

"She hated it. She hated the car culture there. She hated the house. She hated the fact that Papa could not find steady work and threatened to go back to Holland. This went on for several years. I graduated from high school in Ontario and was eager to go to college. I had gotten into UCLA on a scholarship but they still couldn't afford to send me. So I attended a local community college, Chaffey College, which looking back on, was a great experience."

"How so?"

"Well, I had great teachers and small classes. And it was a very pleasant school at the foot of Mount Baldy. I learned a lot, especially about art history and literature. One of my teachers was a Mr. Malone, a handsome British man and an outdoorsman. He skied and sailed. He was also a great English teacher. We read all the great novels of the 20th century, in particular Hemingway and Fitzgerald. All us girls had a crush on him. We would sit in the front row and make goo-goo eyes had him.

"So then you came to Berkeley?"

"Ah no. My mother finally decided to return to Holland for good and begged Papa to do the same since he was going nowhere in L.A. She delivered an ultimatum to him."

At this point, Yvonne was starting to tear up.

"So what happen?"

"Papa, being a proud and stubborn man, said he was staying. It broke my mother's heart but she was determined to leave and so she did, dragging us kids back to Holland. Once again, Papa saw us off at the dock in New York, saying he might return to Holland in a few months if no steady job turned up. But I sensed he was just saying that. He was determined to stay in America no matter what. The last thing he wanted was to live in Holland and admit defeat."

"So what happened after that?"

"Well, to make a long story short, when we returned to Holland, my mother managed to find an apartment. In, addition we had financial support from Papa. So we were doing OK. Of course, I missed him terribly but I was also busy with school. I had enrolled at the University of Leiden in Art History. That's the Harvard of Holland. I did very well, passing my first-year exams but I needed a reading knowledge of Latin and Greek in order to graduate from Leiden. So it would have taken me another four years to graduate even with my two years of community college. I didn't know what to do until Papa came to the rescue."

"How's that?"

"By that time, he was living in Berkeley. He managed to enroll me in Cal at the last minute in the late summer of 1963 based on my Chaffey College transcript. He phoned me telling me what he had done. I had only a day to make up my mind. I decided yes. After that, it was all a blur, arranging the flight and so on. The charter flight was from Paris in a few days, so I traveled to Paris by train, stayed at a home for unwed mothers because it was cheap, saw a little of the city and then flew to San Francisco."

"I still had a couple of weeks before classes started but Papa was renting a room at the Berkeley YMCA, so I had no place to stay until he found an apartment. So I stayed at a dorm at San Francisco State along with a contingent of Peace Corps volunteers. They were fun but I was miserable between jet lag and a bad case of stomach problems. Finally, I got over it and moved into Papa's new apartment on University Avenue. And that's basically my story. I lived with him for two years until I graduated from Berkeley in Art History and then I got a job with Capwell's last year and moved into my own apartment. Voilà, and here I am."

"Wow, that's quite a saga. You ought to write a book about it. Buddenbrooks on the run."

"I suppose, but it's painful. Let's eat," she said as she dove into our freshly served hamburgers, devouring it in just a few seconds, but in a very European lady like manner cutting it up with a knife and a fork.

I had a million more questions but they could wait. San Francisco was still beckoning as the hours ticked off. I asked her if she would like to see the Haight. She said she had never been and was dying to see it. We took the cable car back over Russian Hill and down to Market Street where we hopped on the N Judah and rode it out to Carl Street. We stopped briefly at my apartment where Yvonne checked it out, probably noticing some of Sasha's clothes still hanging in the closet.

"It's very nice," she said diplomatically but much later told me she had really been appalled at squalor, the dirt, the dust balls floating around and the dirty dishes in the sink, to say nothing of Sasha's clothes. While she was being polite, I sensed she was nervous, probably expecting me to make a play, which I did. But after a few minutes of making out, she pulled away saying, "I thought you were going to show me the Haight."

"Oh, yeah, right you are," I replied. "Plenty of time later for relaxing here."

No comment.

We hit the street and I took her on the standard tour. I pointed out the Diggers Free Store across the street. We hiked north on Cole until we came to Haight Street with its array of hip shops. We stopped for a coffee the Victorian Drogstore, browsed in some shops and then hoofed it down traffic-choked Haight to Hippy Hill in Golden Gate Park where we encountered the usual Saturday gathering of characters, many stoned on pot and acid, all swaying to the strains of a flute and an Indian raga guitar player. Yvonne was impressed, saying she wanted to join in the dance but felt out of place all dressed up. "I guess, I'm just too square."

"I know what you mean. I live here and I feel out of it myself. This crowd is too young or maybe too far-out for me."

"Well, I love it. Next time I'm going to dress down and join in."

I suddenly realized that Yvonne and I were almost of different generations even though I was only four years older than she. I was a product of the fifties and she the sixties, albeit, with European overtones. But after further discussion and another look around the Haight and noting the disheveled hippies living on the street, stoned and begging, she did admit, that she could never live like that. "I guess, I'm too Dutch. I like everything nice and clean. Why can't you get high and still be clean?"

"Why not, indeed...Say, I know a couple near here who have a nice clean pad. Let's go see them. It'll expose you to another side of the Haight."

Of course, I was talking about the Daltons, John my old actor friend and his wife Marge the set designer. We walked over to their apartment on Frederick Street and rang the bell. Both were surprised to see us, especially Marge. The last time I was here, they had assumed that Sasha and I were an item. I had not filled them in on the latest. John was especially thunderstruck by Yvonne. He could hardly keep his eyes off her as she held out her hand for a shake in the European fashion.

"Yvonne? That's French isn't it? He said, gallantly kissing her hand.

"Yes, it is, but I'm Dutch. My father liked French names."

Soon we were sitting on their psychedelic patterned couch and Marge was serving us herbal tea in an elegant tea set. (Marge was of English background.) She gazed at Yvonne too with an understanding little smile. Their toddler daughter, Jeannie, waddled over and sat in Yvonne's lap, making herself right at home.

"So how did you two meet?" asked John.

We filled him in on the big encounter.

"Oh, I see."

But John didn't see. Yvonne was like someone from another planet to him. He was used to the hippy Bay Area chicks who never wore makeup, let their hair grow waist long and most likely didn't shave under their arms. Later he told me, he thought Yvonne was stunning but wondered if she wasn't a luxury item. "She looks like she expects the best, Al. Are ready for that? *Mucho dinero.*"

I countered that she wasn't a spoiled rich girl. She worked at Capwells and got a huge discount on her clothes which ate up most of her paycheck. John still didn't see it. But down the road, Marge gave us her blessing. "You two look like brother and sister. Two peas and in a pod."

After a couple of hours of visiting which included an early spaghetti dinner, we returned to my apartment where I put on some music and we sipped on some Chablis that I had. I suggested that Yvonne stay the night. That I would escort her home on the morrow. But she demurred. "Ah, I have to go by Papa's tomorrow morning and clean up his apartment. Allan, I think it would be better to go home tonight."

I didn't push it because I realized this was to be no short-term relationship. We had time. Actually, all the time in the world. Yvonne had told me she had had a couple of boyfriends but no one serious, even though one wanted to marry her. Before she met me, she had been on what she called her butterfly phase. Going out, flirting, partying and in general having a good time.

But now she wanted to see me on a regular basis. Get to know me better. I played the role of a gentleman and escorted her to the Muni Terminal for her bus ride back to Berkeley.

***

Over the next two months, our courtship proceeded at a stately, bourgeois pace. I no longer saw any other women despite constant bugging by Lucy to come over to her place and smoke some pot. I upgraded my wardrobe with a new tweed sport jacket and two pairs of slacks, cut my hair shorter, wore a tie more often even going to classes. Yvonne and I would see each other on the weekends, hanging out in San Francisco, going out to a movie, a party, or just wandering around Golden Gate Park. Other times we would be in Berkeley and browsing in the bookstores, sometimes visiting Jean-Paul and Gerard and Marie. All very civilized, all very proper until one night we listened to the new Stones Album which featured "Let's Spend the Night Together" at Gerard's. After listening to the song on earphones on Gerard's state-of-the-art stereo and having a bit of pot, Yvonne invited me to stay the night at her apartment on Dwight.

The following days and weeks were a blur. Yvonne would stay at my apartment on the weekends. (This was after she had cleaned up my apartment making sure it was spic and span and after I had thrown out Sasha's clothes.) I would spend a weeknight or two in Berkeley at her apartment and then take the Muni back to San Francisco and my classes at San Francisco State. We were both spending a lot of time on the Muni, because my Mercury station wagon had long ago crapped out. Of course, we were also spending a lot of time in bed. In fact, Marie was annoyed that we hardly ever got out of bed on the weekends and she cast irritated glances at Gerard, perhaps wondering if she was missing out.

All appeared to be going well. Where it was headed, I didn't know. Yvonne had said many times that she never wanted to get tied down. Never marry, just have a boyfriend, like me. I, on the other hand, thought a more permanent arrangement might be in the offing, but I said nothing. I just went with the flow.

23. DIRECTOR

In the midst of my courtship with Yvonne in the spring of 1967, I became re-energized at San Francisco State. Thanks to my unemployment checks, I was going full-time taking courses in educational broadcasting, radio production, TV directing, and master's thesis research as well as studying for my orals. I was hoping that I could get out of SF State by the end of the spring semester.

The dullest course was educational broadcasting. I was taking it because plans were afoot that a Corporation of Public Broadcasting was being established and it was rumored that the local educational station, KQED-TV, would be doing a lot more documentaries, an area that I wanted to work in. The Carnegie Report had just come out extolling the glories of a publicly funded network for high-level television programming. No commercials, none of that idiotic, lowest common denominator programming, just pure informative television exploring the issues of the day. In addition, the course was taught by the program director of KQED, a Dr. Smith. I figured he would be a good person to know when I started job hunting.

In the course, Dr. Smith outlined the history of educational broadcasting in the U.S. He explained the Broadcast Communications Act of 1934 that declared the airwaves belonged to the public. Dr. Smith insisted that education and public broadcasting were a logical outgrowth of that landmark act.

KQED-TV had been around since 1954. I remembered it from those days, sometimes watching it at a neighbor's house with its stupid puppet shows and dull teachers standing at blackboards. My kid brother Kenny hated it. He was into *The Mickey Mouse Club* and *Captain Kangaroo* on the commercial stations. But the mothers in the neighborhood had decided that KQED would be good for little kids, because after all, it was "educational." Of course, my father solved the debate smartly by refusing to have a television until 1958. As he used to say, "Read a book kids, listen to the radio. That TV stuff will rot your brain."

But now KQED was on the verge of expansion and proving more interesting. At one point, we toured the station which was housed in a dumpy commercial building south of Market Street. It struck me as a rabbit warren of a place, a rather sleepy operation with old equipment. The stuff we had at SF State was more state-of-the-art. Plus the pace of the place was a crawl. Nothing like the frantic, helter-skelter I remembered from my days KGO-TV when I was helping produce shows for the Sixth Army Headquarters. We watched as a KQED director methodically taped an education show about building blocks for toddlers. The hostesses with a toddler demonstrated the many and varied ways, a child could build different things. Yawn. Still, KQED-TV represented an entrée into the television world.

***

My three-hour night class in radio production was much more exciting. True it was only radio but radio was the broadcast medium that I had grown up with in the 40s and 50s. I used to spend hours listening to *Jack Armstrong*, *The Lone Ranger*, and later, *Gunsmoke* with the deep booming voice of William Conrad. Then there was *Dimension X*, a far-out science fiction drama that featured stories of traveling to other planets, even other stars. I also listened to a couple of local programs that played the top hit songs of the day, programs such as the *Burgie Music Box* and *Lucky Lager Dance Time*.

Radio was intimate. It sparked my imagination. The pictures in my mind were much more interesting than what I saw on TV. I could dimly remember the dramatic voice of Edward R. Murrow on CBS radio during the last days of World War Two. And we often listened to the newscasts of Lowell Thomas and H.V. Kaltenborn. Or Walter Winchell with his "Good evening Mr. and Mrs. America and all the ships at sea." You could just see the radio waves going out over the ocean being intercepted by the ocean liners, the Queen Elizabeth or the Queen Mary.

Our teacher, Dr. Marks, was a fervent proponent of radio. He would stand before the class with an array of radios on a table in front of him dating from a 1920s wireless set through the 30s and 40s, right up to the tinny transistor radios of the 1960s and pontificate on the impact of radio.

"This is it ladies and gentlemen," he said pacing behind the table. "Radio was the true revolution in mass communication. Television is a late comer, still regarded by many as radio with pictures. We will have to see where it goes to reach its full potential. In this course you will learn the basics of simple radio production, how to operate the board, how to voice, and how to work with audio tape and how to produce the typical radio shows—news, talk, sports, drama and documentary. All of these skills are still in demand in the industry with the possible exception of my favorites, radio documentary and drama."

At one point, Dr. Marks illustrated the impact of radio and its power to drive the imagination by playing a recording of Orson Welles' *War of the Worlds*. A program that in 1938 sent people out into the streets, panicked and believing that the earth had been invaded by creatures from Mars.

Some of the kids in the class snickered. As far as this 1960s generation was concerned, radio was yesterday. They were only here because it was considered easier to get into radio as an on-air personality than into television. The goal of most of the guys was to become a radio disc jockey, maybe a sports announcer, and all wanted to get their hands on the board. I saw it as an opportunity to do a radio documentary or maybe even a short drama.

I took the class seriously and spent hours in the studio learning the board with its myriad of dials, learning how to cue records and tapes to integrate into broadcasts and even tried to develop a broadcast voice. These were operations I had seen up close and had some practice in from my time at the broadcast center in the Army. Once again, driving home the point that the Army wasn't a total waste of time.

We had to do various class projects including concocting a little news show with a theme opening and close, doing a short play-by-play of a baseball segment, and a disc jockey show where we alternated chit-chat with spinning records. And finally, we had to do a major project, a half-hour show of some sort. It could be a drama with various actors gathered around a mike reading a script with sound effects. It could also be a variety show, an interview show or a documentary.

I chose to do a radio documentary but when I got into it, I realized would involve a lot of production. At this point, Lin, a little Chinese fellow in the class who wanted desperately to be a radio engineer came up to me and offered to take care of the production end of things if I produced, wrote and voiced the show. That sounded like a fair division of labor, so I said yes. We wanted the show to be current, fresh, and explore some on-going problem in San Francisco. We also wanted it to have a sense of actuality, a sense of being on the street. We settled on the explosion of prostitution in the city.

"That's a pretty big bite, gentlemen," said Dr. Marks when we presented our proposal. "It will take a lot of work but go to it."

I did the initial research consulting the newspapers, public health reports and police reports. Further, I lined up those in the know including a vice cop, a social worker and Roger Grimsby, a local TV news anchor who had recently aired his own series on San Francisco prostitution. Also, I knew from my days of living in the Tenderloin where most of the prostitutes hung out.

I wrote a script outline to guide us on our audio journey which included a brief history of prostitution in the city beginning with the gold rush days and the notorious Barbary Coast. Then, with Lin lugging a Nagra sound recorder, we began the legwork. Our first stop was KGO-TV and an interview with Grimsby. I was surprised that he was so accessible. He had readily agreed to be interviewed when I had phoned him. He greeted us with a hearty handshake in the newsroom. He was a big, bluff guy with every hair perfectly in place, looking as if he was ready to go on the air at any moment. Also, he was quite a newsman who had once worked for the network. He had just returned from Vietnam where he had done a series on local G.I.s serving over there. Or as one of his co-workers sneered through the door, "Don't let him fool you, guys. Grimsby was really doing research on the whore houses of Saigon."

I began the interview by asking Grimsby to give an overall picture of prostitution in the city. He grabbed the mike and launched into a monolog, essentially saying San Francisco had a long tradition of prostitution since its founding. "Where do you think the Native Son comes from? He's the offspring of a gold miner and a whore." Further, he explained that since San Francisco was not only a port town but also a convention and tourist town, it was a natural habitat for call girls and ladies of the night.

Then he added, "By the way, our large homosexual population has its own demands for handsome young men, male hustlers if you like. Then there's the transvestite population, men who dress like women and indeed undergo operations to make themselves like women. Some Johns go for that. In summary, there's a rich array from which to choose."

After another few minutes of interview, I figured we had enough. We thanked Grimsby for his insights, gathered up our equipment and began to leave.

"By the way boys. Send me a copy of the show," said Grimsby from his office doorway. "I would like to hear it. Also, just a tip, keep a copy for yourselves. It could serve as an audition tape for entry into the broadcasting business."

"Will do."

***

Next, we interviewed a vice officer at the San Francisco Police Department. He went through the cop litany of why prostitution was bad for the city, i.e. crime, drugs and pimps but admitted that it could never be wiped out and that maybe, just maybe it should be legalized and controlled like it was in Europe. An enlightened cop.

Then came the woman social worker whose take was the women prostitutes were sorry creatures, trapped in undesirable circumstance, exploited and brutalized by their pimps. And of course, spreaders of venereal disease, even though the city had made efforts to control it with free clinic checkups. She too thought the trade should be legalized and foresaw a day when the ladies of the evening would be treated like regular workers, albeit in the sex trade with full employee benefits, health care and pensions.

A bit pie in the sky, I thought.

Finally, we hit the nighttime streets of the Tenderloin and approached several prostitutes hanging around Ellis and Hyde. They were all made up with heavy eye shadow, low cut blouses, often in hot pants with high go-go boots and bouffant hair. I was struck by how young some of them seemed, in their late teens or early twenties. Here and there, I observed some of the old pros, leaning up against parked Cadillacs or Lincolns with tinted windows. The few cops we saw seemed oblivious to what was going on. I guess they were tired of busting the girls and let them ply their trade within a certain geographic boundary.

Lin and I tried to strike up a conversation with some of the girls, but when they saw we weren't interested in making it with them, they turned away, even after we offered them money for an interview. After an hour in the Tenderloin, Lin and I were becoming discouraged until one outlandish floozy in heavy make-up came up and offered to talk, for a small price.

As we sat in a booth in a nearby coffee shop, "Ricky" as she called herself, opened up about her life as a whore. "I admire what you boys are doing. It's about time somebody did a documentary on how life as a prostitute really is, in all its aspects."

As she talked, her voice became lower and more gravelly. I began to sense that this "she" was really a "he." This was one of the transvestites that Grimsby had mentioned. I thought weird. She had fooled us but I noted that her/his life was not much different from the life of a regular "she" prostitute. But I did have one burning question. What happened when her customers discovered she was a "he"?

"Oh by the time they get to that stage, most don't care," Rickey replied nonchalantly. "Others never make the discovery. We have our little secrets to fool them. And when all is said and done, as the French say, *"Un trou est un trou."* (A hole is a hole.)

Then Lin chimed in, "But you have breasts, and very smooth skin and I couldn't help noticing shapely woman legs."

I was thinking Lin sounded hot for her/him.

"Oh yes, we work hard at that, taking hormones and such, maybe a little surgery, nothing extreme. We still keep our manly equipment."

"Oh," said Lin, embarrassed but still checking his recorder, making sure we got all of this down.

As for myself, I was thinking, as interesting as this was, we needed some straight whores to talk to so I asked Ricky to smooth the way for us. We paid her an extra twenty and she went out into the street and one by one, brought back a female prostitute who was willing to talk for a price. So after a few more hours and four or five interviews, we had our ladies on tape telling us about their life on the streets. And I was about a hundred dollars poorer. But we had our documentary. Now all we had to do was edit it into a half-hour program, no small job.

The next night, Lin came over to my apartment with the Nagra and we listened to the hours of tape interviews, taking notes on sound portions that we could use in the documentary. I then buried myself for the weekend, taking the phone off the hook and not even seeing Yvonne, to write a half-hour radio script. I started with a few brief raunchy and shocking sound bites of present day prostitutes and then backed into a brief history of San Francisco itself and, as noted, it's propensity for ladies of the evening. Here and there I used sound bites from Grimsby, then segued into the modern scene with its problems and tribulations as explained by the vice cop and the social worker. Finally, I led into the interviews with the women, finishing with the transvestite and a summary of where it all might be headed with another sound bite from the social worker on the legalization of prostitution. Along the way, I indicated where music and natural sound might be appropriate and gave the script to Lin so he could cut the audio bites, and collect the music.

A few days later after Lin dubbed off the sound portions onto various audio carts, we reserved the radio studio late one night, and put the show together. This involved Lin at the board cueing the sound carts and blending the music, while I read the script in my best broadcast voice. It was all recorded onto a master tape. It took us all night to finish the thing, but it came out better than expected. The music was perfect, ranging from old style honky-tonk to the latest acid rock. Lin was particularly proud of the production elements which he had blended expertly. He felt it was a network quality production. I didn't disagree.

When we played it for the class and Dr. Marks, they broke out in applause.'

"First class production, gentlemen. There might be a future for you two yet in broadcasting yet."

***

As stimulating as radio was, I had not forgotten about television. My TV directing class was an extension of the TV production class that I had taken the previous semester and it was taught by Dr. Zettl who was constantly urging us to push the envelope.

We were encouraged, even required to produce and direct a musical show and a short dramatic piece, preferably with experimental overtones. Of course, we also had to produce and direct the more mundane interview and news shows. After dispatching those little chores successfully, I decided to do a dance/music show starring none other than Yvonne.

Yvonne had taken modern dance at Berkeley as an elective and from what I had seen, she had an interesting, willowy, undulating style. In addition, she was exotic and beautiful to look at. I thought Ravel's *Bolero*, shortened to ten minutes or so, in a surreal landscape with chroma key effects over her would make an effective little show. It took a little while to convince her to perform. She was worried if her dancing skills were up to par. I assured her that they were. Further, based on some professional stills of her, I pointed out that she photographed great.

"I know," she said. "I've been told that by Powers."

"Powers?"

"Yes, John Robert Powers, the modeling agency. People told me for years that I should try modeling. So one day right after graduation, I went down to Powers in Oakland to find out. They told me they were interested and urged me to get a photographic portfolio which I did. It cost my poor dad a hundred dollars but the results were good."

"Well, did you ever pursue it?"

"No, I needed an immediate income. My father was going broke supporting me. Modeling was too hit-and-miss. That's why I took the job at Capwells as a management trainee. I thought maybe I could do modeling on the side."

"Well, with a dance tape, maybe you could launch a whole new career," I replied cheerily.

"I doubt it, but I'll do it for you. It should be fun."

And yes, it was fun. And after a rehearsal, it was easy. With the *Bolero* music building, I juggled the three camera set up, dissolving and chroma keying to the beat, sometimes focusing close up on Yvonne's concentrated expression, other times watching her in a long shot, as she danced on a small platform in the barren studio with a large mock-up of a melted watch à la Salvador Dali in the background. The music went on and on. I was worried that Yvonne might tire but she hung in there, finding new and different ways to move. At the final climax of the Bolero, Yvonne crumpled gracefully to the platform and the music ended.

The show had been videotaped and we watched the playback with Zettl. Yvonne was pleased with how she had performed and Zettl congratulated me on my direction and effective use of various visual effects including the chroma-key.

Another successful video outing.

***

The final and most challenging project of the course was directing a live dramatic production. I enlisted Jean-Paul who was writing short plays and short stories at the time in addition to his graduate student duties in comparative literature. After I explained the project and how I wanted it to be experimental, he was eager to do it, to see how a symbolic play could be adapted to television, although in general, he disdained commercial television.

Jean-Paul set to work concocting a dramatic piece entitled "The Death of Johann August Sutter." Sutter, of course, was the early California settler who founded Sacramento and upon whose land gold was discovered in 1848. However, Jean-Paul framed the play as kind of an abstract *Waiting for Godot* set in the West. The major characters were Sutter himself, resplendent in his Swiss

Guard uniform, his servant, Kanaka, a hulking Melanesian slave escaped from Hawaii, and a San Francisco prostitute, perhaps the mother of California's Native Sons. The abstract nature of the play was augmented with primitive Oceanic masks that were worn throughout. The plot was as follows:

The trio is on a journey to the shores of the Pacific, seeking riches beyond the far horizon. As they walk along, they complain how long and tiring the journey is, and how the masks make them itch. At one point the prostitute says, "I know neither of you."

Sutter responds, "You slept with us both many times. Don't you remember?"

Obviously, there is a triangle going on here. It later turns out that the prostitute is Sutter's wife. As they journey along, Sutter and the Kanaka engage in dialogue on master/slave relationships, or as Sutter puts "I've chosen you among the thousands of slaves, raised you from dirt to decency."

Kanaka responds enigmatically, "Perhaps that path which I have forgotten, went against the one we walk upon."

Later, the whore/wife complains that she was in effect seduced (perhaps raped) by Kanaka. "He crept into me, Johan, when we were making love," she says.

Now the masks that Sutter and the whore/wife are wearing are burning on their faces as well as itching. Yet Kanaka says his mask is comfortable and roomy enough for all three. Sutter says to his whore/wife they should tear off Kanaka's mask. After accusing Kanaka of murder, rape and plunder, both jump on Kanaka and stab him to death. The play ends as Sutter and the whore/wife turn towards the camera now both wearing the mask of Kanaka.

How all of this was going to translate into a little television drama, I wasn't quite sure. It would no doubt be a static, abstract play against a black backdrop, but it did offer some opportunities for visualization including the use of masks and various totems. My actor friend John Dalton agreed to play Kanaka and do it in black face. At first, I asked Jean-Paul to play Sutter. The thought of Jean-Paul with his little goatee strutting around, getting hysterical amused me. But he would have none of it. So I enlisted Herman, the actor friend of John to play Sutter. I also enlisted my old standby Megan, the drama student, for the prostitute. John's wife Marge agreed to make the paper-maché, masks.

We held a couple of rehearsals where I blocked it out and where Jean-Paul tried to explain the intricacies of the play to John, Herman and Megan. John scratched his head trying to interpret the deeper symbolic meanings of the play. Megan simply played it as written, and in her acting, harkened back to the exaggerated gestures of silent film. Herman hammed it up appropriately as Sutter. He was, after all, an aspiring Shakespearean actor. But I couldn't concentrate on the quality of acting and its interpretation because I was so busy with the abstract set design and the blocking of actors. I left the dramatics to the actors themselves. In fact, I was becoming overwhelmed at the whole process itself. I couldn't imagine how the live dramatic TV directors of the 1950s could put together such complex productions and get it on the air live with relatively few flaws.

Finally, the big day came in late April. My live dramatic TV production. All the cast was assembled and in costumes. Sutter with his regal uniform. Shapely Megan in a skimpy shift, looking like she just got up. Lean, muscular John, bare chest in his overalls. The paper-maché masks and artifacts at the ready. The music: John Cage interspersed with old-timey songs from the Gay Nineties era.

The class was my primary audience, but Yvonne and Marge were on hand as well. Jean-Paul was unable to make it, because he had some big graduate project he was working on at Cal. I thought that maybe he was just sick of the play, seeing its faults and its interpretation by the actors.

Countdown.

"Roll tape. 5-4-3-2-1. Take tape, cue music, up on camera 1."

The play was on....

**

When it was all over, I wasn't quite sure what we had done. Looking over the audience, I got a blank stare and then one or two started clapping. A few more joined in and then all filed out quietly.

Later, viewing the videotape with the actors and Yvonne, I realized what an incoherent mess it was even though I had followed the action as planned. In addition to the standard close-ups, reaction shots and pans and dollies, I had used chroma keys of the Kanaka mask hovering around the set, as well as multiple split screen images of the actors and slow dissolves to indicate the passage of time and place. Still, the play didn't jell. It was too talky, too abstract.

However, when I went to see Zettl about the project, he was ecstatic about it. "You did it, Allan. You broke some barriers. I could truly see the use of television's unique dramaturgical style. It was not perfect. It needs refinement. That will come. Hang in there."

I left his office walking on air with another "A" in my kit bag.

***

The spring semester of 1967 was not all creative fun and games. I had hard-core academics to attend to. I was taking a Master Thesis class and trying to cram for my oral exams. As I said earlier, I wanted to finish my class work at State that semester and then take the fall semester to write my thesis. Yes, San Francisco State required a written master's thesis. It could be a creative project like my little drama but it had to be written up in the prescribed academic style. At the time, SF State had no doctoral program, so they beefed up the master's program to emulate a doctoral program, in hopes that one day they would get one. This was a bummer for a student like me. All I wanted to do was acquire the skills and get the hell out, hopefully with some sort of certification. But the only certification beyond a BA was an MA that required a thesis.

The first step in starting on a master's thesis was a required course on how to go about conducting scholarly research in the media. So far, my courses had been in film and television theory or the practical aspects of production. But lo, there was a whole other body of academic material out there on the media that had to do with communications theory, content analysis, theories of popular culture, legal and economic issues of broadcasting. Much of the stuff had been borrowed from psychology, statistics, law and history.

I decided to stick with the more creative aspects of television. I proposed doing a content analysis of a well-known live television drama, *Requiem for a Heavyweight*. I would explore and document the use of television production techniques that stressed the illusion of depth.

From what I could tell researching the literature including past doctoral and master dissertations, no one had systematically documented depth characteristics in a particular program. This would be a first. It would involve a survey of the production techniques used in television as described in various TV production handbooks and other television production literature. And then I would conduct a rigorous, shot-by-shot analysis of a kinescope of *Requiem for a Heavyweight*. The project would possibly be supplemented by interviews with the director of the play, Ralph Nelson. The results of the analysis would be presented in a statistical manner, along with still photographs of representative shots, and a finally a transcription of the play with a dialogue and a description of the action.

"That's a big undertaking, Mr. Brown," said Zettl, my thesis advisor, sitting at his desk, as he read over my proposal.

"Yes, but I think it's doable," I said. "I don't just want to do another survey of the literature like everyone else. I want to do something with some meat to it."

"I'm with you on that. Go ahead. It will be interesting to see how it turns out. In the meantime, I will try to convince others on the committee that this is a worthwhile project."

"The only thing is don't expect this anytime soon," I said. "It'll probably be six months or so down the road before I get it done."

"I won't. I know that these projects sometimes take years. It took me three years to get my doctoral dissertation done. But don't give up, it's worth it."

I had no plans to give up, but now and then, as I plugged away on the project, I did wonder if it was worth it. I knew it would not be required to get a job in the business, but in the back of my mind, I thought I might teach someday. Also, there was the pride of having a master's degree. Something to show for my years of screwing around at SF State.

***

My Waterloo that spring semester was my master's orals. I had been warned by Zettl that I would be quizzed on a wide range of topics, all central to the burgeoning academic specialty known as "communication arts and theory." This would involve theories of popular culture as well as the signs and symbols of interactive communication. Also, to be covered were the legal and economic aspects of film and broadcasting and last but not least the theory and aesthetics of film and television.

Except for the theory and aesthetics of film and TV, and broadcast business, I had taken virtually no courses in these areas. My plan was to review the texts in these courses on a crash basis which I did and discovered that most of it was bullshit that had nothing to do with film or broadcasting.

The material for the popular culture was interesting. It explored how early oral poets such as Homer and the storytellers of Gilgamesh epics constituted mass media in the ancient days. The course then traced how popular culture evolved through the tales of the troubadours in the Middle Ages to the early romantic novels, to 19th-century newspapers, the music halls of England, the western dime novels and the beginnings of slapstick film comedy.

However, communication theory itself was a bore. It involved theories of the sender, the message and the receiver. Or as one course description outlined it,

> *Communication theory involves communication models, verbal and nonverbal symbols, systems theory, symbolic interactionism, persuasion/compliance-gaining, and communication in various contexts.*

Whatever. It was all Greek to me. Nevertheless, I was confident I would pass my orals. After all, so far San Francisco State had been a breeze after Cal. I had gotten mostly A's. Plus I knew far dimmer students who had passed their orals. So one fine day in late May, I presented myself before my board of inquisition, i.e. two professors from whom I had never taken a course and Zettl. At first, the questions were of a general nature about the role of the media in society and some of the current problems facing the broadcast media in particular. I held forth. No problems. Then Professor Hoag who was big on communication theory began to quiz me. I knew the basic model structure of sender, message and receiver but that was about all. Instead, I did a tap dance talking about persuasion and propaganda techniques based on my Army psy-warfare experience but Hoag wasn't impressed.

"That's all very interesting, Mr. Brown but you seem to lack a basic understanding of the underlying construct of all media studies, namely communications theory."

So much for him.

Then it was Professor Stuart Hyde's turn. He was the chairman of the department and the guru of popular culture. I did better outlining the growth of popular culture from the ancient times to the current crop of crap on network television. Hyde took offense at my attitude, insisting that dramatic network programming such as *Bonanza, Hogan's Heroes,* and *Beverly Hillbillies* reflected the deep inner longings and aspiration of Americans to be enthralled by stories that shaped their life experience. All of this was worthy of serious academic study.

Finally, it was Zettl's turn and as expected, he focused on the film and TV aesthetics and production which I had down cold. Nevertheless, after due deliberation behind closed doors, it was decided I had insufficient background in communication studies and other areas of popular culture and therefore failed to pass my orals.

"Mr. Brown, we recommend that you take or audit a series of classes next semester to bring you up to speed in those designated areas before you try the orals again. Thank you for your time," said Hyde crisply, gathering up his papers.

Zettl looked at me and shrugged. Later he told me to persevere. I was very close to passing but he thought professorial egos got in the way. In essence, Hyde and Hoag were hurt that I had not taken their courses and received their pearls of wisdom.

Shit. It looked like I would be spending the next semester hanging out at SF State if I wanted to pursue this master's degree. I was disappointed but not crushed. Onward.

24. WAR

During the winter and early spring of 1967, I was so involved in school and courting Yvonne that I barely noticed what was going on in the big wide world around me. A glance at the headlines would have told me all was not well with the world and several events were about to touch me personally.

The Vietnam War headed the list. The largest ground operations to date were under way in Vietnam which now had about five-hundred thousand American combat and support troops. The draft was in full swing sucking in over a quarter million men a year and noises were being made about activating the reserves. What? Yes, activating the reserves. Worse yet, buried in a *San Francisco Chronicle* article was a reference to those reserve troops in "control units" as possibly being first on the list to go but no final decision had yet been made. That got my attention.

I was in a control group. Or I thought I was in a control group, a nice, safe control group with a Nürnberg address. I had nearly forgotten about the Army Reserves. It had been three years since I had gone to a meeting. And I had only two more years to go before my six-year reserve obligation was over. As I was mulling this over, my father presented me with another letter from the Sixth Army Reserve District Headquarters asking him if he knew my address. I now dimly remembered the last letter from my Norwegian friend, Eric saying that he had finished his studies was going back to Norway and he that would set up a mail drop at the Hapag-Lloyd/American Express office in Nürnberg. I had thought that would have taken care of it but apparently not.

The resulting conversation with my dad went like this:

Dad: "Allan, either you respond to this letter with your San Francisco new address or I will."

Me: "Why? Just tell them you don't know where I am."

Dad: "I can't do that. First it would be a lie, second, it is your obligation to keep them informed as to your whereabouts, and third, I might be liable myself."

My father was still impressed with governmental authority. He was such a straight arrow. I sighed and told him that I would take care of it. I duly filled out my new address form and waited for the inevitable. A few weeks later I received a letter from the Army Reserves telling me that since I had a U.S. address, I was obligated to join an active reserve unit within 90 days otherwise I would be subject to activation.

"Shit."

It was now late March and in addition to all my other obligations, I had to look for a reserve unit. I phoned up my old unit at the Presidio, the Psy-Warfare unit, and was told it was full. No room at the inn. I did the same for the civil affairs unit down in Sunnyvale and it too was full. Or as the First Sergeant put it, "Good luck, son. You and about a thousand other control group escapees are scrambling for a unit."

He was right. Every reserve controleé was trying to sign up for active reserve units, scared shitless that they might be activated. I telephoned around, eventually talking to a Mr. Morgan at the Sixth Army Reserves District Headquarters. Here was a glimmer of hope.

"Private Brown, I see here you have a broadcast specialist designation. That's a hard one to find a slot for. I think you are going to have to be flexible. There's a unit that has a few openings. It is called Test Company and it meets a weekend a month at Fort Cronkite in Marin County."

"What's Test Company?"

"Oh, they administer Army tests to new recruits and others. It's basically an administrative company. A lot of clerk typists and a few oddball military specialties like yours. Are you interested?"

"I guess."

"OK. I'll notify them that you will show up for the next weekend meeting. Look sharp."

"Uh, sure thing."

Shit, shit, shit. I was back in the Army. Where was my uniform? It was in storage in Martinez. I had my Dad deliver my dress uniform with shoes, boots, shirt and hat, along with my Army fatigues. He arrived at my apartment with the uniform all freshly pressed (thanks to my mother) and zipped up in the cleaner's bag. The rest was in a box.

"Here's your stuff, Allan," he said handing it over.

"Uh, thanks Dad for bringing it," I said pawing through it.

Dad looked around at the apartment, now all fresh and sparkling with new posters on the wall of rock concerts, Impressionists and a Rembrandt.

"Uh, the place looks better since I saw it last," he remarked.

"Well, I have some help cleaning it up," I replied.

(He had not yet met Yvonne. I was keeping her under wraps from my family.)

"Still, it's nice son. Living here, the life of the bachelor," he said sitting down on the couch and looking out the window at St. Ignatius Church across the way.

As we shared a beer, Dad began waxing nostalgic about his bachelor days in the Bay Area before he met Mom back in 1935. But he ended his monolog by noting that he was shocked at some of the characters in the neighborhood. "Those hippies looked like they needed a good scrubbing. Do any of them work?"

"Some do. Most of them just lie around and groove," I replied.

He shrugged. "Let's go eat."

We went out and had a hamburger at McDonald's. As he ate, Dad scoped out the parade of hippies shuffling along to nearby Hippy Hill. He shook his head and then said goodbye. His last words to me before he drove off were, "Do your duty son."

***

Fort Cronkite was a tiny Army base tucked away in the Marin Headlands, practically sitting on a beach. It consisted of two rows of barracks, a mess hall, an administrative building that doubled as an officer's club and not much else.

The most recent reason for its existence was as quarters for a Nike missile crew in the 1950s and early 60s. The missile site sat on top of the hill overlooking the Golden Gate. Before that, the soldiers of Fort Cronkite manned the artillery gun emplacements dug into the hillsides during World War Two. Now Fort Cronkite served as a facility for various reserve units including Test Company.

As I immediately discovered Test Company was a joke. It was filled with losers and misfits that couldn't find any other reserve outfit to take them. At the weekend meetings, we mostly sat around and bullshitted. The officers would watch sports on the large color TV set in the officer's club leaving the unit in the hands of the company sergeant. Occasionally, we would hear a lecture on how to proctor tests in the U.S. Army or be assigned to a cleanup or maintenance detail. Sometimes we would just get lost on the beach right outside our door. Many troops got high on pot for the weekend.

So it seemed a sweet deal, a relaxing way to spend a weekend, almost resort-like when the weather was good. This went on for a couple of months and then responding to pressure from above, the company commander decided he needed to shape the unit up. So he brought in another company sergeant, Earl, who was an out-and-out asshole.

Little Earl immediately had us marching around in parade drills. He also had a hair-brained idea of restoring Fort Cronkite to its former glory. We started by painting all the barracks. When we weren't doing that, we had lectures to attend. The company commander brought in people from the Army Test Command Center to explain what Army Testing was all about.

"The mere handing out of IQ, aptitude, interest and psychological tests is far from the entirety of what we do. We also score the field drills, the efficiency of the administrative process and maintain the records," one bureaucratic Army stiff informed us.

Wow, that sounded really exciting. Not.

Another time, we heard from a Captain Roberts who had just returned from Vietnam. He had been stationed at Cam Rahn Bay. He described the base as an R & R paradise, well away from the fighting. He showed us slides of the place to re-enforce his points.

"There's a great beach, a surfing beach. Also a pool and golf course. Many different kinds of restaurants. Extravagant officers' clubs and enlisted men's clubs. Air-conditioned barracks and accessibility to some of the most beautiful women in South Vietnam."

"Sucky, fucky," came the muttered response. Laughter.

Ignoring the remark, Captain Roberts continued, "Cam Rahn Bay is also one of the administrative centers of the Army Test Command in Vietnam. If you are so inclined, you could volunteer to go on active duty and help the Army out. I guarantee that you will be posted at Cam Rahn Bay or even Saigon."

The good captain found no takers.

***

Getting out to Fort Cronkite was a hassle since I had no car. So initially, I had to take the Greyhound across the Golden Gate Bridge and then a shuttle out to Fort Cronkite. This took about ninety minutes both ways. Then I ran into an old Martinez friend, Jan, who was in a different reserve unit but which met on the same weekends at Fort Cronkite. He now lived in the Sunset District of San Francisco and worked downtown as a buyer for a retail store.

He gave me a ride a few times. But, I must admit that I had skipped a couple of weekend reserve meetings because of an interviewing job that I had started in the summer that required me to work weekends. This inspired Sgt. Earl to threaten me with activation if I continued to miss meetings.

"Private Brown. You must fulfill your reserve obligation."

"I know, but I have this weekend job."

"No matter. The Army Reserves come first. And I fully expect you to go to summer camp with us down at Fort Roberts in August."

"Will do," I said smartly but actually I was plotting to get out that too.

I had yet to go to an Army reserve summer camp. And I didn't plan to start now. I had heard that one could be excused from summer camp due to economic hardship. And now since I was self-supporting, I thought I could file for a hardship exemption. I didn't bring this up with Earl. I would go over his head.

In the meantime, I had my job as an interviewer to attend to. School was out for the summer and I had decided rather than returning to surveying, I would find a job more fitting to my academic background. More about this later, but the bottom line was most of the people I had to interview for a drug prescription study were home on the weekends. And since I was paid per interview, I would be giving up a half month's income if I went to summer camp.

When I explained this to the wimp company commander, all I got was, "Private Brown we expect you at summer camp otherwise in view of your previous absences we will begin to process activation papers."

Now I was pissed. No one at this level would listen to reason. Still, I did not yield. I informed Test Company and the District Reserve Headquarters by registered letter that I could not attend summer camp because of economic hardship. I included a letter from my employer that stated weekend work was required.

So summer camp came and went and I stayed in San Francisco. Initially, I heard nothing. Then a few days before the regular August meeting I received a registered letter back saying paperwork had commenced for my activation. Shit! Now I was in it. No way did I want to go to Vietnam. I had heard they paid no attention to MOS's and just put you in a fill-in position in a grunt unit. I immediately telephoned the office of the Sixth Army Reserve District Headquarters and arranged an appointment with Mr. Morgan.

The office was located in one of the old barrack buildings down by Crissy Field at the Presidio. I waited for a few minutes in the outer office, while a secretary did her nails and talked on the telephone. Then a civilian in a sweaty white shirt and a five o'clock shadow motioned me to come in his cubbyhole and have a seat. (What is it with these civilian defense workers? They always look so disheveled.)

"Private Brown. I have those activation orders that Test Company sent up," Mr. Morgan announced leaning across the desk. "Actually, it's not an order; it's a recommendation. We make the final decision here. I also have your letter asking to be excused from summer camp for economic hardship. Good thing you sent us a copy."

"I thought it might be," I replied.

"Yes, well. Don't worry. We are not going to activate you. We have absolutely no use for your MOS in Vietnam. There are plenty of ex-disc jockeys to do the broadcasting. Nor do we have any use for you in a combat role. As twenty-seven year old E-2, you are a bit too old for that."

"I am?"

"Well, not really. If you were career Army or an enlistee it would be different. But we would have to spend months training you. Frankly, it's not worth it. Tell you what I am going to do. I am going to transfer you out of Test Company to a civil affairs unit in El Cerrito. They have an opening for a public information specialist. It just opened up. How does that sound?"

"Sounds great. That's what I wanted all along."

"Yes, well. Don't blow it. Unlike Test Company, this civil affairs unit is a highly professional outfit, one of the best in the reserves. They expect dedication and enthusiasm. Don't let them down."

"No, sir. You can count on me, Sir." I started to stand up and salute him but then thought better of it. I simply shook his hand, "Thanks a lot, Sir. I really appreciate it,"

"Uh, and by the way, Private Brown, don't miss any meetings and make arrangements ahead of time so you can be sure to attend summer camp."

"Will do," I said skyrocketing out of there.

***

In the summer of 1967, the Vietnam War wasn't the only war going on. The U.S. had its own internal wars in the form of race riots in several

American cities. In June, violence broke in Tampa, Florida and Boston. Everybody was horrified. Was it that bad for blacks? After all, they had just gotten their civil rights legislation passed by congress in 1964. But there was more to come in what would prove to be a long hot summer. Throughout July, there were race riots in Newark, New Jersey in which 27 people were killed. More race riots in Cairo, Illinois, in Durham, North Carolina, and in Memphis, Tennessee. But the granddaddy of them all was in Detroit from July 23rd to the 30th which left forty-dead, two-thousand injured, five thousand homeless, and caused millions of dollars' worth of damage. President Johnson had to dispatch a brigade of U.S. Army paratroopers to put the Detroit riot down.

According to my uncle Jack, the L.A. fireman, they were nervous in Los Angeles too with memories still fresh from the 1965 Watts Riot. And everybody in the Bay Area was wondering when Oakland would go off. It didn't but rumors were swirling about the newly founded Black Panthers arming themselves with weapons to fend off harassment by the Oakland police. This group was led by Huey Newton. Their bible was the little red book of Mao Tse-tung. And to think, they were calling this the "Summer of Love," in the Bay Area.

***

Truly, the so-called "Summer of Love" was more like the summer of chaos in the Haight. It was a war of nerves between the City of San Francisco and the hippies. Thanks to the national news media, tens of thousands of young people were pouring in from all points around the nation and indeed the world. Suitcases painted with "The Haight or Bust," or "Ohio to San Francisco," were a common sight. Most young hippies arrived without a dime to their name. There were just here to groove, get high on the scene or drugs and support themselves by panhandling.

Tourist traffic along Haight Street was now an outright nightmare, backing up for miles. As one observer put it, "Tourists leaned out through their car windows, shooting pictures of the hippies as if they were on some African safari photographing the wildlife."

Gray Line bus tours traversed the Haight hourly. TV news cars regularly patrolled the streets looking for something interesting to film. One couldn't travel more than a block without bumping into a reporter doing a stand-up. Proposals were before the San Francisco Board of Supervisors to make Haight Street a mall. They eventually decided to reroute the city buses instead.

I avoided Haight Street as much as I could, but Yvonne reveled in it, urging me to get with it as she checked out the latest hippy fashion boutiques and head shops for various artifacts. I tagged along trying to keep her from going off the deep end because the Haight was indeed the deep end for many of the hippies. They were like lemmings plunging off cliffs. Hundreds slept on the streets or in the park, often stoned on pot, acid or worse. A number even died of exposure because they hadn't realized that San Francisco near the ocean is cold in the summer. Nights are damp and the temperatures can dip down to low fifties. San Francisco Police Chief Thomas Cahill tried to shut down Golden Gate Park after 10 p.m. with mixed success. There were just too many nooks and crannies in the vegetation for the hippies to hide out in.

As the summer progressed, hard-core drug traffic exploded. Heroin, meth and cocaine were now mainstays on the street. Along with this, turf wars developed. Drug gangs from the ghettos of Oakland and San Francisco were moving in. Owsley's main dispenser of LSD, Superspade, was shot dead. The Hell's Angels and a rival motorcycle gang, the Gypsy Jokers, hung out in the Haight, mostly around Tracy's Donuts, a greasy doughnut shop on Haight. Occasionally, a fight would break out over women or drugs.

Abuse of young hippy chicks continued unabated. Or as Digger publication, *The Communication Company* put it:

> *Pretty little sixteen-year-old middle-class chick comes to the Haight to see what's it all about and gets picked up by a seventeen-year-old street dealer who spends all day shooting her full of speed again and again, then he feeds her 3000 mikes of (12 times the standard dose of LSD) and raffles off her temporarily unemployed body for the biggest Haight Street gang bang since the night before last. The politics and ethics of ecstasy. Rape is as common as bullshit on Haight Street.*

The drug scene got so out of hand, the cops started busting people left and right on the street. At one drug bust in July, police discovered ballet stars Rudy Nureyev and Margot Fonteyn cowering on the roof of a raided building on Belvedere Street. They were in town with the Royal Ballet. All charges were immediately dropped.

Heath Inspectors flooded into the Haight and began closing down various businesses and crash pads citing such violations such as no doors on the bedrooms and dog shit on the floor. The Diggers opened a free medical clinic on Clayton to deal with VD, drug overdoses, hepatitis and other various communal diseases that were sweeping through the hippy communes.

Police Chief Cahill urged the news media to cool it in its coverage of the Haight. As he put it:

> "Any encouragement of the mass media tending to attract more undesirables to the problem areas is a disservice to the community. They are encouraging kids to expose themselves to health hazards, possible arrest and even injury."

At one point in August, George Harrison of the Beatles walked through the Haight and said he had expected it to be "neat and clean, friendly and happy, something like Kings Row," instead he said he found himself surrounded by "hideous, spotty, little teenagers."

Someone handed George a guitar and asked him to sing, "Baby, You're a Rich Man," but after strumming a few cords, George was so stoned, he couldn't remember the words. The crowd began to boo him and George and his girlfriend fled to his waiting limo. The encounter was symbolic. The Haight was going down.

As the summer dragged on, crime increased with muggings, burglaries, and an occasional murder. It was becoming dangerous to walk the streets of the Haight at night. Some of the older hippies began to disappear from the Haight, along with several popular rock bands including *Country Joe and the Fish*. Word was they were buying land and setting up communes in Marin County in order to escape the chaos of the Haight. They wanted a peaceful, bucolic existence where they could get high in peace and maybe grow their own crops of grass. The Diggers had developed Morning Star Ranch in Sonoma County where they grew vegetables for their free food pantries.

Soon only the dregs were left in the neighborhood. And longtime businesses were on the verge of going bust including the Psychedelic Shop and the Drogstore. Hippies were freaking out the tourists now, jumping on their cars and smashing their windows. At one point, there was an outright riot on Haight Street with police moving in and cracking heads. In the melee, a dog was killed by a police riot stick.

The symbolic end of the movement came with the "Death of a Hippy" parade in October which also marked the first anniversary of outlawing LSD. About eighty marchers walked alongside a cardboard coffin with a representative hippy inside and a banner reading, "Death of Hippy Freebie, i.e. Birth of Free Man."

***

While all of this was going on, the anti-war movement was proceeding apace in the Bay Area. This was partly in response to a less than successful prosecution of the Vietnam War. Major ground offensives since the beginning of the year had failed to stem the progress by the Viet Cong and North Vietnamese. A Gallup poll reported that 56% of the American people thought that the U.S. was losing the war and a like number disapproved of Johnson's handling of the war. This at a time when ten thousand American troops had been killed and one hundred thousand were wounded in Vietnam with no visible progress in sight.

In general, the hippies were not too enthralled with anti-war street protests and avoided them especially if there was no music and or acid involved. But many did show up in April at a massive anti-war rally at Kezar Stadium just a few blocks from where I lived. Over one hundred thousand protesters bearing all manner of peace signs had marched from Market Street to Kezar in Golden Gate Park. Most were Bay Area political activists from Berkeley, San Francisco State, Stanford and other nearby colleges; many were joined by faculty and teachers; others were just average people—men, women, mothers and children—fed up by the war. I had missed the march but did go over to the stadium where the program was well underway. It was weird being in this stadium where the 49er's still played. It was never so full on football days.

The keynote speaker, combat photographer David Duncan, talked about his experiences in Vietnam and how that had led to his disillusionment with the war. He finished by telling his audience that anti-war protesters were the best friends that the soldiers in Vietnam had.

Also on hand for the program were Julian Bond, (Civil Rights activist), Eldridge Cleaver (Black Panther Leader), Rabbi Abraham and actor, Robert Vaughn. But not to disappoint the hippies and to lighten things up were performances by folk singer Judy Collins, *Big Brother and the Holding Company* and *Quicksilver Messenger*.

The number of draft resisters increased exponentially during these months. Muhammad Ali (Cassius Clay) refused induction into the Army for what he said was religious reasons. As he put it, "I've no beef with the Vietcong. No Vietcong ever called me 'nigger.'"

He got a five-year prison sentence for his stand but it was reversed a month later by the U.S. Supreme court. However, the World Boxing

Association did revoke his title and license. Ali's refusal to serve highlighted the plight of other draft resisters.

Thousands of young men were still burning their draft cards even though it was now an illegal act according to a law passed by congress in 1965. Draft card burning was usually done as a grand finale of an anti-war protest while the TV news cameras rolled. FBI agents were often in the crowd and took notes on who was burning what. Those who "knowingly" destroyed their draft cards and who were fingered faced up to five years in prison. Despite the law, the cards were going up in flames left and right. Still, draft card burning didn't get you out of serving. You could still be drafted, card or no card.

By far the best way to avoid the draft was to dive into graduate school. Graduate study in theology was a favorite since it combined the graduate deferment with a pacifist record. But not everybody could afford graduate school. Even the undergraduate deferment was out of reach for millions. As in most wars, it was the poor, the minorities and the blue-collar kids who did the fighting. The well off, the far-sighted and the lucky had already joined the military reserves but, as noted, by 1967, it was hard to find a unit that was not filled.

Tens of thousands tried to get status as conscientious objectors but it was nearly impossible unless you had a documented history in one of the pacifist churches such as the Quakers. Even then, you could wind up on the front lines as a noncombatant medic. Those who failed to gain conscientious objector status and who still refused to serve often wound up in jail.

Another route was to convince the Army you were unfit for military service. One trick was to ingest a lot of sugar into your system before taking the Army's glucose tolerance test. If there was too much sugar, the Army might declare you diabetic and exempt you from the draft. Another technique was to act crazy. This was best done with various pep pills, maybe with large amounts of coffee, even better, a tranquilizer prescription for depression. I recalled that Jean-Paul had used that technique to evade the draft a few years ago. Yes, even though he was a French citizen, Jean-Paul was still subject to the U.S. draft.

As mentioned before, the most intriguing dodge was to plead with the Army interviewer that you desperately wanted to serve in order to kill people legally. That would often give the Army pause before inducting you. Perhaps the capper was to declare yourself homosexual and inform the interviewer that you were looking forward to being around men, especially in the showers. This was especially powerful if you had photograph of yourself engaging in sex acts with men. A sure fire way to get out of the draft.

When all else failed, many 1-A candidates simply said, "fuck it" and split for Canada, Sweden or other obscure parts of the world. By 1967, an estimated fifty thousand young men had done just that. The most popular Canadian cities to flee to were Toronto and Vancouver where there were well-established networks that could set you up with a place to live and a job and also advice on how to gain permanent residency in Canada. Of course, many went underground in the U.S., changed their identity, their appearance and hung out in remote corners of the country.

***

By fall, the pace of the anti-war movement picked up. October 1967 was the key anti-war month. It saw a violent protest at the University of Wisconsin against Dow Chemical for manufacturing Agent Orange and napalm. Protesters stormed the building where Dow was recruiting. Police moved in busting heads and dragging students out through broken windows. Here in San Francisco, hundreds of anti-war demonstrators protested outside the Selective Service office. Among the hundreds arrested were folk singer Joan Baez and her sister Mimi Farina.

In Washington DC, on October 21st, an estimated one hundred thousand marched on the Pentagon. Actually, they marched to the Washington Mall with a legal parade and rally permits. Only few hundred hippies led by Abby Hoffman encircled the Pentagon in an attempt to exorcise it. The plan was for people to sing and chant until the building levitated. They were met by a phalanx of some two thousand federal troops as they tried to gain entrance.

The majority of protesters gathered in front of the Lincoln Memorial for two days to listen to speeches by David Dillinger, SDS leader Jerry Rubin and Doctor Benjamin Spock, the baby doctor turned anti-war activist among others. By the time the Washington protest was over, a total of six hundred people had been arrested. Mississippi Senator John Stennis said the march was all part of a communist conspiracy.

***

The action that I was involved in was at the Oakland Induction Center on October 20th. This was the last day of protest at the induction center of the week called "Stop the Draft." At first, I didn't want to go but Yvonne and Gerard's girlfriend Marie insisted.

"Al, this is historic. If we don't go we will be missing out," said Marie the night before.

"Missing out on what?" I said. "That protest is going to accomplish nothing except getting our heads bashed in."

We were sitting around Gerard's apartment, sipping wine and listening to Beatles records.

"You're so square," said Marie, petulant.

Yvonne chimed in, "She's right, Allan. Since, I have known you, we haven't been to a real protest. You just sit back and make snide comments about the protesters. Don't you want to get the troops out of Vietnam?"

"Sure, but..."

At this point, Gerard who had been saying nothing and who I knew was not too enthusiastic either, broke in." What's it going to hurt, Al? We'll just drive down there, park and watch what's going on. The girls can join in the protest if they want. At least I'll have the Green Hornet to getaway, should things get rough."

I nodded, resigned to this futility. "OK, OK. I'll go."

"Great! We'll pick you and Yvonne up at 6 a.m. sharp," said Marie triumphantly.

***

So in the wee, dark hours of the morning of the 20th, we four musketeers drove down Broadway towards the Oakland Induction Center on Clay Street. Marie was dressed for action in Levis, tennis shoes, a jaunty red beret and a black sweatshirt with a red Che Guevara emblem on it. Che, who had recently been executed in the jungles of Bolivia, was her hero. Both Gerard and I were in our regular, everyday clothes of khakis, street shoes, turtlenecks and jackets. Yvonne, on the other hand, was dressed to the nines because she had to be at work later in the morning.

On we went, in Gerard's old bathtub 1950 Hudson with a racing engine. Gerard was in his 1950's hot rod phase. He changed old cars like most people changed shoes.

About a half mile from the Induction Center, we saw police cars cruising around. Then we spotted the protesters on Broadway, marching along by the hundreds, chanting, "Hey, hey LBJ, how many babies did you kill today."

Gerard decided it was time to park and hoof it the rest of the way. We pulled off onto a side street and then walked over to Broadway to join the marchers for the last few blocks before the induction center. Sliding in at the end of the procession, we walked along chanting with the rest. Marie was sorry she hadn't made up a sign.

I couldn't have cared less. I was watching for possible trouble but so far the Oakland cops were cool, lining the sidewalk, arms folded, their white riot helmets glittering in the still illuminated streetlights.

Finally, the procession arrived about a half-block from the induction center, a hulking gray monolith still in morning shadow. In front of the entrance was a double line of police, this group looking more aggressive, batons in their hands at the ready. "No way were these unwashed Commies going to shut down the center," was the unspoken message.

The cops had cleared a path for the buses to deposit the recruits. The protesters had originally declared, they didn't want to shut the induction center down. They only wanted to hand out leaflets to the inductees as they got off the bus. It was all about freedom of speech. It was to be a peaceful affair. For the moment, the police went along with that.

Soon the first of several olive drab buses pulled up and down the stairs came the fresh-faced inductees with manila folders in hand containing their orders. God, they looked young! Some looked like teenagers barely older than Kenny, my fifteen-year-old kid brother. Initially, all was peaceful. A small group of protest leaders quietly handed out leaflets to the inductees as they filed into the center. The leaflets urged them not to join the war machine and invited them to join the protesters. Most inductees just threw the leaflets to the ground. A few stuffed them into their pockets as they entered the building. The cops stood by smirking.

After another two or three buses arrived, things began to get dicey. Some of the more radical protesters started banging on the sides of the bus and chanting, "Hell no, you shouldn't go." The police stiffened but still held back. Then a bus window was broken and someone threw a rock at the cops. A weighted paper bag flew through the air and landed with a splat at the feet of the officers. It was a bag full of shit. Others actively tried to crash the police line to block the entrance.

This was all too much for the cops. Police issued a bullhorn warning to get back. The warning was ignored so the cops started pushing the protesters back. Those who resisted got cracked on the head, knocked down and cuffed. Then all hell broke loose as the police line moved forward methodically cracking heads. We were still hovering near the rear of the gathering. Marie was outraged at what was happening. She wanted to

California Split

plunge forward and mix it up. Gerard was holding her back as she was screaming "Pigs, fascists."

Yvonne didn't know what to do. I could tell part of her wanted to jump in, but she realized she wasn't dressed for it. I knew what to do. We had to get the hell out of there as tear gas started going off. I knew from my Army days how that could fuck you up. I grabbed Yvonne firmly by the arm and led her away. Gerard did the same with Marie and we quickly made it back down the street and out of the crowd. As we did so I glanced back and saw the cops were on the move, almost double-timing down the street, billy clubs swinging, tear gas canisters going off. Protesters fled left and right, tears streaming down their faces. Scores were down on the ground being cuffed. By now we were running, Yvonne not hindered at all by her high heels. Marie now out in front with her sneakers. Gerard and I dashing along.

Finally, we came to the side street where Gerard had parked his Hudson. Quick into the car. Key into the ignition and *vrooom*. Gerard peeled out, race engine gunning. We streaked up San Pablo Avenue heading back to Berkeley, our morning of being active anti-war protesters over.

***

The next day, the head of the induction center, one Lt. Col. James Mc Poland, was quoted as saying that the demonstration had been a big zero. Induction operations were normal, processing about 250 men a day. A nineteen-year-old inductee was also quoted saying, "Somebody's gotta fight. If I have to I'll go to Vietnam."

The war machine went on barely pausing a beat.

As for me, I continued to put on my Army uniform, dutifully going to my weekend reserve meetings now at the civil affairs unit in El Cerrito. I had my old broadcast MOS back and was put in charge of setting up a hypothetical broadcast system for a hypothetical European town that the U.S. Army had hypothetically occupied. The good old reserves. Still fighting World War Two. But I was a good little soldier, obedient to my country because I knew there was no way to beat the war machine once it got its hands on you.

25. NOCE

The same might be said of "Love." There was no way to beat it, once it got your hands on you. Yvonne and I were a number. An item. We were together constantly. This went on for months with no utterings of a formal commitment. We were just happy being together, wandering around San Francisco, out to Playland riding on all the rickety rides, over to the Cliff House, drinking Irish coffee, and gazing at the seals on the rocks.

Other times, we would hike around the ruins of the Sutro Baths overlooking the ocean and I would tell Yvonne how my mother swam here as a little girl. But Yvonne's favorite spot was the Dutch windmill at the western entrance of Golden Gate Park. It was an authentic Dutch windmill, a gift from the Netherlands and once operational. You could see the sail rotating on a windy day.

We also hung out on Hippy Hill, usually with a bottle of ale and a bag of fish and chips and watched the hippies do their thing. Flutes, drums, flowers in the hair, whirling dervishes, and the Hare Krishna issuing their chants. It was old stuff for me, but Yvonne found it delightful.

Of course, we attended a few concerts at the Fillmore and the Avalon. Somehow, the historic Monterey Pop Festival on June 14th got by us. I think Yvonne had to work that weekend.

At one *Grateful Dead* concert in the park, my hippy friend Lucy came up to me and said hello and gave Yvonne, who was as always dressed up for the City, the once over. I introduced her to Lucy but Yvonne barely gave her a glance, concentrating on the music. Lucy was looking a little worse for the wear. Her blue eyes didn't sparkle as much and she had gained weight. Next to Yvonne, she appeared a little seedy. After a few minutes of chitchat, she melted away in the crowd.

I also ran into Clarissa. Yvonne and I were walking along Sproul Plaza outside Sather Gate on the Cal Campus one Saturday when Clarissa, coming the other way with books in her arms, stopped in her tracks and stared at Yvonne and me.

"Ah, hi, Clarissa. How's it going," I said cheerily.

"Ah, it's going fine Al," she said eyeing Yvonne who was all decked out in her burnt orange outfit with the big wide orange hat and looking dazzling. "I don't believe I have met your friend."

"Ah, this is Yvonne Schuster. Yvonne, meet Clarissa."

Clarissa graciously held out her hand and so did Yvonne. But you could sense the fur rise.

"Well, this is a surprise," said Clarissa. "I ran into Gerard a couple of weeks ago. He told me that you were busy these days what with school and so forth," she said glancing at Yvonne.

"Ah, yes I am. How's graduate school? Library school isn't it?" I said

"It's going great, Al. Almost finished. You know how I like to hang out in libraries."

"Yes, I remember. Well, we must be going. Good luck," I said uncomfortable, remembering our last encounter. "See you around."

"A pleasure to meet you, Clarissa," said Yvonne.

"The pleasure is mine. Take care of him," Clarissa said with a wink and walked off.

Later, I heard back from Gerard that Clarissa had phoned him up and wanted to know if my latest girlfriend was for real. Gerard assured her that I was serious about Yvonne. Clarissa then sniffed. "I don't know. She looks like his sister, a flashy sister, maybe too flashy for Al." That was the last I heard from my Grace Kelly blonde.

But it was true. I was constantly asked if Yvonne was my sister. As Jean-Paul later told me after he met Yvonne. "Are you sure you don't have a long lost sister?"

"Not that I know of."

"Well, it's uncanny. Both tall, dark, big smiles. You're good looking and she is beautiful. You both have similar personalities, booming, outgoing, although she does have her European background and mannerisms. Very elegant. *Mon Vieux*, you two are perfect together!"

"Well, thanks for the assessment."

"*De rien*," said Jean-Paul turning back to a German-English translation he was working on.

One evening Yvonne and I were wandering around campus in the twilight. In a redwood grove near the old student union, we came across a little bridge over Strawberry Creek. Here we stopped and I gave Yvonne a long, deep kiss and told her that I loved her. She replied, "That was a brave thing to say. I love you too." We hugged and kissed again.

Love? I had never told any girl that I loved her. Well, maybe Bobbie when we were thinking about getting married. Still, she went off and married Tom. I had been often accused of being an insensitive, unfeeling lout, only interested in one thing. But I guess I was saving myself for my perceived one and only. A girl like Yvonne. Still, I was well aware of the implications of this declaration of love. This was to be no casual affair. But still, there was no formal commitment.

Yvonne was playing out her own fantasy as well. She repeatedly told me that as a little girl, she wanted to run off and live with a painter in Paris. "I never wanted to be like my mother, a stay-at-home housekeeper, cooking and cleaning. She is a good woman, but that life is not for me."

"What happened to the painter fantasy?" I asked.

"Well, when I came to Berkeley, I thought I might change my lover to an architect. There were some really cute guys in architecture. I met a few in my history of architecture class. I even went out with some. They threw fantastic parties. Lots of wild music, pots with bubbling dry ice, strong punch. I had fun but I never met anyone I wanted to be serious about. I was preoccupied with getting my own art history degree. I wasn't going to give that up for anything."

"So what happened to the architect fantasy?"

"Well, I was still working on it after I graduated. I had been going out with an architecture grad student from Stanford. A very handsome, blond fellow but older. I think he was thirty. Jim had spent two years in Japan studying architecture. He was a Frank Lloyd Wright type. He wanted me to live with him in Palo Alto in his wonderful arts-and-craft bungalow. Jim was from a rich family and expected a lot. I think he wanted me to be his mistress. But I couldn't bring myself to do it. We drifted apart. A few months later I met you."

"Me?"

"Yes, you."

"But I'm not a painter or an architect. I'm just a poor graduate student. An ex-fraternity boy."

"It doesn't matter," she said. "In addition to being handsome and a soul mate, I think you are intelligent and creative. Here you are studying film and television."

"Uh, only television at this point."

"Still, I know you will do great things."

"What if I just survey and write?"

"That'll be OK too, but from what you have told me, I don't know if you will be happy just surveying."

"That's true. I am thinking about a career change."

And so the conversation went. But it was not all sweetness and light. Sometimes I was chastised for being too Freddy. This grated on Yvonne.

"Sorry. I'm an ex-fraternity boy."

"Yes, I know. I always hated fraternity boys even though my friend Vail liked them. She always said they had great bodies."

"Well, that's often true," I kidded and then flexed my arm muscle. Yvonne squeezed it and smiled. "Wow."

Then turning serious, she explained, "The one fraternity party I attended, the frat boys were so boorish. Often falling down drunk."

"My fraternity was serious, only sometimes we would get falling down drunk," I countered.

"Well, I'm glad I didn't know you then."

"I wouldn't have qualified?"

"Probably not. But you are obviously a different person now."

"You know what they say, once a frat boy, always a frat boy."

"Yes, but you have lived in Europe. You know about European ways. You speak some French. Perhaps you have 'known' European women.'"

"Well, maybe but I'm still an American."

"I can put up with that."

***

The party continued. During June, we often hung out at Gerard's or across the hall at Dirk's who, as I once mentioned, had decorated his apartment like the desert tent of a Pasha Prince. He also had access to the finest grass around and had a stereo that transported you to a sound only universe. Much better than concert sound. Dirk even had color strobe lights going, if you were so inclined. When the Beatle's *Sergeant Pepper Lonely Hearts Band* came out in June, we sat by the hour, listening to it on headphones over and over again, stoned on pot. Sometimes we just spent the night on the couch at Dirk's or Gerard's, but most often we staggered on back to Yvonne's place and crashed in each other's arms with *Sergeant Pepper* ringing in our ears.

One weekend, Yvonne and I decided to get away from the Bay Area craziness to seek solitude and peace and quiet. Escape to the coast was the idea. Big Sur was too far and too expensive with a rental car so we took a Greyhound Bus from San Francisco to Stinson Beach, about twenty-five miles north of the city.

The day started out sunny but by the time we arrived, it had fogged over. Still, that didn't dampen our spirits. We hustled out to the beach and played in the surf up to our knees even though it was cold and gray water. Then we relaxed on the beach on an old Army blanket that I had. Yvonne had fixed a lunch and I had procured a bottle of Rhine wine.

We ate and drank and cuddled until late afternoon when the sun finally came out of hiding. But by now, we were tired of the beach so we repaired to the ramshackle beachfront motel that we had checked into. This was the first time that we were together in a motel. For some reason, we felt like illicit lovers escaping from the prying eyes of an uptight society which wasn't the case at all. Nobody in liberated Northern California cared what we did. Still, I kept running an old black and white movie in my mind, *The Postman Always Rings Twice*. Illicit and dangerous love affairs that end in death at the seashore. Even Yvonne felt ill at ease.

"This feels very odd, Allan."

"I know what you mean. Do you want to go back to the city?"

"Oh, no, I just feel shy."

"That's OK. Feel shy. I'll sleep in the other twin bed."

"Don't be silly. I'll get over it. Let go eat."

We went out and found a funky seafood restaurant that was featuring local rock crabs. After a hearty meal of that washed down by a pitcher of beer, Yvonne wasn't feeling shy anymore and we retired to our seedy motel room for the night. The next morning, we skipped the bus and hitchhiked back to the city and my apartment on Carl Street. It felt like home.

***

Indeed home. An abode with a woman that I loved. How much better could it get?

Yet, hovering in the background was indeed the specter of commitment. Yvonne continued to insist that she only wanted a lover, a soul mate, a friend, a playmate, someone to bum around with. I wasn't so sure. Maybe I wanted more at this point in my life. I knew that someone like Yvonne didn't come along every day. She seemed to embody everything that I had wanted in a woman. Hopefully, she thought the same of me. And after all, I sensed, it was the woman who ultimately made the choice. Still, we tried to keep it light, unspoken, playful.

About the only hassle was we were both working for a living which cut down on our time together. Yvonne was running the costume jewelry department at Capwells. As a management trainee, it was her job to order stock, display it, educate the sales ladies on what was what in the world of costume jewelry and also to sell it. This took me back to my days at Capwells when I had a Christmas job stocking Tie-Tie wrapping products. I hated it. I hated keeping track of inventory, little bits of ribbons, bows, stickers, cards, everything but the wrapping paper. It drove me nuts. Yvonne felt the same way about her products and wanted to work in the Woman's dress department where she could use her fashion sense and knowledge.

"I don't know why they assigned me to costume jewelry," she fumed. "I think it's obvious that my talents lie elsewhere."

"I agree. You could be a walking advertisement for the latest dress styles."

"Maybe. But it makes me mad when I see who's in the woman's department. The main buyer is a guy. He gets to make trips to Paris, London, Rome and, of course, New York."

"Bummer."

I wondered why she didn't quit and go work for a more upscale clothing store like Joseph Magnin. But she pointed out that she had been at Capwells only a year and that she needed at least two years before moving on. And it paid well. But half of her paycheck went for clothes, bought even at discount. At one point I said, "They ought to pay you for wearing them or at least you ought to get them free."

"You're such a dreamer."

***

Then there was my job as an interviewer for a prescription drug survey that was being conducted in San Francisco. When the spring semester ended my unemployment checks ran out as well. I had to find work. I debated picking up another surveying job. I even contacted Nicarao about summer work but he told me that he was using his eighteen-year-old son as a chainman for Kemp and that work was slow.

"But I'll keep you mind should things pick up."

"Thanks."

I didn't bother to phone the union hall. I had decided that it was time to break away from surveying. Time to try something else more in line with what I was studying. I was on the verge of going around to various TV stations to see if they needed a production assistant which I knew wouldn't pay much but at least I would get my foot in the door. Then I came across a notice at the SF State Placement Office:

Wanted: Interviewers for a prescription drug study in San Francisco. Well paid. Twenty dollars per interview. Work your own hours. Contact: Ingrid at Lundgren Market Research.

I thought, how hard can that be? Knock off four interviews a day, eighty bucks. Be free to roam the city, work at my own pace. I liked the independence that it apparently offered so I applied.

It turned out it was quite a bit more complicated than that. I and about twenty other interviewers had to undergo five days of intensive training on how to interview the subjects who were chosen on a random basis. How to ask questions and record answers in a neutral, non-judgmental manner. We conducted mock interviews with the staff and each other and listened to our leader Ingrid, a heavyset woman with a Minnesota accent, describe how important it was to interview only the subject selected by some random, statistical method.

"You do not substitute subjects because they are hard to pin down or refuse to participate. You must use persuasion. You must tell them how important the survey is for public health reasons, tell them that they will remain anonymous and most importantly offer them five dollars for an hour of their time. We will advance such cash but you must keep accurate expense records."

What Ingrid didn't say was this survey had nothing do to with public health. As I later discovered, it was being funded by pharmaceutical companies who wanted to know how their various drugs were being used and the attitudes towards such drugs.

It turned out most people didn't have a clue what they were taking. While conducting the interview, we would use a chart with color photographs of the pills, such as Valium and Librium so the interview subject could pinpoint what he or she was taking. This was just one part of the interview. The other part consisted mostly of lifestyle and attitude questions toward prescription drugs.

While running around San Francisco doing my interviews, I learned the nooks and crannies of the city. I saw the inside of many homes. Many were nice, some not so nice. A normal family was rare. It was mostly singles or single moms with kids. Often I would have to interview a gay household. After the interview, the gay subject would often offer me a drink. Sometimes if it was the last interview of the day, I would have a beer but usually, I just split when done before the subject got any ideas. But I did see how even gays led a normal life and often for years with the same person.

I was quite good and productive as an interviewer, averaging three interviews a day. But it was hard work running around mostly by bus and cab (travel expenses paid) to interview these people and also working at nights and weekends. I worked on this drug survey most of the summer and then mid-August, Ingrid put me on a different survey relating to alcohol. This was not as good. People had more problems talking about their drinking than talking about legal drugs. I tried to get off but Ingrid would not have it. I was too valuable. I was too productive. So I plugged along with the drinking survey until September and then I kissed the whole thing off so I could go back to school full-time.

Still, the interviewing job was a good experience. I learned just how unreliable opinion polls can be. First, there was the question of random selection. How truly random was it, especially when you couldn't get to the initial randomly selected interviewee and the samplers back in the office had to select another? Second, by merely asking the questions, I often had the impression that people formed their answers on the spot to please me. I suspected that they had no real opinion on the subject before I asked the question and by the next day, it might have changed. The survey designers claimed that all of this was all discounted and that the result averaged out, truly reflecting the opinion and habits of the public. I wasn't so sure.

***

Eventually, the stress of both of us working took its toll. Yvonne was often tired and just wanted to crash on her sofa in front of a little black and white TV set that she had. I was often gone. When I was there, we would get into little squabbles. One thing that bugged me was her messy apartment.

One day, I walked into her walk-in closet and was clobbered by a ton of stuff that came tumbling down from the upper shelves. Yvonne was a pack rat. Her bathroom was messy, the basin smeared with make-up with little bits and gobs of goo here and there, the mirror splashed with soap marks and eye shadow. Her towels were raggedy. The kitchen. Well, we won't go there. Enough to say, the stove could get up and walk away.

"Well, she would say." At least it's clean, maybe except for the oven. I'll get around to that. But I do vacuum every week, clean, dust and polish.

"Yes, but you don't pick up."

"So what! You don't want a girlfriend. You want a housekeeper," she proclaimed. "And in any case your place may be tidy but it's filthy. I found monster dust balls under your bed and your kitchen is worse than mine is. Dishes encrusted with months of goo. You never dust and your windows with the view are filthy. I think I'm the only one who ever cleaned them."

"Touché."

It was true. When she got down to it, Yvonne was a good cleaner upper. In fact, when she was in that mode, she was a different person with her hair done up in a matronly bun, her thick eyeglasses on instead of contact lenses (she was seriously near-sighted) and wearing a shapeless shift. A Dutch house frau, but I didn't dare tell her that.

It was fast becoming apparent that Yvonne was a two for one deal. A glamor puss for the outside world, and a private, almost shy, good little Dutch girl who had learned how to keep a house at her mother's knee, that is when she felt like it or wasn't feeling rebellious.

In addition, she was an excellent cook. Her specialties were Dutch, Indonesian and Surinamese dishes. The Dutch meals were tasty meat, mash potato and cabbage affairs; the Indonesian an exotic, "rice table" production of rice and many different spicy meat and vegetable toppings. The Surinamese, an everyday, healthy stew of odd vegetables, spices, bits of meat, chicken, beans and rice. "This is what the Surinamese eat to sustain themselves," she explained. "It's cheap and easy to fix."

"It is good. Hits the spot. Very flavorful," I would say while ladling up a big spoonful from the pot for a taste.

Of course, after such a meal, her kitchen was a mess. And it would stay that way unless I cleaned it up. So I would while Yvonne flopped down on the couch and stared blankly at the TV set, watching some inane program.

Overall, I guess that this was called "dealing with it." However, these domestic frictions were minor compared to some larger issues we had.

***

Since we were spending all our free time together, I had broached the subject of living together, primarily to save rent. It made sense to me but

Yvonne would have none of it.

"I want my space. I may be old fashioned, but I don't think it's a good idea for couples to live together. It's too Berkeley. They do it for years and wind up nowhere."

This was my first major hint that she might be ready for something more than just being my mistress so I backed off.

But there were other issues as well. One day we were walking along the Berkeley pier and for no apparent reason, she stomped off. I guess we had been arguing about politics. When I told her that I had been a Nixon supporter back in 1960, she got steamed.

"How could you? Tricky Dick. He's a crook."

"Yeah, but that crook might be running for president next year? Also, he just might get us out of Vietnam."

"Oh, I could never vote for that man."

"Uh, you can't vote. You're not a citizen," I countered.

"Well, if I were, I'd vote for any democrat."

"Even Johnson who got us into this mess?"

"Uh, maybe. Anyway, you're so square. You're not radical enough for my taste," she said stomping off.

Indeed, as I later learned, what was bugging her was she wasn't sure she wanted to continue to live in the U.S. Outside of Berkeley and the Bay Area, and New York, she thought most Americans were too provincial. She was also wondering whether it was worth it to abandon Holland for America, a country that had been cruel to her family and caused its breakup. Now that she was involved with me, she was confused. Much later, she told me she felt staying with me would mean giving up her country. "You never had to give up your country. I may seem well adapted to America, but I'm still a foreigner."

"You tell me constantly that you cannot live in Holland anymore," I reminded her. "It's too small, too small-minded."

"That's right," she sniffed

"Well, then become a citizen."

"That's easy for you to say. You have never had to give up your country. Right now my permanent green card is about all I can handle."

She was right. I had no idea what it meant to give up a country. Hence, her depression and confusion that day sitting on the end of the Berkeley pier staring out over the bay.

Still, the implication of all of this was that Yvonne had decided to cast her lot in with me, the American. After a long cozy weekend in late July, I

suggested that maybe we should end all of this confusion and get married. She smiled sleepily and said,
"Yes."

26. HOOKED

A simple yes was all it took and we were betrothed. No elaborate proposal with me on my knees at an elegant restaurant, ring in hand. Just a sleepy Sunday morning in bed. Later over breakfast pancakes with strawberries, I asked Yvonne if she really meant it.

"Of course silly. I've been wondering when you would get around to it."

"What about the lover bit with no commitments?"

"I don't see why we can't go on pretending that we are just lovers when we are actually married. I don't want a bourgeois marriage of house, kids and snotty noses. At least for a while." Smile.

"Uh, OK."

Still, we decided to proceed along the established lines of a traditional betrothal and became engaged. A few days later, I met Yvonne in Oakland and we went shopping for a ring. We were now in the realm of her expertise—jewelry. I discovered that there was something in the Dutch genes that made them instant experts in jewelry. Yvonne had a special eye for precious stones. She could instantly tell quality. And of course, she knew where the best and most reasonable jewelry shops were located. I trudged along behind her as we hit one shop after another. Finally, we entered a small, artsy establishment featuring handmade rings.

"I've known about this place for a while. I just wanted to make sure that this is what I wanted."

"Well, what is it that you want?"

"Here," she pointed to a three-ring set inlaid with small diamonds that formed a golden rose. The center ring, the engagement ring, had the largest diamond. It was a flowery ring set, something out of Art Nouveau school of design. Elaborate, bold and dramatic. No meek little ring set here. Nothing traditional and probably most importantly no huge, kick-ass diamond. As she put, "I don't like those chunk diamonds that dominate a ring. I want something smaller and more organic like these. They seem to grow out of the gold."

I agreed. The set was attractive and looked very well on Yvonne's hand. It suited her personality. So we bought the set on the spot for around $250. I say "we" because I was a little short, with only a hundred dollars to my name. Yvonne kicked in the rest. I vowed to pay her back.

"The important thing, Allan, is we are sharing," she said. "What is mine is yours. By the way, do you want a wedding ring?"

"Ah, not at the moment. Maybe later," I answered.

It should be noted here that wedding rings for men in the 1960s were not all that common in the Bay Area. The joke from the more jaded was, "A wedding ring for a husband? What, wear it through his nose?" In fact, the idea of an engagement itself was rather retro. In the Bay Area, people married right away, lived together, or simply moved on.

The next step was to meet the parents. I had mentioned Yvonne to my parents several times but they took no notice since I had brought several women home over the years, always prefacing it with "Nothing serious, Mom."

However, when I informed them on the phone that Yvonne and I were engaged, my mother gasped, my father merely grunted, "That's nice son. Why don't we all go out to a nice restaurant and get acquainted."

"Ah, sure thing Dad. How about Trader Vic's in Oakland." I said thinking of Don and Nancy's parental meet and greet several years ago.

***

So we all gathered at the Trader Vic's on the appointed day at the appointed time, my parents arriving with Kenny in tow in his best teenager suit.

"Hey, I remember this place," exclaimed Kenny. "They have that great Chinese food."

I introduced Yvonne to Mom and Dad. She shook their hand and said, "So pleased to meet you." Yvonne was in her formal European mode. Really, she was just shy, worried about the impression she would make. I had assured her, she would make a lovely impression decked out as she was in her tan outfit with the silk scarf.

At first, Dad and Kenny just stared at her as if Yvonne was from another planet. My folks had rarely run across an elegant European lady. Of course, I was all suited up, hair cut short and looking like a young executive.

Soon, everybody relaxed and we ordered the standard dinner for six even though we were five. It was a delicious Polynesian feast augmented by a fantastic Rum punch, strong but not too strong. Yvonne and I described how we met, how long we had been going together and what our future plans were, namely we had set no date for the marriage. My mom and dad just nodded. Kenny continued to stare. At the end of the meal, Mom and Dad gave Yvonne a hug and said they would welcome her as a daughter.

Yvonne was touched and a tear welled up in her eye. She had passed the parental test.

Still, I had to explain on the phone to Mom later what Yvonne's background was.

She found it all very interesting and very exotic and would rely on my good judgment about the relationship, saying at the end. "Thank God you found someone. Dad and I were beginning to wonder. I think Yvonne will be good for you. Besides being gorgeous, she seems to have a lot of common sense."

***

The next project was Yvonne's dad, Fred. We had gone out with him to the opera a couple of times. Fred was a worldly man and quite an opera buff. His considerable engineering skills were just a small part of his expertise. He spoke five languages—Dutch, German, Spanish, English and the local Surinamese dialect, Papiamento. He was widely read. His favorite author and philosopher was Goethe. You could tell from looking at him that he was of mixed race, light brown skin, curly hair, the same Indian nose as Yvonne. But he was very elegant and sophisticated in his manner. He said outside of New York, he found Berkeley and San Francisco, the most European of all the American cities. Yet he was struggling, working at short term temporary engineering jobs here and there. For some reason, he couldn't latch onto a permanent job. He attributed it to age. He was fifty-seven. But, I thought it was probably race and his sing-song accent in English.

Yvonne told me that Fred had approved of me after our opera dates. He thought I was a fine young man but now that we were engaged, he wanted to meet with me one on one where it would be expected that I formally ask his permission to marry his daughter.

"It's a European tradition," Yvonne explained.

"I know. That's fine. It was once a tradition here but now pretty much abandoned. People do what they want with or without parental tradition. But I'll do it," I said. "Still, what if he says no?"

"He won't. He's happy to get rid of me," said Yvonne. "I think I've been a burden to him these last two years. He has his own life, his own girlfriend. It's painful."

So one Saturday morning, I met Fred at a coffee shop on Shattuck and we had breakfast. He began telling me his life story. How he grew up in Surinam, went to technical school, became a ship's engineer, sailed the world, and had many "experiences" in Asia, Spain and the South Pacific. How that stood him in good stead to pick a wife. Pause. I felt awkward, not knowing how to broach the subject. He helped me out.

"Ah, so Mr. Allan. That's enough about me. Didn't you come here to ask me something?"

I cleared my throat. "Yes, of course. As you know Yvonne and I are serious, engaged in fact and we would like your blessing. More specifically, I would like your permission to marry her."

He could see I was sweating.

"Relax," he smiled. "Of course you have my permission. You seem to be a fine young man. Yvonne tells me you are studying television and have plans to go into that."

"Ah, yes. They are rather vague right now but in a year or so, I hope to be working in the business. But don't worry. I have other skills too. I have experience in land surveying and can work in that if need be. They pay very well."

"Yes, yes. I'm sure you will do all right no matter what field you go into. You are young. There are many opportunities. I simply want Yvonne to be happy. However, I do think that you should wait until next year to marry."

"Next year?"

"Yes," he paused and then continued. "An engagement needs some period of time so that the couple can come to know each other on a different, let's say more realistic footing. Sometimes, once couples get past the first flush of passion, they discover different people."

"Well, we have set no date yet."

"Good, there is no rush."

End of serious conversation. We chatted on for a while about life in Berkeley and the Bay Area and then I took my leave, with permission in my pocket.

***

When word got around among our friends and acquaintances that Yvonne and I were engaged, reaction was varied. John and Marge thought it was great. They wanted a married couple as friends. Most of the couples they knew were just living together. Jean-Paul thought it would be good for me. "It will focus your mind, *Mon Vieux*." However, he was not so sure about Yvonne. "It is a lot to give up to come and live in this country. I know how she feels."

Other reactions ranged from "Oh, how sweet," to "She looks so young," to "That's nice," to ironic, "Why don't you just live together?" to outright horror "Shit Brown. Why tie yourself down? There's so many fish in the sea."

Reaction from Gerard and Marie was congratulatory but cool.

"That's great, Al and Yvonne," Gerard said, "But don't you crazy kids rush into anything quick."

Gerard glanced nervously over to Marie who was in a funk. About all she could say was, "You two have me to thank. It was I after all who brought you together."

"Ah, not quite," I reminded her. "Remember, you fixed Yvonne up with the French professor."

"Ha, a mere detail," she scoffed. "It all worked out, didn't it, Gerard?"

"Uh, yeah sure."

"Of course, it worked out," said Marie wistfully. Here she and Gerard had been going together for nearly two years, and Gerard had yet to make a move towards formalizing their relationship. He hadn't even urged her to live with him. Gerard still apparently liked his space and freedom. He wasn't ready to commit. Yvonne and I had set a bad example, rushing off and becoming engaged a mere six months after we met.

Around this time, I received a letter from Sasha saying she wanted to move back to San Francisco. Maybe get back together. I had had no contact with Sasha since I left Mexico. She didn't have a clue that I had met Yvonne and was engaged to be married. I had to tell her what was going on. I wrote her a one-page letter explaining my situation but telling her I never would forget her and wished her all the best with her acting career. As far as San Francisco was concerned, I said that was up to her, but I felt that despite her momentary setbacks, her future was in Mexico. A couple of weeks later, I got a postcard from Acapulco, wishing me the best and that if I was so inclined, I could send her some wedding pictures. She ended by saying that she agreed.

Her best chance for success was in Mexico City.

**

Here it was mid-August and as I sent off my rental check two weeks late, it struck us both more forcibly than ever, that it made no sense to pay two rents since we now were engaged. It now made sense to consolidate our living arrangements. The logical answer was for me to move in with Yvonne in Berkeley since I would be carrying a minimal class load at S.F. State in the fall and she could continue her short commute to Capwells.

So I gave notice to my landlord, packed up my belongings and said goodbye to 150 Carl Street at the end of August. But I left with mixed feelings. This apartment had been my home for almost two years. And I had some qualms about moving in with Yvonne. Somehow, I felt I was violating her space. Even though I planned to pay for half the rent, I felt like I was a freeloader. I briefly thought maybe we should find another apartment but Yvonne would have none of that.

"Why move? This place is big enough for both of us," she said. "The rent is reasonable. And a move would be a big hassle."

She was right and I had the feeling we would be moving soon enough. So I became in a sense, Yvonne's kept man.

The next consideration followed logically from the first. Why were we waiting to get married? What were we waiting for? Her Dad's approval? We had that. Although he wanted us to wait in order to know each other better, we felt we knew each other well enough. Essentially, there was no real reason not to get married right away. We could elope. A quick trip to Reno. Get the deed done. After all, we figured the wedding was for us, other people were secondary. I guess we were selfish.

We plunged ahead and picked a date. Tuesday, September 12th. That was a vacation week for Yvonne. And of course, I was flexible. But now I was having second thoughts about Reno. Reno seemed so tacky. Getting married in an ersatz gingerbread chapel by strangers with no friends or family to witness it seemed rather cold. Then there was the Reno curse. Most of the people I knew who got married in Reno divorced a few years later. No, we could do better than that. Thinking back to my days at Ford Ord and how enchanting the Monterey Peninsula had been, I convinced Yvonne we should get married in Carmel, in the midst of Pacific splendor. We would stay at the Highland Inn perched high above the ocean with stunning views. And yes, we would invite our families and friends. It would be half an elopement. But a marriage still on our own terms.

I finalized the arrangements a week before D-Day. We would be married by a Justice of the Peace in Pacific Grove, a town adjacent to Carmel at 11 a.m. on September 12th. The secretary at the municipal hall told me on the phone that it was a cute little municipal courtroom set among the pines. A nice place to exchange our marriage vows. I reserved a room at the Highland Inn for that evening. After that, we planned to stay in Big Sur down the coast.

Finally, I made the phone calls to Mom and Dad telling them of our plans.

Mom: "Oh my God! For real?"

Me: "Yes, yes."

Dad: "Of course we will be there, son."

Me: "Good and bring Kenny along he can be my best man."

Yvonne told her father who was surprised that we were getting married so soon. But he too was delighted. He would certainly be there, even though it required taking an unpaid day off work.

We phoned Gerard and Marie and when we told them of our plans, Marie sounded ecstatic but then said that she was in a wedding in Los Angeles that weekend and didn't know if she and Gerard would make it back in time. She had some family obligations down there. I said, "Well, make it if you can."

Yvonne had also invited her best friend Kathy but for some reason, Kathy couldn't make it either. Yvonne suspected that Kathy was still angry with her for going off and getting married. In Kathy's eyes, I had busted up their close friendship. So Kathy was out. It was too bad that none of our closest friends could make it, but ultimately, it didn't matter. The wedding was for us.

And that was it. Wedding arrangements were made. It took all of a few hours on a weekday morning. What a contrast to my brother's wedding to Nancy! Their wedding that had been planned for months and while fancy, it had been very stressful for them.

Yvonne immediately went off to shop for a wedding dress.

27. THE KNOT

The following Monday, the day before our wedding, I rented a car from Budget on Shattuck Avenue and we set off. We crossed the bay at the San Mateo Bridge and took Route 92 over hills to Half Moon Bay. From there we drove down Highway One towards Monterey and Carmel. It was one of those bright, sunny days when you could see forever across the Pacific. It was on a day like this that I was with Tami on the beach at Big Sur. No. I shouldn't think of that. I was about to get married. God, why was my mind doing that?

I glanced over to Yvonne who was happily looking out the window at the seascape. I felt an urge to pull over and rush down to a secluded beach and ravage her but I didn't. Instead, I dwelt on the fact that here I was about to get married and I was thinking about another woman. Why was I doing that? Was I getting cold feet? Or was it a sign that maybe I couldn't be faithful to one person. Perhaps I had known too much variety. Still, I realized that variety was illusory. Yvonne was the one. I shoved all these thoughts out of my mind as we drove along on our scenic way to Carmel.

A couple of hours later we were on Seventeen Mile Drive outside of Carmel, admiring the spectacular seascape and noting the lush green golf course dotted with well-heeled golfers. Then we were on the outskirts of Carmel. I navigated my way up Ocean Drive, the main drag in town, and turned off onto a side street. A few seconds later, we pulled up in front a quaint little gingerbread cottage, the vacation home of a fraternity brother of mine who had generously offered it for our use.

The cottage was a one-bedroom affair built in the twenties when Carmel was an out-of-the-way art colony. At first, I had proposed that I should stay at a nearby motel in order to preserve some sense of traditional decorum. I mean, a groom really shouldn't sleep with his bride-to-be the night before the wedding. That was too much even for me. We needed separation. We needed the anticipation of the real wedding night. But Yvonne protested.

"That's a waste of money, Allan. Here, this cottage has twin beds. We can sleep apart. That should satisfy your bourgeois sense of decorum."

"OK, OK."

We then turned our attention to the last minute details of getting this quasi-elopement off the ground. It was rather disorganized. When I last talked to Mom and Dad, they weren't sure if they would drive down on the morning of or stay overnight somewhere. Fred said he would leave Berkeley early and drive down on the twelfth. All I knew was the parents said they would be there at the municipal hall at the appointed hour. So much for logistics.

I rushed off to order a bouquet for the bride while Yvonne stayed behind, unpacked and fooled with her dress and other accessories. When I came back, she modeled her dress for me. It was stunning—a chic, but simple white woolen A-line dress with long sleeves, ending six inches above the knee. She complimented it with white pantyhose, white shoes and a mini white bridal veil. Of course, Yvonne set the outfit off perfectly with her long dark hair and long elegant legs.

As for me, I was planning to wear my dark blue suit that I had bought in New York in my junior executive phase. It still looked good.

That evening we dined at a Mexican restaurant. Yvonne had only a taco salad, being careful about what she ate because sometimes Mexican food didn't sit well on the stomach. Later, we watched TV in our tiny cottage and like little children dutifully fell asleep in our separate twin beds on the eve of our fast approaching fate.

***

September 12, 1967. D-Day. Or rather W-Day. The day of our wedding. A day that Yvonne and I would vow to be together for better or for worse. It was enough to give any couple pause. Forever was a long time. Still, our path was set. We plunged ahead.

I was up early at seven and went out for a newspaper and some coffee and rolls. I was too nervous to have a regular breakfast. So was Yvonne. Back at the cottage, we munched on rolls and sipped coffee while perusing the *San Francisco Chronicle* as if nothing special was going on that day.

Indeed the news of the day was tame aside from a headlined story about singer Frank Sinatra having his two front teeth knocked out by the manager of the Las Vegas Sands Casino. No headlines from Vietnam. Anti-War protests were being planned but not for a month. It was just an ordinary day except for one small detail. OUR MARRIAGE!

We didn't talk much. We both knew what we had to do. I had to go fetch the wedding bouquet that I had ordered. Yvonne had to dress, a project, she told me that would take a long time and a project that she preferred I not be around for. That was OK. I would gladly get lost for an hour or so.

I went back out and wandered up and down Ocean Avenue on foot for a while. Then I got into the rental car and drove out to Seventeen Mile Drive. Slowly, the time passed and before I knew it, it was ten o'clock and I was back at the cottage showering and getting dressed. Yvonne had laid out my wedding suit in the living room and had shut the bedroom door while she was putting on her makeup. I wasn't supposed to see her until the very last moment. OK. OK.

Finally, the moment of departure arrived—10:30 a.m. I knocked on the bedroom door and announced it was time.

"OK. Just a minute. I have more touch up to do."

I thought, "Jeez, she has had all morning to get ready."

Patience.

A few minutes later, Yvonne emerged from the bedroom. Needless to say, she was spectacular in her white wool mini dress with the aforementioned accessories. Yet at the same time, she had the air of a blushing bride with flushed cheeks and shy, downcast eyes. Too perfect to even touch. All I said was, "Fantastic," and handed her the wedding bouquet.

Without a further word, we got into the rental and drove off to Pacific Grove.

***

Everybody was there when we pulled up in front of the municipal hall, an elegant little building that looked as if it belonged in New England. Fred, Mom, Dad, Kenny and surprise, Don. Don had flown down from Kennewick, Washington where he was now living and working for Ranney, a water system construction company.

"We can't have an older brother getting married without a Best Man, can we," said Don.

Apparently, Kenny had given way to Don in the Best Man role. Really, I had never given it much thought. Either one or both was OK with me. I hoped Kenny's feelings weren't hurt.

Everyone looked presentable. Don was in his power business suit. Dad was in his best "go-to-work" suit, Mom, lovely in an elegant summer dress and Kenny with his thick horn-rimmed glasses, looking like a teen intellectual in his narrow lapel, almost too small "go-to-church" suit. Fred looked a little rumbled with papers stuffed in his suit coat pocket, hair slightly mussed. He had just barely made it in time after a long drive through traffic. Dad, Mom, Don and Kenny had stayed overnight in Monterey.

After a few minutes of greetings, hugs and kisses, the moment had arrived. We filed into the municipal hall and were greeted by the secretary who led us to a courtroom where we met the judge who was to do the deed. I had expected some white-headed geezer in a black robe. This fellow was a tall, hip looking guy with gray at his temples, in a well-cut business suit. He shook our hands, made a little chit chat and then he said, "Shall we begin?" No procession here, but there was some background wedding music. Mom, Dad, Fred and Kenny sat down on courtroom benches. Yvonne and I with Don off to my side stood up front before the judge. The ceremony began.

I don't remember the exact words. I guess I was in a daze. Later I recalled, it was the standard ceremony and I remember saying "I do." I remember Don handing over the ring and I remember slipping the wedding ring on Yvonne's finger and saying, "With this ring, I do thee wed." That's about all.

When it was over, Yvonne was beaming. She pulled her veil pulled back and we kissed. The deed was done. We shook the judge's hand, thanking him and made our way back out into the sunshine. The whole ceremony had taken less than ten minutes. Unreal, I thought. I didn't feel any different. But Yvonne was obviously walking on air with a victory smile. She had got her man.

I felt harpooned. But happily harpooned.

Everybody took photos of one another. Yvonne and I in a score of poses. One having me look into my nearly empty wallet after paying the judge. Another of us gazing into each other's eyes. Photos of Mom and Yvonne, Fred and Yvonne, Dad and Yvonne, Kenny, Don and Yvonne. And a family photo with Yvonne taken by Fred. All on a little Kodak Instamatics and on my father's new reflex Mamiya/Sekor camera. Then we got into our respective cars and drove off to the Highland Inn for a wedding lunch.

***

The Highland Inn, four miles south of Carmel, was once a cute tucked-away hotel on a pine-studded hillside overlooking the ocean. That was back in the 1920s. Now it was a major, large-scale resort that my mother and father had stayed at and raved about. I had filed it away in my memory as a great place for a romantic, albeit, expensive getaway. But you only get married once (hopefully) and screw the eighty-dollar a day cost which, by the way, was footed by Dad as part of our wedding present.

Up the long winding drive we went. A doorman in a vaguely alpine get-up greeted us. We checked in and were led to our accommodations, a one-bedroom white cottage up the hill with a front porch and a stunning view of the Pacific. Yvonne, still beaming, said it was perfect. I concurred.

Yet no time to tarry. It was back down the hill to the main building where we met up with the rest of the family now in the lobby waiting for a table in the dining room. A few minutes later, we were led to our table in the corner with yet another view of the ocean and the rocks below. Again, perfection.

The wedding lunch: an elegant buffet with seafood, prime rib, perfectly done vegetables, a fresh salad bar and for desert a little wedding cake that my mother had ordered special. We all stuffed ourselves like pigs and of course washed it down with French Champagne and other assorted wines. Many toasts, much laughter, crazy stories from Mom and Dad and Fred. Even Don and Kenny got a few words in edgewise. And all the while, Yvonne still flushed with the victory look.

Later after lunch, before they left, Dad took me aside and gave me two hundred dollars. So did Fred. So we were fat for the remainder of our three-day honeymoon. Mom also informed me that she was planning a reception at our house in Martinez so all our friends from Berkeley could wish us well, along with a few from Martinez.

"Thanks, Mom. But you don't have to," I replied.

"Nonsense," she said. "You both deserve a reception. After all, it's not every day our eldest son gets married."

After they drove off, Yvonne and I hiked back up the hill to our cottage. Back at the cottage, we were still both wired. Too antsy to relax. On a patio just below us, Yvonne spotted a ping-pong table with paddles and balls at the ready.

"Let's play Allan. I don't think I have ever played you."

"Ah, sure. Why not?" I said, thinking "ping pong" on our honeymoon? I felt a bit sorry for her because I was a pretty good player. I would take it easy.

So still dressed in our wedding finery, we began to play. After the first couple of serves, I was fighting for my life. Yvonne served and volleyed that little white ball with skill and panache. It turned out she was an ace player, beating me handily the first few games.

"Where did you learn to play like that?"

"Oh, I didn't tell you? Ping-pong is popular in Holland. I played there and then was on a girl's team in high school. Pretty good, wouldn't you say?

I nodded, amazed at discovering a side of Yvonne that I had known nothing about.

Following several more ping-pong games, we felt pleasantly tired and relaxed and decided to return to the cottage and take advantage of our luxurious accommodations.

Later, stretched out on the big king size bed, with the late afternoon sun streaming in through the Venetian blinds, I marveled at her long, sleek body, at the perfection of her skin, at her crystal clear blue eyes. Suddenly, I had a sense of possession, a sense of having her forever. She was mine. I was hers. Until the end.

28. BIG SUR

The next day, we were up bright and early, both relieved that the wedding day was over. Although the wedding was as simple and as painless as we could make it, it was still stressful. After all, a lifetime commitment was no small thing. After a leisurely breakfast at the Highland Inn, we hit the road for the rest of our *voyage de noces*.

Our first stop was Mission Carmel, an eighteenth-century adobe mission founded by the Spanish padre, Father Serra. It was the good Father Serra who established a string of missions up and down the California coast and who was instrumental in enslaving the local Indians under the guise of saving their souls.

The Spanish styled church and the courtyard with the high adobe walls inspired me to take some fashion photo shots of Yvonne, now dressed in a perky red, white and blue striped mini-dress. She posed as if she were a Vogue model in archways, behind see-through wrought iron gates and against mud brown adobe walls.

Then it was back in the car and down Highway One to Big Sur where we were going to spend the rest of the day and the night. As we drove along the coast, the gently rolling countryside around Carmel gave way to high plunging hills, canyons, redwood gorges and spectacular seascapes. It was this landscape that had attracted hermits, visionaries, dropouts, painters and writers for years, most notably Henry Miller. During the 1950s, Beats, like Kerouac and Ferlinghetti, used to hang out here, getting stoned on pot or on simple meditation. Now Big Sur was a magnet for hippy communal types finding their groove with nature.

Soon, we came to the Limekiln Bridge, in the heart of Big Sur. The graceful concrete and steel bridge spanned a dramatic gorge with a creek running under it, a perfect blend of the man-made integrated with nature.

I noted some shacks and lean-tos far below and tiny figures on the beach. The place looked inviting so I turned off on a dirt road that appeared to lead down to the beach. Bump, bump, bump, down the rutted road we went in the rental with Yvonne holding on tight and me trying not to drive off the road. We finally came to the end of the road about fifty yards from the beach. A couple of husky hippy dudes with chest-length beards approached the car, not looking too friendly.

I got out and said hello.

"Hello, yourself man. You have business here?" said the older of the two.

"Hey, this beach is open to the public, isn't it?"

"Don't know but we hang out here. We like it for ourselves," one said eyeing me and then Yvonne still in the car.

"We just want to take a short stroll around," I explained. "We'll be gone in no time."

One whispered something to the other.

I got the drift. "Hey, don't worry. I'm not the Man. Just a newlywed tourist."

Then both smiled. The younger said, "Yeah, we were wondering. That shit colored car sure looks like a narc car.

"Nah it's just a cheap rental," I replied, wondering how many other pissed off hippies were around here.

"Cool," nodded the elder. "Sure man, take a look around."

Yvonne got out of the car and we hiked over to the coarse gravel beach and walked around a bit and then seeing the two hippies watching us from afar, we headed back.

"You really are newlyweds?" said the elder as we approached.

"Yes, freshly minted."

"Far out. Come on over to my shack and let's share a joint."

"Uh, OK," I said somewhat against my better judgment. We hiked up the canyon along the creek until we came to a clearing with several lean-to shacks scattered about. And there, under one shelter, sitting on a sleeping bag, was a young woman with a baby suckling at her breast. She smiled at us but said nothing.

"My ol' lady," the older hippy explained as he lit up a joint and then passed it over to us. "How about a little wine to go with that." He poured some wine from a jug into a coffee cup.

We sat on stumps in front of the shelter, sipping the wine, taking only one puff on the joint before handing it back.

The elder hippy shrugged, took a deep drag for himself and then said, "Married, huh?"

"Yep. All married up," I replied.

"That's nice. Straight but nice. Me and my ol' lady don't need that piece of paper."

"Whatever works for you," I said nodding and then changing the subject, "Don't you get cold down here. All that fog and such."

"Nah, not really," he said looking over his domain. "We just build a big bonfire if it gets too dank. It's a great life." Then the elder hippy fell into a hacking cough fit that sounded tubercular to me.

I looked around. There was a small garden. "So you grow your own food," said Yvonne brightly.

"Oh, yeah, we try," said the younger. "But we have to shop now and then up in Carmel. It's a bummer. Got to panhandle first. Sometimes we get busted. Still, it's a great life."

We chatted for a while longer and then Yvonne and I thanked them for their hospitality and started back for the car. The elder followed along. At the car, he shook my hand and then still holding it, he said, "Say, man, I could use a little bread. Supplies are low, here."

"Bread?"

"Yeah, just a little cash to get by," he said. "Like, give me your address, I'll pay you back"

"Ah, sure, don't worry about it," I said, realizing that I didn't have much choice down here in a gulch with god knows how many drug-crazed hippies hanging about in the forest and the weeds. I pulled out my wallet and handed him a five-dollar bill.

"Thanks, man," he said, eyeing my wallet stuffed with cash. "Ah, say, maybe you could advance me another five spot. That'll keep me and my ol' lady good for a while.

"Sure, sure," I said, handing him another five and then quickly slipped into the driver's seat and started the engine.

He stepped back. "Thanks, man. Have a great trip. Have a great marriage."

We drove off, relieved to get out of there.

***

We turned around and headed back up Highway One. After this encounter at Limekiln, we both needed a stroll on a nice, safe, state park beach. Pfeiffer Beach with its long sweeping vista was just the ticket for our peace of mind. By now, the day was warm for the coast, somewhere in low seventies and the Pacific glittered like a jewel. We hiked along the beach for a while, happy together, dodging the surf at the water's edge. Yvonne said she loved being near rough water. It reminded her of the North Sea in the winter.

"Yes, but you have to admit the scenery is better here," I said.

"Of course, but the North Sea is in my blood," she replied. "I don't care if it's cold and gray and the beaches are dull and flat, it's my heritage."

"Well, someday we will see it."

"Of course. How about next year, Allan? I haven't been back to Holland for four years. Also, I would like you to meet my mother and sisters, Jeanette and Ingrid."

"Certainly," I said now realizing that many trips to Europe would probably be in our future.

We hung out at Pfeiffer Beach for an hour and then getting hungry, we hiked back up the trail to the car and drove down to the Nepenthe Restaurant.

Even though it was a weekday, the Nepenthe was in full swing. Its vast sundeck with the stunning views of the ocean far below was jammed with diners, drinkers, loungers and hangers-on. Nobody worked nine to five around here, especially on a nice day. We found a table near the edge of the deck that somebody had just left and by and by, a free-spirit waitress came up and took our order—the Nepenthe ambrosia burger and two steins of the local brew. Then we settled back and mellowed in the warm sun, yet cool air with the fresh ocean smell, and listened to the sound of soft Buddhist chants and ethereal eastern music punctuated by the tinkling of wind chimes.

I could see how one could spend a lot of time here chilling. Even the name Nepenthe evoked escape. In Greek, the loose translation of "nepenthe" was "the one that chases away sorrow."

The Nepenthe had been around since the late forties, the site originally owned by Orson Wells. It was a place famous for the views, chimes, bonfires, moonlight dancing and its burgers that we were now enjoying. There was also the distinct smell of pot in the air and even stronger—hashish. Beer was good enough for us.

Eventually, feeling sleepy with the beer and the scene, we were ready for a nap so we checked into the nearby Big Sur River Inn where we had reservations. It was a much smaller hotel than the Highland Inn. But cozy and charming in its woodsy chalet way. Our room was small too but no matter, it had a queen size bed and a view of the woods outside, now dabbled with the late afternoon light. We crashed on the bed and soon it was.... ZZZ.

That evening, we were back at Nepenthe for dinner. We sipped on Chablis while we watched the sun go down, at first saturating the horizon clouds in a blaze of golds and reds and then sinking, sizzling into the sea. Soon the fires were going in the barbecue pits as a fog bank moved in, cooling the coast. We debated eating inside, but Yvonne said the spirit of the place had to be experienced outdoors. So I in my jacket and she in a sweater, we dined on grilled salmon outdoors on a table lit by candlelight and clicked glasses in another toast to our journey through life together.

***

A week and a half later, Mom held her reception. It was rather nice affair at our Martinez house. Plenty of goodies to eat, including another little wedding cake and a stack of wedding presents which Yvonne and I opened like kids on Christmas morning. (In those days, one opened wedding presents in front of the guests, a practice rare today.) Just about all of our friends were there. Marie and Gerard who apologized profusely for not making our wedding. Jean-Paul and his current girlfriend, looking very French, opining on this and that. Dirk running around taking photos. Dirk, in his Dashiki and wild Afro hair said he was returning to his African roots. Yvonne's friends, Kathy and Vail. My old high school friend Bob and his wife Gloria. (Boy he had gained weight.) Jan, another old high school friend and fellow Army reservist.

Then there were Mom's neighborhood friends, Lucille from down the street and Cal, the former professional baseball player. And of course, Don and Nancy who had flown in from Kennewick and Kenny looking very grown up and bedazzled by the Berkeley crowd. Not to be outdone, Dad was running around beaming, taking pictures with his slick Mamiya/Sekor camera. I could tell he was impressed with the bevy of lovelies in his house and also happy that his eldest son finally had a wife.

So Yvonne and I stood there, she in her burnt orange dress, I in my New York business suit, amid the toasters, the waffle irons, the dishes, and the coffee makers, looking like a perfectly matched couple—all captured in photos. A moment frozen in time.

29. GRIND

A few days later, it was back to grind. Although we were married, we carried on as much before. What was that mad interlude in Carmel all about? Just kidding, of course. Yvonne resumed her commute to Capwells. I, now living in Berkeley, had a much longer commute to San Francisco State. First, I had to take the Muni Bus over to the San Francisco Muni Terminal and then hop on the M line trolley that went out to San Francisco State on 19th Avenue. It was about a ninety-minute operation one-way. I got a lot of reading done. Still, I was desperately missing my Carl Street apartment and vowed to move back to San Francisco at the first opportunity, thinking that maybe Yvonne could indeed land a job at Joseph Magnin in the city.

Although I was only taking two courses, TV News and Master Thesis, I was spending about three hours a day auditing classes to make up for the deficiencies that I had displayed in my orals in communication theory and popular culture. This was a boring, tedious exercise. I could barely stay awake in the classes while the various professors droned on. However, I did make sure that the department chairman Stuart Hyde knew I was auditing the classes he had suggested. Occasionally, I would engage in class discussion.

Actually, some of the most interesting things going on at SF State were outside the classroom. In particular, black student politics. It should be noted here that by the fall of 1967, the term "Negro" had disappeared overnight from the college campuses and the news media. It was now replaced with "black" or "Afro-American." Dashikis and luxuriant afro hairstyles were the order of the day. Actually, I thought the style worked very well on the blacks. At least they were honoring their African roots. And everywhere one turned on campus, there were posters of Huey Newton sitting in a wicker chair in his Black Panther get-up, holding a trident in one hand and a rifle in the other. Newton was now in jail awaiting trial, accused of fatally shooting an Oakland cop.

The central issue at San Francisco State was whether black students should have their own college within a college. In other words, a black student union that would have its own offices, its own finances, its own faculty, its own courses, etc. I used to see the activist blacks sitting in the cafeteria by the hour in their berets, dashikis, Army fatigues and boots. Many had beards. They would argue at length over the particulars of a black student union (BSU) and whether to engage in protests and demonstrations to achieve their goals. In November, some of them did take action. Members of the BSU broke into the offices of the student newspaper and beat up the editor who had to be hospitalized. This was a preview of the turmoil to come at San Francisco State.

Even though student revolution was in the air, I was intent on doing my studies and getting out. I felt ancient. At twenty-seven, I felt too old to be a student any longer. Dare I say it, I was eager to launch a serious career. Maybe being married only a few short weeks had matured me. Of course, I was still bogged down in my thesis which was proving to be a much greater project than I had anticipated. And I seriously doubted whether it was worth the effort. I didn't need a master's degree to get a job in broadcasting. But Yvonne insisted that I continue.

"You've come all this way, Allan," she said. "You should finish what you started. You never know, you might want to teach."

"OK, OK, as long as you are willing to support me."

"For a while," she replied.

So I proceeded to round up of scores of books on television production, aesthetics, and dramaturgy, including Zettl's *Television Production Handbook*. Also, I checked out books on theater design, acting and directing along with newspaper and magazine articles on *Requiem for a Heavyweight*. Further, I had reference works on conducting a content analysis of visual material, along with several unpublished dissertations on television dramaturgy. I read them all and took copious notes based on a preliminary outline that I had concocted for my thesis now entitled, "Depth Characteristics of Requiem for a Heavyweight."

As already mentioned, my thesis advisor, Dr. Zettl had warned me it might be a daunting task. As I delved into the literature, I began to see what he meant. I had to isolate each and every technique the clever directors of the live TV dramas had done to enhance the depth characteristics of the image. This was taking weeks, several hours a day. I compiled stacks and stacks of note cards and filed them under various topics. I estimated that the research of just this portion of the project would take me the entire semester. Then I had to procure the kinescope and do the visual analysis. My head ached even to think about it. But I plugged away.

While researching my thesis, I also had to cram for my orals which were scheduled for mid-January. I had notebook after notebook filled with the collective wisdom of my audit professors. I did consult some of the texts for the course but concentrated on what was said in lecture. I figured what these egomaniacs really wanted to hear was their own pearls of wisdom regurgitated.

When I wasn't involved in school and Yvonne wasn't working, we hung out with our friends or just strolled around Telegraph and the campus. Essentially, I was bored with Berkeley even though it was as active as ever in the anti-war movement. As already described, our big involvement came with the Induction Center protest in October. Other than that, we were out of it.

Yvonne was tired of Berkeley too and also tired of Capwells. She wasn't looking forward to the Christmas crush in retailing. During that time, Capwells required their management trainees to work ten and twelve-hour days, six days a week, all without overtime pay, since the management trainees were on salary. She had gone through one Christmas crunch and didn't know if she could handle another.

"It's maddening. I don't want to do what I did last year. They were supposed to give me extra time off to make up for my extra-long hours last year but they never did."

"You ought to unionize," I suggested.

"Don't be silly. We are supposed to be management. Only the sales clerks are unionized. They get the overtime."

"Hey, go on strike anyway. Blood suckers."

***

My only real interest at San Francisco State was the night course I was taking in television news. It was given by Mel Kampmann, the news director at the local NBC affiliate, KRON-TV. This was a nuts and bolts course in real world local TV news. We didn't have tests; we didn't have to produce a news show (which I had already done). We only had to watch the local TV news shows, take notes on the stories they covered and then write a short paper at the end of the semester describing what we got out of the course. Almost a blow-off course, except it gave us valuable insights into the workings of local TV News.

Aside from some general discussions about the problems and conundrums of covering local news, each week Kampmann would bring in a member of his news team who would explain exactly what he did. For instance, the news producer. His job was to organize the newscast, oversee the writing of it, and then get it on and off the air without a hitch. Then there was the assignment editor whose job it was to decide along with the news director what stories to cover and how to cover them on a daily basis. The assignment editor had to also assign reporters and film crews to the various stories and make sure they were completed in the field in time to be edited and gotten on air. Then there were the reporters who explained how they went about covering their beats in politics, education, sports, crime, or spot news of accidents and disasters. We also heard from the cameramen who shot the film and the film editors who edited the film. The main anchors, Art Brown and Jerry Jensen, dropped by for one class and told us what they did, at times rather defensively: "We are more than just readers. We have long experience as journalists and the awards to prove it. So when we read, we give credibility to the newscast."

And finally, there was the weather girl, Karna, a former model who stood at the weatherboard and told the audience whether it was warm or cold, foggy or sunny or rainy. She was essentially visual eye-candy but she took her job very seriously and was bucking to become a full-fledged news reporter.

The course was capped by a tour of the newsroom and studios at KRON-TV, studios still housed in the basement of Chronicle building at Fifth and Mission. Kampmann told us that a new state-of-the-art station was completed on Van Ness Avenue and that the news operation would move in there shortly.

Our class of twelve watched as the reporters oversaw the final editing of their film news packages. We watched as newswriters frantically pounded out last minute scripts in the newsroom for the 6 p.m. show that was about to air. We watched as the on-air director marked his scripts with cues to indicate which visual source he would be on—studio camera, camera card, film chain, etc. We watched as the 6 p.m. producer calmly walked into the control room with his stack of scripts in one hand and a stopwatch in the other. And finally, we watched, as the on-air director put the whole thing on the air like a master juggler with scores of balls in the air and never once missing a beat or going to black. It was indeed a heady experience and it harkened back to my days in the control room at KGO-TV in helping put on the Army public service show. At the time, I was appalled at the helter-skelter of a live TV production but now over two years later with experience in film and in my own student TV productions, it dawned on me that maybe this TV news business is what I would like to be doing in some capacity. And perhaps, just perhaps, Mel Kampmann was my entrée into this world.

I thought that maybe I could start as a newswriter. News writing seemed like a do-able job. I thought I could write in what appeared to be television's simple conversational style. I had spoken with one newswriter, Vic Burton, who had been sitting in the corner at a small typing table banging out a last minute script. He said ninety percent of the show was written by newswriters

"So what do the anchors do? Just sit there and look good?"

"Just about. Sometimes they write something. Most of them are more than just a pretty face and can do actually reporting. But the bulk of the writing and editing supervision is done by the writers and the reporters."

"No kidding."

***

Mid-January, I took my orals for my master's and did much better. The irony was they didn't ask me much about communication theory or popular culture. Instead, they focused on TV aesthetics and my thesis which I had down cold. In any case, they gave me a pass and wished me good luck in my future endeavors, apparently thinking I was through with San Francisco State. Actually, I still had one more course to go, another semester of Master's Thesis. I wanted to get at least some credit for this ever ballooning project. But since, there was no class to attend, I was effectively done with trooping out to San Francisco State. Now, I had the choice, indeed the luxury, of spending all the time on my thesis but I was also anxious to get started in the TV business. I was feeling guilty at being a financial burden to Yvonne. We needed more cash rolling in as we were trying to save for a trip to Europe in the fall. Thus it was I began my job hunt.

I had been subscribing to *Broadcast Magazine*, the bible of the industry. The back listed pages of job availabilities in both radio and television. Most of the television opportunities were in small market operations. They had jobs in production, news reporting, producing, or even anchoring. That might be a logical place to start except all the California jobs were in the sticks, places like Eureka, Santa Maria, Salinas, Merced, etc. All out of the question. With Yvonne's job at Capwells, I had to find something in the Bay Area. Most were entry-level gofer jobs but even these jobs were in high demand and often not advertised.

I decided my best bet was to use the contacts that I already had in the industry. I started with Mr. Smith, the program director of KQED. In his course last spring, he had mentioned that they would be expanding their production staff in the fall. This in anticipation of funding from the newly formed Corporation for Public Broadcasting. I wondered if they were still hiring.

Mid-February I contacted Smith. Yes, he remembered me and remembered that I was good at TV directing. He had seen some of my work. He said they were still looking for assistant directors. If I was interested to come on over for an interview.

I typed up a resume emphasizing my TV and radio projects. Then I put on my suit and tie, and took the Muni to KQED south of Market Street. After a few minutes wait in the dingy waiting room, Mr. Smith came out of his office and greeted me warmly. Mr. Smith, a gracious man, courtly man, was very different from most of the hyperkinetic types that I had met in commercial TV land. He scanned my resume, noting the radio documentary.

"Hmm... that's interesting. We do a lot of documentaries here but right now there's nothing open in that area."

"That's an area I would like to work in," I replied. "Do you expect any openings in the near future?"

"Ah, possibly but competition is very stiff. We recruit nationally for the documentaries. We get the best here, people who have a track record. And if we set up a unit, they hire their own production staff. Your best, bet, Allan, is to start working here in a general production capacity. As an assistant director and such. Down the road you could possibly segue into documentary."

"OK, what does an assistant director do?" I asked. "Does he actually get to direct?"

"Ah, sometimes on the easier shows, the taped shows. Mostly an assistant director does whatever the director wants him to do. Set up the shows, procure props, hand hold guests. In general, take care of the myriad of details in order to get a show on the air. And I'm afraid, even fetch coffee."

I remembered my tour of the station last spring when I watched a KQED director methodically direct an education show about building blocks for toddlers. The hostesses demonstrated the many and varied ways, a child could build different things. Not too exciting, but being an assistant director was a way in.

"Well, I might be interested. Can we take look around?"

"Sure," said Mr. Smith and he gave me a quickie tour. I saw the same TV director, half asleep, now directing an interview show with some boring educator in town looking at the San Francisco Public schools. This was an even bigger yawn than the building block show.

"I'll tell you what Allan," said Mr. Smith at the end of the tour. "I'll talk this over with the staff but with my recommendation, I'm sure that they would be willing to take you aboard initially as an intern."

"An intern?"

"Yes, we start all prospective hires out as interns, even though you will be doing assistant director work."

"Do you pay interns?"

"Well, no. Not for the first few months at least. It's standard operating procedure at KQED but I'm confident it will all work out and we will ultimately hire you as a paid staff member." He smiled.

I frowned.

Seeing the frown on my face, Mr. Smith added. "Are you still interested?"

"I'll have to think about that," I said, inwardly feeling very insulted. I was used to working for good union wages, probably double of anything I might make here. No way was I going to work for free, entrée or not into the world of broadcasting.

"Well, let me know within the week," said Mr. Smith. "We do have other interviewees."

"Certainly."

That was the end of KQED-TV for me. I was so pissed, I never phoned back.

***

Ironically, a few months later, KQED launched one of the most innovative television news shows in history. The reporters and writers of the *San Francisco Chronicle* who were on strike for fifty-two days participated in a show called "Newspaper of the Air," anchored by Mel Wax. They sat around a city news desk and discussed the news of the day. Everybody knew their stuff but the most informed and most insightful were a couple of grizzled city editors wearing green visors who would hold forth on national and international news.

At the end of the program, the managing editor would create a mock up of a front page on a large butcher paper easel explaining why he headlined one story or another, where that story would be placed and what photos would be used. As an added bonus, the Chronicle political cartoonist would display an array of cartoons he had drawn that day, and the most relevant and witty one would be chosen for the front page.

Had I been able to work on that, I might have just said yes to Mr. Smith.

30. KRON-TV

The pressure to find a job increased when Yvonne was laid off from Capwells in late February. It seemed her resistance to working six long days a week during Christmas season had been held against her and when it came time to evaluate her performance as a management trainee, she received a low rating, although her sales figures were way up. Of course, Capwells had no intention of keeping all the trainees they had hired. Their employment had been on a trial basis for a year to 18-months. Then Capwells took the meat ax, keeping only a few of the so-called outstanding trainees. In any case, Yvonne was stunned.

"It's all about the culture," I said. "If you're not a true believer in the world of retailing, you're suspect."

"But, my department was doing so well," she lamented.

"It doesn't matter. For some reason, they sensed you didn't fit into their maniac culture. The joint is too downscale for you, anyway," I insisted. "I think you'd do much better at Joseph Magnin or some other high-end retailer."

"Well, we'll see," she sighed. "I have some vacation money. We can live on that for a while."

I urged her to file for unemployment right away which she obediently did.

***

So now, my screwing around with my master thesis seemed so frivolous. We had to get cash rolling in. It was so tight that a big night out was strolling down Telegraph Avenue and sharing a twenty-five cent ice cream cone. Was surveying again in my future? It was a sure thing and well paid. But was I giving up too easily on working in television?

I had sent out my resume to other California stations, including the ones in the sticks and heard nothing back. I even went to a career counselor in San Francisco to get some advice on my job hunt. The gentleman, an ex-personnel man at IBM, re-wrote my resume to make it more marketable and urged me to deal with only the man at the top.

"Avoid all personnel offices," he advised. "They are paid mainly to fend off job seekers, especially in glamor professions like broadcasting."

"So what do I do?"

"You compile a list of the station managers or the presidents of the broadcast groups, whoever has the power to hire and send them your resume, along with a professional photo. If they like what they see, they'll pass it on down to the news director with a note something like, "Why don't you talk to this young man." It'll be a suggestion the underlings can't ignore."

"Uh, OK. I'll give that a try."

"It's a proven method," he insisted. "Just remember in any large organization, there are only a few who make the real decisions. It's your task to make contact with them."

It was a lot of theoretical talk, but the counselor did make a certain amount of sense. I had a photo portrait taken of me in my business suit with a fresh, well-groomed haircut. I looked like an archetypical junior executive on the make. I sent out some revised resumes with my photo.

I also went over to the Cal Placement office to see what they had since it was job recruitment season. I scanned the list of corporations coming for interviews. Hmm, the ad agencies looked interesting. I knew that all of them were doing a lot in television commercial production. They were looking for TV/film people. I signed up for one interview with the Leo Burnett Ad Agency to see what was what but then I got cold feet and canceled it. I had decided to stick with television. Nonetheless, I got a telephone call from the Leo Burnett recruiter urging me to come by.

"Mr. Brown, I see you canceled your interview appointment. That's too bad because we would really like to talk to you," said a polished voice on the phone.

"Uh, after due consideration, I think I'm going to look in the area of television news," I replied.

"Oh, that's fine. Very glamorous. Although you must know that unless you are working in a major market as a reporter or an anchor, it doesn't pay very well."

"I'm aware of that."

"On the other hand, we at Leo Burnett are doing wonderful, exciting things in film and television and we pay well even for those just starting out. Looking at your resume, I see you have a nice photograph of yourself and a varied background, a varied work history, indeed a degree in history from Berkeley, time abroad, plus knowledge of television and film production. That's what we are looking for. Somebody with a broad background, awareness of the world and also with technical expertise."

"Gee, I'm flattered," I replied. "But aren't you headquartered in Chicago?"

"Yes, we are. But we have branches in all the major cities with a rather large production oriented branch in Los Angeles. Still, you would have to spend a year or so in Chicago before we sent out into the field. In any case, why don't I reschedule your appointment and we can talk about this further."

"Sure," I said, weakening.

***

After talking to the Leo Burnett recruiter, I felt down in the dumps. Here was a golden opportunity, yet I really didn't want to work in advertising selling soap or cars. Plus, the prospect of leaving California for the Midwest was not too appealing. I liked Chicago when I visited it several years ago when I was going around with Bobbie but to live there, was another story.

The next day I phoned Mel Kampmann, the news director of KRON-TV, asking if he would see one of his former students. I phrased it as wanting to get some job hunting tips for a job in TV news. He said "Sure, come on over tomorrow around lunch time. I'll show you the new studios."

So I took the Muni over and walked up Van Ness Avenue until I came to the spanking new station. It was indeed impressive—an ultra modern block-long building, something in the style of I. M. Pei. I waited in the marble lobby for a few minutes until Kampmann showed up, coming out of an elevator with Jerry Jensen, the KRON-TV anchor.

Kampmann shook my hand and then said, "Let's go up to the newsroom where we can talk."

We took the elevator up to the third floor and he led me through the newsroom, a rather large room full of new desks, electric typewriters and an assignment area which consisted of a semi-circular desk full of squawking police radios. Since it was noon, there was not much activity going on. Only the assignment editor, a hippy looking guy, was on duty with an assistant. The 6 p.m. producer was reading the newspaper. As Kampmann explained, the reporters were out in the field, the producer on lunch and the afternoon newswriters had yet to arrive for their shifts.

He led me into his glass-enclosed office. I was wondering if this was the tour—a bums rush through the newsroom, but it was apparent he wanted to talk about something.

"Have a seat Allan."

I sat down. He leaned back in his swivel chair and then looking me over, said, "Do you remember what I said in class about timing and luck often being determinants in a career in television news."

"Ah, yes I do," I replied, wondering what he was driving at.

"Yes, well this could be your lucky day. Our courier, Vince, just quit this morning. He's going back to Boston. Something about family problems. Great kid, sorry to lose him. But now we have the slot open and here you are coming to see me about how to get a job in TV News. Do you think you would be interested in starting out as a KRON courier?"

"Ah, maybe. What does a courier do?"

"Well, assuming you have a valid driver's license, you drive around San Francisco and indeed the Bay Area and pick up the film from crews in the field and rush it back to the lab for processing. Once processed, you rush it back to the station for editing for air. It's a critical, rush, rush job but you have a new VW Bug to zip around in. While we don't encourage you to get speeding or parking tickets, we don't sweat it either. How well, do you know San Francisco and the Bay Area?"

"Rather well, I've been driving around here for years."

"There are other duties as well which Vince will explain to you and I might add, there should be opportunities to work on the desk when our assignment editor, Evan, is off or maybe get involved in show production on the weekends. We do expect you to work weekends. The pay is one hundred dollars a week plus the opportunity for a lot of overtime, double time on Sundays."

Hmm, I thought. That wouldn't be half of what I could make surveying. Still, it was an entrée into the television news business and I didn't foresee staying in this job long. It would be a stopgap while I looked for a better position. After a pause, I answered, "Ah, when do you want me to start?"

"How about tomorrow. Vince will show you the ropes for a few days and then you'll be on your own."

I took a deep breath and then said, "OK."

When I reported back to Yvonne, she couldn't believe it. "Just like that. You walk in and Mr. Kampmann offers you a job?"

"Yeah, as he said just luck. In any case, television moves fast. It doesn't pay much but I plan on a lot of overtime and with your unemployment checks, we should be in good shape for while."

"I hope. Just don't give up your thesis."

"Don't worry, I'll get it done.

***

When I said television news moved fast, that was an understatement. The next few weeks were an unbroken blur. In addition to major breaking news such as the assassination of Martin Luther King Jr. in Memphis and a shootout between the Oakland Police and the Black Panthers, there were my duties as a courier to attend to. Vince showed me the ins and outs of getting around town, getting over to the lab, all the short cuts and the alleys. He showed me how to get down to the airport in rush hour, how to beat the traffic on the Bay Bridge. We did this in a brand new VW Bug with the KRON-TV logo and a big circle "4" plastered on the hood, the doors and the rear of the car. This was our ticket to speed up and down San Francisco's hills and park in any illegal spot that we chose with the cops looking the other way.

Part of my job was to deliver reporters to their film crews in the field. Other times, I drove station VIP's to various functions around town. Quite often, this meant a free meal or at least free *hors d'oeurves* at the event. While making these rounds, I got a glimpse of the San Francisco's movers and shakers—Mayor Joseph Alioto; Melvin Belli, the flamboyant defense lawyer; Herb Caen, the Baghdad-by-the Bay columnist; Dianne Feinstein who was then active in civic affairs; Casper Weinberger, the Republican state director of finance and also on the Board of KQED; and Jesse Unruh, Speaker of the California State Assembly. No sighting of Governor Reagan though. He avoided San Francisco if he could help it. Then there was John Fell Stevenson, one of Adlai Stevenson's sons, a transplant from Illinois who was active in San Francisco social circles. I thought he was cool, urbane, and Eastern but I could never figure out what he did other than bask in the veneration of San Francisco society.

Also, every evening, I had to fetch of a pile of late editions of the *San*

Francisco Chronicle that came out around 8 p.m. Vic Burton, the 11 p.m. news producer, always wanted to see what the paper was headlining. Half of the 11 p.m. newscast seemed to come from that edition. That was one of things that shocked me. Watching the newswriters rewrite newspaper stories from the bulldog edition of the *Chronicle*. The theory was the papers wouldn't hit the street until 10 p.m., so few people would have seen it by the 11 p.m. News. It would still be fresh news.

Sometimes I stood in the Chronicle press room and watched the "bulldogs" roll off the presses, headlines going by so fast it made you dizzy. Other times, I would go upstairs and hang out the Chronicle city room. The city room was a relic left over from the turn-of-the-century with its low hanging lights, its ancient, circular editor's desk around which old editors in visors sat scanning wire copy. Fire and police radios squawking, teletypes clacking. Off in the corners, rewrite men at their desks on the telephone with reporters, banging out copy. It was still the world of ink-stained wood and tobacco splattered linoleum. It was the smell of men who didn't change their shirts too often, the smell of ink and day-old burnt coffee. It was a scene right out of Ben Hecht's "Front Page."

Occasionally, I had to dig up old stories from the Chronicle newspaper morgue for the KRON reporters so they would have some idea of the background on a particular story. The creaky newspaper librarian one floor above the city room was always more than happy to find a particular story that she had carefully sorted, cataloged and stuck in one of the many thousands of manila folders piled about. I would grab the folder full of yellowed clippings and hustle back to the station.

But as noted, the most critical part of my job was to transport the film from the crew to the lab. Sometimes I had to go as far as Vallejo, Hayward or even Martinez if big news was breaking to fetch the film. Then it was a road race back to San Francisco. Once at the film lab on Golden Gate Avenue, I would always urge the processor to push the film in order to develop it faster. There was often film from KGO News waiting for processing too. But KGO-TV, located across the street, usually had no one around to lobby for its film, so mine would take priority. Once the film was processed, I would jump back in the VW and race over to KRON-TV, parking in the underground garage. Then I would run up four flights of stairs and hand the film off to the film editor for cutting.

After I had been doing couriers duties on my own for a couple of weeks, Kampmann pulled me aside, "I don't know how you do it, Allan, I don't know how many traffic laws you have broken, but you are the fastest courier we have ever had. Keep up the good work."

That was me, Johnny Rocket.

When news was slow or there wasn't much film being shot, I would hang out at the assignment desk and help the assignment editor, Evan White, monitor the radios. I quickly learned the codes that the police and the fire used around town. Listening to these radios was key to getting on the scene of a fire or a crime scene before any other news outfit. I managed to pick up on a few calls for shootings and fires. I also picked up the desk duties fairly rapidly and often ran the desk on weekends when no regular assignment editor was on the job. I think Evan had mixed feelings about me. He was younger than I and in spite of is hippy beard and dress, was a very serious fellow. To him, I was probably the archetypical eager beaver gunning for his job down the line. Still, I was a big help to him and he let me know it.

"You seem to have a knack for this shit, Brown. If I ever leave this dump, I'll recommend you for the job."

"No thanks, Evan. My interest lies in the production side of things."

"Well, it pays to know about the whole news operation, to be able to do any job."

Essentially, the jobs that interested me were the producing and news writing jobs. Dick Riley and Vic Burton were the 6 p.m. and the 11 p.m. news producers respectively. They wrote and organized the show. Helping them were four or five newswriters who wrote readers, voice-overs and oversaw the editing of various news film packages with the reporter. Their other duties included ordering slides, artwork, and monitoring the daily electronic feeds from the network. They also wrote the national and international stories with the accompanying videotape.

I used to follow one of the *über*-newswriters around, Bill Magee. A cool guy with a pen always stuck behind his ear and a stopwatch on a chain around his neck. He never broke a sweat when the pressure was on to get a news film package on the air. It was from him that I learned the rudiments of working on a film package.

Usually, but not always, the newswriter and the reporter viewed the film together. As the writer screened the film, he would scribble on a large yellow legal pad noting the times of various scenes and sound bites with a stopwatch. Then he and the reporter would discuss which sound bites and video to use and the reporter would go off to write his script. Once written, the reporter would usually record his script on audio carts that would later be synced up to the film package.

(This historic note: film with magnetic audio strips was not yet in widespread use in TV news. The magnetic strip allowed the reporter to record audio directly onto the film.)

Meanwhile, under the supervision of the newswriter, the film editor would cut the film to match the carts and integrate the chosen sound bites into the package. If there was time, the on-air director would prerecord the audio carts and film package on videotape, so when it aired there would be no screw-ups. Most often there was no time and so the whole exercise was done live on a crash basis with fingers crossed. Hence the importance of getting the film back from the lab at the earliest possible opportunity. And hence, the importance of being able to work fast under deadline pressure, a skill at which Magee excelled.

Other times Magee would just screen the film and instruct the editor to cut a voice-over, visuals only and then he would write a script to match the video. Sometimes, Magee would screen an interview and pull a sound bite and then write a script setting up the sound bite and the piece would air like that.

Of course, I wanted to get involved in this but being a lowly courier I could only watch during the week. However, Kampmann was desperate for help in these areas on the weekends. Nobody wanted to work weekends, so he let it be known that I could be used for minor newswriter chores when my courier duties would allow.

Thus it was that I eased myself into writing readers, voice-over copy and monitoring the news feeds. Although I had no formal training in writing for TV news, I had a simple conversational style to begin with and I soon picked up the technique for TV news script writing. The hardest part was boiling complicated stories down to twenty or thirty seconds of copy. Also, I had to write in a way that complimented the film or videotape that was airing, not repeat what someone could see visually.

My big breakthrough came when I proposed to the weekend producer that I do a film package compiling the week's top news stories. Jerry, the weekend producer, was hot on the idea. It would fill up a four or five-minute news hole that he had on nearly every weekend news show, a hole that he would usually fill with inane features off the network feeds. He floated the idea by Kampmann who said go ahead, but he didn't want it to interfere with my other duties.

Thus it was that I would arrive at work on the weekends, hours before my official start time and comb through the week's scripts, isolating the top stories. Then I would break them down, shorten them, and rewrite a summary script. Then I would go off to the early film editor, and we would go through the film and re-edit the stories for the package. At first, the film editor, an old guy who had been there for years, was hesitant to do this and asked Kampmann if it was OK. Kampmann said yes but wanted the film restored to its original package.

All of this was a lot of work for the film editor and he would bitch, but since he was being paid overtime to do it for Johnny Eager Beaver, he would shrug and forge ahead. When it was done, the packages usually looked great on the air. They were fast moving and informative and most importantly, they filled up a four to five-minute time slot on the weekend shows. Kampmann complimented me and advised me to make sure that the packages were dubbed on videotape before being dismantled. "You can use these as a resume tape, when you decide to go on to bigger and better opportunities in TV land."

What I was doing did not go unnoticed by the other newswriters who while reluctant to work the weekends, were concerned about my nonunion status in performing such functions. Most were solid Midwestern types who had moved to San Francisco for the job. Most were married and had modest houses in Concord or Pleasant Hill and commuted to work. Their wants were simple, except their chief want was job security and with me around, some were nervous. Although, I did indicate that I would willing to join their union, the Writers Guild, if and when I was officially hired as a newswriter. That seemed to mollify them for a bit.

Then there was the secretary Alice who was doing a slow burn. She wanted to get into the production end of things too and when heard of my weekend production, she went ballistic and stomped into Kampmann's office threatening to quit unless she could do something like that too. You must remember, this was a time when except for the weather girl, there were hardly any women working in local television news. Kampmann tried to appease her by telling her how vital she was doing her secretarial duties and gave her a raise. Alice still fumed.

***

Since I was often working seven days a week, sometimes twelve hours a day, the long commute from Berkeley was a real pain. So I convinced Yvonne that we had to move back to San Francisco. She was still unemployed and happily collecting her unemployment checks. We found a large studio apartment at Willard and Parnassus with a spectacular view of Golden Gate Park and the hills of San Francisco. It was also on the edge of the Haight.

Yvonne loved it and it was easy to get downtown where she could hunt for a job in retailing. We moved in May and it felt great to be back in San Francisco.

With only a half-hour commute to work, I had more time to mess around with my thesis in the morning since I didn't usually go to work on the weekdays until eleven or eleven thirty. By now, I had procured a kinescope of *Requiem of a Heavyweight* and had set up an editing bench in an alcove in the apartment. I was going through the kinescope frame by frame noting on a checklist various depth characteristics. With a special camera set up, I would photograph the frame if it were particularly representative of the point I was trying to make. It was tedious but necessary work and gradually I was able to document these elusive depth techniques which I was confident would prove my thesis once and for all. But this kind of research was only good for about two hours a day. The rest of the time, I was immersed in my duties as a courier/newswriter.

***

One day, Yvonne came by the newsroom on one of her pilgrimages downtown. She was wearing a fetching miniskirt, sweater and had a saucy beret on her head. With high heels, she looked like a French woman of the night. I introduced her around and Dick Riley, the 6 p.m. producer, practically fell out of his chair. He took her hand and with a grand continental gesture gave it a lingering kiss, murmuring, "What a lovely Mademoiselle."

Later, he said, "Hey there Brown, how do you rate such a fetching wife?"

"Just lucky, I guess."

"Lucky is not the word for it. You are going to have to become an anchor to afford that."

Needless to say, Riley was annoying. A tall, stooped shoulder fellow in his fifties with a shaved, bald head and a large handlebar mustache. Recently divorced, I guess he was just horny. And as he let everybody know, his true passion was as a jazz trumpeter. In fact, Riley played around town with the top groups. Still, working for KRON News was his bread and butter. He compared producing to a jazz riff. As he put it, "You have to stay loose and often improvise when the shit is coming down such as the film is not being ready. You have to be able to juggle a lot of balls in the air at once."

For some reason, Riley showed me the ins and outs of producing a show. "It's not simply a matter of stacking and timing scripts, Al. I strive for flow, rhythm, and maybe a little artistry." It was advice that I later took to heart when I got my chance to produce

I got another piece of advice from Ed Hart, the sportscaster who had spent time in Fresno before making it to San Francisco. He took me aside one day and said, "Al, you're a good looking kid. I'd say a natural for reporting, maybe sports anchoring down the road. But, if you ever want to go on air, you're going to have to go to the boondocks. Fresno, Sacramento, wherever they give you a shot. Don't hang around here too long or you'll wind up as a permanent newswriter."

Hmm. That was an interesting piece of advice. Did I want to go on the air? Well, maybe but I was also fascinated by the concept of producing a news show and controlling the whole creative enterprise. I thought that maybe my natural talent lay behind the scenes like a puppet master pulling the strings. But I also realized that on-air personnel got the recognition and the money. Then there was the issue of moving to a minor market to get on the air. I didn't want to leave the Bay Area for the time being because a European trip was pending in the fall. With me now racking up overtime, we were saving enough money to make such a trip possible. Any major new direction in TV news would have to wait until we returned from Europe. Meanwhile, I continued being Johnny Rocket, hustling film and becoming a budding newswriter.

Allan Brown

31. NEWS STORM

After a couple of weeks at KRON-TV, I realized that I was in the middle of a perfect storm of blockbuster news events sweeping through 1968. I had a front row seat to many of those news stories which later proved to be historic.

The year started with the siege of Khe Sahn, a Marine forward base under attack from the North Vietnamese. Also in January, the North Koreans seized the USS Pueblo, a naval intelligence ship, off the coast of Korea and held the crew prisoner. By the end of January, the Tet Offensive had begun with the North Vietnamese and Vietcong attacking major South Vietnamese cities and briefly occupying the American embassy in Saigon. In the Battle of Hue, thousands of homes were destroyed in house-to-house fighting, inflicting heavy civilian casualties.

In other words, the war was not going well for the U.S. military.

In February, General Westmoreland requested two-hundred thousand more troops but his request was denied. Rumors flew that Westmoreland would soon resign. And in fact, he did resign two weeks later was replaced by General Creighton Abrams.

In the midst of this Richard Nixon, back from the political dead, announced his candidacy for the Republican nomination for president. We in California remembered well how Nixon had lost to Pat Brown in the 1962 California gubernatorial election and who then told the press, they wouldn't have Nixon to kick around anymore.

On the Democratic side, peace candidate Senator Eugene McCarthy unexpectedly came within a hair's breadth of beating President Johnson in the New Hampshire March Primary. Johnson was suddenly perceived as vulnerable. At this news, Senator Robert Kennedy declared he too would be a candidate for the Democratic presidential nomination. Kennedy had previously said he would not seek the nomination.

Sensing that his political future was doomed because of the war, President Johnson told the nation on March 31st that he would not seek re-election. His vice president, Hubert Humphrey, announced his candidacy shortly thereafter.

April was barely underway when Martin Luther King Junior was assassinated in Memphis Tennessee. This was a shocker that we witnessed unfold on the network feeds coming into the newsroom. We saw video of the Memphis motel and later the still photographs of civil rights activist Jesse Jackson standing with King moments before the shot rang out, and then a photo of Jackson and the Reverend Ralph Abernathy on the balcony pointing in the direction of the gunfire as King lay at their feet. All of this was followed by major riots in Memphis, Washington DC, Chicago and Baltimore. Two months later the alleged assassin, James Earl Ray, was arrested at Heathrow Airport in London.

Everybody at KRON expected a riot to break out in Oakland right after the King assassination but nothing happened. Some later credited the Black Panthers for keeping the city cool. However, on April 6, two days after the assassination, the Oakland Police and the Black Panthers got into a shootout. When it was over, 18-year old Panther Bobby Hutton was dead. The Panthers claimed that Hutton was attempting to surrender when the police gunned him down. The Oakland police claimed that Hutton was running towards police, refused to stop when ordered and appeared to be concealing something in his hands, possibly a weapon. It turned out Hutton was unarmed.

This is where the KRON-TV news team sprang into action with extensive coverage and I made many trips into the heart of the Oakland ghetto retrieving the film from the camera crews. The KRON Volkswagen attracted attention. I kept my doors locked and expected a rock through my windshield at any moment. Again, nothing happened. Oakland remained cool, although over two thousand people attended Hutton's funeral.

The other Black Panther story perking along was the impending trial of Huey Newton who was still in jail following the fatal shooting of an Oakland police officer back in October. Newton was being portrayed as a martyr and a revolutionary in the black community. The Panthers held demonstrations and vigils throughout the spring and summer months leading up to the October trial, with their chants of "Free Huey."

I had to admit the Panthers were a scary looking bunch, marching together with their black berets and fists in the air, proclaiming "Black Power." Of course, Newton was eventually convicted of voluntary manslaughter and sentenced from two to fifteen years in prison, a conviction that was overturned in 1970.

***

Student protests over the war also dominated the news that spring. San Francisco and New York saw the largest student strikes yet against the war organized by the Student Mobilization Committee. Tens of thousands of protesters marched in the streets. Students shut down Columbia University and hundreds of thousands of high school and college students boycotted classes in a nationwide protest to end the war.

In May, there was more trouble at San Francisco State. Police were called in to remove students from the San Francisco State administration building after a nine-hour sit-in. The students wanted an end to Air Force ROTC on campus and were demanding programs to admit more minority students and the hiring of minority professors. I was out there at SF State among some four hundred protesters as the cops extracted the students from the buildings. KRON-TV captured it all on film. It felt weird being there as a member of the press since I was technically still a student at SF State.

I remembered, Zettl shaking his head at the student unrest at SF State and worrying what it would do the reputation of the school. "These kids don't realize what a jewel this place is. I have seen real repression at educational institutions in Germany. These administrators are doing their best to appease the more radical elements here but it doesn't seem to satisfy anybody."

***

We also covered less spectacular local news stories throughout the year such as the routine political dogfights at City Hall, crime in the Haight Ashbury and celebrity news. One day Woody Allen came to the newsroom to promote his latest movie and appearances in town at a local comedy club. He joked and jived for about a half hour with us before being interviewed on the air. Then there was the controversial opening of the movie *2001 A Space Odyssey* in which most of the audience was high on acid or pot in order to better groove on the special effects concocted by Stanley Kubrick. Stories like these had a minor impact. But there were other important stories that would affect San Francisco and the Bay Area for years to come.

An immediate one was the decision of the Board of Supervisors to kill once and for all, the proposed extension of the Embarcadero Freeway which now terminated abruptly at the foot of Broadway. The original plans called for continuing it along the waterfront and eventually hooking up with the Golden Gate Bridge and US 101. Had it been completed the freeway would have blocked the view of the bay casting a hulking shadow over Fisherman's Warf and other San Francisco waterfront attractions. KRON filmed the charts and the models of what San Francisco would look like with such a freeway and then contrasted it to the present jewel-like open vistas of the bay.

Another on-going story was the effort by environmentalists to slow down development that was filling in large portions of the bay. The San Francisco Bay had once spread out over 700-square miles; now it was reduced by over a third to 420-square miles. Efforts were also ongoing to clean up bay pollution. These issues were usually aired in stuffy conference rooms with charts but occasionally the parties would hold news conferences on the sites of proposed fill-in projects which made for more visual interest.

We also periodically covered the construction of Bay Area Rapid Transit (BART) throughout the Bay Area and Contra Costa County. In San Francisco, most of Market Street was torn up as they dug the BART subway tunnel.

BART was of more than passing interest to me. As noted earlier, I had worked on BART surveying the right away near Hayward back in 1965. Now I was being bugged by the union to take a shift job as a surveyor on the subway.

"Overtime is unlimited. We need you down there on Market Street, Brown," they said.

It was tempting. I had seen the survey crews working along Market Street. It seemed like an easy gig. Just lay down a little line and elevation for the crews as they dug. And it would have been big money. Much more than I was earning now. But, I told the union that I was on a different career track.

"Television News?" said the voice not quite comprehending it.

"Yeah. That's what I was studying at S.F. State."

"Well, good luck," said the voice. "And by the way don't forget to take a union withdrawal card. You might want to come back to us someday."

"Ah, sure."

I did take out a withdrawal card because you never really knew.

On the grimmer side of local news, bodies were turning up here and there throughout the Bay Area. Police believed a single serial killer was on the loose. Eventually, the killer communicated with the cops by letter sent to the local newspapers signing them the Zodiac Killer.

***

Then there were little noticed hi-tech stories buried in the business pages that didn't rate television news coverage. Most of these stories emanated from around Sunnyvale on the Peninsula, an area which had long been home to Hewlett-Packard, Fairchild and Lockheed. Now that area was filling up with curious little start-up companies engaged in wonkish visions of what computerization could do. 1968 saw the founding of Intel. Intel was said to be developing something called a "microprocessor chip." This was supposed to lead to a dramatic miniaturization of the hulking IBM computers that now filled a room to perform routine bookkeeping and accounting chores. Also, the Stanford Research Institute gave one of the first public demonstrations of a computer mouse, windows and networking. Not to be outdone, Hewlett-Packard introduced the first programmable desktop calculator. Still, the personal computer revolution that the visionaries were predicting would be years away.

***

Back on the political front, Senators Eugene McCarthy and Robert Kennedy were going at it hammer and tongs in the Democratic Presidential Primaries. Vice President Humphrey, for the most part, was relying on favorite son candidates in Florida, Ohio and Indiana.

By the end of May, McCarthy had won five primaries and Kennedy four. But so far, where Kennedy and McCarthy had competed head to head, Kennedy beat McCarthy. However, McCarthy did beat Kennedy in the May 30th Oregon Primary. Thus, the California Primary on June 5th was seen as critical for both.

Kennedy campaigned in the barrios and in the slums of the California's major cities while McCarthy stumped the universities and the colleges before anti-war crowds. And for sure, KRON was there to cover it.

Both candidates showed up in our newsroom for in-studio interviews. McCarthy impressed me the most. He was like a college professor patiently explaining why the Vietnam War was a mistake to an uninformed public. Yvonne was taken by him too, so much so that she volunteered to work in his campaign offices in San Francisco even though she couldn't vote. She was by no means alone. Hundreds of counter-culture types began working for McCarthy. They had "cleaned up" for Gene, shaving their beards, cutting their hair short and donning khakis and button down shirts.

Robert Kennedy was a different story. In person, I thought him brusque, and opportunistic, always in a hurry to get to his next campaign appearance. But he always had time for a pretty face. Yvonne once encountered Robert Kennedy after he gave a speech in the Greek Theater at UC Berkeley before I met her. As she described it, he was walking down a side path from the theater by himself and she was coming the other way. He smiled at her; she smiled back and held out her hand. He shook it, all the time staring at her with his piercing blue eyes. Yet no words were exchanged and both moved on.

However, I still remembered the newsreels of Robert Kennedy as an assistant to another McCarthy, Senator Joe McCarthy conducting his communist witch-hunts in the early 1950s, and more recently Kennedy's tough guy role as an Attorney General under his brother, John Kennedy. Some speculated that his crackdown on the mob led to his brother's assassination. Now here, all of a sudden, he was a caring compassionate, liberal Senator worried about the plight of the blacks and the Hispanics. I thought he was milking the Kennedy myth for all it was worth.

Both McCarthy and Kennedy engaged in a debate a few days before the election. It was generally considered a draw. Finally, it was California Primary day. It was expected this primary would give the winner a decisive push toward being the party's nominee.

KRON, like most of the local California news media, had a crew down in Los Angeles at Kennedy's headquarters on the day of the primary. I had pleaded to go down to act as a field producer for the crew, or even a gofer but Kampmann said no. I was needed in the newsroom for my regular courier duties. So I along with the others sat and watched the election news feeds come into the newsroom as the primary day unfolded.

By early evening, it was clear that Kennedy had narrowly defeated McCarthy. There was a groan in the newsroom as many were McCarthy supporters. Nevertheless, we watched the live coverage with interest as Robert Kennedy came out to give his victory speech at the Ambassador Hotel. We watched as the pro-Kennedy crowd cheered him on. We watched as he joked with his well-wishers with a big shit-eating grin on his face, and a lock of hair that kept falling down on his forehead.

We watched as he finally made his way to the back of the ballroom of the Ambassador Hotel and disappear from view into a crowd of campaign workers. And then screaming and chaos ensued. Kennedy had been shot. Later we saw video of campaign workers in funny straw hats crowded around a blood-soaked Kennedy. Someone covered him with a sheet. Kennedy would die of his wounds twenty-six hours later. Of course, the alleged assassin, Sirhan Sirhan, had been immediately arrested and his little .22 caliber revolver seized. Suddenly, the Democratic nomination for the Presidency was up for grabs.

***

While the country was reeling from the Robert Kennedy assassination, the Republican Party was perking along with Nixon winning primary after primary, despite the strong showing by our very own Governor Ronald Reagan. Although, not officially a candidate, Reagan's name had been entered into several primaries. Other than Reagan, Nixon's main opponent was New York Governor Nelson Rockefeller.

Until California, Nixon had won all the primaries but when it came to the California Primary, Reagan walked away with victory giving him a plurality of votes. It was tempting to root for Reagan because that would mean he would have to give up the California Governorship in order to be president. Many Democrats in California figured that it was better that Reagan be in Washington rather than screwing up California. Reagan officially announced his candidacy for the nomination at the Republican National Convention convened in Miami in early August. Still, Nixon won the nomination on the first ballot.

The Democratic Convention held in Chicago in late August was in stark contrast to the relatively calm Republican Convention. Initially, coverage of the convention itself was a hoot. Yvonne and I laughed as we watched ABC with conservative pundit Bill Buckley and liberal author Gore Vidal spare with one another over the proceedings. At one point, Vidal told Buckley to shut up. Buckley responded telling Gore to stick to his fictional pornography and called him a "faggot."

As noted, the nomination was up for grabs, although it looked like Humphrey was the favorite choice by rank-and-file Democratic delegates. Outside the convention hall, the streets and parks of Chicago were filled with protesters for the entire week— organized by Abbie Hoffman, Jerry Rubin and other assorted Yippies and all spoiling for a fight. It was an understatement to say that the Chicago cops were ready for them. They along with the National Guard were ready to crack heads. And crack heads they did on several occasions. The Chicago Police charged into crowds of protesters, swinging batons, shooting off tear gas, spraying mace and making hundreds of arrests. Many were calling it a police riot. Or as Mayor Daley put it, "The policeman isn't there to create disorder. The policeman is there to preserve disorder." It was, of course, a telling slip of the famous Daley tongue.

It was all for naught for the Democrats. In November, Richard Nixon defeated Humphrey. Nixon was elected President with 43% percent of the popular vote. Humphrey received 42% of the vote while the third-party spoiler, George Wallace got 13% of the vote, most of that from the South.

***

Still, there was much more to this perfect storm of 1968 news. Overseas, Soviet and Warsaw Pact forces had invaded Czechoslovakia to put an end to protests, (student and otherwise) over communist rule. President Alexander Dubcek was sent to Moscow in handcuffs. Thousands of young people faced down Soviet Tanks rolling through Prague. Eighty-three people were killed. For the moment, Soviet-style communism was firmly re-established.

In October, hundreds of students were killed in and around the University of Mexico in Mexico City following student protests. Two weeks later, American black athletes raised their fists in the black power salute during the Summer Olympic medal ceremonies also in Mexico City.

In November, another extended student strike at San Francisco State occurred. The students were protesting the war in Vietnam and demanding a larger Black studies program. The campus was shut down for two months. Police were called in. At one protest, the acting president S.I. Hayakawa tried to disconnect the student loudspeakers. But as he did so, his tam-o-shanter cap was knocked from his head. Nevertheless, he became a hero to the California right wing. The campus didn't reopen until after Christmas break.

By the end of 1968, some 530-thousand troops were still in Vietnam. More than sixteen-thousand American soldiers had died in that year. Twenty-eight thousand South Vietnam troops had also perished. And the war? Despite all the protests, the chaos and the mayhem, there was still no sign the war was winding down.

After September, Yvonne and I watched much of this turmoil on European television and read about it in the headlines of the *International Herald Tribune*. For us, California and the United States were now on the far side of the planet. Here is how that came about.

32. FLIGHT

Mom and Dad drove us to the San Francisco Airport one fine morning in late August. Both Mom and Dad were worried about us. Earlier, on the phone, Mom asked me why Yvonne and I were doing this.

"After all, Allan, You now have a job in a field that is promising and a wife to support. Running off to Europe and all doesn't seem like a wise thing to do."

"We'll only be gone a couple of months," I replied. "Yvonne hasn't seen her mom or sisters for years."

"Yes, but two months is too long. Why not go for a few weeks? That way you can keep your job when you get back."

"Uh, I don't think so mom. I've burned that bridge for the time being."

***

Indeed, I had. In fact, I was on the verge of being fired when I informed Kampmann that I was quitting.

"Probably just as well, Allan," he had replied. "The higher-ups are upset at you for your little stunt."

The "little stunt" that Kampmann was referring to was my debut as an on-air director. I had been under pressure to send a news film package off to KNBC in Los Angeles. It required being dubbed from film over to videotape but no director was about to do it. So I sat down in the director's chair in the control room and had it dubbed over myself. At the time, I thought it was no big deal. It was a dumbshit job anybody could do. In fact, it was fun telling the TD to roll the videotape and then roll film and proceed with the dubbing.

A day later, word got around at what I had done and I was confronted by the shop steward for the on-air directors.

"Al, is it true that you made the dub?"

"Ah, yeah. Is there a problem?"

"Yes, a big problem. You've been here long enough to know that it only the on-air director does that. It's part of our union jurisdiction."

"Yeah, I know you're in a union, but that was such a piddling thing. None of you guys were around and the tape had to be shipped."

"Doesn't matter. We're in the middle of negotiations. Possibly on the verge of a strike. The suits that run this place would like nothing better than a platoon of scabs to take our place. I'm going to have to file a grievance about your action."

"Really?" I replied, "I'm hardly a threat to you guys. I'd never do scab work. I'm in a couple unions myself."

And I thought that was the end of the matter. But a few days later, a grievance was filed and the station manager was upset. He didn't want a strike. He didn't want trouble so the word was he wanted to get rid of the troublemaker, namely me. Of course, he was going to let Kampmann do the dirty work. Hence, my timely resignation.

About the same time, Kampmann announced to the newsroom that he was resigning as well to take a job in Philadelphia with a Westinghouse station. He was being brought in to launch a new news format, something called Action News. It was supposed to be fast-paced, chock full of flashy graphics and many, many film and videotape stories. Well, good for him. My departure was even timelier.

I was going to quit anyway in order to go to Europe. We had been diligently saving money since spring for the trip. We basically lived on Yvonne's unemployment checks and I banked my salary. By the end of summer, we had four thousand dollars saved up. However, the length of the trip was not yet settled. I had envisioned a two-month stay but Yvonne wanted to stay longer, through Christmas. OK, OK.

There were also other factors at play about our leaving San Francisco. We were both tired of the Bay Area scene and all its craziness. It was deja-vu, the same thing over and over again for the past five years. I was tired of the hang loose, go nowhere lifestyle. I would look around and see perennial graduate students in their thirties. I had already been a student for ten years. It was old. Yes, I had a job in television, my career path, but the Bay Area was small-time in the world of TV news. I wanted to try out for the networks again in New York. This even though Vic Burton who was to become Mel

Kampmann's replacement as news director had offered me a full-fledged newswriter's job when I returned.

"You've earned it, Allan," said Vic. "You've mastered the skills. You know the town. I think you would do well, probably even produce down the road. Don't worry about this little directing tiff. It'll blow over."

"Thanks. I'll think about it."

"Yeah, but don't stay over in Europe too long. I'll have to hire someone by January."

It was nice to know that I had a place to come back to after Europe, but I was also entertaining thoughts of trying to get a job at one of the network bureaus over there. I knew NBC had a large bureau in Paris. I knew they hired field producers to scout out stories all over Europe. I figured my knowledge of French and a little bit of German would make me marketable. Also, by now, I had a videotape reel of all my weekend news summaries, along with the scripts. I was loaded for bear.

***

Before we could leave, I had to clear it with my civil affairs reserve unit in El Cerrito. The immediate threat of activating reservists had passed. Control groups were once again an option. I had informed the company commander that I was moving to Europe at the beginning of August and would be looking for a reserve unit there.

"Hard to find. You might have to join up in Germany but otherwise, we'll have to put you in a control group," he told me.

I thought to myself, "Gee, that's too bad," then I said would try my best to look for a unit.

"Also it looks like you'll be missing our summer camp down at Camp Roberts," he noted. "Too bad you can't delay our departure, can you?"

"Ah, no, I don't think so," I answered still sticking to my story that I was leaving early August. But inwardly congratulating myself that I had so far escaped reserve camp during my entire six-year obligation.

Actually, the civil affairs unit in El Cerrito had not been too bad. We had interesting weekend meetings with lectures on how to run the administration of small German towns, right out of the World War Two playbook. But there was also a bit of drilling and regular Army stuff. I had managed to hitch a ride on a regular basis from one reservist who lived in San Francisco and worked for IBM. When I told him I was leaving for Europe, he was envious.

"You lucky dog. I wish I could do that. Maybe IBM will transfer me."

"Give it a try."

"That's the problem with a regular job," he lamented. "The fuckers get you tied down, get you in their gun sights. The Army Reserves knows where you are when you have a regular nine to five."

One reserve weekend was guest weekend. Friends and families could come and watch us perform. The deal was if someone showed up with you, you could get out of the rest of the day. Yvonne accompanied me and thought the whole thing was a hoot.

"You don't march very well, do you?" she laughed. "Your bad attitude was showing."

"Hey, we are civil affairs soldiers. We don't have to be Army spit and polish."

***

By the last week in August, we had all our affairs in order. We had given notice to our landlady. We also had given most of our furniture away on a temporary basis to Herman and his girlfriend. We stored two large trunks of clothes in Martinez, along with another suitcase full of my research material for my thesis. I had effectively put my thesis on hold. I had completed all the research with the kinescope and had developed my photos. Everything was in order. Now all I had to do was write it. I vowed I would, somewhere down the road.

We had said goodbye to our friends but not to Jean-Paul, nor to Marie and Gerard because they were already in Europe. Jean-Paul had returned to Paris with his girlfriend early summer and Marie and Gerard were still on an extended honeymoon in France. They had married back in April. I was Gerard's best man. Marie had the same victory look that Yvonne had displayed when we were married a year ago.

***

And so it was, on Wednesday, August 28, 1968, Yvonne and I climbed aboard a charter Air France flight bound for Paris. Minutes later, we were winging our way over San Francisco Bay, deep blue in the morning light, then over the hot brown hills of northern California. Later, the green forests and mountains of the Great Northwest, and eventually over the white blank of the Arctic. As it turned out, this polar flight to Europe would take us away from California for years. Yvonne and I would visit, but never live in the Golden State again. But that's another story.

THE END

www.ingramcontent.com/pod-product-compliance
Lightning Source LLC
Chambersburg PA
CBHW021757220426
43662CB00006B/87